U.S.A.

TWENTIES

Volume 4

Magazines and Magazine Publishing — Politics, Local

GROLIER

First published 2005 by Grolier,
an imprint of Scholastic Library Publishing,
Old Sherman Turnpike
Danbury, Connecticut 06816

Set ISBN 0-7172-6013-5
Volume ISBN 0-7172-6017-8

Library of Congress Cataloging-in-Publication Data
U.S.A. twenties.
p. cm.
Includes bibliographical references and index.
Contents:—v. 1. Advertising–Cushing Harvey—v. 2. Dance–Harding, Warren G.— v. 3. Harlem renaissance–Lynd report—v. 4. Magazines and magazine publishing–Politics, local—v. 5. Popular music–Sports—v. 6. Sports, professionalism and–Young Plan.
ISBN 0-7172-6013-5 (set : alk. paper)—ISBN 0-7172-6014-3 (v. 1 : alk. paper)—ISBN 0-7172-6015-1 (v. 2 : alk. paper)—ISBN 0-7172-6016-X (v. 3 : alk. paper)—ISBN 0-7172-6017-8 (v. 4 : alk. paper)—ISBN 0-7172-6018-6 (v. 5 : alk. paper)—ISBN 0-7172-6019-4 (v. 6 : alk. paper)
1. United States—History—1919–1933—Encyclopedias, Juvenile. 2. Nineteen twenties—Encyclopedias, Juvenile. I. Title: USA twenties. II. Title: U.S.A. 20s. III.
Grolier (Firm)

E784.U13 2004
973.91'5—dc22 2004040604

For information address the publisher:
Grolier, Scholastic Library Publishing,
Old Sherman Turnpike,
Danbury, Connecticut 06816

Printed and bound in Singapore

For The Brown Reference Group plc

Project Editor:	Sally MacEachern
Editors:	Rachel Bean, Mark Fletcher, Henry Russell
Designer:	Ron Callow
Picture Researcher:	Clare Newman
Index:	Kay Ollerenshaw
Production Director:	Alastair Gourlay
Managing Editor:	Tim Cooke
Editorial Director:	Lindsey Lowe
Consultant:	Dr. Eric Leif Davin, University of Pittsburgh

ABOUT THIS SET

This book is part of a six-volume reference set that provides a detailed portrait of all aspects of the United States in the 1920s—political events, scientific advances, cultural and social trends, and famous personalities. The decade opened in the aftermath of the First World War and closed on the threshold of the Great Depression. It is perhaps best known as the Jazz Age and the era of Prohibition, the ill-fated attempt to outlaw alcohol that turned gangsters into tycoons. Yet the twenties also saw the dawn of the ages of air travel, radio, television, and the talkies—new technologies that would change the world.

Above all, the twenties were a paradox. On the surface they were politically conservative. In 1920 U.S. voters, disillusioned with the idealism of Democrat Woodrow Wilson, elected the first of three successive Republican administrations, each of which favored big business. Yet although there was a consequent decline in the power and influence of organized labor, there remained strong progressive and radical movements. Their ultimately unsuccessful attempts to ally themselves into a cohesive political force would have a lasting influence on U.S. politics.

In foreign policy the United States tried to extricate itself from overseas involvements but found it difficult to do so—after World War I the nation was too great a power to be isolationist. The federal government placed heavy tariffs on imports in the hope of protecting domestic industries, but they had the opposite effect, contributing to an international recession that gravely damaged U.S. exports.

There were other contradictions in U.S. life. According to conventional economic indicators, the United States was thriving. The introduction of mass-production techniques in many industries created prosperity, which was reflected in the huge rise in the availability and affordability of consumer goods—automobiles, phonographs, washing machines, and so on. But the underlying trend—largely unnoticed at the time—was toward economic meltdown. The crisis duly came with the stock market crash of 1929.

Arranged in alphabetical order for ease of reference, *U.S.A. Twenties* contains nearly 300 articles illustrated with fascinating images of the period and, where appropriate, maps and diagrams for further clarification. Many of the entries contain boxed features that provide extra detail. Each entry concludes with cross-references to related articles.

Every volume has a complete set index to help students find their way around the whole set, together with a comprehensive timeline, a reading list, and useful websites for further research.

CONTENTS

MAGAZINES AND MAGAZINE PUBLISHING

The twenties saw the launch of many new weekly and monthly magazines, some of which, such as *Time* and *Reader's Digest*, have survived into the 21st century.

In the late 19th century the introduction of new printing methods and the development of cheap paper made from ground wood enabled newspaper publishers to cut their costs significantly. They invested some of the savings in editorial content and layout, and almost immediately there was a significant rise in the circulation of newspapers in America.

Increased readership attracted more advertising revenue than ever before. This boom period attracted further investment and inspired diversification from newspapers to magazines. The era saw the birth of several new periodicals. Some were opinion journals such as the *Atlantic Monthly*, the *Nation*, and *Harper's*. The largest readerships, however, were won by magazines that catered to Americans' increasing leisure time and appetite for consumer goods—publications such as *Cosmopolitan*, the *Ladies' Home Journal*, and the *Saturday Evening Post*. By the dawn of the 20th century publishers were no longer just selling reading matter; they were delivering readers to advertisers. The advertisers were eager to target as much of the population as they could. Daily newspapers were quite useful for this purpose, but they reached only local audiences. The longer lead time of weekly or monthly magazines enabled their publishers to distribute them from coast to coast, so they were clearly the best places for commercial businesses to advertise.

The growth of the magazine market was interrupted by World War I (1914–1918), but it was followed by another resurgence, led by the start of news weeklies. The first of these was *Time*, which was founded by Henry Luce and Briton Hadden (*see box on p. 7*). The inaugural issue hit the news stands on March 2, 1923. *Time* sought to attract busy readers who did not have "time" (hence the title) to read a daily newspaper by organizing its news pages into separate compartments such as national affairs, business, and science. From the beginning the publication tried to achieve a style of reporting and analysis that would set it apart from newspapers. This approach was inspired principally by Hadden, who wanted *Time* to be important but fun. That accounts for its tone, which many people criticized as too light for serious news and more suited to its extensive coverage of celebrities (including politicians), the entertainment industry, and pop culture. The idiosyncratic *Time* prose style was famously parodied by the author Wolcott Gibbs: "Backward ran sentences until reeled the mind. Where it would end, knows God." The magazine pioneered, and came to epitomize, group journalism, in which teams of researchers, writers, and editors prepare articles collaboratively.

Time magazine's most famous feature soon became its annual Man of the Year (later renamed Person of the Year) contest, in which the magazine recognizes the individual or group of individuals who "for better or worse, has most influenced events in the preceding year." Despite its name, the award is not always given to a human: Ideas and machines have also won it. The tradition of selecting a Man of the Year began during a slow week in 1927, when *Time* editors were stuck for stories to write about. Recycling the year's earlier events, they came up with the idea of a cover story about Charles A. Lindbergh being the "Man of the Year." The second winner was automobile manufacturer Walter Chrysler; in 1929 it was Owen Young, an economist in the Hoover administration; in 1930 the Indian political and spiritual leader Mahatma Gandhi became the first foreigner to win the award.

Pioneers

One of the most important publishers of the twenties was Bernarr Macfadden (1868–1955), who published *Physical Culture* and was the pioneer of health and bodybuilding magazines. He was also the publisher of confession magazines, such as *True Story*. In 1929 he bought *Amazing Stories* from Hugo Gernsback.

Another publisher was the ambitious entrepreneur William Roy DeWitt Wallace. Wallace was born in St. Paul, Minnesota, in 1889. After attending Macalester College (1907–1909) and the University of California at Berkeley (1909–1911), he returned to Minnesota to work as a book salesman and publicist. He joined the army in 1917 and was wounded in World War I. While he was convalescing, he read a wide range of books that fascinated him, but that he realized he would never have had time to look at if he had not been in the hospital.

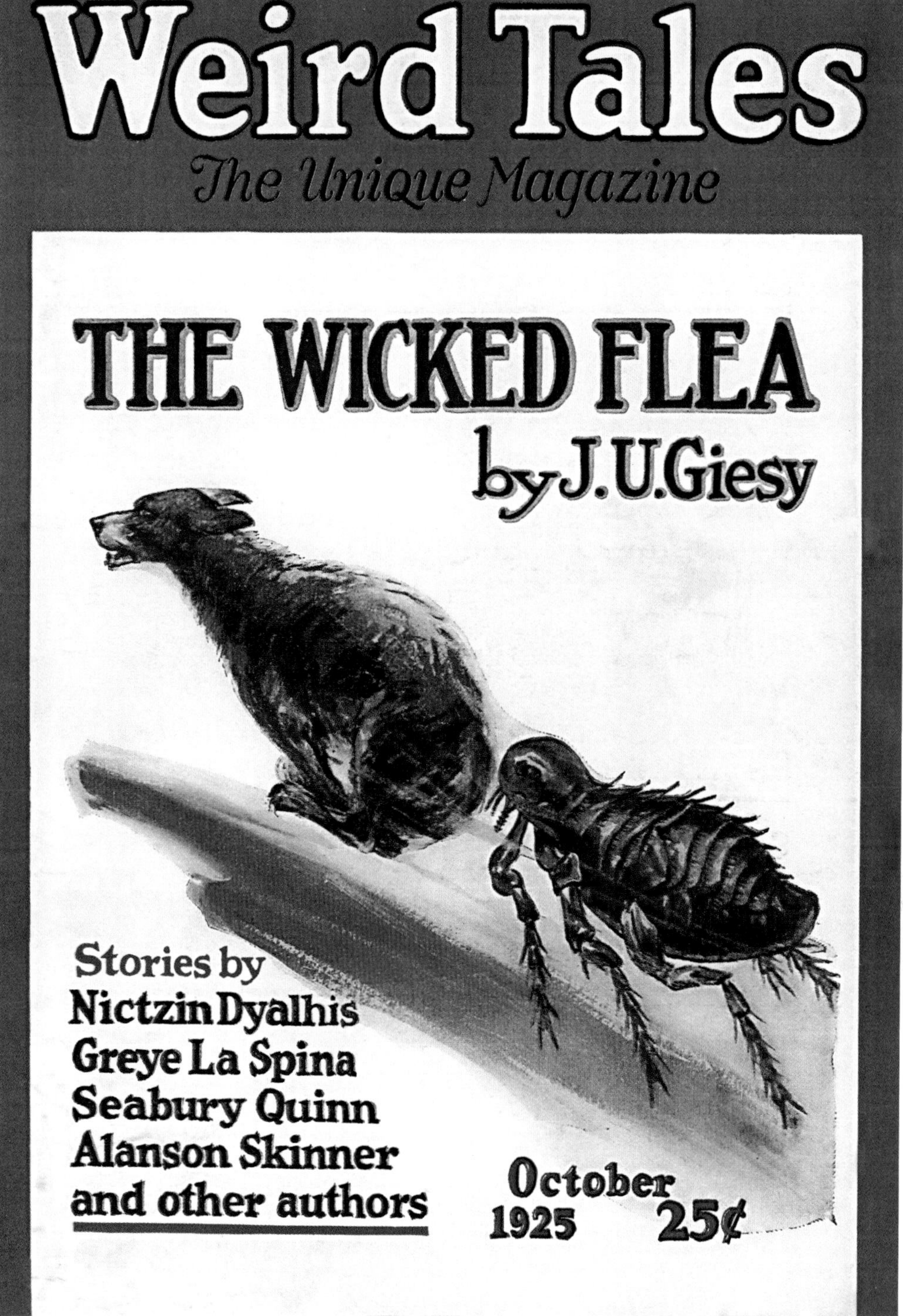

***Weird Tales: The Unique Magazine* was the world's first fantasy magazine. First published in 1923, it stayed in print for another 30 years. It published obscure, odd, macabre, and far-fetched pulp fiction.**

This gave him an idea: In 1920 he submitted to publishers across the United States a sample magazine containing condensed versions of articles that had previously appeared in books and periodicals. Every one of them turned him down. Undeterred, Wallace and his wife Lila Bell Acheson (1889–1984) published the magazine themselves from home, printing 5,000 copies that were sold exclusively by mail to 1,500 subscribers and priced at 25 cents. The first issue came out in February 1922 under the title *Reader's Digest*. By the end of the decade it had inspired many imitators and with a circulation of 200,000 had become the biggest-selling magazine in the English-speaking world. The success of their publishing business brought the Wallaces great wealth, and they donated millions of dollars to a wide range of philanthropic causes and institutions, including New York City's Metropolitan Museum. Wallace died in 1981.

Science fiction magazines

Another publishing pioneer of the era was Hugo Gernsback (1884–1967), who in 1926 published *Amazing Stories*, the world's first science fiction magazine, which featured stories by Jules Verne and H.G. Wells among others. An inventor of electrical gadgets himself (he invented the first home radio set in 1905 and pioneered early television), he published the first radio magazine, *Modern Electrics*, in 1908. Gernsback encouraged his writers to imagine scenarios for the future, and his magazines predicted many future inventions, including radar and television. He also came up with the term science fiction to explain the type of writing he published—fictional stories that were based on an accurate scientific basis. In 1929 he was forced into bankruptcy by Bernarr Macfadden, who immediately bought *Amazing Stories*. Nevertheless, Gernsback quickly bounced back and published two new successful science fiction magazines: *Science Wonder Stories* and *Air Wonder Stories* (later merged to become *Wonder Stories*). Today he is

This *Illustrated Detective Magazine* cover is from February 1930. Detective magazines helped launch the careers of writers Erle Stanley Gardner, Raymond Chandler, and Dashiell Hammett.

honored as one of the founders of science fiction—the annual science fiction Hugo Awards are named after him.

Not every magazine thrived, however. Among those that did not was *The Smart Set.* The publication had launched the career of F. Scott Fitzgerald (1896–1940), but its sales suffered from the general perception—fueled no doubt to some extent by its rather arrogant subtitle, "A Magazine of Cleverness"—that it was too smart for its own good. By 1918 it was in financial trouble, and two of its owners—critic and essayist H.L. Mencken (1880–1956) and theater critic George Jean Nathan (1882–1958)—began casting around for a new idea for a title with mass-market appeal, the profits from which could be used to shore up the high-brow monthly.

Eventually they decided to try periodicals that would cash in on the popular pulp fiction market. Their first two attempts, *Parisienne* and *Saucy Stories*, were based on dime novels and were fairly well received by the reading public. Thus encouraged, Mencken and Nathan decided to bring out a mystery magazine. Their publication was inspired by *Detective Story*, the circulation of which had grown steadily since it was launched in 1915. When it came to choosing a title, they decided on a reference to *The Smart Set*, the cover of which featured a line-drawing of Satan in a black mask; from this they got the idea of the new logo, a thin black pirate's mask with a dirk and a flintlock pistol crossed behind it, and hence the title. *Black Mask* was first published in April 1920, with a cover price of 20 cents. Each issue was 128 pages and contained 12 stories. The first issue described itself as "An Illustrated Magazine of Detective, Mystery, Adventure, Romance and Spiritualism," although the subtitle was constantly revised and eventually dropped. Spiritualism did not even make it to issue two. Western fiction was added later.

Mencken and Nathan snobbishly deplored *Black Mask* on aesthetic grounds, and they refused to have their names put on the masthead—for them the publication was a moneymaker, nothing more. They sold the magazine in November 1920 to the other owners of *The Smart Set.* The new version of the magazine,

MAKING TIME

The two founders of *Time* magazine were Henry Robinson Luce (1898–1967) and Briton Hadden (1898–1929). Luce, the son of American missionaries, was born in Tengchow (now Penglai), China, and educated from age 10 at a British boarding school in that country. He first came to the United States in 1913, when he went to attend the Hotchkiss School in Connecticut. There he became editor of the school magazine. His assistant was fellow pupil Briton Hadden, a native of Brooklyn, New York. Luce and Hadden went on together to Yale University, where again they were editor and assistant editor respectively of the *Yale Daily News*. After graduation the two men went their separate ways for a year while Luce went to Oxford University, England, to study history, but they were later reunited as newsmen on the *Baltimore News*. In 1922 both men quit to start their own news magazine. They needed $100,000 but raised only a total of $86,000 from 74 investors. Yet they were confident that their magazine would appeal to a mass audience and determined to go ahead. The launch of the first issue was accompanied by a mission statement by Luce: "In an age when people are bombarded by information," he said, "we are, ironically, becoming less informed. *Time* is dedicated to keeping busy men and women well informed by making information more readily accessible."

Although the two men alternated annually the titles of president and secretary-treasurer, in fact Hadden was always the editor and Luce the business manager of *Time*. Hadden gave up writing himself in order to devote all his energies to training his staff. "Let all stories make sharp sense," he told them. "Omit flowers. Remember you can't be too obvious."

By 1927 the magazine was well established and had achieved a circulation of 175,000. In December 1928 Hadden fell ill with a sore throat. He died on February 27, 1929, a week after his 31st birthday. Luce carried on alone. Despite the Depression, a second magazine, *Fortune* (1930), soon became profitable. *Life* magazine, which Luce began in 1936, grew into the world's most popular weekly picture magazine.

The publisher and editor Henry Luce photographed in 1937. Luce founded three of the United States' most successful magazines: Time, Fortune, *and* Life.

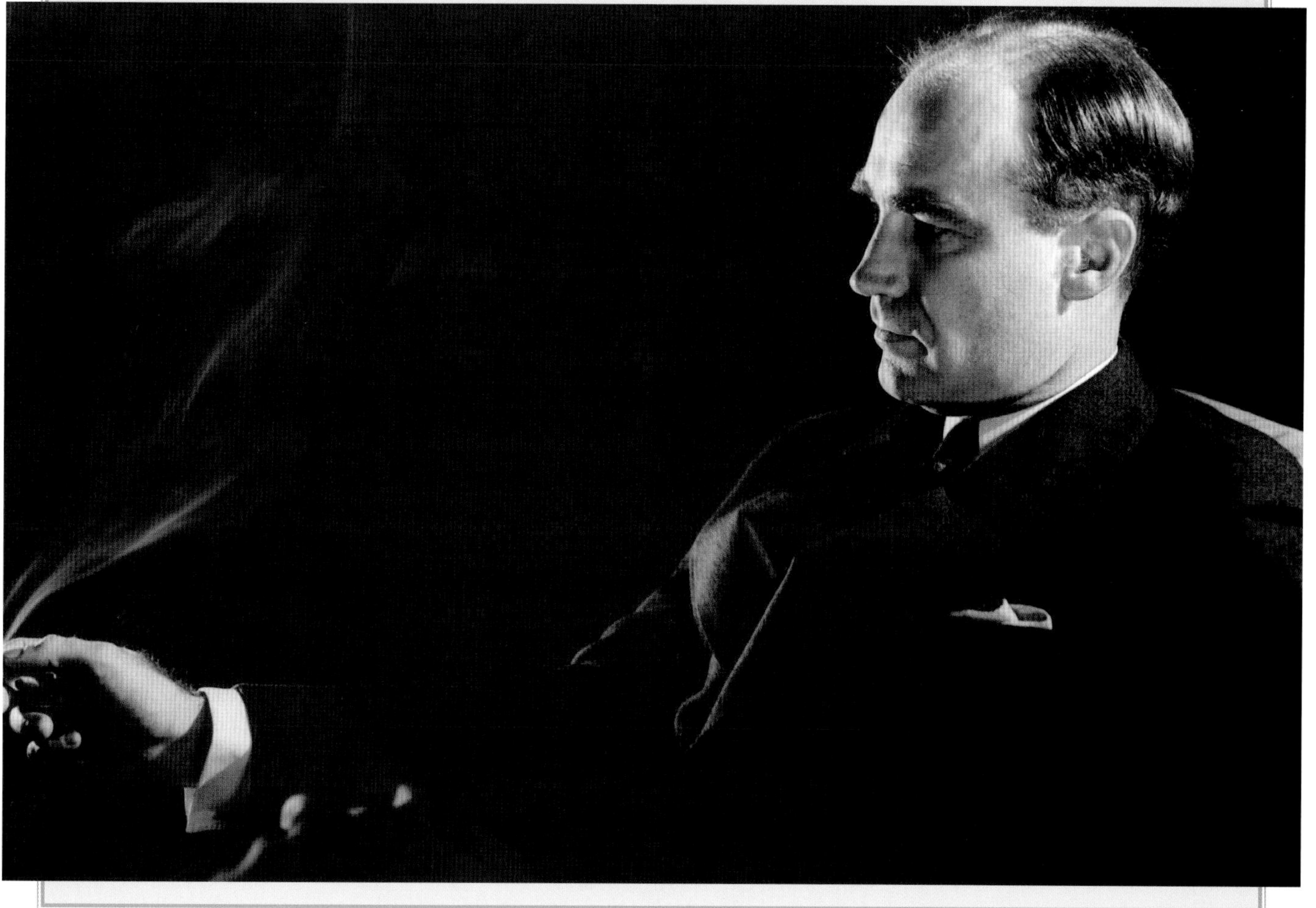

This Bud Fisher comic from 1919 stars the characters Mutt and Jeff. The five-frame comic strip shows Jeff trying out Mutt's magnifying eyeglasses. Jeff puts the glasses on in a New York restaurant to eat a steak.

however, attracted increasing advertising revenue and went from strength to strength. In October 1922 George W. Sutton, Jr., was appointed editor. A month later *Black Mask* ran the first stories by Dashiell Hammett (1894–1961) under the pseudonym "Peter Collinson." On May 15 the following year it published "Three Gun Terry," a story by Carroll John Daly whose protagonist, private eye Terry Mack, is now regarded as the original hard-boiled detective. The long and distinguished line of fictional sleuths who were unsentimental and made no moral claims, but brought a ruthless honesty and dedication to the job, later came to include Hammett's Sam Spade and Raymond Chandler's Philip Marlowe. Also in 1923 the magazine published the first work of Erle Stanley Gardner (1889–1970). His stories were phenomenally successful, and he went on to write 90 million-selling novels, many of which had as their protagonist the Los Angeles lawyer-sleuth Perry Mason.

On October 1, 1923, *Black Mask* published Hammett's first Continental Detective Agency tale, "Arson Plus." In 1926 the author asked for a rise; his request was refused, and so he quit. Almost immediately, *Black Mask* circulation dropped. Hammett brought out his first two novels—*Red Harvest* and *The Dain Curse*—in 1929. In both books the narrator was the anonymous Continental Op (operative). In 1930 Hammett published his most famous novel, *The Maltese Falcon*, with its hero Sam Spade.

Comics

In late-19th century America comic strips began to appear in the Sunday supplements of various newspapers. The earliest was *The Yellow Kid* by Richard Felton Outcault, which first appeared as *Down in Hogan's Alley* in the *New York World* in 1895. In 1896 Outcault was poached by rival publisher William Randolf Hearst. In March 1897 Hearst's *Sunday Journal* began publishing a weekly compendium of strips that sold for 5 cents. These were the seeds of a multimillion dollar industry. In 1911 Krazy Kat made his first appearance in the cartoon strip section of George Herriman's newspapers. By 1916 the prototype "funny animal" was starring in his own color Sunday strip.

The year after Krazy Kat's debut, in an attempt to boost circulation, the *Chicago American* came out with a special cartoon-based promotion. Readers who clipped six coupons from the newspaper could receive an 18-by-6-inch landscape book about Mutt and Jeff, a pair of characters originally created by Bud Fisher in 1908. Despite the fact that this comic sold a remarkable 45,000 copies, it was not for another 18 years that such a special would appear again. In the meantime, magazines filled the gap in the market. In 1922 a reprint magazine, *Comic Monthly*, appeared with each issue devoted to reprints of a separate comic strip.

In January 1929 George Delacorte (1894–1991), working for the pulp publisher New Fiction Company, published *The Funnies* No. 1, the first four-color comic newsstand publication featuring original comic pages rather than reprints. Its cover price was 10 cents. Until No. 5 it was a weekly publication the same size as the free Sunday supplements, making confusion easy and ensuring its failure. In an attempt to save the publication, Delacorte reduced the cover price of No. 25 to 5 cents. Even that was not enough to save it: *The Funnies* ceased publication with issue No. 36. Among *The Funnies* historic firsts was the publication of work by Victoria Pazmino, the first published female comic book artist.

The New Yorker

In 1925 Harold Ross (1892–1951) founded *The New Yorker* and became its first editor. The weekly magazine was primarily literary, but also covered almost the whole gamut of contemporary artistic and political matters of topical interest. *The New Yorker* was glossy and well written, and pioneered the single-line-caption cartoon. From the start *The New Yorker* established an exceptionally high standard of reporting—especially in its famous biographical "Profiles." Writers on *The New Yorker* included Alexander Woolcott, Robert Benchley, H.L. Mencken, and Dorothy Parker.

SEE ALSO:

Books & Publishing • Cartoon & Animation • Fitzgerald, F. Scott • *New Yorker* • Mencken, H.L. • Parker, Dorothy • Pulp Magazines

MARATHON DANCING

The 1920s was a period of wild living and fleeting fads, including crazes for strange record-breaking contests such as dance marathons. These events developed from voluntary, fun activities to one of the most widely attended and controversial forms of commercialized theater.

The craze for dance marathons began in 1923, when 32-year old Alma Cummings danced nonstop for 27 hours, wearing out six different partners, breaking the previous record set in Britain and gaining brief national acclaim for her feat. Her achievement and moment of fame inspired others, most often women, who wished to share her glory and break her record. More local spectacles and contests were held, which dancers could enter solo or with a specific partner, and which celebrated the spirit and endurance of both winners and losers. Dancers aimed to break records, propelled by the excitement of competition, the possibility of brief fame, and cheered on by family and friends. Local dance studios all over the country held marathons. They included McMillan's Dancing Academy in Houston, whose proprietor set a number of firsts in the promotion and development of marathon dancing. He charged admission to spectators and awarded the winner of a 65.5-hour marathon in April 1923 a cash prize for her achievement. McMillan embraced a flair for the spectacular and encouraged contestants to entertain the crowds in any way they could. However, he also seemed to care for and protect his contestants in a way that vanished in later marathons.

Commercializing the craze

After 1923 marathons began to change shape. Sports and entertainment promoters realized that good money could be made from commercializing and standardizing the events. Unlike other fads for record-breaking contests—such as flagpole sitting, which was popular between 1924 and 1929 and saw people perching for ever longer periods on top of poles—dancing had movement and variety, and took place in venues perfect for entertaining audiences. The contests became endless, grueling marathons that would continue for weeks, regulated by rules and heavily promoted to audiences. They were no longer driven primarily by dancers' desire to set records or to enjoy "15 minutes of fame." Rather marathon dances were staged and shaped by promoters driven by the prospect of making money. Presented on a much grander scale, they offered nonstop entertainment hosted by a master of ceremonies and interspersed with performances and specialty numbers, live band music, and audience participation in addition to the contest element.

Each marathon had its own set of rules that governed the dancing, sleeping, eating, bathing, and bathroom breaks of its round-the-clock dancers. Rules often demanded that couples register and stay together, stating that if one partner dropped out, the other had to leave too. They regulated rest periods: 15 minutes

THE DANCE DERBY OF THE CENTURY

On June 10, 1928, Milton Crandall, a veteran promoter and publicist of theatrical events, staged a monumental contest at New York's Madison Square Garden that enshrined the type of mass-entertainment spectacle the dance marathon had become by the late twenties. He called his contest "The Dance Derby of the Century," setting the tone for marathons to follow. Some 91 couples participated in the event, which challenged the attention, strength, and endurance of both dancers and spectators.

Crandall's "Derby" was the most famous and financially successful of the marathons, especially before the 1930s, and was the first to fully exploit the thin line between reality and theater. Creating an ambiance drawn from horse shows, ballrooms, and vaudeville, the event offered everything from exhibition dancers and variety performers to Shipwreck Kelly, the record-holder for flagpole sitting, as well as special "unexpected" guests such as Mary "Texas" Guinan, one of the most infamous speakeasy hostesses of the Prohibition era (*see p. 93*). Crandall knew how to exploit the press to afford his show publicity and coverage, scandalizing and dramatizing the event's daily occurrences. The contest ran until 2:00 P.M. on June 30, when a health commissioner came in and closed it down. The $5,000 prize money was split among the eight couples who remained after the 481 hours of dancing.

for every hour of dancing, often in separate quarters for men and women, during which they could sleep, change clothes, or have a massage—which contestants paid for themselves. Although healthier for the dancers than the earlier nonstop contests, the rest periods allowed the marathons to continue for days, weeks, and even months. The increasingly complex events also drew on the services of more and more people, from judges, musicians, and entertainers to nurses, doctors, masseurs, and souvenir and snack sellers.

Tests of endurance

Although dance marathons were never a test of finesse or technical ability, later contests were much more a question of stamina and endurance, of outliving your opponents, often at a risk to health and well-being. Couples would dance popular dances of the day, including the fox trot, waltz, and Charleston, for as long as possible, while judges watched to verify that their knees did not touch the ground. Rules stated that contestants did not need to dance as long as they stood in a dance position and kept their feet moving. Every so often, however, they were made to take part in a sprint, or quick competition of waltz or fox trot, earning the winning couple prestige and extra money.

To break the monotony of constant dancing for spectators, promoters added distractions, usually performances by both contestants and by guest artists. They invited professional dancers and teachers to enter contests, often paying them to participate. Specialty acts from vaudeville, exhibition dancers, even boxing matches were added to the spectacle. In addition, the competition element and constant proximity of the dancers combined with exhaustion and mental stress to create real dramas and conflicts. Promoters were quick to exploit these stories and rivalries, especially through the newly created tabloid newspapers. They also hired eccentric and ostentatious personalities sure to create exciting situations, and many marathons featured "unexpected" guest appearances by local celebrities such as theatrical agents and performers. The contests combined professional and amateur entertainment, creating real life and theatrical drama.

Like professional wrestling, much about the contests was staged, but both contestants and spectators alike bought into the staged excitement and competition. Spectators could cheer, make wagers, and root for their favorite team, even interacting with the dancers, chatting with them and throwing them money. Contestants were enticed by the potential for fame and fortune, from prizes of several thousand dollars to performing contracts, and were fueled by the audiences' support and applause. In this form

Contestants take part in a marathon in California in April 1927. Some 300 couples competed for a cash prize of $1,000 for dancing a 15-mile (24-km) route between Venice and Los Angeles.

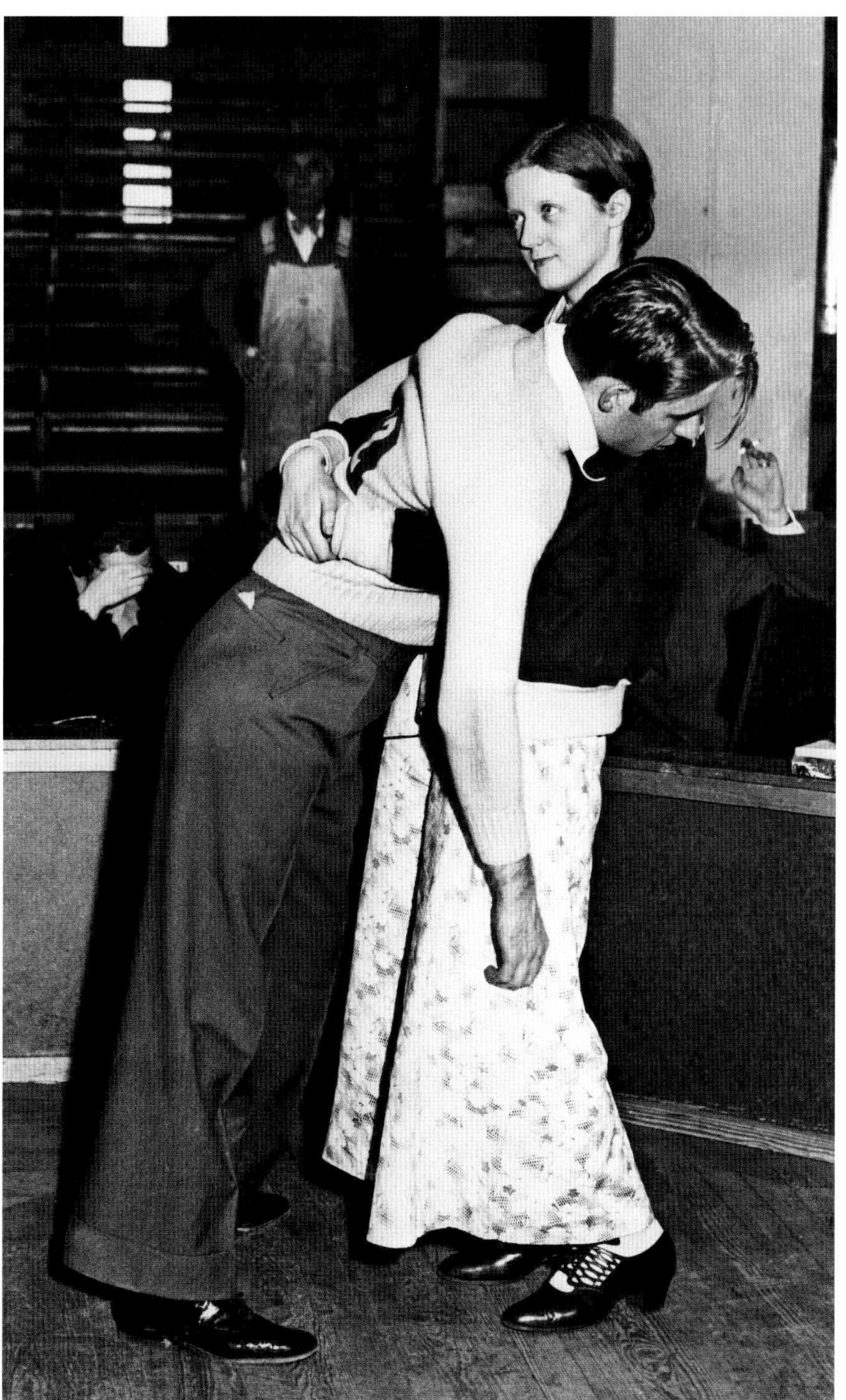

A female contestant holds up her exhausted partner after more than 1,000 hours competing in a dance marathon in 1932.

of episodic entertainment spectators would return day after day to follow their heroes and see more drama unfold.

Many contestants viewed themselves as professional entertainers and traveled the country competing in one marathon after another. Especially during the Depression of the 1930s marathons offered work, shelter, food, potential for extra money, and hope. Marathon dancing became more and more a craze that exploited the poor to entertain the rich. Contestants dreamed of careers in films. Although many found roles as extras, only the few who were already performers, like June Havoc and Red Skelton, found fame and careers in entertainment after their marathon days.

Dancing in the Depression years

During the first half of the 1930s dance marathons developed on an ever-larger scale, drawing on the amount of time spectators and contestants—out-of-work victims of the Depression—had on their hands. The dance marathon record of 5,154 hours, 48 minutes was set from August 29, 1930 until April 1, 1931. The chance of fame and fortune was there for contestants, but often at the cost of humiliation in ever more complex endurance and elimination contests, or even worse, mental and physical health problems—two contestants even danced to their death. The contests of the thirties were certainly a far cry from the fun, record-seeking craze that they had been in the twenties.

By the mid-1930s the popularity of marathon dancing began to decline. It was one of many leisure activities to suffer as money became less and less available in the Depression years. It proved to be a passing fad alongside more enduring forms of entertainment such as sports, theater, music, regular dance, radio, and movies. Objections to the contests on moral grounds—some people thought that the events "corrupted" the contestants, especially the women—had always existed and were fueled by rising opposition from the communities in which promoters staged their marathons. Many people were suspicious of the promoters, local theater owners objected to the competition, and few local police forces welcomed the extra work involved in monitoring the events. The fad finally lost its attraction with the outbreak of World War II. A film starring Jane Fonda about a dance marathon couple, *They Shoot Horses Don't They*, was released in 1969.

SEE ALSO:

Dance • Fads & Crazes • Games & Pastimes • Leisure Activities

Margaret MEAD (1901–1978)

Margaret Mead made the science of anthropology accessible to ordinary people. Anthropology is the study of human beings and human culture. Physical anthropologists study peoples' physical characteristics, while cultural anthropologists study how people live throughout the world.

Cultural anthropology was a new area of study in the 1920s. As a female anthropologist, Mead was able to gain access to women and children in some of the world's remotest regions. Her research greatly increased the West's understanding of their cultures. Mead invented the phrase "generation gap" and was one of the first scientists to study child-rearing, linking it to societal influences. She believed that cultural factors are fundamental determinants of behavior, a view that has been questioned by some later anthropologists.

Margaret Mead was born in Philadelphia, Pennsylvania, on December 16, 1901. The eldest of five children, Mead had a happy childhood. From an early age she was taught at home by her paternal grandmother. Her mother and grandmother were both feminists who encouraged in Mead a self-belief and an interest in observing everyday objects.

An undated photograph of Margaret Mead taken between 1930 and 1950. By then she was a bestselling author with an established reputation.

Education and research

Mead studied at Barnard College, New York, under anthropology professor Franz Boas (1858–1942) and his assistant Ruth Benedict, who became Mead's lifelong mentor. Mead gained her master's degree from Columbia University in 1924.

In 1925 Boas sent Mead to do fieldwork in American Samoa. Because anthropology was a new science, fieldwork techniques were still being established and refined. Nonliterate peoples who had had little contact with the West were considered "primitive" and therefore simpler to study than industrial societies.

Mead was able to study Samoan women and children at close hand. Her brief was to examine Samoan adolescents to see whether they experienced the same teenage problems as American teenagers. Her first book, *Coming of Age in Samoa* (1928), the findings of her research, described how Samoan teenagers passed through adolescence without experiencing the emotional roller coaster usual in Western society. She suggested that if they could get through puberty unscathed, so might American and European teenagers.

Mead's accessible style and outspoken coverage of sexual issues made the book a popular and controversial bestseller, introducing anthropology to a wide audience for the first time. In 1926 she became an assistant curator at the American Museum of Natural History, an association with the museum that continued until her death.

When she finished her Ph.D. in 1929, Mead went to Manus, in the Admiralty Islands, with her second husband and fellow anthropologist, Reo Franklin Fortune. Her research formed the basis of *Growing Up in New Guinea* (1930), which was another popular success.

During the 1930s Mead undertook field research in New Guinea and Bali. She was one of the first anthropologists to realize the potential of film and photography for research. She and her third husband, Gregory Bateson, filmed their Balinese subjects so that other anthropologists could study their material. When Mead's third marriage ended after 15 years, she and her daughter, Catherine Bateson, set up home with another anthropologist and her child in Greenwich Village, New York. Mead continued to write prolifically, producing more than 40 books and over 1,000 articles and monographs.

She became became president of the American Anthropological Society in 1960, curator emeritus at the Museum of Natural History in 1964, and the first president to be elected by the membership of the American Association for Advancement of Science in 1974.

A deeply committed activist, Mead often testified on social issues before Congress and other government agencies. She said, "I have spent most of my life studying the lives of other peoples—faraway peoples—so that Americans might better understand themselves."

SEE ALSO:

Feminism • Lynd Report

MEDICINE

At the start of the 20th century standards in medicine rose considerably. By the 1920s a number of research institutions had been opened, both by the government and by charitable organizations. Other developments included advances in bacteriology, anesthetics, and surgery.

The medical profession—one of the old learned professions—came of age in the first three decades of the 20th century. Declining death rates in both Europe and the United States helped dispel engrained suspicions of doctors. Medical standards rose sharply, and improved sanitation and the achievements of bacteriology raised the public's awareness of the need for better public health provision.

When the United States entered World War I in 1917, the medical examination of potential recruits to the army revealed a startling lack of physical fitness in the nation's youth. Nearly one-third of them were turned down on physical grounds. Other alarming statistics were provided by the American Labor Legislative Review in 1919. Wage-earners were losing 250 million working days a year because of illness, costing the country, at an average of $2 a day, at least $500 million a year. About two-thirds of the people who were too ill to work were without medical care. More than 15,000 American women died every year from complications in childbirth, and 250,000 babies died in the first year of life. Those findings were more important in pointing to the need for health provision than for medicine itself (most studies conducted between 1918 and 1928 concluded that the chief cause of inadequate medical attention was the poverty of large numbers of the population). They also acted as a spur to an improvement in medical practice.

In the 19th century the United States had lagged behind Europe in medical research. However, by the end of the century, thanks to the work of people such as Louis Pasteur in France, the value of

THE RADIO MEDIC

Of the breed of radio quacks who flourished in the 1920s the most notorious was "Doctor" John Brinkley (1885–1941), who set up his own radio station in Milford, Kansas (where he also ran a rejuvenation clinic), to sell his medical specialty—restoring male potency by grafting goat glands (he avoided the word "testicles") into the groin. Brinkley was on the air twice a day, and in 1930 his station, KFKB ("Kansas First, Kansas Best"), was given a Radio Digest Award as the most popular station in America. It is improbable, given the near certainty of tissue rejection, that a single goat gland was ever inserted into anyone, although hundreds of patients testified to being cured.

Brinkley diversified, first into children's ailments and then to supplying patent remedies he advertised on the radio to pharmacists across the country on a royalty basis. Brinkley grew rich and ambitious. He was narrowly beaten in 1930 and 1932 as an independent candidate in the Kansas gubernatorial elections. However, this did him little good. In 1932 Kansas revoked his license to practice medicine, and the Federal Radio Commission closed KFKB.

A photograph of John R. Brinkley from 1920. Brinkley was the archetypal quack, who spread his bogus therapies via radio broadcasts on his own radio station KFKB.

The Rockefeller Institute building in New York on York Avenue and 66th Street. The oil magnate John D. Rockefeller paid millions of dollars from his charitable foundation to found this independent medical research center.

research, especially into infectious diseases like smallpox and tuberculosis, was becoming clear. In 1901 the American Medical Association was reorganized to give a new emphasis to research, which in turn meant reforming medical training at colleges and teaching hospitals. John D. Rockefeller, Jr., established an independent Institute for Medical Research into which his charitable foundation poured millions of dollars. The government established its own laboratories at Bethesda, Maryland. The American College of Surgeons was founded in 1913. Another feature of the time was the founding of medical centers such as the Medical Center, New York (attached to Columbia University and the Presbyterian Hospital) and the Mayo Foundation for Medical Education and Research, Rochester, Minnesota.

Medical reform

Two reports issued in 1909 focused national attention on the task confronting the medical profession. Irving Fisher's (1867–1947) report for the Committee of One Hundred, established in that year, emphasized the importance of preventative medicine. Abraham Flexner (1866–1959), the director of Rockefeller's Institute, produced a report for the Carnegie Foundation for the Advancement of Learning that inaugurated sweeping reforms in medical training. Flexner, one of the country's most prominent educational reformists, toured U.S. medical schools and discovered that even the better schools concentrated on lecturing at the expense of laboratory work on cadavers and neglected important subjects like bacteriology, pathology, and organic chemistry in favor of old-fashioned run-throughs of symptoms and diagnoses. To this catalog of woe Flexner added that state licensing boards validated without much scrutiny the ill-prepared products of a negligent teaching system. He concluded that the country had too many doctors, arguing that when "six or eight ill-trained physicians undertake to gain a living in a town which can only support two, the whole plane of professional conduct is lowered."

Medical reformers had to battle against the efforts of antivivisectionists, anti-

POTIONS AND REMEDIES

Despite the advance of medical science in the early 20th century, quacks peddling secret potions and miracle remedies and "sectarian" doctors offering alternative therapies continued to thrive in the 1920s. It was estimated that thanks to the ignorance and gullibility of sections of the population, $500 million a year were being diverted from legitimate medicine into their hands. In 1932 there were 1,420,000 regular doctors practicing in the United States and 32,000 sectarians.

The most renowned and successful producer of home remedies was Lydia E. Pinkham, who claimed that her Vegetable Compound could cure any female complaint. The compound consisted of a blend of herbs and alcohol. Pinkham first started selling her compound for $1 in 1875. Although there was no scientific proof that her concoction worked, thousands of woman bought it, and Pinkham's business made as much as $300,000 a year at its height. However, by the 1920s, when there were stricter regulations, the Lydia E. Pinkham Medicine Co. was forced to stop making unsubstantiated claims for its compound.

By far the largest group of nonregular practitioners were osteopaths and chiropractors. While osteopaths and chiropractors prospered, pharmacists suffered. Throughout the 1920s the number of doctors' prescriptions declined, forcing pharmacists to rely for their income more and more on general retail trade in household goods—hence the rise of the "drugstore" that sold almost everything except drugs.

An old man tapping Seneca oil (a crude oil that quacks and hawkers claimed could cure all ailments) from a barrel on a horse for a woman and two girls in the 1920s.

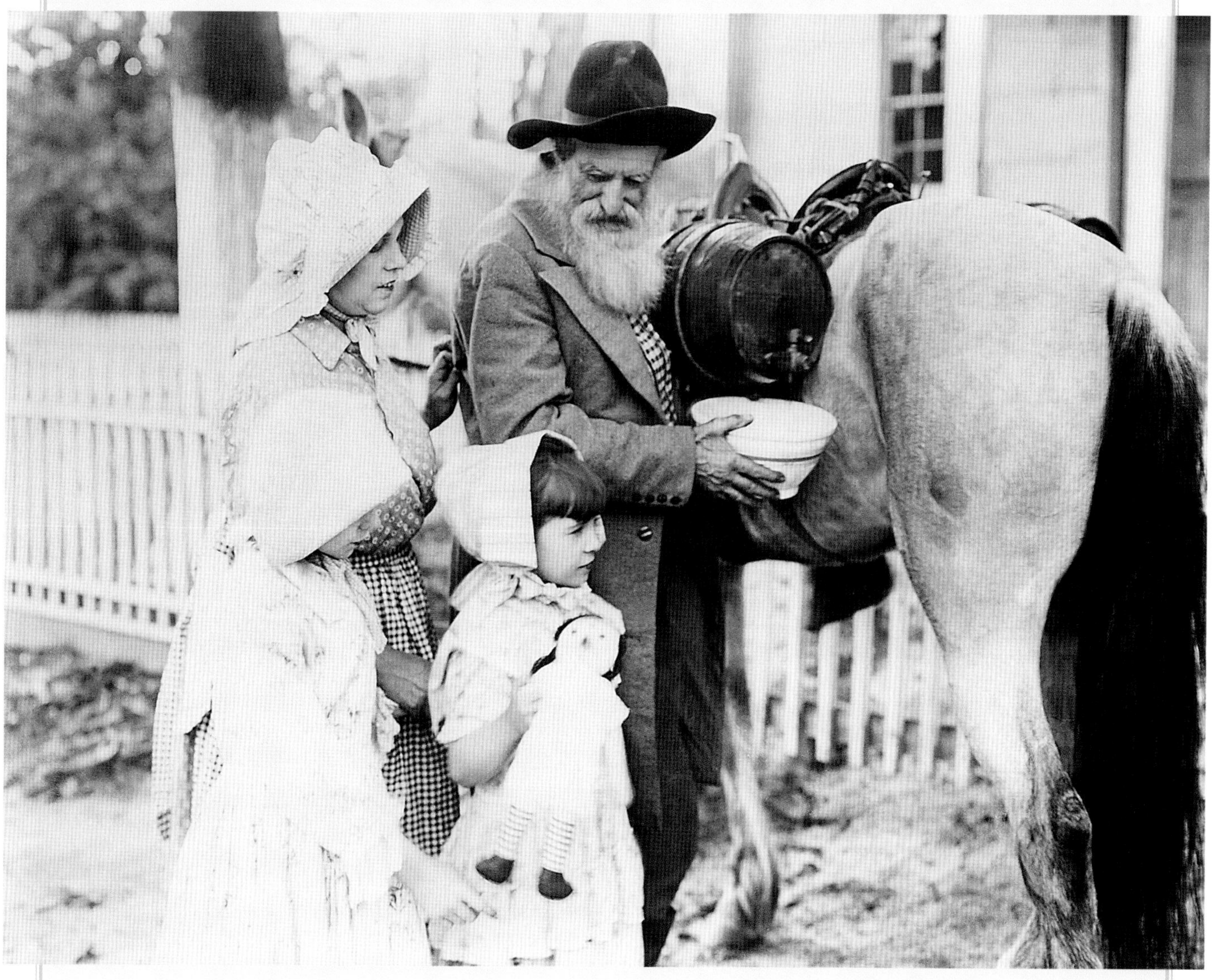

PAYING FOR MEDICINE

In the 1920s the American Medical Association (AMA) and most doctors opposed compulsory state national health insurance because they did not want the state to interfere in medical issues. They were also concerned about income levels, particularly for doctors working in the public health sector. The AMA established a Bureau of Medical Economics to study the financial position of doctors and published a journal devoted entirely to the business side of the profession. The bureau reported in 1931 that the lowest average income occurred among doctors involved in public health work, while the highest was among surgeons. The former earned about $5,000 annually, the latter about $13,000. In general, salaried practitioners made less money than doctors who derived their income from patients' fees. It was among salaried doctors that most of the one-quarter of the profession who earned less than $3,500 were to be found. Some organizations—universities, industrial concerns, and in a few instances benevolent foundations and charities—experimented with forms of health coverage during the period.

vaccinationists, and Christian Scientists (who reject medical intervention) to stem the advance of medical knowledge and practice by cutting off funds for research. Even so, Flexner's report galvanized the medical profession. Over the next two decades universities established chairs in premedical studies and even in clinical fields, setting scientists free to devote most of their time to research. A growing proportion of the staff in medical schools and teaching hospitals were given full-time appointments, which enabled doctors to make careers in the classroom and the laboratory. Rising standards in medical schools and teaching hospitals were accompanied by an increase in student applications.

Despite ingrained prejudice among male doctors and in the AMA, there were a number of notable women doctors during the twenties. They included Dr. Florence R. Sabin (1871–1953), who became an influential role model for other women. From 1901 to 1925 Sabin conducted research on the origins of the lymphatic system, blood vessels, and white blood cells, and from 1924 to 1926 she was the first woman to serve as president of the American Association of Anatomists.

Surgery

Improvements in surgery in general constituted one of the great success stories of the decade. Surgery benefited considerably from the experience of operating on wounded soldiers during World War I and from advances in anesthesia such as the use of avertin (tribromethal alcohol) as a rectal anesthetic. Surgery came to supplant some older treatments, notably in orthopedics, where operations replaced the use of straps and braces.

Hospitals

Surveys undertaken by the American College of Surgeons before World War I disclosed that many hospitals had no laboratories and no X-rays. The college therefore came up with a list of requirements relating to the keeping of records as well as the availability of research, diagnostic, and therapeutic facilities, which every hospital had to satisfy before it could be placed on the college's approved list. The new regime produced quick results. In 1918 only 13 percent of 692 large hospitals were approved by the college; in 1932 the college inspected 1,600 hospitals and approved 93 percent of them.

In the United States and in Europe research in the fields of immunology and chemotherapy, of which so much had been expected after German doctor Paul Erlich's 1909 discovery of the "magic bullet"—salvarsan (an arsenic compound)—which was to prove effective against syphilis, remained in the doldrums. In other fields parts of Europe made more headway than the United States. Germany, for example, had made vaccination against smallpox compulsory in 1874 and almost eliminated the disease. In the U.S. vaccination remained voluntary at a federal level, and only some state legislatures made it compulsory. In 1924 one-fifth of all smallpox cases in the world were in the United States. Where maternity centers were set up for prenatal care, maternal mortality dropped, as in New York, to less than 2 deaths per 1,000 mothers, as low as in progressive countries such as Denmark; but the national average in 1929 was still 6 deaths per 1,000.

Deaths from typhoid fever and tuberculosis declined sharply. But despite improvements in X-ray technology and electrocardiography, deaths from heart disease rose dramatically, as did cancer and diseases of the kidneys. X-rays were effective when used with radium treatment to get rid of minor and incipient noncancerous tumors. The rise in degenerative diseases, such as cancer and heart disease, was accompanied by the continued failure to find a prevention or cure for chronic diseases like arthritis. The rise in degenerative, as opposed to infectious, diseases was largely a reflection of the fact that people were living longer.

Rising rates of cancer and heart disease were ill portents for the future, but at the end of the 1920s the United States was much better placed to face the medical future than it had been 10 years earlier. *The Encylopedia of Social Sciences* gave its judgment that whereas only recently "the standard of medical education in the United States was incredibly low," by 1930 American medical schools ranked equal with those of any other country and were on the whole better equipped.

SEE ALSO:

Birth Control • Cushing, Harvey • Drugs & Drug Use • Healthcare • Population • Poverty • Rockefeller, John D., Jr.

Andrew MELLON (1855–1937)

Andrew William Mellon—financier, industrialist, and secretary of the Treasury to three consecutive Republican presidents from 1921 to 1932—was so powerful a figure that it was said three presidents served under him.

Mellon was the son of a wealthy Pittsburgh banker. He graduated from the Western University of Pennsylvania (now the University of Pittsburgh) in 1873 and entered his father's banking house in 1874. He proved so capable that his father transferred the bank's ownership to him in 1882.

Mellon branched out from banking into industrial activities. He helped establish the Union Trust Company and Union Savings Bank of Pittsburgh, the Gulf Oil Company, the Aluminum Company of America (Alcoa), and the Union Steel Company. By the early 1920s Mellon was one of the richest men in the country.

Secretary of the Treasury

In 1921 President Warren G. Harding appointed Mellon to head the Treasury—a position he was to hold until 1932—with a brief to reform the tax and tariff systems. Deeply conservative, Mellon believed in running government to suit big business. In 1920s terms that meant high protective tariffs and low taxation.

The first was achieved by the Fordney–McCumber Act of 1922, which imposed the highest import tariffs in American history. Mellon used the large budgetary surplus produced by tariffs to lower taxation for the rich and to reduce the national debt from $24.289 billion in 1920 to $16.185 billion in 1930. Mellon believed in the trickle-down effect—tax cuts for the rich would encourage them to create wealth that would trickle down to those who were less well off.

When Mellon joined the Treasury, the cost of running the government was $6.5 billion. At the end of his first three years the annual budget had been reduced to $3.5 billion, and the national debt had been reduced to $2.8 billion. In November 1923 Mellon introduced what became known as the Mellon Plan, which used surplus revenues to lower taxes. It became law as the Revenue Act of 1924.

Mellon's policies did much to fuel the 1920s economic boom, and for most of the decade he was a popular figure. The start of the Depression brought him under increasing criticism as his policies worsened its effect on ordinary people. In 1932 he resigned to become U.S. ambassador to Britain for a year before retiring.

Although Mellon had resigned the presidency of the Mellon National Bank and directorships in 60 corporations when he entered the cabinet in 1921, he put his investments into a family corporation that continued to make large sums of money. In 1935 his 1931 income-tax return came under federal investigation, but he was cleared four months after his death.

Andrew Mellon in 1925, when he was secretary of the Treasury under Calvin Coolidge. Frail, soft-spoken, and outwardly unassuming, he shook hands by the fingertips and wore only dark suits, the jackets always buttoned.

In 1913 Mellon gave $10 million to the Mellon Institute of Industrial Research; in 1937 he donated his art collection, valued at $25 million to the government, plus $15 million to build the National Gallery of Art in Washington, D.C.

SEE ALSO:

Business • Economy • Industry • Protectionism • Taxation • Trade • Wall Street Crash

H.L. MENCKEN (1880–1956)

H.L. Mencken was one of the most influential literary critics and social commentators of the 1920s. Known for his scathing satirical style and attacks on the weaknesses of American life, he also supported emerging writers and produced a highly regarded study of American English.

The "Great Iconoclast" and the "Sage of Baltimore" were just two of the nicknames given to Henry Louis Mencken during his lifetime. A man of many talents, Mencken was a satirist, critic, journalist, editor, author, and linguist. During the twenties he was the leading intellectual critic of the social and cultural life of America, and a mentor to the younger generation. His biting satire and criticism made his newspaper columns and collected volumes of writings essential reading for most of the decade.

H.L. Mencken, as he always signed himself, was born on September 12, 1880, in Baltimore, Maryland, to parents who were descended from German immigrants. His upbringing, in a German American family, exerted a strong influence all his life. He championed German culture and values, and his pro-German stance led to his newspaper articles being stopped during World War I (1914–1918). Mencken also remained loyal to the city of Baltimore, where he lived all his life.

Mencken was eager to be a newspaper reporter from an early age. However, on his father's wishes he briefly joined the family's successful cigar business. He left when his father died unexpectedly, and in 1899 Mencken joined the *Baltimore Morning Herald* as a cub reporter. Four years later he became the paper's editor.

H.L. Mencken photographed in 1932 by the photographer, critic, and novelist Carl Van Vechten (1880–1964).

AMERICAN MERCURY

The first issue of *American Mercury*, with its distinctive green cover, appeared in January 1924. The magazine was primarily a social commentary, although it included poetry and writing by new writers. It was an immediate hit and became a status symbol. In its first editorial, Mencken set out the magazine's aim: "The editors are committed to nothing save this: to keep the common sense as best as they can, to belabor sham as agreeably as possible, to give a civilized entertainment." At the peak of its popularity in 1927 the magazine's circulation reached 77,000. As well as publishing new literary voices, the magazine published criticism on all kinds of topics. The articles, representing a wide variety of approaches and opinions, set out to provoke using humor, irony, and satire. One regular feature was the "Americana" column. It presented clippings, notes, and public announcements drawn from a wide range of sources from across the country and was intended to illustrate the stupidity and prejudices of the American population.

Mencken flirted with the idea of being a novelist or poet. In 1903 he published a volume of poetry; but as he read more widely, he became convinced that his talent lay not in creative writing but in criticism. After working at the *Herald*, Mencken joined the *Baltimore Sun* in 1906 and worked there intermittently until 1941. Initially employed as editor of the Sunday edition, Mencken had time on his hands and started to write editorials and theater reviews. He soon stopped reviewing when he realized that all his pieces were negative, but he continued writing editorials.

Social critique

Mencken's editorials provided a platform for the so-called "ideological warfare" that he perfected during the twenties. Among his many targets were provincialism, snobbery, organized religion, Anglo-Saxon culture, and the American middle class. In 1908 he became literary critic of *The Smart Set*, a New York monthly magazine where he worked for six years as book reviewer and nine as coeditor with the drama critic George Jean Nathan (1882–1958). Mencken believed that the writer's duty was to present the "unvarnished truth," and his literary reviews supported the work of new authors such as Theodore Dreiser (1871–1945) and Sinclair Lewis (1885–1951). The magazine gave Mencken a national audience, and it was during this period that he found his outrageous and provocative voice.

As well as his biting social criticism, he was interested in the development of language, particularly the differences between American and British English. In 1919 he published *The American Language*, a study of the differences and a record of American phrases and idioms. The book was updated and reprinted several times during Mencken's lifetime.

In the twenties Mencken's reputation as the country's leading literary and social critic was cemented with the publication between 1919 and 1927 of *Prejudices*, a six-volume collection of essays. In these writings he examined and often satirized every aspect of American life. Nobody was exempt from his razor-sharp wit, from politicians to the average middle-class American, whom he nicknamed the "booboisie." He relished the controversy he caused.

When in July 1925 he attended the Scopes Trial—the trial of John T. Scopes, a high school teacher in Dayton, Tennessee, charged with violating state law for teaching the theory of evolution—Mencken was as much a celebrity as a reporter, and his excoriating reports for the *Baltimore Evening Sun* did not disappoint his fans. He called Tennesseans "gaping primates of the Cumberland slopes" and wrote a savage obituary of the anti-evolutionist lawyer William Jennings Bryan (1860–1925). Such was the antipathy he caused among local people in Dayton that many people expected him to be run out of town.

For most of the decade Mencken's main platform was the magazine he cofounded and edited with Nathan, the *American Mercury* (*see box above*). The magazine was the journalistic phenomenon of the decade and was aimed at a middle-class audience from college students to business leaders. During the 10 years he edited the magazine, from 1923 to 1933, Mencken reached the height of his influence and popularity. With the onset of the Great Depression, however, the wit that had served him and his reading public for most of the decade suddenly seemed inappropriate, and Mencken's influence waned dramatically at the start of the 1930s. He resigned from the *Mercury* in 1933, his economic conservatism alienating the readers he had once attracted.

During the 1930s and 1940s Mencken found his satirical style out of fashion. Nevertheless, he continued to write and publish both in newspapers and books. He found temporary happiness in his personal life when he married the writer Sara Powell Haardt (1898–1935) shortly before his 50th birthday in 1930. Her untimely death five years later left him alone with his writing, whereupon he immersed himself in diary writing.

His career was cut short by a stroke on November 23, 1948, which left him unable to read or write. He died in his sleep in Baltimore on January 29, 1956. His will specified that works such as his diary, *My Life as Author and Editor*, and *Thirty-Five Years of Newspaper Work* could not be published until 35 years after his death. When they finally appeared in the late 1980s and 1990s, controversy over his opinions flared up once more.

SEE ALSO:

Dreiser, Theodore • Lewis, Sinclair • Literature • Magazines & Magazine Publishing • Pulp Magazines • Scopes Trial

MEXICAN AMERICANS

Mexicans began to emigrate to the United States in large numbers after the Mexican War (1846–1848) in response to an increasing demand for cheap agricultural labor in the Southwestern states. The economic boom of the 1920s attracted ever greater numbers.

There were several reasons for the increased demand for Mexican labor in the late 19th and early 20th centuries. In 1882 there was a ban on Chinese immigrants; this was followed by the exclusion of the Japanese in 1924. World War I (1914–1918) had caused European emigration to the United States to dry up while at the same time boosting the demand for unskilled labor as world markets for American food expanded.

Mexico was the nearest source of cheap agricultural labor—cheap by U.S. standards, but alluring to Mexicans. Eager to escape low wages, high taxes, and unemployment in their native country, "Chicanos," as they came to be called, boarded railroad cars that took them thousands of miles from the Mexican central plateau to the American border states and beyond.

The 1910 census estimated that there were 162,000 Mexican-born residents in the United States. That may have been an underestimate. By the beginning of World War I Mexicans had replaced blacks and American whites as the most important ethnic group in California agriculture and had become essential to cotton and vegetable farming throughout the Southwest. Sugar-beet farming drew Chicanos as far north as Michigan, Minnesota, Ohio, and the Dakotas, where they were willing to do the stoop labor that Americans and earlier immigrant groups now refused to do. By 1927 Mexico supplied almost all of the United States' beet-pickers. Tomato-harvesting, which was even more arduous, brought Mexican families to Midwestern states such as Indiana. Between 1890 and 1930 one-eighth of Mexico's population headed north to work.

Nonagricultural work

Businessmen and professionals also looked to greener pastures north of the Rio Grande. Many had backed the losing side in the Mexican Revolution (1910–1920). They tended to distance themselves from the poorer emigrants, taking pride in a supposed "pure" Hispanic ancestry that they believed made them superior to the Chicanos. A Mexican merchant summed up the difference in attitudes when he described Chicanos as "mostly Indians of the lower uneducated class of peons" (landless laboring class).

Not all unskilled Chicanos found work on farms. According to a 1928 survey, 75 percent of workers in the Texas construction trade were Mexican. The first few hundred Mexicans to make their way to Chicago were railroad workers recruited from the Texas–Mexico border in 1916. By 1930 there were 30,000 Mexicans in Chicago, the second largest concentration of Mexicans in the United States after Los Angeles. In 1930 Los Angeles had a population of about 1 million, 90,000 of whom were Mexicans.

In the agricultural off-season Chicanos worked in steel and automobile factories, oil and sugar refineries, textile mills, mines, and furnaces. The 1930 census recorded that, for the first time, more than

COMMUTERS

More people go back and forth daily over the Mexican–American border than across any other international boundary. In the 1920s the flow was less constant than it is now and the numbers were fewer, but there were already a significant number of Mexicans who had jobs in the United States while continuing to live in Mexico. Some of them returned home every night; others stayed in the United States during the working week and returned to Mexico on weekends. No law was passed by Congress to allow such a breach of conventional immigration controls to operate, but in a series of rulings in 1927 the Immigration and Naturalization Service gave official backing to a commuter system that had its origins in the 19th century. The government took the view, as it did with regard to Canada, that relations with Mexico were so close that tight immigration rules need not be enforced. It was a pragmatic and sensible arrangement, given the high demand for seasonal Mexican labor. Mexicans were also exempted from national immigration quotas laid down in the National Origins Act of 1924.

Mexican Americans lay irrigation pipes in Ventura County, California, in about 1920. Water shortages prompted a number of irrigation projects in the twenties to provide farmers with water and stimulate economic growth.

half of Mexican Americans lived and worked in towns and cities.

Urban Chicanos tended to take jobs in occupations previously filled by earlier immigrant groups who had worked themselves up the economic and social ladder. They moved into empty rundown housing near their places of work, such as the Hull House area in Chicago near the steelworks and the dockyard districts adjoining the meatpacking plants.

Harsh conditions

Hard as their lives were, industrial workers were better off than farmworkers. A mineworker might earn $5 a day; tomato-pickers were paid $1.50. Crop-picking was muscle-aching drudgery, performed from daybreak to nightfall in all weathers. Near-starvation wages often meant living on a diet of bread and beans.

As "agribusiness" developed, associated with extensive irrigation, farms grew ever larger. By 1929 large-scale farming accounted for 60 percent of U.S. fruit and vegetable production. Agribusiness depended on "fluid" migrant labor. Whole communities of Mexicans followed the harvest, moving from place to place by truck and living in temporary settlements of shacks, called *barrios*, or camping in barns or empty slaughterhouses. Women and children, often in defiance of labor laws, joined the men in the fields (*see box on p. 22*).

The Spanish-speaking *barrios* had advantages in that Chicanos had their own shops and bars, and drew comfort from living among their own people. However, they were created as much by prejudice as by the Chicanos' desire to stick together. Many Southwestern communities had restrictive agreements against the leasing or selling of property to Mexicans, Jews, and other "undesirables."

Many Hispanic Americans had served in the U.S. armed forces during World War I. In 1921 veterans formed the Mexican American organization Sons of America to break down prejudice against Mexican Americans. Cultural organizations to preserve Mexican traditions also came into being, along with welfare organizations to provide social security in the absence of government benefits.

MEXICAN SCHOOLS AND THE "MEXICAN PROBLEM"

In the late 1920s Americans began talking about the "Mexican problem." The term came from a book published in 1928 by Robert McLean, *That Mexican! As He Really Is North and South of the Rio Grande*: "With his inherited ignorance, his superstition, his habits of poor housing, his weakness to some diseases, and his resistance to others, with his abiding love of beauty, he has come to pour his blood into the veins of our national life. 'That Mexican' no longer lives in Mexico ... The 'Mexican Problem'... reaches from Gopher Prairie to Guatemala."

The Mexican problem included segregated, underfunded, and overcrowded schools, generally staffed by substandard teachers. Such schools offered an inferior education to that provided by ordinary state schools. In rural districts teaching hours were reduced to allow children to work in the fields. Some state governments—most notoriously Texas—thought that migrant child labor was too important to the agricultural economy to provide schools of any kind for child workers.

The overriding purpose of Mexican schools was to promote assimilation and Americanize Mexican children. Academic subjects were considered less important than vocational training and general knowledge less important than learning how to behave and think like an American. The less "Mexican" pupils became, the higher their grades and the more respect they earned from their teachers and their non-Mexican neighbors.

Mexican American children in a kindergarten class at Lincoln Elementary School, San Gabriel, California, in 1924. Teachers discouraged Mexican children from speaking Spanish.

Mexican Americans were much like other immigrant groups. However, they did not feel as uprooted as immigrants who had crossed the ocean; it was easier for them to keep in touch with and visit friends and family back home. Their close family ties, with three generations often living under the same roof, provided support and stability.

A high proportion of the "guest workers" were single males who thought of themselves as temporary residents, traveling away from home for adventure and the aim of saving money before returning home. As a result, they seldom took out naturalization papers. In 1930 only 5.8 percent of Mexican-born residents in the United States had become naturalized—the lowest percentage of any immigrant group. The good thing about Chicanos not being citizens, as far as employers were concerned, was that they could not vote for programs such as social security. It also meant that few first-generation Mexican Americans had the vote, allowing politicians to ignore them. During the Depression, when jobs were scarce, tens of thousands of Mexicans were forced to return to Mexico.

SEE ALSO:

Agriculture • Immigration • Industry • Mexico • National Origins Act, 1924

MEXICO

The twenties were a period of relative peace and prosperity for Mexico as the country emerged from 10 years of revolution and bloody civil war. However, as the new government embarked on a program of social and economic reform, relations with the United States remained strained.

The relationship between the United States and its southern neighbor, Mexico, was difficult at the start of the 1920s. The Mexican Revolution of November 1910 had continued to play out for much of the succeeding decade. Historians estimate that the long and bloody struggle between constantly shifting factions cost the lives of about an eighth of the population. The U.S. government was horrified by the peasant uprisings that convulsed Mexico and by the 1911 overthrow of the dictator Porfirio Díaz (1830–1915), who had ruled since 1876. To the United States the dictatorship of Porfirio Díaz had made Mexico a secure neighbor and a stable economy worth investing in.

American investment

After he had consolidated his power, Díaz had embarked on a modernization program that included the creation of infrastructure such as railroads, roads, and telephone lines, and the promotion of industry. Because the government was in debt and had few cash reserves, Díaz had turned to foreign investors, offering them extremely favorable terms to attract their capital. By 1910 the vast majority of the country's oil and mining rights, railroads, and natural resources were owned by foreign—mainly American—corporations. In 1910 the United States and Mexico did business together worth $117,000,000. American economic power was felt throughout the Mexican economy. However, despite Díaz's policies—or to some extent, because of them, since they favored foreign investors and the landowning elite—Mexico remained an essentially peasant state. The population was predominantly rural, comprising tenant farmers. Fewer than 3 percent of Mexican families owned land. Three million agricultural workers earned 35

This photograph shows Porfirio Díaz in around 1911, the year in which he was ousted from the presidency. During the 34 years of his repressive regime he initiated a program of modernization that relied heavily on U.S. investment.

cents a day and lived in a system of peonage (laborers who were bound in servitude through debt). Widespread poverty and dissatisfaction with Díaz's policies, which benefited a small elite and American interests, formed the backdrop to the Revolution.

Revolution and nationalism

At the start of the Revolution as many as 75,000 Americans lived in Mexico. When the Revolution erupted, between 200 and 500 U.S. citizens lost their lives, and some 45,000 of them fled. The anti-American riots and rhetoric of the Revolution, with its avowedly nationalistic stance, shocked the United States. The U.S. government turned against the liberal president Francisco Madero (1873–1913) who had wrested power from Díaz and been elected in 1911. It feared that he would make too many concessions to rebel leaders and that the worsening unrest in the country seriously threatened U.S. business interests. In 1913 Madero was overthrown and assassinated by the head of the armed forces, General Victoriano Huerta (1854–1916), who embarked on a repressive military dictatorship. Huerta promised to protect foreign interests in the country. However, America's new president, Woodrow Wilson (1913–1921), had admired Madero as a reformer and reacted with alarm to his bloody overthrow. Wilson refused to recognize Huerta and urged him to hold democratic elections; when Huerta refused, Wilson gave his support to Madero's follower Venustiano Carranza (1859–1920).

Carranza won control of most of the country by 1915. However, the revolutionary forces that backed him split, and civil war raged between Carranza's followers and those of his chief rivals, Pancho Villa (1878–1923) and Emiliano Zapata (1879–1919). In 1916 Villa initiated an attack against Americans in the town of Columbus, New Mexico, to demonstrate Carranza's lack of control in northern Mexico and as a reaction to the United States cutting off his arms supply; 17 Americans were executed. Two months later Villa attacked Columbus, New Mexico, killing about 17 Americans. Wilson sent a punitive expedition to Mexico under General Pershing to hunt for Villa, and relations between the governments deteriorated. They improved

Venustiano Carranza and the officers who backed him in his fight for the presidency pose in front of the presidential chair in 1916. Alvaro Obregón, who succeeded Carranza as president, stands to Carranza's right.

DWIGHT D. MORROW

After Mexico was readmitted into the international fold in 1923, the United States appointed James Rockwell Sheffield (1864–1938) as ambassador to Mexico, a post he held from 1924 to 1927. Sheffield was a New York Republican with no diplomatic experience. Convinced that Mexico presented a Bolshevik threat to the United States, he did nothing to improve understanding between the two countries.

In contrast his successor, Dwight D. Morrow (1873–1931), was one of the greatest ambassadors to serve in Mexico. A lawyer turned banker, Spanish-speaking Morrow was an old school friend of President Calvin Coolidge (1923–1929), who offered him the position in 1927—he held the office until September 1930. Morrow's appointment marked the start of the most successful period of cooperation between the United States and Mexico. His work showed how much one man can influence relations between two countries.

Morrow loved Mexico and worked hard in his new role. Famed for his charm, he ignored many of the traditional diplomatic formalities and soon became a confidant of President Calles. He played an active role in settling the Cristero Rebellion (*see box on p. 26*) and gained limited recognition for the oil and land holdings of American citizens dating from before the 1917 constitution. Morrow also involved himself in the promotion of artistic and cultural ties between the two countries. The aviator Charles A. Lindbergh (1902–1974)—Morrow's future son-in-law—and actor Will Rogers (1879–1935) were just two of the American stars Morrow brought to Mexico on goodwill tours. He commissioned Mexican artist Diego Rivera (1886–1957) to paint a series of murals at the Palace of Hernán Cortés, Cuernavaca, in 1929. He is also widely credited with conceiving the idea for the *Mexican Art Show*, which opened at the Metropolitan Museum of Art in New York in 1930. Morrow's great contribution to U.S.-Mexican relations provided a precedent for the "Good Neighbor Policy" that underlay U.S. foreign policy in the 1930s.

slightly, but remained difficult after U.S. forces withdrew and Carranza was elected president in 1917. Mexico's neutrality during World War I (1914–1918) angered Wilson, who interpreted the country's stance as being pro-German

President Carranza (1915–1920) rejected the Monroe Doctrine—under which the United States assumed the right to police the central American region—and developed a nationalistic agenda. His principal objective was to place Mexico in a position to solve its own problems without relying on the United States. The new Mexican constitution, drawn up in 1917, was a comprehensive framework for social, economic, and political reform; it included a statement of Mexico's right to own its own subsoil resources—its mineral and oil rights—thereby setting the scene for a showdown with the country's mighty northern neighbor.

The chance of improved relations

At the start of the twenties, however, an opportunity existed for Mexico and the United States to forge closer ties. Many of the major protagonists of the Revolution were now dead or retired. President Wilson had left the White House. Pancho Villa had retired. Emiliano Zapata, the revolutionary leader who had fought for social reform, namely land redistribution, had been assassinated in 1919. Carranza had been assassinated in 1920 at the end of his term in office, when he tried to force the election of his chosen successor, Ignacio Bollinas. Carranza's former supporter Alvaro Obregón (1880–1928), dissatisfied with the outgoing president's lack of progress on social reform, had staged an almost bloodless coup with two other powerful leaders, Plutarco Elías Calles (1877–1945) and Adolfo de la Huerta (1881–1955). Obregón was elected president in December 1920. Under his government a period of relative peace and prosperity ensued, and the reforms of the 1917 constitution were put into practice. However, despite the leadership changes in the United States and Mexico, the first half of the twenties saw relations between the two countries as strained as they had been in the 1910s.

President Warren G. Harding (1921–1923) did not share Wilson's belief that democracy could be installed overnight in Mexico. Harding reverted to a hands-off approach. His policy of nonintervention made political life in Mexico difficult. Obregón's administration found itself dealing not only with the U.S. State Department; it was also approached directly by every American group with a vested interest in Mexico, from the U.S. Department of Commerce, the Catholic Church, and private banks in New York to the mayors of small towns on the U.S.–Mexico border. The Mexican government had to tread a careful path between these different groups with their varied demands. To make matters even more difficult, the United States refused to officially recognize Obregón's administration.

While the United States continued to withhold diplomatic recognition of the new postrevolutionary Mexican government, the rest of the world followed suit. The United States considered Obregón too radical; the major obstacle preventing U.S. recognition of his administration was the 1917 Mexican constitution, specifically Article 27, the clause about ownership of subsoil rights. U.S. Secretary of the Interior Albert B. Fall (1861–1944), with the backing of American and British oil companies, tried to force Obregón to repeal Article 27 in exchange for U.S. diplomatic recognition.

At the same time, U.S. banks hoped to persuade the Mexican government to repay its national debt, which had grown substantially during the civil war. While Washington refused to recognize Mexico, the mayors of many small American

THE CRISTERO REBELLION

From 1926 many Mexican Catholics engaged in an anti-government, anti-Calles uprising. They were outraged by the Mexican president's enforcement of sections of the 1917 constitution that aimed to control the power of the Catholic Church. Hundreds of thousands of peasants from the central-west region of Mexico rose up against the Calles regime. In the United States American Catholics pressed the U.S. government to take a stand against Calles.

After he became president in 1924, Calles issued laws to implement the constitutional changes needed to separate church and state. In response the Mexican clergy went on strike. All churches closed, and public worship was suspended from July 31, 1926. Peasant uprisings and armed hostilities followed. For the next three years Mexican peasants, particularly in the states of Jalisco and Michoacán, continued to fight government forces. U.S. Ambassador Morrow (*see box on p. 25*) helped end the stalemate, which lasted until 1930, by negotiating the return of religious instruction, which was, once again, allowed in churches. The name Cristero came from the rebels' rallying slogan, "*Viva Cristo Rey!*" (Long Live Christ the King). A member of the Cristeros, José de León de Toral, assassinated President Obregón in 1928.

Plutarco Elías Calles pictured in 1931. The anti-Catholic measures implemented by Calles during his presidency precipitated the Cristero Rebellion.

border towns lobbied for Mexico to be re-admitted into the diplomatic fold to generate further business with their close neighbor. For its part, Mexico wanted to gain diplomatic recognition from the United States to reap the benefits of wider international recognition that would follow. It also wanted to be able to influence the development of the Pan American Union across the Americas, thereby preventing the United States from dominating its growth.

Much to the irritation of the United States, Mexico was eager to support other social revolutions within its vicinity in order to lessen its political isolation. To this end, when President Plutarco Calles took office in 1924, Mexico started to develop a strong bond with Cuba, which was also struggling in its relationship with the United States. During the same period the Mexican government supported the Nicaraguan guerrilla Augusto Sandino (1893–1934) in his fight against the United States from the mid-1920s.

The oil industry

The early twenties were also a watershed in the Mexican oil industry. Much American agitation about events in Mexico was caused by the large amount of capital investment U.S. companies had made in the Mexican oil industry. The changes that took place at the start of the decade eventually led to the expropriation of foreign-owned oil companies in 1938. When President Obregón assumed office, he consolidated his political power base to such a degree that he and his successor, President Calles, were in a position to impose new taxes and regulations on the oil industry. However, by the mid-twenties tax revenue from oil had dropped due to an 80 percent decline in oil production. Having increased in the 1910s, oil prices started to slide in 1920. In an effort to compete internationally, companies laid off thousands of workers between 1921 and 1922. The workers, to protect their position, retaliated by creating larger unions and working closely with the Obregón government. When the economy picked up in 1923, workers secured wage increases and improved benefits. However, this temporary improvement could not disguise the fact that the Mexican oil industry of the twenties was a shadow of its former self. To the south, Colombia, Peru, and Venezuela increased production; by the end of the decade Mexico's share of the oil market was significantly reduced.

President Obregón initially refused to concede the mineral rights in his dealings with the American government. However, when Adolfo de la Huerta led a rebellion against him on the eve of the 1924 presidential elections, Obregón relented. In exchange for U.S. recognition of his government Obregón gave ground on the question of mineral rights. The timing of U.S. recognition was a signal to any Mexican thinking of challenging Obregón's appointed successor, Calles, that such a move would be unwise.

Once Mexico was readmitted into the international community, its relationship with the United States stabilized. U.S. vested interests in Mexico now had to toe the diplomatic line. For its part, Mexico had achieved international diplomatic recognition, and Calles was eager to emphasize that acceptance of Mexico's new government was a pattern that could be repeated elsewhere in Latin America.

Culture and national identity

President Calles wanted to create the idea of a Mexican nation that would unite the disparate peoples of Mexico for the first time. He restored public awareness of the ancient civilizations of the Aztecs and Mayans, which had been systematically destroyed by the Spanish conquerors in the 16th century, and their legacy. He also promoted Mexico's mixed Indian and Spanish heritage as a cause for celebration and pride rather than shame. Education and culture comprised the two key components in this new idea of Mexican nationhood.

The initiative to promote Mexican education and culture had begun in 1920, when José Vasconcelos (1882–1959) became minister of education. Vasconcelos believed in democratizing education and art. He initiated major reforms in the schools system, particularly rural schools. With a large budget at his disposal, he also embarked on an ambitious program of public art works. He favored large murals celebrating Mexico's history and people in public places where they could be seen by ordinary people. These monumental frescos painted by artists such as Diego Rivera (1886–1957), José Orozco (1883–1949), and David Siqueiros (1896–1974) comprise Mexico's most significant contribution to 20th-century art.

Mexican muralist Diego Rivera at work in 1933 on his famous mural for the Rockefeller Center. Rivera lived in the United States from 1930 to 1934. His work and that of the other Mexican muralists influenced the public art of the American Federal Arts Project.

MIGUEL COVARRUBIAS

Covarrubias (1904–1957) was the first Mexican artist to achieve success in the United States. He was born in Mexico City in 1904 and started work as a caricaturist for the Mexican press in 1920. Known in Mexico as *el chamaco* (the kid), his biting satirical drawings soon drew the attention of the Mexican poet José Juan Tablada (1871–1945). Tablada helped Covarrubias secure work in New York City, where he moved in 1923. He worked as a caricaturist for *Vanity Fair* magazine between 1924 and 1936. In 1925 he started at *The New Yorker* and published his first book, a collection of portraits, *The Prince of Wales and Other Famous Americans*. It established his reputation in America. Covarrubias played an active role in New York's intellectual life throughout the twenties, particularly the Harlem Renaissance. In the mid-1920s he started work on sketches of Harlem life and published them in a second book, *Negro Drawings* (1927). In addition to contributing regularly to *Vanity Fair*, *The New Yorker*, and *Vogue* magazine, Covarrubias worked as a set and costume designer for New York theaters. He helped organize the 1928 *Applied Arts of Mexico* exhibition at the Art Center of New York and the 1930 *Mexican Art Show* at the American Federation of the Arts.

Cultural exchange

There was an enormous vogue for Mexican art and culture in the United States during the twenties. Some left-wing American writers and artists had been attracted to Mexico during the Revolution. While the U.S. government saw the Revolution as a threat to its political and economic ideals, writers such as John Reed (1887–1920) saw it as offering an alternative, and attractive, means of social reform. During the 1920s, as Mexico started its postrevolutionary reconstruction, Americans started to travel to Mexico attracted by the low cost of living, warm climate, and creative possibilities offered by a country and society different from their own. Among those who moved to Mexico during the decade were the writers Katherine Anne Porter (1890–1980) and Anita Brenner (1905–1974)—whose *Idols behind Altars* (1929), a study of Mexican art and culture, was the most influential book about Mexico in the United States—the photographers Edward Weston (1886–1958) and Tina Modotti (1896–1942), and the architect and designer William Spratling (1900–1967).

American artists tended to have a romanticized view of Mexico. They idealized the rural way of life, contrasting it favorably with the capitalism they felt had taken over the United States. They often represented Mexico as a timeless rural idyll, excluding any mention of urbanization and mechanization.

The traffic in artists was not all one way. Some of Mexico's greatest painters—including Diego Rivera, José Orozco, and David Siqueiros—traveled to the United States at the end of the twenties and beginning of the thirties. Others, like the caricaturist Miguel Covarrubias (*see box above*), moved north earlier. Mexican artists, intellectuals, and writers were attracted to the United States partly because economic rewards were greater but also because they recognized the growing importance of the United States as a cultural center.

During the 1920s Mexican art was increasingly promoted in the United States, particularly folk art, which became highly collectable. The first major exhibition of folk art arrived in Los Angeles in 1922—following a show in Mexico City the preceding year—and was a great success. Other exhibitions followed, culminating in the *Mexican Art Show* at the Metropolitan Museum of Art in New York in 1930.

It was not only exhibitions that brought Mexican art and culture to America. Starting in the 1920s, American magazines ran illustrated articles about Mexican colonial architecture and folk art. Anita Brenner's *Idols behind Altars* and her articles and columns for American newspapers and magazines played a significant role in stimulating American interest in Mexico. So too did *Mexican Folkways*, a bilingual magazine published in Mexico City between 1925 and 1937 by the American anthropologist Francis Toor.

American architects as well as artists drew on Mexico for inspiration. During the twenties movie theaters, skyscrapers, and private houses were designed in the so-called "Mayan Revival" style, which borrowed its structural forms and decorative motifs from pre-Colombian civilizations. The Mayan Theater movie palace in Los Angeles, opened in 1927, was one of the best examples. With its lavish interior loosely modeled on archaeological and imagined Mayan buildings, it offered audiences a taste of an exotic ancient world.

A changed relationship

The 1920s marked a change in relations between Mexico and the United States. Once the United States granted Mexico diplomatic recognition, the two neighbors settled into a pattern of political acceptance. The United States had to accept that its position of dominance in Mexico was over and that Mexico was an autonomous nation. For its part, Mexico had to accept that the United States would always be its neighbor. The work of Dwight D. Morrow, in his role as U.S. ambassador to Mexico, helped improve relations, as did the cultural exchange between the two countries. Artists from both nations were inspired by each other's cultures, and their visits helped stimulate the young travel industry.

SEE ALSO:

Art • Central America • Foreign Policy, U.S. • Latin America • Mexican Americans • Nicaragua • Pan-Americanism • Photography

Edna St. Vincent MILLAY (1892–1950)

The first woman to be awarded the Pulitzer Prize for poetry, in 1923, Edna St. Vincent Millay's themes of love and death were popular during the 1920s. Her poetic achievements were often overshadowed during her lifetime by her rebellious beliefs and behavior.

Edna St. Vincent Millay—known to her family and friends as Vincent—was born, the oldest of three daughters, in Rockland, Maine, on February 22, 1892. Her mother encouraged her daughters to be independent and ambitious, qualities Millay developed throughout her life.

As a child, Millay studied to be a concert pianist, but stopped when her hands proved too small to span the keyboard. The lyrical quality of music is evident in much of her poetry. While at Vassar, between 1913 and 1917, Millay wrote poetry, plays, and short stories for her college magazine. Her first book of poetry, *Renascence and Other Poems,* was published in 1917. The 214-line title poem, with its mystical description of life, God, and death, written in 1912 when Millay was just 20, caused a sensation.

Edna St. Vincent Millay in 1940. Her verse varied from the fashionably cynical to some of the finest lyrics and sonnets in American poetry. Conservative in form, their content often shocked contemporary readers.

A bohemian life

After graduation Millay moved to Greenwich Village, New York, to pursue her writing career. She became an early member of the experimental Provincetown Players, acting in and writing plays for them, and a leading light in the bohemian society of the Village. She also published two poetry collections, *A Few Figs from Thistles* in 1920 and *Second April* the following year. With their publication, Millay became the spokeswoman for her generation with her meditations on feminism and free love. Her poetry captured the upbeat postwar mood and the rebellious attitude of the young.

Millay, slim and attractive, soon had a string of suitors, including Edmund Wilson (1895–1972), then an editor at *Vanity Fair.* He helped her secure a commission from the magazine, and in 1921 Millay sailed for Europe. She lived there for two years, sending back regular articles under the pseudonym Nancy Boyd, and finally earning some money.

In 1922 Millay contributed eight sonnets to *American Poetry: A Miscellany* and published a pamphlet of her poem *The Ballad of the Harp-Weaver.* She was rewarded with the Pulitzer Prize for poetry in 1923, the first woman ever to win it.

On her return to New York in 1923 she met Eugen Jan Boissevain, a Dutch businessman. The couple were married on July 18, 1923. Boissevain, eager to support his wife's career, devoted his life to running their household so that she could concentrate on her poetry. They spent the next few years traveling, first in the United States, where Millay gave poetry readings, and then to Asia and France.

On their return they bought a remote farm, Steepletop, in Austerlitz, New York. There Millay continued to work. In 1926 she wrote the libretto for an opera, *The King's Henchman,* which received good reviews at the Metropolitan Opera, New York, and when published in book form sold out four printings in 20 days.

A champion of human rights and women's issues, Millay protested, and was arrested, in Boston against the execution of the anarchists Sacco and Vanzetti. In 1927 she donated the proceeds from her poem "Justice Denied in Massachusetts" to their defense. In 1928 *The Buck in the Snow and Other Poems* was published. In 1929 she was elected to the National Institute of Arts and Letters.

Millay continued in the thirties to produce socially conscious poetry, and following the outbreak of World War II (1939–1945) she began writing "verse propaganda." The strain of that commitment may have contributed to her nervous breakdown in 1944. Millay died of a heart attack at Steepletop on October 19, 1950. Her final collection, *Mine the Harvest,* appeared posthumously in 1954.

SEE ALSO:

Greenwich Village • Jazz Age • Literature • Poetry • Theater

Robert A. MILLIKAN (1868–1953)

One of three Americans awarded the Nobel Prize in physics in the 1920s, Millikan was an outstanding scientist who made numerous important discoveries. He was also renowned as a teacher and for his ability to make science understandable and interesting to the general public.

Robert Andrews Millikan was born in Morrison, Illinois. He graduated from Oberlin College, Ohio, in 1891, and obtained his doctorate at Columbia University in 1895.

Millikan's greatest contributions to theoretical physics were made during his academic career at the University of Chicago from 1896 to 1921. In 1909 he began a series of experiments to accurately determine the electric charge carried by a single electron (one of the subatomic particles in an atom). His initial measurements of water droplets were not accurate enough. When he switched to oil drops in 1910, he not only obtained accurate results but also proved that this quantity was a constant for all electrons, thus demonstrating the atomic structure of electricity.

In 1916 Millikan provided experimental verification of Albert Einstein's (1879–1955) equation describing the photoelectric effect. He also discovered a more precise determination of Planck's constant—originated by Max Planck (1858–1947)—which describes the behavior of particles and waves on the atomic scale.

Robert A. Millikan in 1923, the year he was awarded the Nobel Prize in physics for "his work on the elementary charge of electricity and on the photoelectric effect."

Teacher and researcher

Millikan satisfied his desire to combine teaching and his own high-level research by making the classroom and the laboratory mutually enhancing elements in his work with graduate students. The best students flocked to him because he conducted courses in the most up-to-date fields of physics—electromagnetism, X-rays, electron physics, and quantum theory. He was one of the first academics to make use of his students' experiments to further his own investigations.

Millikan was lured away from Chicago in 1921 to become director of the Norman Bridge Laboratory of Physics at the recently founded California Institute of Technology (Caltech) in Pasadena. He was hugely influential in attracting major scholars to Caltech and making it one of the world's leading research institutions. He also played a major role in persuading the Rockefeller Foundation to fund an aeronautical research center at Caltech, thus enabling southern California to become an international leader in the aircraft industry. In 1923 Millikan was awarded both the Nobel Prize in physics and the prestigious Hughes Medal of the Royal Society in London, England.

Not always popular because of his anti-Semitism and his sometimes brusque manner with colleagues, Millikan was nevertheless widely admired for his brilliant research, his dedication to teaching, his government work during World War II (1939–1945) developing antisubmarine devices, and his ability to popularize science. He was a powerful advocate of the benefits to society that close links between business and scientific research could bring, and his many publications brought science to the public in accessible prose that *Time* magazine said made "scientific complexities charming as well as awesome."

The son of a Congregationalist minister, Millikan argued that science and religion were compatible. *Evolution in Science and Religion,* a defense of Darwinian evolution, was published in 1927 amid the hysteria unleashed by the Scopes Trial.

SEE ALSO:

Compton, Arthur H. • Physics • Scopes Trial

MISSISSIPPI FLOOD

In 1927 the Mississippi River burst its banks in a catastrophic flood that inundated about 26,000 square miles (67,300 sq. km) of land, killed 313 people, drove 700,000 from their homes, and caused an estimated $300 million of property damage.

The Mississippi River is one of the major rivers of the world. It forms the heart of a great inland water system formed by the Ohio, Missouri, and Mississippi rivers and their tributaries. Its drainage area stretches from the western Appalachians to the Rocky Mountains, covers about 40 percent of the country, and includes all or part of 31 states. The river rises in Minnesota and discharges into the Gulf of Mexico.

From the mid-19th century the Army Corps of Engineers attempted to control the river's regular flooding. A vast amount of time and labor was invested in building levees—earth and stonework dikes designed to hold back the river. However, the Mississippi carries a vast load of silt (some 500 million tons annually) down to its delta in the Gulf of Mexico, and the levees, by preventing the river from depositing silt on the floodplain, gradually caused the river level to rise. The engineers responded by building ever-higher levees—in places the river was

Flooded countryside 6 miles (10km) west of Elaine, Arkansas, between the White and Mississippi rivers on May 7, 1927. The flood waters began to recede in June and July, leaving thick layers of mud behind them.

SINGIN' THE BLUES

As the floodwaters began their inexorable rise, many blues artists were inspired to write songs about their experience. The blues of the Mississippi Delta were forged by deeply felt personal experience, which was communicated in a raw, sung narrative, accompanied by little more than a slide guitar. The overwhelming tragedy of the flood soon found its way into blues music, and some 25 or 30 flood-related records were made. Artists like Charlie Patton and Alice Pearson actually experienced the flood, and their songs are raw and immediate. Blind Lemon Jefferson, from Texas, recorded a flood song and frequently performed in the Delta in small theaters in towns like Greenwood and Greenville. The most famous song about the flood, "Back Water Blues" by Bessie Smith, was recorded just before the flood in February 1927, but may have been inspired by the steady buildup of rain during that winter.

actually flowing above ground level. Reservoirs, cutoffs, spillways, and jetties to drain water, straighten the river, and speed up its flow would have helped lessen the impact of the levees, but the government was insistent that they were the best way to control the mighty river.

In 1922 the river flooded six Delta counties. What would have been a minor flood before the levees were constructed left 20,000 people homeless. However, the Army Corps continued to insist that levees would prevent any further floods.

The great flood

Violent storms in the fall of 1926 dumped tons of water into many of the tributaries that fed the Mississippi. Rainfall during March and April of 1927 was unusually heavy—Greenville, Mississippi, for example, received 8.12 inches (206mm) on April 15—and the Mississippi started to rise. Levees began cracking; and as the pressure of continuous rainfall built up, 10 different flood crests moved down the river. The authorities continued to maintain a blind belief in the levee system.

The Durina Levee, 30 miles (48km) south of Cairo, Illinois, was the first to be breached on April 16, flooding 175,000 acres (70,820ha.). When the levee at Mounds Landing broke on April 21, downtown Greenville was flooded with 10 feet (3m) of water, and a million acres were flooded. In New Orleans the city authorities voted to dynamite the upstream levees on April 29, opting to sacrifice Louisiana's rural land and homes to save the city from flooding.

The flood lasted for more than six weeks, with 47 recorded levee breaks. The Mississippi River Commission recorded a record 2,278,00 cubic feet (65,500 cubic m) of water flowing into the Delta every second. By the end the river had inundated 26,000 square miles (67,300 sq. km) of land, submerged thousands of homes, and left over 600,000 people destitute.

The relief effort

In the immediate aftermath of the flood towns struggled to cope. Relief committees appointed by individual towns were charged with rescuing, housing, and feeding thousands of refugees, as well as livestock. The authorities seized all privately owned boats, wagons, and trucks, and confiscated food and supplies from the local stores. Many people were evacuated to other towns.

Over 53 percent of the victims were black, and from the outset the racial segregation of the South permeated the relief effort. Faced with many thousands of black victims, relief committees agonized about whether to feed blacks in communal kitchens alongside whites. When arrangements were made for the black refugees' evacuation, plantation-owners objected that this would depopulate the Delta of its labor force, and many whites agreed. Relations between the races deteriorated, and there were outbreaks of lawlessness. Debates like these caused outraged comment in the newspapers of the North.

President Coolidge (1923–1929) put Secretary of Commerce Herbert Hoover in charge of federal flood relief. Hoover traveled through the flood zone and made detailed plans. His program called for camps for flood refugees, retraining programs, and financial credit provided by the government. He made the first nationwide radio address on the subject of flood relief and became a national hero. The crisis was an effective springboard for his 1928 presidential campaign.

In effect, however, the vast majority of the relief was provided by local agencies and private charities. The American Red Cross set up 154 refugee camps, caring for more than 325,000 people in a reconstruction program that lasted until May 1928. Millions of dollars were spent on clothing, food, seed for planting, furniture, and vocational training, as well as on an immunization program that fought rampant smallpox, malaria, typhoid fever, and pellagra. Despite these efforts, there were persistent rumors that the Red Cross was discriminating against black victims. It reacted by setting up a Colored Advisory Commission, but thousands of blacks left for the North. Within a year 50 percent of the Delta's African American population had left the region.

Hoover set up the Tri-State River Commission, establishing full federal control over the entire Mississippi River. This was a step that greatly expanded federal involvement in local affairs, foreshadowing the dominant role of central government in the 1930s New Deal era. Federal control of rivers resulted in many new programs, such as federally subsidized flood insurance, flood relief programs, and a series of new, more effective flood-control works.

SEE ALSO:

Blues • Hoover, Herbert • Smith, Bessie

MODERNISM

The early part of the 20th century saw the introduction of many new ideas in science, politics, psychology, and culture. They led in turn to new movements in art. One of the most significant of them was modernism, which affected art, architecture, literature, and design.

Modernism is the term used to describe a wide range of artistic movements that came to represent the culture of the 20th century. These movements did not always share the same goals and were sometimes reactions against each other. Some fields, such as painting, were transformations of existing artistic practices, and others, such as photography, sprang from the new technologies of industrialization. These movements all shared, however, a sense of shock, discontinuity, and abstraction, and a strong preoccupation with modernity.

Modernity was the new condition of rapid industrial development, secularization, and urbanization that transformed European societies from the mid-19th century. They changed the basis of social relations and not only caused a break with past customs and values but also created conditions of continual change. Huge numbers of people migrated to cities and to other countries. Cities were transformed from haphazard clusters into planned structures.

The birth of modernism is generally located in Paris in the mid-19th century. Paris was then developing from a compact medieval city with narrow, winding streets to a grand city with wide boulevards, and this new appearance and the new urban life it generated provided "modern life" as subject matter. This was evident in the writings of the poet and critic Charles Baudelaire, who advocated the portrayal of "modern life" in the arts, and in the paintings of Edouard Manet, who depicted the public spectacles of the new streets, parks, and bars as high art. Modernism later affected all countries with a European culture. Since modernism was an urban phenomenon, different cities became cosmopolitan centers at different times: Paris continuously from the mid-19th century to 1939, Berlin and Vienna in the 1890s, Moscow and St. Petersburg before the Revolution, London before World War I (1914–1918), and New York in the 1920s.

The Cafe-Concert by Edouard Manet painted in 1878. Manet was one of the first French artists to paint everyday "modern" life in Paris: His paintings typically depict scenes of ordinary people in bars or on the city streets.

THE MUSEUM OF MODERN ART, NEW YORK

The Museum of Modern Art, New York, became one of the most important and influential museums of modern art in the world, but it was not founded with this intention. It was established in 1929 to display the private collections of modern art of its founders, almost all from the Rockefeller family. They were not the pioneer collectors of modern art in the United States, and the permanent collection was actually quite small. Alfred Barr, the first director, aspired to expand the collections beyond painting and sculpture to drawings, prints and photography, typography, industrial design, architecture, stage design, furniture, decorative arts, and films, which were then not thought of as being worthy of display in a museum. The Museum of Modern Art profited from his administration to become an authority in all these areas. Exhibitions such as "Modern Architecture: International Exhibition" (1932), "Machine Art" (1934), and "Bauhaus 1919–1928" (1938) were pioneering exhibitions of contemporary modernism in the United States, while "Modern Architecture in California" (1935), "T.V.A. Architecture and Design" (1941–1942), and "Built in the USA" (1944) attempted to show the United States as a fully modern country. After World War II the museum, conscious of its new global position, opened a Department for International Programs supported by the Rockefeller Foundation to exhibit American art in Europe and East Asia such as "The Skyscraper USA" and "Built in the USA: Post-War Architecture" (both 1953).

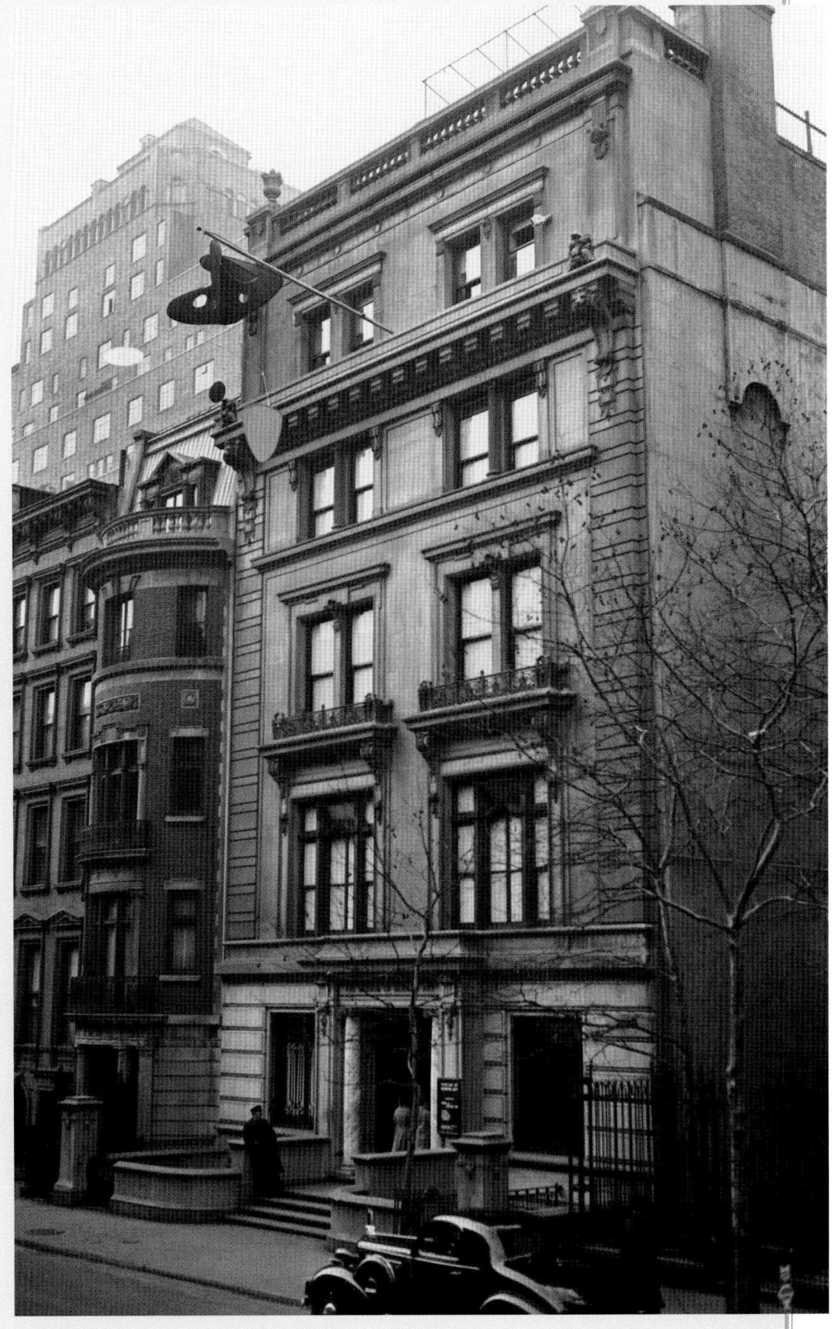

The exterior of the Museum of Modern Art in New York in 1936. The museum moved to this site at 11 West 53rd Street in 1932. It moved into a larger building in 1939.

Modernism found strong exponents in painting, photography, architecture, literature, and music, and was supported by critics, historians, and theorists. Because these fields had different histories and production practices, they were affected by modernism at different times and in different ways. They all shared an opposition to the low artistic standards of mass culture and the assumption that the viewer, reader, or user should be an unconscious consumer. While many artists who sought to transform mass culture were allied to left-wing politics, others, especially writers, supported right-wing politics.

Painting was a recognizable representation of modernism because of the immediacy of its production. Popular culture in the late 19th century and early 20th century was intensely visual; advertising, entertainment, propaganda, and fashion all became widespread in cities. The intellectual movements in fine art, therefore, had to distinguish their value: to show themselves as self-evidently modern, to dismiss the work of previous art movements as outdated and conservative, to promote abstraction as historically inevitable, to question the roles of artist and viewer, and to insist on the autonomy of art and the artist. Many of the movements were very short-lived. But once the sense of public outrage and scorn had passed, much of the work, for example, Impressionism, quickly moved into mainstream culture. The artists were directly supported initially by a system of private galleries and wealthy collectors and later by public museums, which ensured their recognition and success.

Similar conditions applied to architecture. During the urban expansion of the late 19th century and early 20th century there was an enormous amount of building, but very little consensus on an appropriate style. Popular building styles were an eclectic combination of features from previous epochs despite incorporating enormous advances in construction technology.

The Modern Movement, a term that included a wide range of architectural interests, grew out of the Art and Crafts Movement in Britain and developed rapidly in other European countries and in various isolated places in the United States. Reinforced concrete construction developed in France and posed new challenges to and opportunities for architects; by the beginning of World War I the craft element had begun to seem inappropriate. The architecture of the Modern Movement usually appeared as white, undecorated, fragmented cubic forms. Such was the success of this architecture that by 1932 it was known as the International Style, although, like painting, it was restricted to a tiny intellectual minority.

The first phase of modernism was over by World War I, but modernism continued to develop during the 1920s and 1930s. After World War II (1939–1945) it became the dominant cultural expression. By the 1970s its political, social, and artistic basis was widely challenged. As modernity itself developed and transformed, new artistic approaches replaced the earlier utopian ideals.

Modernism in America

In no country other than the United States were the conditions of modernity so advanced in 1920, but with so little modernism. There had been particularly rapid industrial development and urbanization in the previous 40 years. The United States had welcomed and received huge numbers of immigrants from Europe, and the secular state allowed freedom to some persecuted minorities such as Jews. World War I had accelerated industrialization, urbanization, and immigration in the United States and increased the divide between it and Europe.

Artistically and intellectually, however, the United States seemed dwarfed by Europe. Educated people tended to look to Europe, particularly the French capital, Paris, as the exemplar of artistic achievement. American intellectuals were faced with the dilemma of being both modern and American; they were pulled between the desire to participate in the objective and abstract world of modern ideas and the desire to represent particularly American concerns. The American heritage included Native American culture, the African American population in the big cities in the North, and the unique American landscape, especially in the Southwest. All of these characteristics were to appear in American artists' work during the 1920s.

The appearance of a modernism in America can be traced to the years around 1900 in a small group in New York around Alfred Stieglitz (1864–1946). Stieglitz was a photographer who opened a gallery that was to become a center of intellectual life in New York. One of his most famous photographs, of the Flatiron Building in a snowstorm taken during the winter of 1902–1903, represented his interest in "modern life" but utilized the new technology of photography. Stieglitz not only showed the work of artist-photographers such as Paul Strand (1890–1976) at his gallery but introduced the work of French artists, including

INDUSTRIAL BUILDINGS AND MODERN ARCHITECTURE

The architects of the Modern Movement in Europe believed that their work was motivated by an objective response to function rather than a subjective taste in aesthetics. They supposed American engineering, then the most advanced in the world, to be an expression of a new, rational world. The German architects Walter Gropius (1883–1969) and Erich Mendelssohn (1887–1953) illustrated "daylight" factories in Detroit and grain elevators in Buffalo in *Jahrbuch des Deutsche Werkbundes* (*Yearbook of the German Design and Industry Association*) (1913) and *Amerika: Bilderbuch eines Architekten* (*America: A German Architect's Picture Book*) (1926) respectively. The influential Swiss architect and city planner Le Corbusier (1887–1965) illustrated North and South American grain elevators in *Vers une Architecture* (*Toward a New Architecture*) (1923). "Daylight" factories were multistory concrete-framed buildings with repetitive horizontal windows used for car production; grain elevators were collections of enormous concrete storage cylinders. The architects' interest waned, however, once they had experimented with the forms in masterpieces such as the Bauhaus, Dessau (1925–1926), and the Villa Savoye, Paris (1929–1932).

After World War II these forms were used throughout the world in a very literal way by less discriminating architects, which led to modern architecture being widely discredited by the 1970s. The publication of *A Concrete Atlantis* by the British architectural historian Reyner Banham in 1986 explained them not as abstract forms in unison with a universal order but as pragmatic designs rooted in particular industrial processes.

Auguste Rodin, Henri Matisse, Pablo Picasso, Georges Braque, and Paul Cézanne. In 1916 Stieglitz championed the artist Georgia O'Keeffe (1887–1986) at exactly the time when he felt that the Impressionistic style of his early work was no longer appropriate. From 1917 to 1925 he developed a direct form of photography: portraits of O'Keeffe, studies of New York, and cloud series. O'Keeffe was one of the first artists to use Native American art, which she observed during her stays in New Mexico, as part of abstract compositions.

The tension between nature and urbanism was evident in artistic work throughout the 1920s. Photographers such as Paul Strand and painters such as Edward Hopper (1882–1967) used the "modern life" of New York City as subject matter. Charles Sheeler (1883–1965) began taking photographs of vernacular architecture and moved to industrial structures such as factories, which Charles Demuth also painted. The photographer Edward Weston (1886–1958), on the other hand, started in New Mexico and California, and moved to Mexico City in 1923.

The 1920s were also an age when literature focused on the realities of "modern life." Many American writers preferred to live abroad, particularly in Paris. Ezra Pound (1885–1972) was one of the most important influences on modern poetry; he left the United States for England in 1907; in the early 1920s he moved to Paris and in 1925 to Italy. *The Cantos*, written from 1925 onward, were an extraordinary mixture of historical myths. T. S. Eliot (1888–1965) moved to London in 1914; *The Waste Land* (1922) is regarded as one of the greatest works of modern poetry, whose fragmented nature reflects the episodic experience of "modern life." Gertrude Stein (1874–1946) lived in Paris from 1903 until her death in 1946; she was an author as well as patron of the arts. F. Scott Fitzgerald (1896–1940) moved to New York City in 1920 and to France in 1921; his most famous novel, *The Great Gatsby* (1925), depicted the empty lives of the rich in 1920s New York. Ernest Hemingway (1899–1961) depicted the dissolute lives of American expatriates in Paris in novels such as *The Sun Also Rises* (1926). Other writers remained in the United States. John Dos Passos (1896–1970) presented the decadent lives of 1920s New Yorkers through a series of the intertwined narratives in *Manhattan Transfer* (1925). John Steinbeck (1902–1968) started writing about the poor of Monterey, California. William Faulkner (1897–1962) set his stories in Yoknapatawpha, an imaginary county in Mississippi, in which he dealt with the decline of Southern values and the mistreatment of blacks.

The poet T.S. Eliot in 1954. Eliot emigrated from America to London, England, in 1914. His poem *The Waste Land* (1922) is considered by critics to be one of the most important modernist works.

The discovery of African American culture was an important part of modern culture in America. A large number of blacks emigrated from the South to New York City during and after World War I as part of the process of industrialization and urbanization, where they congregated in Harlem. Jazz, which developed there out of its roots in New Orleans, was enormously popular and has become regarded as an authentically American contribution to music. Among classical composers Aaron Copland (1900–1990) studied in Paris under conductor and musical composition teacher Nadia Boulanger (1887–1979) and wrote his first symphony in 1925. His work incorporated jazz, Mexican, and Shaker influences.

In other fields of the arts modernism did not have such a hold. Despite being at the forefront of modernity, the movie industry in Hollywood had little interest in modernism. In architecture there was not much modernism until the 1930s, although two important modern movement architects, Richard Neutra and Rudolph Schindler, did design several houses in Los Angeles in the 1920s. The popular styles during the 1920s were Beaux Arts for public buildings and art deco for skyscrapers.

By the end of the 1920s the artistic situation had changed significantly. American museums such as the Museum of Modern Art, New York (*see box on p. 34*) were founded. It not only showed modern art but pioneered many other fields as well. During the 1930s there was an influx of European intellectuals such as the musician Arnold Schoenberg and the architects Walter Gropius and Ludwig Mies van der Rohe. During the Depression federal programs sponsored many artists. By the end of World War II the U.S. had acquired a distinctive style in music, dance, art, and architecture.

SEE ALSO:

Architecture • Art • Classical Music • Design • Jazz • Literature • Lost Generation • Off-Broadway • Painting • Photography • Pound, Ezra

MONETARY POLICY

The monetary policy of a government is its attempts to control inflation and to influence the business cycle—the tendency of economies to grow quickly or "boom" and then to decline rapidly or "bust"—by changing the quantity of money in circulation (the money supply) and by adjusting interest rates, the cost of borrowing money.

The monetary policy decisions of the 1920s were of particular significance given what was to follow—the Wall Street Crash of 1929 and the Great Depression. Some economic historians have argued that the monetary policies of the U.S. policymakers and America's central bank, the Federal Reserve System (the Fed), led to the crash and the disastrous economic decline. Others have doubted that the Depression could have been averted or made less severe with different choices.

By the postwar period of the 1920s U.S. monetary policy had become the responsibility of the Fed, which began operations in 1914. The Fed is said to be "independent within government"; although the Fed makes its own decisions on interest rates and other questions, it must work within the framework of the government's main economic objectives.

The early and mid-1920s

Having only recently begun operations, the Federal Reserve System was quite new to its decision-making role with regard to monetary policy. It took time for the Fed to discover which of the policy tools at its disposal were most effective in controlling inflation (the general level of prices), the money supply, and activity in the economy more generally.

There was almost universal support among economists and politicians for a Fed policy that targeted inflation since high price rises are unpopular with both voters and customers. However, stable prices could—and in fact did—disguise underlying economic imbalances. Some economic critics today believe that the Fed overrelied on low inflation as the main indicator of the correctness of monetary policy during this time.

Broadly speaking, the early and mid-1920s saw the Fed pursuing a relaxed monetary regime—it used its policy tools in order to maintain the easy availability of credit at moderate interest rates. The economy was growing overall, with the industrial, consumer goods, and retail industries booming. Dependent as many of these key industries were on the nation's increasing spending spree, few policymakers saw any reason to curtail people's enthusiasm for borrowing, spending, and consuming. However, most modern studies agree that monetary policy was too easy—dangerously lax, even—during this period.

Speculative fever

As the decade went on, many ordinary people began to see speculation on the stock markets as a good way to "get rich quick." Some borrowed heavily to finance

MONETARY POLICY TOOLS

During the 1920s (as today) the Fed was able to use three main policy tools to achieve its goals: reserve requirements, the discount rate, and open market operations.

The reserve requirement is the ratio of a bank's financial reserves (held with the Fed) as compared to the deposits it can lend out. For example, if the Fed sets the reserve requirement at 10 percent, then for every $90 that a bank lends, it is obliged to hold a reserve of at least $10. By increasing or reducing the required reserve ratio, the Fed can influence the money supply and interest rates. If the reserve requirement is high, for instance, banks are unable to lend out so much money; this creates an upward pressure on interest rates because credit is in short supply. The reverse is true for a low reserve requirement.

The discount rate is the interest rate at which the Fed is prepared to lend out its financial reserves to commercial banks. By increasing the discount rate, the Fed can make borrowing more expensive for banks. That encourages banks to reduce their lending and so increases interest rates. The reverse is true if the Fed decides to lower the discount rate.

Since the midtwenties the most effective monetary policy tool available to the Fed has been open market operations—the sale and purchase of U.S. government securities (treasury bills and bonds). When the Federal Reserve sells government securities, they are paid for with bank deposits and bank reserves. This creates tighter monetary and credit conditions because, with lower reserves, banks cut their lending, and interest rates rise. When the Fed buys government securities, its payments for them provide the banks with additional reserves. This loosens credit conditions because the banks are able to increase their lending, and interest rates fall.

The Federal Reserve Bank Building, New York City, in 1924, shortly after it opened for business. The vaults were 86 feet (26m) below street level and by 1927 contained 10 percent of the world's entire store of monetary gold.

this gamble. Meanwhile, gold began to flow into the United States from Europe after World War I (1914–1918), as America's allies and the defeated nations of Germany and Austria began to repay their debts. These gold inflows expanded the money supply, but did not lead to high inflation because the money was channeled into securities markets where it helped fuel the stock market boom.

In 1927 a mild recession (a decline in production and employment) in the United States and a balance-of-payments crisis in Britain inclined the Fed toward a further easing of monetary policy. The resulting fall in interest rates helped offset the decline in domestic economic activity. However, with credit more easily available and cheaper than ever before, many critics believe that the Fed encouraged the speculative fever that was taking hold across the nation.

Monetary policy and the crash

In early 1928 the Fed at last became sufficiently alarmed by the soaring share prices to act. Fearing the stock market boom was an unsustainable "bubble," it moved to tighten monetary policy—between January and July 1928 the Fed raised the discount rate (*see box on p. 37*) from 3.5 to 5 percent. At the same time, it engaged in extensive open market operations to drain reserves from the banking system. In August 1929 the Fed stepped up its attack on speculation and tightened credit further by raising interest rates to 6 percent. With higher interest rates and speculators becoming nervous that stocks were overvalued, share prices started to fall rapidly. On October 29, 1929, the speculative bubble burst.

In the opinion of most economists the Federal Reserve's initial reaction to the crash was entirely appropriate. Between October 1929 and February 1930 credit conditions were eased—the interest rate was lowered to 4 percent and the money supply increased, partly through the Fed's purchase of government securities.

However, the easing of monetary and credit conditions proved to be temporary. Interest rates were hiked again in 1931, making loans more expensive and deterring people and corporations from borrowing. Between 1929 and 1933 the money supply contracted by one-third. The result was a sharp contraction in economic activity and a huge rise in unemployment; overall the U.S. economy shrank by 27 percent in the three years after the crash. Although the Fed's monetary policy succeeded in halting the stock market boom, it may well have done so at the price of contributing significantly to the economic disaster that followed.

SEE ALSO:

Banks & Banking • Consumer Goods Revolution • Credit • Economy • Gold Supply • Keynes, John Maynard • Stock Market • Wall Street Crash

J.P. MORGAN, Jr. (1867–1943)

In 1913 J.P. Morgan, Jr., inherited J.P. Morgan and Company, Inc., the investment bank started by his father, J.P. Morgan. Known as the "wizard of Wall Street," he maintained J.P. Morgan (often called the House of Morgan) as the United States' leading bank throughout the 1920s.

John Pierpont Morgan, Jr., was born on September 7, 1867, the second of four children and only son of John Pierpont and Frances Louisa Tracy Morgan. Known as Jack to distinguish him from his father, he graduated from Harvard University in 1889. In 1890 he married Jane Norton, with whom he had four children.

After working briefly for the Boston bank of Jacob C. Roberts, Morgan joined his father's bank in 1892. He served a short apprenticeship in New York before being sent to work in the firm's London branch in 1898. Morgan's seven years in London turned him into a great Anglophile. He maintained an estate in Great Britain throughout his life.

Inherited wealth and power

When his father died in 1913, Morgan became heir to an estate of more than $50 million and took control of the House of Morgan. Very different from his dominating, ebullient father, Morgan relied on boardroom consensus to make decisions. During World War I (1914–1918) Morgan made his own mark on his father's bank.

When the Allied governments were looking for a financial agent to purchase arms, Morgan's pro-British and French stance and his connections with Paris and London made him the obvious choice. Through his initiative the House of Morgan became the sole purchasing agent in the United States for Britain and France. Between 1915 and U.S. entry into the war in 1917 the bank handled orders for more than $3 billion worth of arms, netting commissions of $30 million.

By the end of the war New York had replaced London as the world's financial capital, and so Morgan shifted his focus to the domestic market. During the 1920s the bank sold $4 billion of stocks and bonds for U.S. companies. Although the bank was no longer as preeminent as it had been under his father, the House of Morgan remained the United States' and the world's leading investment bank throughout the decade. Its reputation was based on the quality of its clients and its reputation for fair and honest dealings.

J.P. Morgan, Jr., was an active layman in the Episcopal Church and a philanthropist who gave $36 million to charitable and public institutions during his lifetime, including $9 million to the Metropolitan Museum of Art.

Morgan was a strong internationalist. He also supported the administrations of Warren G. Harding and Calvin Coolidge. In 1924 he represented the Coolidge administration at the conference that created the Dawes Plan to restructure Germany's international debt. Morgan saw to it that his bank underwrote massive German loans.

When the Wall Street stock market collapsed in 1929, Morgan was in Europe trying to sort out a new refinancing of the German debt. He led the way for other banks to pour money into the ailing stock market but failed to stop the collapse. The House of Morgan survived the crash but lost half its capital.

During the thirties both Morgan and his bank came under government scrutiny. Morgan's personal reputation suffered when he revealed that he had used loopholes to avoid paying tax between 1930 and 1932. The 1933 Banking Act forced his firm to separate its investment banking from its commercial banking activities and split in two. Morgan remained head of the commercial bank.

In 1924 Morgan endowed the Pierpont Morgan Library, New York, as a memorial to his father. It housed his father's library of rare books and manuscripts. He died of a cerebral stroke while on holiday in Florida on March 13, 1943.

SEE ALSO:

Banks & Banking • Dawes Plan • Europe, Postwar • Reparations • Stock Market • Wall Street Crash • World War I

Thomas Hunt MORGAN (1866–1945)

In an academic career spent chiefly at Columbia University and the California Institute of Technology (Caltech), Thomas Hunt Morgan established himself as a pioneer of experimental zoology and a leading geneticist, winning the Nobel Prize in physiology or medicine in 1933.

Thomas Hunt Morgan was born in Lexington, Kentucky, in 1866. Early in life Morgan showed an interest in natural history. In 1886 he received the B.S. degree from the State College of Kentucky (later the University of Kentucky) in zoology.

Morgan's doctoral dissertation (1890) at Johns Hopkins University on the evolution of sea spiders (pycnogonids) demonstrated that although they resembled crustaceans such as crabs and lobsters, sea spiders were actually more closely related to spiders (arachnids). His dissertation was essentially a work of morphology, which classified animals chiefly by a description of their form. Morgan was soon dissatisfied with the highly speculative nature of morphology, and he became interested in experimental embryology before allying himself with a new school of biology called developmental mechanics, which was associated with the German professor Hans Driesch (1867–1941).

Developmental mechanics was based less on description and classified animals more according to their functioning. In that spirit Morgan, in collaboration with Driesch, conducted experiments to discover how the developing egg produces a complex adult organism with differentiated structures. His major publication in the field of embryology was *The Development of the Frog's Egg* (1897).

Thomas Hunt Morgan in 1933, the year he was awarded the Nobel Prize in physiology or medicine "for his discoveries concerning the role played by the chromosome in heredity."

Columbia University and Caltech

As professor of experimental zoology at Columbia University from 1904 to 1928 Morgan shifted his interest to the study of the physical basis of genetic inheritance. He concentrated on the fruit fly (Drosophila) and gathered around him a group of students who worked in a laboratory that became famous as "the fly room." It was there in 1913 that one of Morgan's students, Alfred Sturtevant (1891–1970), produced the first "genetic map," demonstrating that genes—discovered by Austrian botanist Gregor Mendel in the 1860s—were not metaphorical but real, separate entities precisely distributed along the length of chromosomes (threadlike parts of the cell nucleus that contain all the information a cell needs to carry out its life processes).

The Mechanism of Mendelian Heredity, written by Morgan, Sturtevant, and two other students, was published in 1915. It contained the first experimentally backed proof that genes, regularly distributed in constant numbers on a species' chromosomes, were the transmitters of inherited characteristics. This discovery was the most important advance in the study of genetics since Mendel's founding of the science.

It was followed by Morgan's masterly survey of the science of genetics, *The Theory of the Gene* (1926). More than any of his colleagues Morgan, by his results and those of his students, significantly raised the scientific status of biology.

Morgan moved to Caltech in 1928, where he remained until his death. He established a school of biology, which added further luster to the research institute's growing international reputation. He was awarded the Darwin Medal by the Royal Society in London, England, in 1924 and the Nobel Prize in physiology or medicine in 1933.

SEE ALSO:
Medicine

MOVIE INDUSTRY

The American movie industry came of age in the 1920s, becoming a highly organized, multimillion dollar concern. Hollywood flourished as the home of the major studios, leading actors and actresses enjoyed unprecedented stardom, and people flocked to the new movie palaces.

The movie as we know it today developed in the first decades of the 20th century and has come to be seen as both an art form and a popular entertainment that characterizes the century. Like photography, the movie industry is linked to technological developments; but unlike photography, it also depends on very complex systems of production, distribution, and exhibition.

Early developments

Early forms of cinema developed simultaneously in several European countries—France, Germany, and Great Britain—and in the United States at the end of the 19th century. Early experiments with moving pictures followed the principle of the Zoetrope, a popular parlor toy in which a sequence of still pictures fixed to the inside of a rotating drum were viewed through a slot to produce the effect of a moving picture. The novelty of moving pictures exerted such a fascination that even though only very short movies could be made, they still attracted audiences. Some of the first movies lasted only 20 seconds and consisted of a single shot—they were known as "animated photographs" or "living pictures." Not only were movies very short, they were also combined with live entertainment; projectionists could vary the speed of projection and add their own accompanying music or commentary.

Inventors of cinematic equipment acted as both moviemakers and projectionists. They were based in New York City, which

***In the Movies*, an illustration by artist Henry Mayer from the September 26, 1914, issue of *Puck* magazine. The cartoon shows eight scenes of moviemaking and one of movie viewing.**

A lobby card advertising the United Artists' movie *Little Lord Fauntleroy* (1921), which starred Mary Pickford. Known as "America's sweetheart," Pickford played the role of both Little Lord Fauntleroy and his mother.

was fast becoming the nation's leading urban center, and the first studios and cinemas in the United States were all located in or around the city. As cinema developed, New York's blossoming theater and entertainment industry would also provide a ready supply of actors. While the French Lumière brothers toured the United States with their *cinématographe*—a projector that also functioned as a camera—Thomas Alva Edison (1854–1932) set up the first of his Kinetoscope parlors in New York City in 1894. These establishments featured Edison's Kinetoscopes, viewing devices that enabled an individual to watch a short motion picture that had been made using Edison's Kinetograph cameras. Realizing that the future of cinema lay in projection, Edison acquired the patents to the Vitascope projector in 1896.

Nickelodeons

Movies in the United States were shown in both established vaudeville houses, which attracted a middle-class audience, as well as in tents at fairs and in rented shops, which were oriented toward poorer audiences. Nickelodeons sprang up around 1905—the first one was in the working-class steel town of Pittsburgh. These often makeshift theaters were housed in converted storefronts and showed an hour's worth of films for an admission price of 5 or 10 cents. By 1910 nickelodeons had become so numerous that some tried to gain a commercial edge by moving upmarket and introducing small-time vaudeville acts. Although cinema had its origins in working-class entertainment, it was the support of a middle-class audience that fueled the growth of the movie industry. The move into established theaters led to the use of the term "movie theater" and was to have enormous consequences in the 1920s.

During the years immediately preceding World War I (1914–1918) moviemaking developed from the activities of a collection of inventors and enthusiasts working informally into a highly structured industry. This transition came about partly because of the demand for a steady supply of new movies from the new movie theaters. To protect their interests, the major producers formed the Motion Picture Patents Company (MPPC) in 1908 to regulate production and share profits. The MPPC was led by Edison and Biograph, the most powerful—although not the most productive—companies, and leased its movies to licensed movie theaters. The establishment of the MPPC led a group of independent producers to form a rival organization, the Independent Moving Picture Alliance, the following year. They moved to Hollywood—as did some MPPC members—because land was cheaper, there were no labor unions, and there was more sunlight, making possible year-round filming: Most movies were shot outside.

The studios and the star system

The increased complexity of the film production process and commitment to demanding schedules led to increased specialization and the formation of enormous studio complexes. Producers controlled finance and schedules, directors controlled the set, and camera, lighting, set building, makeup, and costume became skilled professions. Initially all film was orthochromatic black and white, which meant it was sensitive to blue light only. For this reason it could not reproduce flesh tones accurately, and actors and actresses had to wear heavy makeup to appear natural on film, including green lipstick and eye shadow, which gave them a lurid appearance in reality; sets were restricted to only a few colors. In 1912 the Eastman Kodak company developed for the Gaumont Corporation a panchromatic black-and-white film, which was sensitive to red and green light as well as blue. It could reproduce a greater range of tones but was less sensitive, so artificial lighting techniques had to be developed. As audiences became more familiar with moving pictures, directors began to experiment with more complex sequences and editing. As feature movies became standardized at around 1,000 feet (305m) of film, or 60 minutes, directors had the opportunity to introduce narrative films with an identifiable and coherent story, and to experiment with different shots such as the closeup. They were able to depart from the conventions of theater for the first time and to begin to establish definite artistic conventions for cinema.

Movies soon came to be made on what was virtually a production-line system and depended on movie "stars" who were placed under contract to individual studios. While the contracts only stipulated that an actor or actress perform in a specific number of movies during a specified period, they were not really contracts for labor: Stars' images became the property of the studios, which built up often totally fictional portraits of their personal lives for public consumption. The rewards for actors and actresses were astonishing sums of money. Realizing their worth, actors Charlie Chaplin (1889–1977), Douglas Fairbanks (1883–1939), and Mary Pickford (1893–1979), along with leading director D.W. Griffith (1875–1948), founded the United Artists Corporation in 1919 to free themselves of the studio system. They achieved great success in the 1920s with films such as *The Mark of Zorro* (1920), *Little Lord Fauntleroy* (1921), *Robin Hood* (1923), and *The Gold Rush* (1925). However, they were unable to meet the huge demand for films, and United Artists remained an anomaly in the studio system.

To avoid the restrictions of the MPPC, independent movie producers bought their own movie theaters, especially big theaters in major cities. To further increase their profits, they began to export, principally to Europe. World War I brought European film production to a standstill and gave an impetus to the production of movies in Hollywood. By 1920 the studios in Hollywood were independent no more: Universal Pictures, Paramount Pictures, Metro–Goldwyn–Mayer, and the Fox Film Corporation dominated not only the American market but also the markets of all Western countries, in some accounting for as much as 80 percent of the market share.

Dramas and comedies

Two genres epitomized the films of the 1920s: melodrama and comedy. As the film industry became standardized, these genres proliferated and for marketing purposes were divided into subgenres. Films became categorized as Western, crime, horror, or costume melodrama, and as chase or farce comedy. The carefree moral and social values of the time were depicted in many melodramas, such as Cecil B. DeMille's *We Can't Have Everything* (1918) and *Why Change Your Wife* (1920), Erich von Stroheim's *Foolish Wives* (1922) and *Greed* (1923–1925), and Ernst Lubitsch's *The Marriage Circle* (1924) and *Lady Windermere's Fan* (1925). In the late 1920s films depicted the very contemporary attitudes of the "flapper," played mainly by Clara Bow (1905–1965), Colleen Moore (1902–1988), and Joan Crawford (1908–1973). Costume melodramas were mostly epic films with high investments and high returns; among the most acclaimed were Rex Ingram's *The Four Horsemen of the Apocalypse* (1921), D.W. Griffith's *America* (1924), and Raoul Walsh's *The Thief of Baghdad* (1924). The Western was America's most

Renowned escape artist Harry Houdini (1874–1926) and his wife Beatrice with the production crew of *The Man from Beyond* (1922). Houdini played the lead role in the movie, which reached its climax when Houdini saved the heroine from being washed over Niagara Falls.

CATHEDRALS OF MOTION PICTURES

A "cathedral of motion pictures" was how the impresario Samuel "Roxy" Rothafel described his new movie palace at 7th Avenue and 50th Street in New York City, designed by Walter W. Ahlschlager in 1927. It was the largest cinema ever built, seating 5,800 people. In his book *New York* (1930) French writer Paul Morand described the Roxy in its heyday, conjuring up not only the splendor of the building but also something of the mysticism of the experience of moviegoing. He likened the cinema itself to the biblical temple of Solomon, in which "the brazen doors of the Ark of the Covenant open into a hall with golden cupolas, in old style, and a ceiling with storied panels. Satan has hung this disused sanctuary with scarlet velvet; a nightmare light falls from bowls of imitation alabaster; from yellow glass lanterns, from branching ritual candlesticks: the organ pipes, lit from beneath by greenish lights, made one think of a cathedral under the waves, and in the walls are niches awaiting sinful bishops." He went on to describe the physical vastness of the images projected onto the screen. To him they seemed to turn humans into titans and their mouths into "crevasses of the Grand Canyon." He called an onscreen kiss "a whole propaganda of the flesh which maddens, without satisfying, these violent American temperaments."

The Roxy was demolished in 1960 in favor of an office block. While many movie palaces were torn down, some were restored to other uses such as theaters and concert halls. One cinema, the Central Park in Chicago designed in 1917, has survived intact as a church.

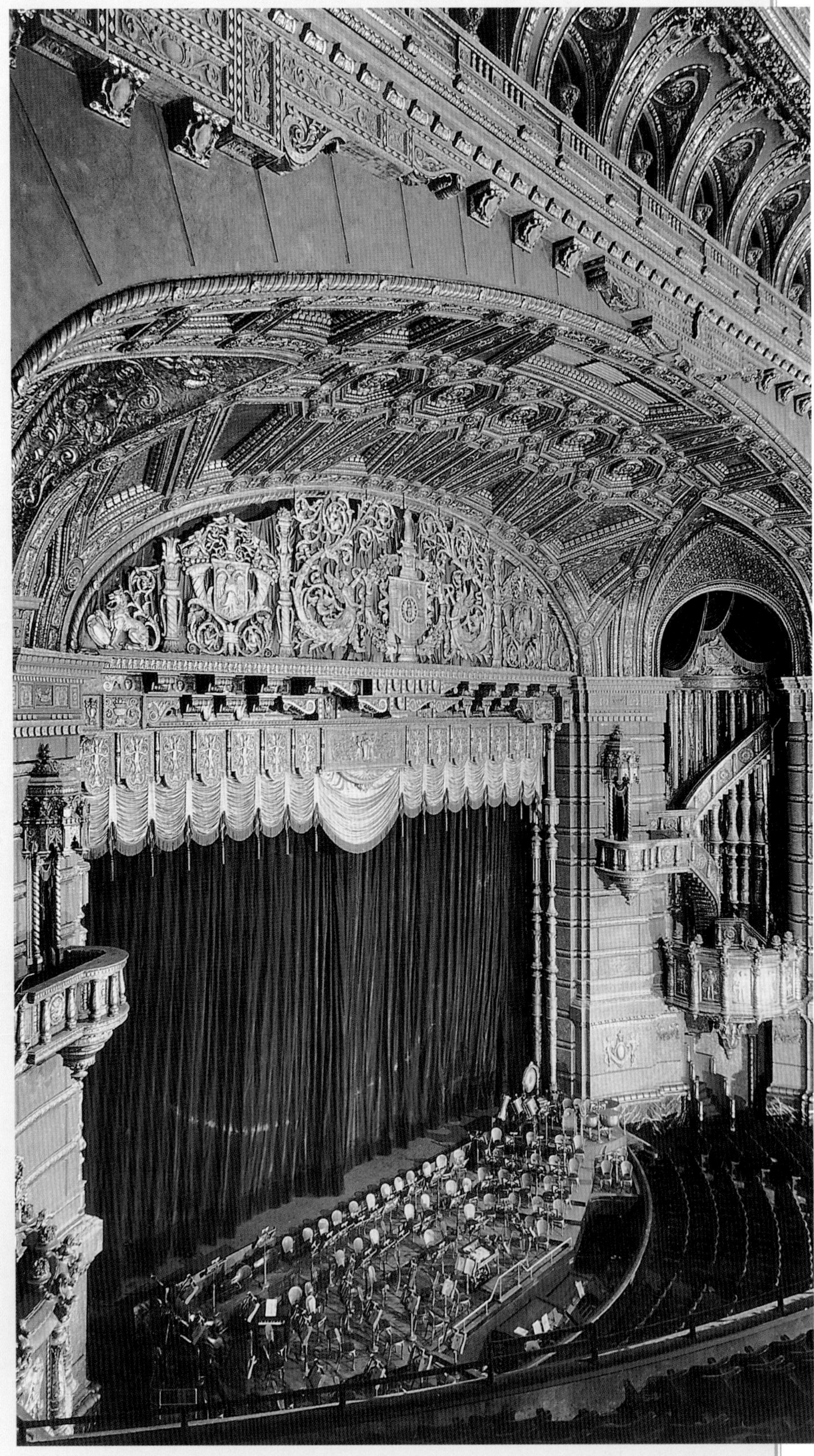

A photograph of the Roxy's lavish interior taken around 1927.

original contribution to film genres. It gained great popularity in the 1920s and flourished up to the 1960s, adapting to various changes in the movie industry. Westerns were generally produced quickly and cheaply, but some epic films were made, including James Cruze's *The Covered Wagon* (1923) and John Ford's *The Iron Horse* (1924).

The rise of movies came at a time when popular comedies were at the peak of their success in theaters. The genre was quickly adapted to film and turned into a whole new tradition. By 1912 comedy was recognized as important enough to justify the creation of the Keystone Comedy Studio as a subsidiary of the New York Motion Picture Company. Under the leadership of director Mack Sennett (1880–1960) Keystone made comedies that were an anarchic caricature of the new everyday life of suburbs and cars, and often depicted massive destruction of material possessions. Charlie Chaplin started out on the road to world fame with his "Little Tramp" character at Keystone in 1914. Feature-length comedies began with his *A Dog's Life* in 1918, followed by the films of Buster Keaton (1895–1966), Harold Lloyd (1893–1971), and Harry Langdon (1884–1944). Comedy evolved so precisely to fit the silent movie format that when the talkies arrived in the late 1920s, Keystone went out of business.

Cartoons, serials, and documentaries

Tricks of animation were used in early films, but animation as a distinctive genre appeared between 1906 and 1910. Films initially showed an artist's hand drawing followed by the drawing starting to move. In the 1920s animated films remained short—one-reel in length—and were mainly adapted from existing comics. Producers promoted cartoon characters in the same way as film stars. In the 1920s Felix the Cat, produced and marketed by Pat Sullivan and drawn by Otto Messmer (1892–1983), was the most famous American cartoon character of the period, dominating the international market. The popularity of Felix the Cat waned with the arrival of sound, which was skillfully exploited by Walt Disney (1901–1966).

The film industry also used serials (stories broadcast in regular installments), profiting from a formula established in magazines and newspapers. Serials were very popular during the nickelodeon years since they were short and easy to produce, and encouraged a return audience. Their popularity diminished as audiences became more discerning. However, they survived through the 1930s as B movies for children, generally based on heroes from comic books, until the advent of television, which proved to be a better vehicle for the format.

Some early films were nonfictional. In the 1920s the documentary title was given to films that had a cultural dimension to them, starting with Charles Sheeler's and Paul Strand's *Mannahatta* (1921), which depicted an almost abstract view of urban existence. So-called "city symphony" films, which presented portraits of particular cities and urban life, found more acceptance in Europe and flourished there in the 1920s. Other early documentaries included Robert Flaherty's *Nanook of the North* (1922), which showed the life of Inuit people in the Arctic, and Merian C. Cooper's and Ernest B. Schoedsack's *Grass* (1925), which followed the Bakhtiari nomads of Iran. These films were not strict anthropological studies and romanticized the lives of the indigenous people they showed. Documentary films were often shown as shorts or in alternative venues such as art galleries.

The prize for the studios was growing audience numbers in the new urban centers, and they soon owned chains of theaters in all the major cities. In the drive to attract middle-class audiences, managers tried to make cheap theaters more attractive. The first of the luxurious theaters was the Strand, built for the impresario S.L. Rothafel in New York City in 1914; the Million Dollar Theater in Los Angeles was opened by Sidney Grauman (1879–1950) in 1918. The cinema, like the skyscraper, was a new building type in which American architects excelled in size and decoration. The great movie palaces of the 1920s were highly eclectic, ranging in style from French baroque and Spanish Renaissance to Oriental, using highly decorative details and creating "atmospheres" with artificial lighting. The architect Thomas W. Lamb designed the first major cinema in New York City, the Regent Theater in 1913; he subsequently designed cinemas for the Roxy cinema chain, including the Strand, and by 1921 had designed 300 cinemas in a neoclassical style. Chicago-based architect John Eberson (1875–1964) specialized in creating movie theater interiors that evoked the appearance and atmosphere of Italian or Moorish gardens, using special lighting techniques.

Movie palace developers

Balaban & Katz in Chicago were the most successful movie palace developers; they employed the architects C.W. and George L. Rapp, who worked in the neoclassical style. Their first movie theater, the Central Park, opened in 1917, followed by the Riviera in 1918, the Tivoli in 1920, and the Chicago Theater in 1921. Location was the key to Balaban & Katz's success. They chose sites close to public transport in the new suburbs. So successful did the Riviera become in the 1920s that it was the center of the Uptown entertainment district. The facades of Balaban & Katz's movie palaces were brightly colored with enormous electric signs, a novelty when electricity was just becoming available for private consumption. The interiors consisted of enormous vestibules, grand staircases and lobbies, luxurious seating, and opulent decoration. Children's play areas allowed mothers to see films during the day. All services were administered by uniformed ushers. Another attraction for audiences was the air-conditioning installed by Balaban & Katz in all their movie theaters. It was based on industrial systems used in the city's meatpacking plants and was pioneered in the Central Park in 1917. Air-conditioning allowed movie theaters to remain open—and comfortable—during the hot summers in Chicago, when they would otherwise have had to close.

The success of the Balaban & Katz movie theaters could be clearly seen, not least by the Hollywood studios. Balaban & Katz joined the Famous Players–Lasky Corporation to form the Paramount

SERGEI EISENSTEIN

The career and films of the Russian director Sergei Mikhaylovich Eisenstein (1898–1948) were diametrically opposed to both the production system and the linear narratives perfected in Hollywood. After the Bolshevik Revolution in Russia in 1917 there was a climate of experimentation in the arts; paralleling the political changes taking place, artists created new forms of writing, theater, architecture, and cinema. The Bolshevik Party was initially happy to work with Eisenstein since his films glorified the revolution, and he enjoyed considerable artistic freedom. *October* (1928) was a fictionalized account of the revolution. Instead of the usual linked images in narrative sequences, Eisenstein created expressive montages of disparate shots to increase the psychological impact of his films. *Potemkin* (1925) became one of his most celebrated films, known particularly for its "Odessa Steps" sequence. Long shots raking across the steps that lead to the harbor in Odessa are juxtaposed with closeups to express the violence of the scene, in which czarist soldiers massacre the city's citizens.

Such was Eisenstein's fame that he made a brief, albeit unsuccessful, visit to Hollywood in 1930. On his return to the Soviet Union he found a new cultural climate: Stalin had clamped down on all dissent and promoted socialist realism in the arts. Eisenstein's work was discredited. Unable to produce films, he taught at the State Film Academy. He returned to filmmaking in 1938 with *Alexander Nevsky*, a medieval epic based on the great 13th-century Russian leader of the same name. Made when a German invasion of Russia was imminent, the film conformed to Stalin's desire to justify and glorify his regime through analogy to Russian history. Although the structure of the film was more conventional than Eisenstein's earlier work, it was still expressive.

Picture Corporation in 1925. Samuel Katz formed the Publix theater chain with movie palaces throughout the East Coast, Midwest, and Canada. The movie palace formula lasted only during the 1920s. In the Great Depression services were closed and staff fired to reduce costs; the tearooms gave way to popcorn and soft-drink concessions.

Accompanying music

Early film stock and equipment were not advanced enough to carry sound tracks, but movie shows had been full of sound since the inception of cinema. A special type of theatrical sound was devised for the cinema. Nonfiction movies were often accompanied by a lecturer, and early fictional movies could be accompanied by comments on the action or have the dialogues spoken. Above all, movies were accompanied by a variety of music, which ranged from improvisations to full scores, and from a piano or small ensemble to a full orchestra. These accompaniments sprang from the tradition of incidental music for the theater, which was adapted for the new medium. During the 1910s music for opera had the greatest influence on film music, since it was often used as a continuous accompaniment to stage drama. Music was an integral part of the silent movie experience and encompassed the work of established composers from Camille Saint-Saëns (1835–1921) in the French film *L'Assassinat du Duc de Guise* (1908) to Dmitry Shostakovich (1906–1975) in the Russian film *The New Babylon* (1929), made at the end of the silent movie era.

When films were shown as part of vaudeville shows, the music hall orchestra would accompany the movie, and the music was prepared for the film in the same way as for the live show. During the nickelodeon years the film was accompanied by solo piano; music in these unrefined settings was often ruined by unskilled performers and out-of-tune instruments. With the advent of the movie palace in the 1920s music became a very important part of the show, and ensembles were common. The grand movie palaces had their own orchestras and theater organs; the Publix theater chain was the largest employer of musicians in the United States in the 1920s. Conductors came to share the eminence of movie stars, and some enjoyed considerable fame as composers of film music.

The importance of music led to an increased demand for scores especially composed for film, as well as for the publication of film music. The first score to be specially written for a movie was composed by Joseph Carl Breil (1870–1926) for D.W. Griffith's epic *Birth of a Nation* (1915). Famous scores of the 1920s included Mortimer Wilson's for Raoul Walsh's film *The Thief of Baghdad* (1924). While full original scores were written for special films, the main rule was to use a music compilation. Compiled scores became the norm for important movies, and copies of these works were distributed with the film. The production of scores was dictated by finance, and the majority of feature films had no score; the music had to be devised by the performer. To supply this need, the publication of music anthologies and catalogs became an established business. Such publications included a variety of pieces of music in a single volume to accompany a range of moods and occasions. They included *Motion Picture Music* (1924) by Erno Rapée, which contained 370 pieces under 53 headings. By the mid-1920s the repertoire of film music boasted tens of thousands of pieces, from arrangements to original compositions.

Color and sound

Although all film was black and white, many attempts were made to produce color projection prints. Initially they were colored by painting the projection prints by hand. A stenciling process was patented by the French Pathé company in 1906. The first color film, sensitive to only two colors, was developed by Eastman in

1915. Technicolor developed a more successful process and made its first experimental movie, *The Toll of the Sea*, in 1922. Color films did not become popular until the late 1930s, however.

The inclusion of sound had been the goal of inventors from the beginning of motion pictures. Edison had made a synchronized phonograph, and it became a popular system, but the Western Electric system of recording sound directly on the film proved to be more promising. This system took the form of a separate track parallel to the images with modulations in tone that could be read by a sensor and turned into sound by an amplifier. The sound track necessitated a standard speed, and a projection rate of 24 frames per second became standard. Sound could be easily incorporated into movie theaters: The capital investment in the new technology was offset by dispensing with the musicians and vaudeville acts. It required a larger change in the studios, however, since the stages that had been used for silent films had to be changed radically to incorporate sound recording.

The introduction of sound changed the nature of the moviegoing experience in other ways. Once a movie contained all the images and sound necessary for its performance, it ceased to be a communal experience shared among the original studio, musicians, projectionist, and audience, and became a standard product in which the experience of each individual was the same at each performance. The biggest changes, however, were in the stars and the movies. Unlike the silent films, talkies from Hollywood were immediately restricted to English-speaking countries. This limitation led to a temporary decline in Hollywood's output between 1929 and 1932 as national industries made films in their own languages. At first American producers made the same film in different versions for different countries, but this solution proved too expensive. From 1933 they bounced back to consolidate their grip on international cinema production by either dubbing or subtitling their movies.

During the 1920s the Hollywood studio system became by far the largest film producer in the world. However, with the rapid pace of change and innovation in the industry, movies from this era were largely forgotten—their presentation restricted to art cinemas. With the arrival of sound, the original music for silent films was also forgotten. The nickelodeon piano came, erroneously, to epitomize the accompaniment to silent films. Since the 1980s, however, there has been an interest in unearthing the original music through archival research and the recreation of authentic scores and sound experiences.

SEE ALSO:

Cartoon & Animation • Chaplin, Charlie • Disney, Walt • Eastman, George • Griffith, D.W. • Hollywood • Houdini, Harry • Pickford, Mary • Vaudeville

Actor Lon Chaney (1883–1930) in character as Mr. Wu conducting the all-female band that provided the music for MGM's movie *Mr. Wu* (1927). Musical accompaniment and sound tracks were important components of silent films.

MUSICALS AND MUSICAL THEATER

American musicals came of age in the 1920s, when a succession of brilliant shows captivated audiences. Their combination of improbable plots, love stories, chorus lines of beautiful girls, and show-stopping tunes captured the optimistic energy and escapism of the postwar era.

Musical theater had been a popular form of entertainment in America from the early 1800s and flourished with renewed vigor in the postwar years of the twenties. Revues, often lavish productions that showcased the talents of varied performers, grew out of the traditions of English music hall, burlesque—theatrical entertainments with a comic, often mocking content and character—minstrel shows, and the popular variety theater known as vaudeville. The book musical, a format that used popular-style songs and dialogue to tell a story, also drew on these sources. It included musical comedies as well as operettas, which were often written by European-born composers and drew on European traditions of light opera.

In the 1920s musicals enjoyed immense popularity, particularly in the theaters of Broadway. More theaters were built in New York between 1900 and 1930 than in the whole of the preceding century, and Broadway itself featured in the titles of many songs and musicals from the era.

The Broadway musical

If anyone can be singled out as the father of musical comedy it is the librettist, lyricist, and composer George M. Cohan (1878–1942). His musicals such as *Little Johnny Jones* (1904) and *Forty-Five Minutes from Broadway* (1906) were

A drawing of a tap-dancer from between 1920 and 1940. Tap-dancing became popular in revues and musical comedies during the twenties.

distinguished by their thoroughly American setting, their colloquial dialogue and lyrics, and their popular melodies. Like his musical heirs, Cohan was happy to use any plot, however far-fetched and improbable, as long as it could support the required complement of songs, dances, routines, and humorous episodes.

In the early years a musical came into being because a producer had a star, or a group of stars, under contract. A play would then be stitched together to highlight the performers' talents. The production always followed the same formula: The curtains opened to reveal a chorus line of dancing girls. Each act closed with a major production number. A love story was the crux of the plot; the girl always won the boy, and the villain always got his just punishment.

Show time

The great musicals of the 1920s started with *Sally* (1920), a production by Florenz Ziegfeld (*see box below*) that starred Marilyn Miller (1898–1936), with whom he was having a passionate affair. Miller was petite, blonde, and a competent singer and dancer, but it was her enchanting stage persona that gave her star quality. *Sally* is the story of a poor dishwasher whose dancing talents lead her to stardom. Ziegfeld commissioned a score from composer Jerome Kern (*see box on p. 50*), which included the famous "Look for the Silver Lining." The show ran for 570 performances and toured for over a year, winning nationwide acclaim. Success and adulation made Miller, already known for her fiery temper, less and less manageable. Confident of her new-found star status, she never missed an opportunity to torment the adoring Ziegfeld, who was married at the time to the actress Billie Burke (1885–1970).

Miller went on to star in two more Broadway hits: *Sunny* (1925) and *Rosalie* (1928). Her stage career did not last for long, however. By 1933 she had retired; she died aged 37, a victim of a tempestuous marriage, chronic health problems, and heavy drinking.

No, No, Nanette

No, No, Nanette was the quintessential musical comedy of the 1920s. It was such a hit in Chicago, where it first appeared in 1924, that it stayed there for a year before transferring to Broadway in 1925. It enjoyed international success for the rest of the decade. The lighthearted story of a

ZIEGFELD'S FOLLIES

Florenz Ziegfeld was born in Chicago in 1867 and made his early reputation as a producer of Broadway musicals showcasing the talents of the music-hall sensation Anna Held (about 1870–1918), to whom he was unofficially married between 1897 and 1913. In 1907, at her suggestion, he began to produce a musical revue based on those staged at the famous Folies-Bergère theater in Paris, France. Creative visual spectacles with comedy and a chorus line of beautiful, scantily clad girls, the revues were an instant hit with audiences. After a highly profitable 70-performance run the show went on a brief tour. The *Follies* became an annual event, first appearing at the New Amsterdam Theater, New York, in 1913. Ziegfeld oversaw every aspect of the *Follies'* production, and the revue was soon the hottest property on Broadway. Ziegfeld was a well-known philanderer, and chorus-line girls who caught his fancy often found themselves elevated to star status overnight. In the 1920s the *Follies* enjoyed longer runs than ever, with 541 performances for the 1922 show and 520 for the 1924 production. At a time when the average Broadway musical was budgeted at $25,000, Ziegfeld spent $170,000 on his revue. He went on to produce a number of famous Broadway musicals, culminating in the acclaimed *Show Boat* (1927). However, his lavish productions were out of step with the economic recession that set in after the stock market crash of 1929, and despite several attempted comebacks, he never regained his former glory. He died in 1932.

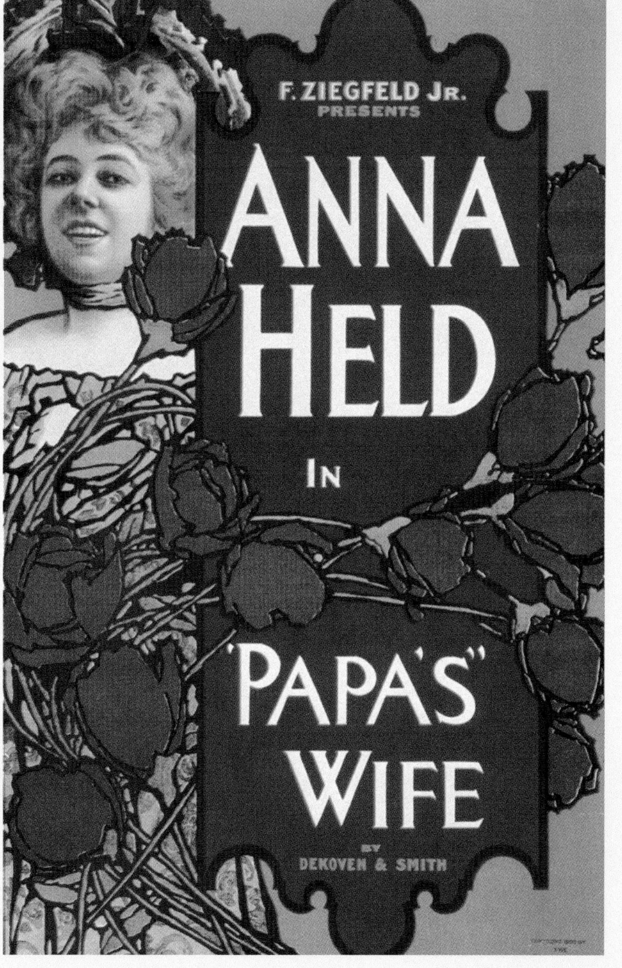

A poster advertising Ziegfeld's production of the musical Papa's Wife *(1899), which showcased the talents of Anna Held.*

JEROME KERN

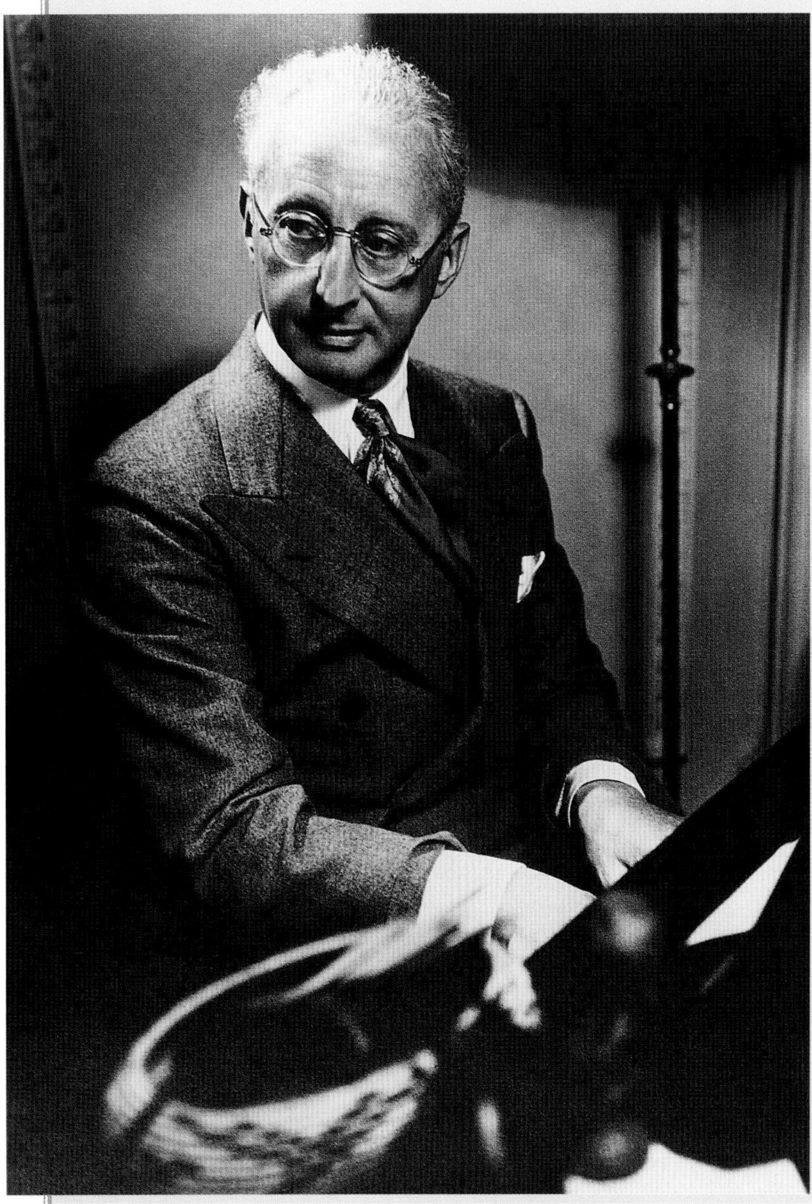

The composer Jerome Kern (1885–1945) studied at the New York School of Music and in 1903 in Heidelberg, Germany, and also spent time in England learning about musical comedy in the theaters of London's West End. Working with two Englishmen, playwright Guy Bolton (1884–1979) and novelist P.G. Wodehouse (1881–1975), Kern began to write musicals that turned to modern American life—especially new dance crazes—for their inspiration. Popular shows created by this team include *Very Good, Eddie*, *Oh, Boy!*, and *Oh, Lady! Lady!*

The pinnacle of Kern's musical career came in 1927 when he wrote *Show Boat*, for which Oscar Hammerstein II (1895–1960) contributed the book and lyrics. The production opened at the Ziegfeld Theater and ran for 575 Broadway performances. Recognized as a classic among musicals, *Show Boat* is based on a novel by Edna Ferber and was the first American musical with a serious plot drawn from a literary source. It is set on board one of the many American riverboats that featured traveling shows in the mid-1880s. It follows the lives and loves of the troupe that work aboard the *Cotton Blossom*. It is a key work in the history of the American musical, remarkable for the ways in which song, humor, and production numbers are integrated into a single and inextricable artistic entity. It is famous for a great story, moving lyrics, and music that is played and loved the world over. Its songs include "Why Do I Love You," "Can't Help Lovin' Dat Man," "Bill," and "Ol' Man River."

Jerome Kern photographed after 1930.

Manhattan heiress who eludes her fiancé for a weekend in sinful Atlantic City, and her philandering, Bible-publishing father, the show was considered a failure when it went on tour prior to its Chicago opening. The producers acted decisively, demanding a complete overhaul. The composer Vincent Youmans (1898–1946) and lyricists Irving Caesar (1895–1996) and Otto Harbach (1873–1963) came back with a score that was rich in popular hits, including the songs "Tea for Two" and "I Want to Be Happy."

George Gershwin (1898–1937) went some way toward bridging the wide gap between classical music and the popular tunes of Tin Pan Alley, a place where musical songs were pitched to music executives in the hopes of selling the rights to them. He won success as a composer of light music, of songs and musicals, but also experimented with a new form of classical repertoire that incorporated jazz rhythms, exemplified by *Rhapsody in Blue* (1924). In 1924 his musical *Lady, Be Good!* opened at the Liberty Theater, starring brother and sister act Fred (1899–1987) and Adele Astaire (1897–1981), old friends from Gershwin's time working in Tin Pan Alley. The production was a major breakthrough for Fred Astaire, who sang and danced his way to stardom in a series of Hollywood musicals in the 1930s. The show was also widely acknowledged as the first mature example of the American musical, establishing Gershwin as a leader in the jazz-oriented style. Gershwin went on to write a succession of musicals, many with

RODGERS AND HART

Songwriter Richard Rodgers (1902–1979) and lyricist Lorenz Hart (1895–1943) were famous for their lighthearted, effervescent musical comedies, such as *The Garrick Gaieties* (1925). However, some of their popular songs were surprisingly bittersweet, and Lorenz Hart was adept at capturing the heartbreak of unrequited love and romantic frustration. Together with the librettist Herb Fields (1897–1958), Rodgers and Hart wrote *Dearest Enemy* (1925), a musical set in the American Revolution in which a New York housewife performs her patriotic duty by entertaining, and distracting, a group of British officers. They had even greater success with *A Connecticut Yankee* (1927), based on Mark Twain's tale of a modern American who is transported to the court of King Arthur. This setting gave the team a chance to playfully meld the medieval with the American idiom, with spectacular results: "Thou Swell" is a Rodgers and Hart classic. William Gaxton played the leading role to critical acclaim, becoming Broadway's most popular leading man. Depression-era Broadway was not so kind to Rodgers and Hart, and after a series of expensive flops they went to Hollywood. They continued their collaboration in the 1930s, with successful shows such as *The Boys from Syracuse* (1938), *Pal Joey* (1940), and *By Jupiter* (1942).

Richard Rodgers (left) and Lorenz Hart (right) in 1936.

lyrics by his brother, Ira, including: *Oh, Kay!* (1926), *Strike up the Band* (1927), *Funny Face* (1927), and *Girl Crazy* (1930).

Broadway operettas

Not all the hit musicals of the 1920s were based on recognizably American themes. Many were operettas—productions similar in structure to an opera but often with wildly improbable, romantic plots interspersed with songs, orchestral music, dancing, and dialogue—written by European-born composers. The Czech composer Rudolf Friml (1879–1972) wrote 20 operettas over the course of his long career. His three biggest hits were *Rose Marie* (1924), *The Vagabond King* (1925), and *The Three Musketeers* (1928), which ranged confidently between the wilds of Canada and the streets of revolutionary Paris.

Hungarian-born composer Sigmund Romberg (1887–1951) worked for the New York impresario Jacob Schubert and was a prolific writer of Broadway musical scores. His best-known operettas include *The Blue Paradise* (1915), *Blossom Time* (1921), *The Desert Song* (1926), and *The New Moon* (1928). Like Friml's operettas, these works covered an improbable range of settings, from the deserts of North Africa to colonial New Orleans. *Blossom Time* was a fictitious love story involving the Austrian composer Franz Schubert (1797–1828), which adapted many of Schubert's classic melodies. The show toured all over the country, sometimes to its detriment—a touring company performing *Blossom Time* became a byword for second-rate, provincial theatricals. Nevertheless, Romberg's lush melodies, the sheer ambition of the stories and their entertaining escapism helped make the show enduringly popular.

Black musicals

One of the longest-running hit musicals of the 1920s was one of the least written about. *Shuffle Along* (1921) was written, produced, and performed entirely by black Americans, and could be seen at New York's 63rd Street Music Hall. It was conceived by the black comic duo of Flournoy Miller (1887–1971) and Aubrey Lyles as a "play with songs." Nominally there was a plot about a mayoral race in the fictional "Jim Town," but in essence the show was a musical revue, featuring songs by Eubie Blake (1883–1983) and Noble Sissle (1889–1975), including "Love Will Find a Way" and "I'm Just Wild about Harry." In many ways the show adhered to the old minstrel show stereotypes; black American dancers darkened their skin with blackface makeup and sang songs praising the beauty of paler, "seal-skin brown" skin. The show gave several major stars their first major break, such as Ethel Waters (1896–1977), Paul Robeson (1898–1976), Josephine Baker (1906–1975), and Adelaide Hall (1901–1993). The musical didn't play to exclusively black audiences: whites anxious to be part of the latest trend rushed to see *Shuffle Along* as well.

It was more common to see black performers in shows that were created by white composers and producers. The popular series of *Blackbirds* revues, staged by Lew Leslie, began in 1926. The *Blackbirds* revue of 1928 opened at the Liberty Theater and played for 518 performances. The score by composer Jimmy McHugh (1894–1969) and lyricist Dorothy Fields (1905–1974) included the hit song "I Can't Give You Anything But Love." However, racial stereotypes still persisted: Burnt cork was used to darken the skin of some performers, and one of the backdrops featured a huge portrait of a smiling "pickanniny" eating watermelon.

Dancing the night away

No musical was complete without a line of beautiful tap-dancing girls. Tap-dancing was a uniquely American form, an eclectic mixture of Irish jigs, clog dances, and African rhythms, which probably originated in the slave plantations of the Deep South in the 18th century. In the 19th century tap was developed and performed by famous black Americans, such as William Henry Lane and Rastus Brown. During the early 20th century, and especially the 1920s, jazz music evolved alongside tap-dancing, and original compositions were written to accompany the dancing. Musician Duke Ellington (1899–1974), for example, composed "Bojangles" as a musical portrait of the famous tap-dancer Bill "Bojangles" Robinson (1878–1949), a frequent performer at the Cotton Club in Harlem, New York City. Broadway musicals were quick to incorporate the exciting rhythms of tap, showcasing the individual talents of dancers such as Fred Astaire and providing the exhilarating spectacle of a line of beautiful girls tap-dancing together with well-drilled precision.

JEANETTE MACDONALD AND *THE LOVE PARADE*

The silent screen director Ernst Lubitsch (1892–1947) turned his talents to musical comedy in 1929. He cast around among Broadway stars for his film, but found that their stage-based techniques did not translate well to the screen—they appeared too exaggerated. However, he struck gold with Jeanette MacDonald (1903–1965), who had been singing, dancing, and acting on Broadway for nine years. Her first big singing part came in 1923 in *The Magic Ring*, in which she was billed as "the girl with the gold-red hair and the sea-green eyes." Next came roles of increasing importance, for which she received much attention, in the musicals *Tip Toes*, *Bubbling Over*, *Yes, Yes Yvette*, *The Studio Girl*, *Sunny Days*, and *Angela*. In 1929 Lubitsch teamed her up with the French cabaret performer Maurice Chevalier (1888–1972) to make the movie *The Love Parade*, a light-hearted operetta with a melodic and witty score. MacDonald plays the queen of a European country who falls in love with a scandalous playboy diplomat played by Chevalier. She almost immediately became one of Hollywood's top attractions and the first movie star whose success was built on her ability to sing.

WARNER BROS.
Supreme Triumph
AL JOLSON
in
The JAZZ SINGER

An advertisement for *The Jazz Singer* from a January 1928 issue of *Motion Picture News*. The movie, the first with synchronized speech, music, and sound effects, prepared the way for the popularity of talkies and musical films.

Numerous stage schools sprang up to equip girls for careers on Broadway. A job dancing in a chorus line was seen as the first step on a career ladder. "Spotted" by an eagle-eyed producer, a talented girl could emerge into the spotlight, and stardom beckoned. But high standards were rigorously applied. In the words of Florenz Ziegfeld: "Beauty, of course, is the most important requirement and the paramount asset of the applicant. When I say that, I mean beauty of face, form, charm, and manner, personal magnetism, individuality, grace, and poise." Training was rigorous; chorus girls spent hours every day rehearsing their numbers under the exacting eyes of choreographers, producers, and directors.

Hollywood musicals

The late 1920s saw the advent of cinematic sound, and with it the birth of the musical film. Warner Brothers was the first pioneer of sound, experimenting in the mid-1920s with Vitaphone, a system that coordinated large phonograph disks with filmed images. A number of films used recorded orchestral scores and sound effects, but no dialogue—from the outset it was assumed that the audience would not be interested in listening to actors speaking. All this changed in 1927, when Al Jolson (1886–1950) appeared in *The Jazz Singer*, the first film to use recorded song and dialogue. Although it was enthusiastically received, and much discussed, it only reached a small audience because so few cinemas at the time were wired for sound. However, Warner Brothers, the producer of the film, had seen the future. Within a year it had equipped a nationwide chain of theaters with sound systems. When Al Jolson reappeared in 1928 in *The Singing Fool*, they were ready. Rapt audiences watched Jolson play a professional singer who loses his son, and his heart-rending performance of "Sonny Boy" topped the charts. The film broke all box office records, and Hollywood woke up.

All the major Hollywood studios scrambled to jump on the sound bandwagon. Theaters rushed to convert to sound, and producers desperately cast around to find sound projects. They bought up the rights to thousands of existing songs and commissioned Broadway composers to start writing screen musicals. The most successful musical film of the 1920s was *Broadway Melody* (1929), a revue-style movie featuring a backstage plot with a score by Nacio Herb Brown (1896–1964) and Arthur Freed (1894–1973). Irving Thalberg (1899–1936), head of production at MGM studios, shot the film in just four weeks. A series of *Broadway Melody* films followed. The 1929 film was produced for just $379,000 and made $1.6 million on its initial release, even scooping an Academy Award—the first given to a musical. It was to be the beginning of a long line of musical successes for MGM in the 1930s.

SEE ALSO:

Broadway • Cotton Club • Dance • Hollywood • Jazz • Jolson, Al • Opera • Popular Music • Vaudeville

NATIONAL BROADCASTING COMPANY

Formed in November 1926 by the Radio Corporation of America (RCA), the National Broadcasting Company (NBC) opened with 24 stations on November 15 and almost immediately became the most powerful radio network in the United States.

In 1925 RCA and its partners Westinghouse Electric Corporation and General Electric (GE) acquired a virtual monopoly on U.S. radio transmissions over phone lines by buying the entire broadcasting business of RCA's main competitor, American Telephone and Telegraph (AT&T). One condition of the deal was that the seller would not try to compete with the buyer for seven years.

From RCA's point of view there were originally two reasons for the purchase. The first was to establish entertainment networks that would induce people to buy RCA radio sets so they could listen to the shows. The second was to use the power and influence of a national network as part of its aim of getting its technology adopted as the industry standard. Once the business was established, however, NBC struck an even richer vein—advertising revenue.

The opening night

NBC began broadcasting across its newly acquired network at 8:00 P.M. EST on November 15, 1926. A total of 24 stations in the East and Midwest participated in the inaugural hook up. The four-hour broadcast cost more than $50,000. The largest item of expenditure was the fees of the many famous performers, who included the New York Symphony Orchestra, soprano Mary Garden, comedian Will Rogers, comedy duo Weber and Fields, and Vincent Lopez and his orchestra.

No broadcaster could sustain such a high level of expenditure, but NBC had no intention of even trying to do so. Its vast network of wholly owned subsidiaries gave it great leverage: manufacturers of automobiles, tobacco, and other consumer goods were eager to sponsor shows with mass appeal, and the bigger the radio audience, the higher the rates that the broadcaster could charge.

Commercial success

This strategy worked extremely well: In subsequent broadcasts advertising effectively defrayed the costs of production. The face of U.S. radio changed quickly as a direct result: In 1925 only 21 radio stations were commercial (7 percent of the national total); in 1926 that rose to 11 percent; by 1930 there were 223 commercial stations (59 percent of the total).

THE BIRTH OF THE CHIMES

In the early days of NBC, at the end of every program an announcer would read out the names of all the stations that carried it. The network grew so quickly that this soon became impracticable, and a series of chimes was adopted as a corporate signature or call sign. There are several versions of how the chimes came to be. According to one version, a set of hand chimes was purchased for $48.50 from the Lesch Silver Company of Manhattan, and between 1927 and 1928 NBC studio technicians experimented with a seven-note sequence of chimes: They eventually adopted G–C–G–E–G–C–E. This proved too complicated to be struck repeatedly and accurately by a live performer, so the jingle was reduced to four notes, G–G–G–E. Then two of the Gs were dropped and a C was added to make G–E–C. It was generally agreed that this sounded better, and it was certainly easier to play. People pointed out that the chimes were also the initials of General Electric Corporation, but NBC claimed that this was a coincidence. The three-note sequence was first broadcast on November 29, 1929; it was struck every hour and half hour. In 1950 the chimes were the first audio trademark to be accepted by the U.S. Patent and Trademark Office. According to other versions, the chimes were invented by a local radio station, and NBC obtained permission to use them. They can still heard on radio on weekdays.

Comedy team Joe Weber (1867–1942) and Lew Fields (1867–1941) took part in NBC's opening network program on November 15, 1926. They were popular for their slapstick antics, dialect jokes, and burlesques of popular plays.

Within a year of its launch NBC was operating two national networks: NBC Red (the original chain of stations) and NBC Blue (launched January 1927). The Red flagship was WEAF in New York. Originally established by AT&T, it broadcast most of the established shows; one of its biggest sponsors was the American Tobacco Company. Most programs on the Blue network did not have sponsors. NBC later set up several other networks, starting with the White (or Watchtower) network, a religious station.

In January 1928 NBC produced a 47-station coast-to-coast program, "The Dodge Victory Hour," sponsored by the Dodge Motor Company to promote its new Victory Six automobile. The linkup featured big-name popular entertainers, including Al Jolson in New Orleans, Fred Stone in Chicago, Paul Whiteman in New York, and Will Rogers in Beverly Hills. Part of Rogers's act was an impersonation of President Calvin Coolidge, the first time an impressionist had been heard on air. The total audience was estimated at 35 million, and the following day the headline of the *New York Times* read, "All America Used As a Radio Station."

A rival appears

NBC did not go unchallenged for long. In 1927 New York talent agent Arthur Judson (1881–1975) and Columbia Records both launched independent networks, which quickly merged but continued to lose money. In 1928 the company was bought by William S. Paley (1901–1990) of La Palina Cigar Company and renamed the Columbia Broadcasting System (CBS). Realizing that the key to radio's success was large audiences that would attract advertisers, Paley offered programming free to affiliated stations in return for having part of their schedule devoted to sponsored network shows. From 22 stations in 1928 the network grew to 91 stations in five years. Although the companies were vying for the same market, they were different in structure and ethos: CBS was an independent programming enterprise, while NBC was basically a marketing initiative.

SEE ALSO:

Amos 'n' Andy • Advertising • Communications • Radio & Radio Industry

NATIONAL ORIGINS ACT, 1924

The National Origins Act of 1924 severely restricted immigration by establishing a system of national quotas that discriminated against immigrants from southern and eastern Europe and virtually excluded Asians. The policy stayed in effect until 1965.

The United States Immigration Commission reported in 1911 that only about one-fifth of all wage-earners had native, white parents; almost three-fifths of them were of immigrant origin. By 1924 roughly one-third of the total population was of foreign stock.

During the first wave of immigration in the 19th century nearly three-quarters of immigrants came from northern and western Europe and were predominantly Protestant. These "old stock" immigrants, broadly speaking, shared the same origins and religion as the original 17th-century colonists. But by 1910 fewer than one-quarter of immigrants were of "old stock"; the remaining three-quarters were "new" immigrants from southern and eastern Europe and from Asia. Most of the new European immigrants were Roman Catholic, some were Orthodox Christian, and a signficant minority were Jews.

The "old" immigrants had much in common with the new land in which they arrived and so found it easier to assimilate; the "new" immigrants were, for the most part, unskilled and from ethnic and linguistic backgrounds that made it harder for them to be stirred into the melting pot.

Their arrival provoked a wave of nativism—an attitude of hostility toward people perceived as not conforming to American national values. Popular pressure built up for restriction of the "wrong" kind of immigrant, and prejudice against Asians, Jews, and Roman Catholics was rampant. There were widespread fears that immigrants of "inferior stock" would bring disease and madness. Societies such as the American Protective League (APL) reported on "disloyal" activities and helped whip up a frenzy of fear that white Anglo-Saxon Protestants (WASPs) were committing "racial suicide" by accepting more immigrants. Trade unions were concerned that the labor market would be flooded by immigrant workers, particularly Asians.

It hurt immigrants—and assisted those people wishing to erect barriers against further immigration—that they were closely associated with the Socialist Party and other radical political movements. Immigrant groups were also prominent in the movement to keep the United States out of World War I (1914–1918), and American public opinion began to focus on the idea that true patriotism meant rejecting all foreign values. Organizations of superpatriots such as the National Security League harassed foreigners of all kinds, often with the approval of state and local officials. The Ku Klux Klan added its voice to the chorus against "polyglotism"; its constitution promoted the "ideals of a pure Americanism."

JOHNSON AND REED

The authors of the National Origins Act were Senators Hiram W. Johnson (R-CA) (1866–1945) and David A. Reed (R-PA) (1880–1953). The following passage illustrates Reed's argument in favor of the act:

"There has come about a general realization of the fact that the races of men who have been coming to us in recent years are wholly dissimilar to the native-born Americans; that they are untrained in self-government—a faculty that it has taken the Northwestern Europeans many centuries to acquire. America was beginning also to smart under the irritation of her 'foreign colonies'—those groups of aliens, either in city slums or in country districts, who speak a foreign language and live a foreign life, and who want neither to learn our common speech nor to share our common life. From all this has grown the conviction that it was best for America that our incoming immigrants should hereafter be of the same races as those of us who are already here, so that each year's immigration should so far as possible be a miniature America, resembling in national origins the persons who are already settled in our country...."

The bill passed in the Senate with only six dissenting votes and came into full effect in 1929.

IMMIGRATION QUOTAS

The table below was published in the 1929 Statistical Abstract of the United States. It shows annual national immigration quotas under the 1924 Immigration Act.

Northwest Europe and Scandinavia		Eastern and Southern Europe		Other Countries	
Country	*Quota*	*Country*	*Quota*	*Country*	*Quota*
Germany	51,227	Poland	5,982	Africa (other than Egypt)	1,100
Great Britain & Northern Ireland	34,007	Italy	3,845	Armenia	124
Irish Free State	28,567	Czechoslovakia	3,073	Australia	121
Sweden	9,561	Russia	2,248	Palestine	100
Norway	6,453	Yugoslavia	671	Syria	100
France	3,954	Romania	603	Turkey	100
Denmark	2,789	Portugal	503	Egypt	100
Switzerland	2,081	Hungary	473	New Zealand & Pacific Islands	100
Netherlands	1,648	Lithuania	344	All others	1,900
Austria	785	Latvia	142		
Belgium	512	Spain	131		
Finland	471	Estonia	124		
Free City of Danzig	228	Albania	100		
Iceland	100	Bulgaria	100		
Luxembourg	100	Greece	100		
Total	142,483	Total	18,439	Total	3,745
Total %	86.5	Total %	11.2	Total %	2.3

(Total Annual immigrant quota: 164,667)

Source: Statistical Abstract of the United States (Washington, D.C. Government Printing Office, 1929), 100

From 1919 to 1920, during the Red Scare, anticommunist feelings ran high as a rash of industrial strikes disrupted the economy, and terrorist bombs sent a ripple of fear through the country. Immigrants as a whole were branded as unpatriotic, a danger to the American way of life, and a potential threat to the American form of government. In fact, the weight of immigrant political influence came down on the side of conservatism, partly because so many eastern and southern European immigrants came from peasant, Roman Catholic backgrounds.

The door is closed

Between June 1920 and June 1921, 805,228 immigrants entered the United States—an almost 800 percent increase on the figures for 1918. In 1921 Congress passed an emergency measure to slow down immigration, using the 1910 census as the base for determining quotas and limiting total annual immigration to 350,000. Yet many felt that there were still too many immigrants. In 1924 Congress gave in to the pressure of public feeling and passed the Johnson–Reed National Origins Act (*see boxes opposite and above*). The act had three main features. It set an annual limit of 164,000 on the total number of immigrants to be allowed into the United States. By the time that the act came into force in 1929, the figure had been lowered to 150,000.

The act excluded new immigration from Japan and China entirely. The Japanese government made heated protests, and May 26, the effective date of the legislation, was declared a day of national humiliation in Japan as its already strained relationship with the United States plunged to a new low.

The act laid down as its guiding principle that the number of immigrants to be allowed in from any one country could not exceed 2 percent of the number of people of that national group reported as living in the United States in the 1890 census. Since the influx of "new" immigrants from southern and eastern Europe had largely taken place after 1890, that ensured that the majority of immigrants from 1924 onward would be from the "old" Protestant stock. They made up, in fact, about 85 percent of the new quota. Because the Republican administrations of the twenties were trying to build closer ties with the countries of South America, the whole of the Western Hemisphere was exempted from the operation of the quota system laid down in the act.

SEE ALSO:

Anarchism • Asian Americans • China • Japan • Ethnic Conflict •Immigration • Ku Klux Klan • Latin America • Political Radicalism • Racial Stereotypes • Red Scare

NATIVE AMERICANS

Marginalized and poverty stricken, Native Americans were some of the most disadvantaged members of U.S. society in the 1920s. However, the decade was also a time of transition. Reformers fought for recognition of native rights, and a number of initiatives led to later reforms.

As World War I (1914–1918) ended and the United States entered the Roaring Twenties, Native Americans were one part of the population who did not enjoy the prosperity and benefits of the economic boom. They were recovering from a population low around the turn of the century, when their numbers had dropped to approximately 250,000. They were also experiencing the consequences of the Dawes General Allotment Act (1887), under which their reservation lands were divided and apportioned to individuals—both Native American and nonnative—for farming. American Indians on reservations lived in poverty. Their health was poor, many were starving, infant mortality was twice that of mainstream Americans, and life expectancy was short, at approximately 43 years—it was about 55 years for white Americans. Unemployment was high and the educational system inferior to that of white Americans. In 1929, when the stock market crashed and the United States entered the worst economic recession in its history, the majority of Native Americans were already living in destitution.

In spite of efforts to destroy their culture and traditions, by 1920 Native Americans had neither vanished nor assimilated (integrated into white society). However, they were virtually invisible in U.S. society. Only romanticized elements of their culture were found in the popular media, culture, and the arts—in paintings, architecture, movies, and dime novels.

Signs of change

The first piece of legislation in the twenties that had the potential to improve the situation for Native Americans was the Synder Act, passed by Congress on November 2, 1921. The act authorized the Bureau of Indian Affairs to direct the expenditure appropriations for Native Americans throughout the United States under the supervision of the secretary of the interior. The act included expenditures for health, education, employment, administration of Native American property, and irrigation. Up until this time appropriation requests for Native Americans were often defeated on the floor of Congress.

Assimilation and allotment

Organizations devoted to native rights had existed since the late 19th century. However, the policies that many of them advocated differed from those that came to the fore in the early 20th century. The Indian Rights Association, founded by white Americans in 1882, was dedicated to providing equal protection of the law, education, citizenship, and individual land title to Native Americans. Its members believed that this objective could best be achieved by assimilating American Indians into mainstream white culture, by removing their tribal lifestyles and values, and by educating them in white ways. The association was a significant driving force behind the General Allotment Act and subsequent federal assimilationist policy. The Dawes General Allotment Act of 1887—named for Senator Henry L. Dawes (1816–1903) of Massachusetts, who sponsored the bill in Congress—was a comprehensive attempt by the federal government to create a new role for Native Americans. It aimed to assimilate them into mainstream white society by teaching them to be farmers and to value individualism and property ownership. To achieve this goal, the act made provision for reservation lands to be allotted or divided. Heads of families generally received 160 acres, single individuals over 18 years of age received 80 acres, and other tribal members 40 acres. The allotments were to be held in trust by the federal government for 25 years, after which time title, or ownership, passed to the individual. The act allowed surplus lands not allocated to tribal members to be sold to nonnatives, such as homesteaders.

Allotment was devastating for Native American society—politically, culturally, and economically. Private ownership of land was not a broadly held Native American value. Indian traditions held that land, Mother Earth, was to be used communally and was sacred. Additionally, farming was not a way of life for all Native Americans—especially the western tribes, many of whom were hunters and gatherers—and where it was, it was often the role of women.

Allotment diminished the importance of tribal governments and leaders because the federal government dealt directly with individuals, especially in the distribution of supplies, food, and payments. By 1934, when allotment ended, the peoples on more than 100 reservations had lost 90 million acres, 60 million of which had been sold as surplus to settlers. During the allotment era corruption, graft, and bribery were commonly used to gain lands from Native Americans. Many dishonest settlers and speculators used questionable means to acquire land, purchasing it at unfair prices, buying inheritance rights, or gaining guardianship over Native American minors. The federal government also granted rights of way to railroads and telegraph lines across Indian lands. Government officials often allotted Native Americans less desirable land, which was unsuitable for agriculture, while they sold more attractive land to settlers as surplus. To make matters worse, the federal government's promises of assistance—in the form of money, supplies, and technical advice—rarely materialized, which left Native Americans unable to compete with white farmers. These factors contributed to many American Indians leasing or selling their lands to whites. Two million acres of tribal lands passed into white hands each year between 1903 and 1933. Allotment weakened tribal governments, devalued Native American culture and traditions, and damaged communal and family life.

By the early 20th century the failure of the Dawes General Allotment Act was becoming apparent. Although the Indian Rights Association had been well-intentioned, many of its policies had been damaging, and a new generation of activists and reformers emerged. They included Native American individuals and, for the first time, Native American organizations such as the Society of American Indians, founded in 1911, and the National Council of the American Indians, created by Gertrude Simmons Bonnin in 1926 (*see box on p. 63*). Along with nonnative bodies such as the influential Indian Defense Association established by John Collier in 1923 (*see box on p. 65*) these groups launched campaigns focused on the consolidation of Indian land rights, cultural retention, and self-government. The efforts of these organizations were largely responsible for changing attitudes toward Native Americans in the 1920s and for shaping the reforms of the 1930s.

Land rights

Land rights continued to be a central issue in Native American affairs in the 1920s. Forcible land seizure had long defined U.S. policy toward American Indians, and attempts to appropriate land did not stop in the twenties. The most high-profile instance, and the one that galvanized and unified the efforts of reformers, concerned the Pueblo peoples of New Mexico.

New Mexico became part of an independent Mexico in 1821. After the U.S. victory over Mexico in the Mexican War (1846–1848) New Mexico was established as a territory of the United States in 1850; it became a U.S. state in 1912. The region had a history of disputes and violence between Pueblo peoples and

Native American tepees next to the Columbia River in the northwest of the United States photographed around 1922. Traditionally many American Indians lived in temporary settlements as they moved around in search of food.

Members of a Pueblo delegation visit Washington, D.C., in January 1923 to lobby against the Bursum Bill. They hold canes given to their ancestors by Abraham Lincoln to symbolize their land rights.

residents with Spanish and U.S. ancestry. Most of these disputes centered around land claims. In 1921 Senator Holm O. Bursum (1867–1953) of New Mexico drafted a bill, known as the Bursum Bill, designed to give nonnatives the right to former Pueblo land and water. In 1922 the Pueblo peoples of New Mexico and Arizona united to form the All-Pueblo Council; 20 Pueblos organized and joined with white reformers led by John Collier in a campaign to defeat the Bursum Bill. The last unification of Pueblo people had occurred in 1680 with the Pueblo Revolt against the Spanish, which had succeeded in driving the colonists from Pueblo territories for 12 years. In 1923 the Pueblos sent a delegation to Washington, D.C., to press their case. They were successful, and the Bursum Bill was defeated. The Pueblos were victorious partly because the bill came at a time when the detrimental effects of allotment were becoming very apparent, and partly because advocates of Native American rights united in their campaign under the effective leadership of John Collier. The result of fighting the Bursum Bill was the drafting and passage of the Pueblo Lands Act in 1924. The act established the Pueblo Lands Board to address disputes caused by earlier sales of Pueblo lands. The board's duties included establishing ownership and awarding compensation to Pueblos adjudged to have suffered earlier unlawful land losses.

The question of citizenship

One event that had focused attention on the inequitable treatment of Native Americans—and also black Americans—in U.S. society was World War I. The entry of the United States into the conflict in 1917 affected tribes in two main ways. First, the federal government cut back on Native American healthcare, education, and welfare services. Second, an estimated 10,000 young Native American men served in the U.S. armed forces at a time when most American Indians were not even allowed to vote, except for some specific cases in which citizenship was granted at the expense of tribal citizenship, treaties, or special statutes. The government encouraged Native Americans to enlist, and Native American males were asked to register for the draft although no draft occurred. On some reservations, including Navajo, Goshiute, and Fort Hall, tribal peoples protested, citing the fact that Native Americans were not classed as citizens. The war did bring a few minor benefits: It created some employment opportunities for Native Americans as farm laborers, and some Native American lands were leased for wartime agricultural production.

Native Americans who served in the armed forces in World War I were granted full citizenship in 1919. However, other Native Americans had to wait until 1924 and the Citizenship Act, which conferred citizenship on Native Americans who had not become citizens under other acts, and who were born within the territorial limits of the United States. The act did not require Native Americans to renounce their tribal citizenship or rights. Native Americans became, and remain, citizens of three political entities: the United States, the state they live in, and their tribal nation. They have the rights and privileges of each. As U.S. citizens, Native Americans are protected by the Bill of Rights and are required to register for the draft. As state citizens, they are eligible to vote and receive state services. As tribal citizens, they receive tribal and federal benefits. Citizenship was granted because of Native American participation in World War I and to motivate further assimilation into mainstream society.

State suffrage did not automatically follow the passage of the Citizenship Act for Native Americans. Many states continued to deny Native Americans the right to vote because they did not pay taxes or were under guardianship. For instance, Native Americans were not allowed to vote in Arizona and New Mexico until 1948, and in Maine until 1954. Many Native Americans who were allowed to vote did not exercise their right.

CULTURAL TOURISM

By the 1920s large numbers of tourists were visiting the Southwest to see the Native American communities there and to buy the artifacts they made, particularly Hopi pottery and Washoe basketry. The interest had in part been stimulated in the late 19th century by the highly successful marketing campaign of the Atchison, Topeka, and Santa Fe Railway, which focused on the landscape and indigenous population of the region to attract tourists. Entrepreneurs such as Fred Harvey soon exploited growing interest in the Southwest, setting up emporiums where tourists could buy Native American crafts as souvenirs of their visit. Interest in Native American crafts had also been stimulated in the late 19th century by anthropologists and museums, such as the Smithsonian Institution, which was eager to preserve artifacts produced by cultures that many people considered doomed to perish. To satisfy the demand for Native American artifacts, growing numbers of Indians became craftspeople at a time when there was widespread poverty and unemployment in their communities. They included the Hopi-Tewa potter Nampeyo (about 1860–1942) and the Washoe basketmaker Louisa Keyser. While their artifacts drew on traditional wares, they were made specifically for U.S. collectors and tourists.

The Hopi-Tewa potter Nampeyo photographed around 1903 decorates one of the large jars for which she was famous.

Water and mineral rights

It was not only land rights and the right to vote that featured in government dealings with Native Americans in the twenties. Two government actions early in the decade revealed little regard for Native American water and mineral rights. The first was the Colorado River Basin Compact (1922), negotiated by Secretary of Commerce Herbert Hoover (1874–1964). It was drawn up to protect the water rights of the seven states through which the Colorado River flowed and was precipitated by concern that the rapidly growing state of California would lay claim to more than its fair share of water. The compact apportioned water from the Colorado river system between the Upper Basin states (Colorado, New Mexico, Utah, and Wyoming) and the Lower Basin states (Arizona, California, and Nevada). Despite the large number of Indian reservations on these lands, Native Americans were excluded from the proceedings.

The compact contained a clause stating that the agreement did not affect the obligations of the federal government to Indian tribes. A precedent for federal obligations had been set out in the 1908 court case *Winters v. United States*. In this case the Supreme Court had ruled that the Fort Belknap Reservation in Montana had prior right to reserve the amount of water necessary for the functioning of the reservation under the terms of the federal government agreement that had created it in 1888. However, the exclusion of Native American participation in the Colorado River Compact to all intents and purposes ignored their water rights. The compact formed the basis of the still contentious water politics of the West and has greatly affected Native Americans in the region.

A similar disregard for Native American rights was shown toward the Navajo over the question of oil and mineral rights. In 1922 oil was discovered on the Navajo Reservation, and the California company Standard Oil wanted to lease the land to drill for oil. However, the U.S. government could not legally lease the land without the consent of the Navajo. At the time the Navajo had no formal governing body, and power was decentralized among many headmen. In May 1922 the U.S. government called the leading headmen to a meeting, but the Navajo leaders rejected all leasing applications. Secretary of the Interior Albert B. Fall (1861–1944) then used a number of maneuvers to secure approval, including the creation of a Navajo Business Council comprising three members to sign and approve oil leases. Fall was soon to be discredited for his corrupt dealings in other oil reserves in the Teapot Dome Scandal. In 1923 the Business Council was enlarged and renamed the Navajo Tribal Council, and the federal government supervised the election of its

Members of the Committee of One Hundred, an advisory group on Indian affairs, photographed on December 13, 1923. At the center stand President Calvin Coolidge and Ruth Muskrat, a leading Cherokee reformer and activist.

PROMINENT NATIVE AMERICAN WOMEN

In the early 1900s white, male-dominated society and its ethnic and racial prejudices left little room for recognition of Native American women's achievements. Yet a few American Indian women did gain attention outside their communities. They included Native American craftspeople such as the potters Nampeyo and Maria Martinez, whose work, often produced under the auspices of white entrepreneurs, was highly collectable (*see box on p. 61*), the author and campaigner for Native American rights Gertrude Simmons Bonnin (1876–1938), and the writer Mourning Dove (1888–1936). Around 1900 Gertrude Simmons Bonnin, a Sioux Indian from South Dakota, had several stories published in *The Atlantic Monthly* and *Harper's Monthly* under the pen name Zitkala-Sa (Red Bird). Based on her own experiences, these works explored the tensions of maintaining traditional Native American identity during a period of assimilation; they were republished in 1921 in the anthology *American Indian Stories*. As well as writing and promoting Native American culture, Bonnin was an activist for American Indian rights. She was involved with the Society of American Indians, the first reform organization to be administered entirely by Native Americans, and in 1916 became its secretary and moved to Washington, D.C., to lobby the Bureau of Indian Affairs. After the society disbanded, she remained an influential activist and in 1926 founded the National Council of American Indians. She was a member of a team charged with investigating corruption against Native Americans in Oklahoma in the mid-1920s when oil was discovered on their lands and was an adviser to the Meriam Commission in 1928. Mourning Dove was a Salishan Indian from Idaho who also received attention during the twenties for her writing. Her novel *Cogewea the Half Blood* was published in 1927 followed by her anthology *Coyote Stories* in 1933. Although heavily edited to appeal to white readers, the books provide important insights into Native American traditions.

This photograph of the Sioux writer and political activist Gertrude Simmons Bonnin appeared as the frontispiece to her book American Indian Stories, *published in 1921.*

members. The council was formed specifically for the purposes of mineral leasing. Once in place, it gave authority to the Department of the Interior to negotiate all future oil and gas leases on behalf of the Navajo Nation. Concerns about government administration of income generated from Native American lands and resources—particularly the transfer of appropriate sums due to American Indians—has been a long-running source of contention. They were at the center of *Cobel v. Norton* (1996), a court case that remained unresolved in summer 2004.

Reform initiatives

During the twenties advocates for Native American rights began to make small inroads into official policy. A significant milestone in this respect was the Committee of One Hundred. The committee, made up of U.S. citizens, was formed to advise the Republican administration on Indian affairs. When it convened in Washington, D.C., on December 12 and 13, 1923, it became the first official study of Indian affairs to be conducted in the 1920s. The committee made suggestions for changes, especially to education, but the Bureau of Indian Affairs neglected its recommendations. Reformers, realizing their work was far from finished, intensified their efforts. Their demands in 1924 and 1925 led Secretary of the Interior Hubert Work (1860–1942) to commission a comprehensive study into the situation of Native Americans, which became the primary catalyst for change.

The Meriam Report

Hubert Work commissioned the survey in 1926 from the Institute for Government Research. Anthropologist Lewis M. Meriam headed the study, and under his

NATIVE AMERICAN INFLUENCES IN ARCHITECTURE

Native American design motifs influenced American architecture in the twenties, especially in the Southwest. In this region the buildings of the Pueblo peoples had long influenced the structures of later European arrivals. Based on cubic modules with few window openings and made from mud brick and stucco, they were perfectly adapted to the hot climate. Frank Lloyd Wright (1867–1959), always responsive to local environments, drew on the forms of Pueblo buildings—as well as those of the Mayans of Mexico—for a series of houses he designed in Los Angeles in the twenties.

Other architects drew on Native American culture in more superficial ways for the decorative motifs that adorned their buildings. Art deco, a style that became popular in America in the twenties and thirties, was highly eclectic, drawing on many diverse cultures and sources for decorative features. The so-called "Pueblo deco" was a Southwestern variation. Two of the best known examples were constructed in Albuquerque, New Mexico: the KiMo Theater and the Franciscan Hotel. Carl Boller, a Kansas architect, designed the KiMo in 1927. He drew on the pueblos around Albuquerque as well as Navajo imagery and Western folklore for the extravagant decoration of his movie theater. El Paso architect Henry Trost designed the Franciscan in 1923. Another example from 1923 is the El Navajo Hotel in Gallup, New Mexico. Designed by Mary Jane Colter, it featured Navajo sand painting designs in the lobby. While the El Navajo and Franciscan hotels have been demolished, the KiMo survives as the most famous example of Pueblo deco architecture.

The KiMo Theater in Albuquerque, New Mexico, designed in the Pueblo deco style by Carl Boller in 1927.

JOHN COLLIER: REFORMER

John Collier (1884–1968) was a sociologist, educator, and reformer who played a key role in the reassessment and assertion of Native American rights from the 1920s until his death in 1968. He learned about Native American life from his visits to Pueblo Indian settlements in New Mexico. During Christmas 1920 he traveled with his family to Taos, New Mexico, to visit Mabel Dodge Luhan (1879–1962), a writer from New York City who was married to a Taos tribal member, Antonio Luhan. As Collier learned about Taos traditions and witnessed tribal dances, he became fascinated with Native Americans and their culture.

He became a major reformer for Native American rights in 1922, when he led opposition to the Bursum Bill, which proposed to confirm non-Indian claims to former Pueblo lands. Collier organized public gatherings and an effective publicity campaign, eventually setting up the American Indian Defense Association to support his fight. He served as executive director of the organization from 1923 to 1933 and the American Indian Defense Association became the strongest reform group fighting for Native American rights in the twenties. The association published its own bulletin, *American Indian Life*, although *Sunset* magazine was the primary voice for reformers.

Collier attacked allotment and assimilation, calling for Native American involvement in federal policy-making. He was instrumental in bringing Native Americans to Washington, D.C., to meet with congressmen. Individuals from the All-Pueblo Council were the first to travel to the capital in 1923, and their visit assisted the passage of the Pueblo Lands Act (1924), which was designed to resolve disputes concerning nonnative ownership of former Pueblo lands.

John Collier works at his desk in 1933, shortly after his appointment as commissioner of Indian Affairs.

A variety of groups supported Collier, including the General Federation of Women's Clubs and the Association on American Indian Affairs. Collier's view that Indians required defense rather than "civilizing" was revolutionary, as was his insistence on programs that would fit the interests and needs of tribal peoples.

Collier was appointed commissioner of the Bureau of Indian Affairs in 1933 under President Franklin D. Roosevelt (1933–1945), an office he held until 1945. As commissioner, Collier led the effort to implement the recommendations of the Meriam Report (1928) through the Indian Reorganization Act (*see box on p. 69*) and the Indian New Deal. He was an ardent believer in cultural pluralism rather than assimilation for Native Americans.

direction a team of experts gathered data and prepared the report. One of the principal investigators was the Native American Henry Roe Cloud (*see box on p. 67*). Published in 1928, the report is considered the most significant inquiry into Native American affairs in the 20th century. Its official title is *The Problem of Indian Administration*, although it is more popularly known as the Meriam Report.

The Meriam Report revealed poverty, suffering, and discontent among Native Americans. It showed that American Indians suffered from poor health, disease, malnutrition, and short life expectancy. It recorded infant mortality rates (the number of babies who died before they were one year old) of 190.7 per 1,000, far higher than than the rates for any other ethnic group. It also found that measles, pneumonia, tuberculosis, and trachoma—an infectious eye disease—were rampant on reservations. Native Americans had an average annual per capita income of only $100—around a tenth of the national average. The report also revealed that the Bureau of Indian Affairs was not meeting the needs of Native Americans, and that Native Americans were excluded from managing their own affairs.

The Meriam Report brought public attention and sympathy to the deplorable living conditions of native peoples in the United States. It also acknowledged the value of Native American economic, social, religious, and ethical concepts. In so doing, it changed the federal government's attitude toward American Indians. The report strongly advised that the federal government should develop and build on tribal values instead of trying to destroy them, and should support self-sufficiency. It recommended an end to allotment and the closure of boarding schools that were sited far away from reservations and required the removal of children from their families and communities. The report stressed the need for a comprehensive educational policy, systematic economic planning and development, better-paid and more efficient personnel in the Bureau of Indian Affairs, Native American use of native lands, the strengthening of community life, clarification of law and order on the reservations, and settlement of any outstanding legal claims. Although the Meriam Report was still based on ideas of assimilating Native American peoples, it did urge greater respect for their culture.

Implementing reforms

Implementing the recommendations of the Meriam Report was the responsibility of Charles Rhoads (1872–1956), whom President Herbert Hoover (1929–1933) appointed commissioner of Indian Affairs in 1929. Rhoads was a Quaker and a

Charles Rhoads (second right) and J. Henry Scattergood (second left) are sworn in as commissioner of Indian affairs and assistant commissioner, respectively, in the Department of the Interior on July 2, 1929.

PROMINENT NATIVE AMERICAN MEN

During the twenties a number of Native American men were in the public eye, including the politician Charles Curtis (1860–1936), the educator Henry Roe Cloud (1884–1950), the physician and reformer Carlos Montezuma (about 1866–1923), and the sportsman John Levi.

Charles Curtis was the son of a soldier, Orren Arms Curtis, and Ellen Gonville Pappen, who was one-quarter Native American. She was descended from the Kaw and Osage peoples of Kansas, and Charles Curtis spent his early youth with the Kaw tribe. He later became a lawyer and entered Republican Party politics, serving as a Kansas congressman for 14 years and a senator for 20. In 1928 Curtis was elected vice president under Herbert Hoover, a position he held until 1933. He was the first person with Native American ancestry to reach such high office in the United States.

Henry Roe Cloud was one of the most influential figures in the reform of Native American education from the mid-1910s until his death in 1950. He was born on the Winnebago Reservation in Nebraska and attended Genoa, Nebraska, Indian School, and Santee Normal Training School, a mission-run Indian school, where he converted to Christianity. His teachers there encouraged him to enter Mount Hermon School in Northfield, Massachusetts, as preparation for college. This Cloud did and proceeded to win a place at Yale University, where he studied psychology and philosophy. After graduating in 1910, Cloud continued his studies: he was awarded a master's degree in anthropology in 1912 and, having also studied at Auburn Theological Seminary, New York State, was ordained as a Presbyterian minister in 1913. During this period Cloud became an active member of the Society of American Indians, a reform group founded in 1911. He also pursued plans to open a preparatory school for Native Americans in the West. In 1915 his Roe Indian Institute (later renamed the American Indian Institute) opened in Wichita, Kansas, becoming the only Indian-run high school in the country. In 1923 Secretary of the Interior Hubert Work selected Cloud as a member of the Committee of One Hundred. Three years later Lewis M. Meriam selected him as a principal investigator for the Meriam Report. In 1931 Cloud began his government career as a field agent in Indian affairs. Two years later John Collier, commissioner of Indian affairs, appointed him president of Haskell Institute in Lawrence, Kansas (now the Haskell Indian Nations University), one of the most prestigious posts in Native American education.

On January 31, 1923, Carlos Montezuma, a Yavapai, died at Fort McDowell, Arizona, from tuberculosis. He was one of the first Native American physicians, a Yavapai leader, and a national activist advocating Native American emancipation. Wassaja, his Yavapai name, was born in Arizona in around 1866. In 1871 he was captured by Pima Indians and sold to a photographer, Carlos Gentile, for $30. Renamed Carlos Montezuma, he worked his way through college and became a Chicago doctor. He traced some of his Yavapai relatives to the Fort McDowell reservation and, witnessing the prisonlike conditions there, became an ardent campaigner for Native American rights, including land and water rights. He was a member of the Society of American Indians.

John Levi, an Arapaho Indian from Oklahoma, attended Haskell Institute from 1921 to 1924. Considered one of the greatest Native American athletes from Haskell, he was on the 1923 All-American football team. While at Haskell, John Levi also played baseball and excelled at track events. In the twenties and thirties Haskell attained national prominence for its sports programs, especially in football and track.

Educationist Henry Roe Cloud photographed in 1939.

banker by profession. Following World War I, he had gone to France to help with war relief work. He was well acquainted with Native American issues because his father, James E. Rhoads, had helped establish the Indian Rights Association, an organization of which he himself became chairman in 1927. J. Henry Scattergood (1877–1953), Rhoads's friend and associate from his war relief work in France, was appointed assistant commissioner of Indian affairs.

At first reformers were pleased with the appointment of Rhoads and Scattergood. During their tenure both men attempted to upgrade the personnel of the Bureau of Indian Affairs, emphasized local day schools rather than boarding schools, and encouraged employment of Native Americans with respect for their culture. However, the Bureau staff and Congress did not always endorse their policy changes, and much of their proposed legislation did not pass the first time it was presented. Rhoads and Scattergood were impeded in implementing initiatives for reform not only by entrenched attitudes toward Native Americans but also by the worsening economic recession that gripped the country after the stock market crash of October 1929. As the Great Depression of the thirties set in, economic recovery was the issue that preoccupied politicians.

Reforming education

Reformers of the 1920s discovered extensive mismanagement within the Bureau of Indian Affairs, which fueled their demands for change. Native American education was one of the areas on which they focused. Federal schools for Native Americans were inadequate and badly lacking in quality.

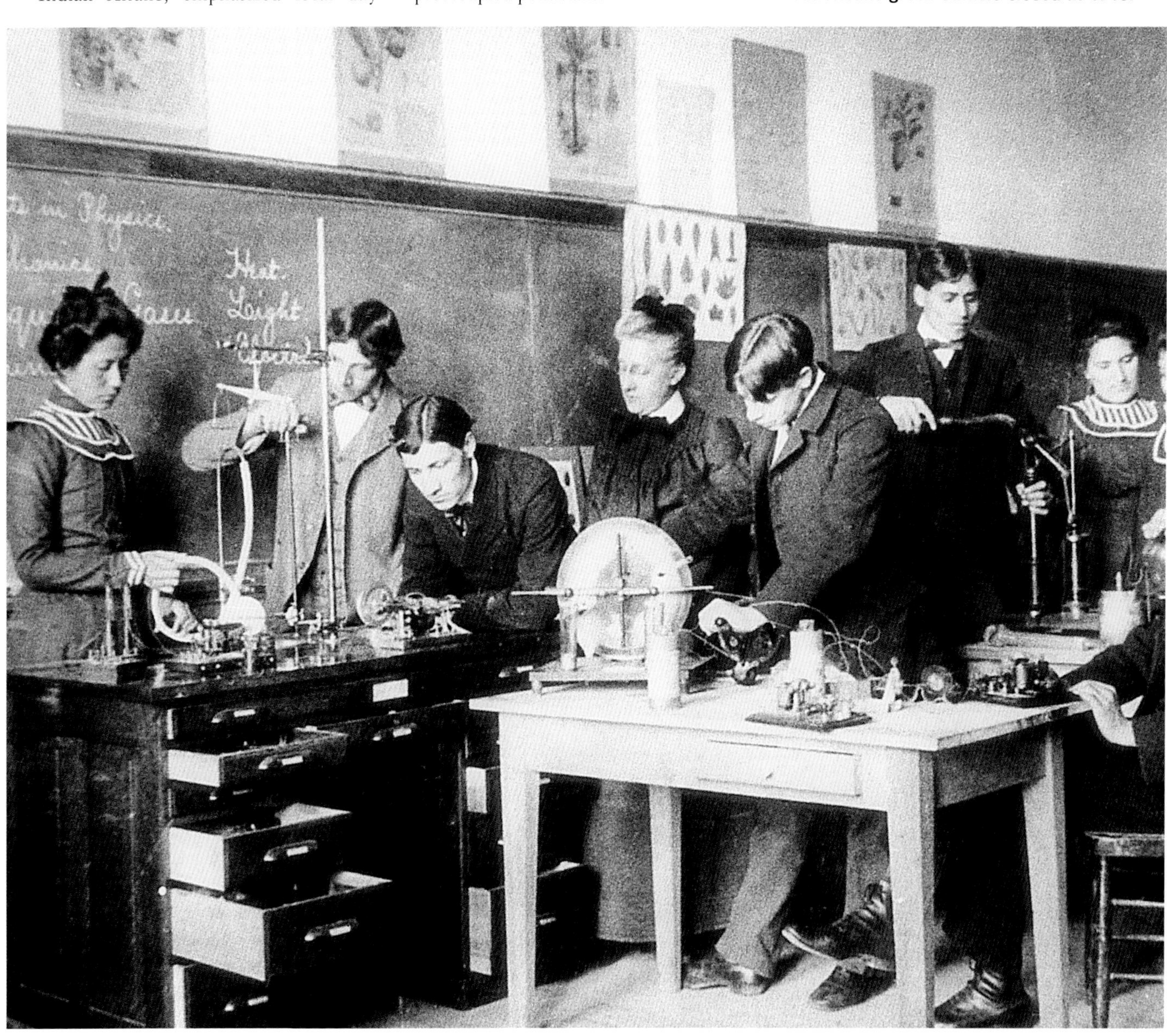

Pupils conduct experiments during a physics class at Carlisle Indian Industrial School, Pennsylvania, in 1915. During the 1910s and 1920s opposition to boarding school education for Native Americans grew. Carlisle closed in 1918.

THE INDIAN REORGANIZATION ACT, 1934

The Indian Reorganization Act of 1934, also known as the Wheeler–Howard Act, was the outcome of the Meriam Report and its recommendations. The motivation behind the act was the desire to end the dispersal of Native American lands through allotment, to encourage Native American land reforms, and to improve the economic situation of American Indians. The act aimed to decrease federal control of Native American affairs and increase Indian self-government. It prohibited further allotment of native lands, extended existing periods of trust and restrictions on the seizure of Native American lands, restored to tribal ownership any remaining surplus reservation lands, and prohibited the transfer of restricted Native lands except to Native American tribes. In addition, the act authorized the acquisition of lands for Native Americans, exempting them from taxation, encouraged the conservation of forestry and grazing, and empowered the secretary of the interior to declare newly acquired lands for Native American reservations or to add to existing reservations. The act also encouraged tribes to adopt written constitutions and charters in order to give them the power to run their own affairs. It made provision for implementing Native American preferences in appointing staff to positions in agencies that dealt with their affairs. It also allowed tribes to form business corporations. Finally, the act created a revolving credit program to help fund tribal land purchases, education, and organization. The Indian Reorganization Act helped improve living conditions for many Native Americans. It laid the groundwork for an improvement in their economic position, improved the staff and services involved in education and healthcare provision, and prompted greater Native American interest in voting. The act's basic aims were reinforced by further legislation in the 1960s and 1970s.

Few had a high school curriculum, none were of comparable quality to public schools, vocational training was inferior, and lessons were unrelated to reservation life. The government ignored the recommendations for education produced early in the 1920s by the Committee of One Hundred. Reformers increased their demands until the publication of the Meriam Report in 1928.

The education section of the Meriam Report was prepared by W. Carson Ryan, Jr., an educator and expert in educational surveys. The report was extremely critical of Native American education, revealing shocking conditions, especially in the boarding schools. Like the Dawes Allotment Act, boarding schools had played a fundamental part in the government's policy of assimilation. Like the Allotment Act, they were supported by reformers as well as politicians, who believed that removing Native American children from their homes and communities, teaching them English, and providing a vocational education in agriculture or industry would diminish their tribalism and prepare them for integration with white society. In the words of Captain Richard Pratt (1840–1924), who founded the first federally administered boarding school in Carlisle, Pennsylvania, in 1879, the main objective was to "kill the Indian and save the man."

The Meriam Report showed that boarding schools were severely overcrowded and had high rates of disease, and that they provided inadequate student care and poorly trained teachers, and relied on student labor to support the school. The report recommended that education should become the primary function of the Bureau of Indian Affairs, whose other functions should pass to more specialized agencies. It suggested that education should be geared to all age levels, should include Native American culture, and should be connected to local communities. It urged the construction of local day schools and the reform of boarding schools. Charles Rhoads was largely unsuccessful in his attempts to implement the educational reforms set out in the report. However, he did lay the groundwork for improvements in Native American education in the thirties.

The New Deal reforms

In 1932, as the United States sank deeper into economic depression, Franklin D. Roosevelt (1933–1945) won an overwhelming victory in the presidential election based on his promise of reform. The following year he appointed John Collier as commissioner of Indian affairs and gave him responsibility for leading the government's New Deal for Indians (1933–1945). The political climate was more open to change, and Collier experienced more success than Rhoads and Scattergood as he accelerated the trends started by the Meriam Report and the previous administration. Congress did not always support Collier's policies, and some of his proposed legislation was not enacted or funded. However, the passage of the Indian Reorganization Act in 1934 marked a milestone in Native American policy and the realization of reforms suggested in the Meriam Report (*see box above*). Collier also implemented improvements in education as outlined by the report, including bilingual education, teacher training in Native culture and traditions, and the replacement of boarding schools with day schools. Collier and the Indian New Deal brought about dynamic changes in Native American policy. However, in spite of their reform legislation, bureaucratic conflicts, economic recession, entrenched attitudes, and World War II (1939–1945) often hindered implementation. The campaign for recognition of Native American rights continues in the 21st century.

SEE ALSO:

Architecture • Art • Poverty • Racial Stereotypes • Schools & Universities • Unemployment

NAVY

The era was marked by two significant events: the test bombing of the battleship *Ostfriedland* by warplanes in 1921 and the Washington Naval Treaty in 1922. As a result of these two events the U.S. Navy shifted its focus from building large battleships to developing new aircraft carriers.

In the first three decades of the 20th century the most powerful weapons of war were battleships. At the beginning of the 1920s the largest of these armored so-called "battlewagons" could displace up to 40,000 tons and carry guns of 16-in. caliber, capable of firing a high-explosive shell 12 miles (19km). Despite the apparently unassailable position of battleships as the superweapons of the time, the U.S. Navy nevertheless began to develop a new type of warship: the aircraft carrier. The aircraft carrier would prove so successful that within 25 years, during the naval battles of World War II (1939–1945), it would make the battleship almost obsolete.

Air power was the key to this success, and in the first years of the decade a great debate took place as to the future role of warplanes in the U.S. military. Navy traditionalists were wedded to the belief that the battleship was the key component of the service and the nation's first line of defense. The idea that aircraft could destroy these mighty war machines was considered absurd. In the summer of 1920 this view was shown to be dangerously shortsighted. In a series of bombing tests off the Virginia coast, beginning on June 21, former Imperial

The USS *Arizona* in the Panama Canal in about 1921. In the same year Great Britain, Japan, the United States, France, and Italy agreed to reduce the numbers of their battleships as part of an international disarmament agreement.

German Navy warships and a submarine were subjected to a series of attacks by Navy, Army, and Marine aircraft.

The tests culminated on July 21, when eight biplane bombers of the Army Air Corps directed from the air by the corps's assistant chief Brigadier General "Billy" Mitchell (1879–1936) destroyed the battleship *Ostfriedland*. The Navy had only wanted the raid to assess the extent of the damage bombs might cause its battleships. Mitchell, however, wanted to prove the destructive potential of air power once and for all, and ordered the attack pressed home. *Ostfriedland* sank under a rain of bombs.

Brigadier General "Billy" Mitchell standing in aviator's clothes next to one of his airplanes in the early 1920s. Mitchell was instrumental in establishing the aircraft carrier as the key weapon on the seas.

Although senior Navy personnel refused to recognize the full implications of Mitchell's demonstration, the politicians in the administration of President Warren G. Harding's (1921–1923) did not. In October 1921 the organization of the Navy's air service, which had been founded in 1911, was formalized with the creation of the Navy Bureau of Aeronautics. The bureau was to take charge of all training and assignments as well as taking responsibility for the design, construction, and repair of all Navy and Marine Corps aircraft. Although the use of aircraft in the Navy was no longer a point at issue, there still remained unsolved problems as to how warplanes were to be integrated into the fleet and how best they could be deployed.

To help solve these problems, the U.S. Navy commissioned its first aircraft carrier in March 1922 (*see box on p. 72*). Congress authorized the construction of two further carriers in July 1922. The *Lexington* and the *Saratoga*, like the *Langley*, were conversions, but this time the parent vessels were warships—two unfinished battle cruisers. In November 1924 the *Langley* was promoted from its experimental status and reported for duty with the fleet, becoming the Navy's first operational carrier. In January 1925 it received its first squadron of aircraft and in March took part in fleet exercises off California, which for the first time involved the carrier and its squadron in simulated combat operations. Further innovations soon followed, with aircraft making the first night landings on *Langley* at sea off San Diego in early April. In October 1926 fighter aircraft from *Langley* undertook the first simulated dive-bombing attack on the Pacific fleet. Diving vertically from over 12,000 feet (3,658m), the bombing was so accurate that the new tactic was introduced on a large scale in December during an exercise that deployed six Navy and Marine squadrons.

THE *LANGLEY*

The *USS Samuel P. Langley*—named for the inventor of the first mechanically powered, heavier-than-air craft to fly—was not a purpose-built aircraft carrier. The ship started off as a coal-carrier and was converted by having a flight deck built on top of its superstructure to allow warplanes to take off and land. The *Langley* was an experimental vessel, and its main purpose was to solve the two great problems facing warplane operations at sea: how to launch an aircraft at sufficient speed for it to take off safely, and how to prevent it from racing off the end of the flight deck when it landed.

Early methods to provide solutions to these problems involved a catapult powered by gunpowder to launch the aircraft and steel wires on weights stretched across the deck to catch it on landing. By late 1922 these experiments had proved successful enough for the first carrier takeoff to be attempted. On October 17 a Vought VE-7 biplane was successfully launched off *Langley*'s deck while the ship was at anchor. Encouraged by this success, the first carrier landing was achieved on October 26 by an Aeromarine 39B aircraft while *Langley* was at sea off the Virginia coast.

As the crew and airmen on the *Langley* perfected combat tactics and the new skills required to make a carrier work—such as aircraft handling at sea—the building program on the second generation of carriers moved forward. In November 1927 the *Saratoga* was commissioned into service. The *Lexington* was accepted into service a month later. Both vessels took part in fleet exercises in January 1928, the *Saratoga* with a complement of 69 aircraft launching a successful mock air raid against the Panama Canal. The success of these exercises led Congress to authorize the construction of the first purpose-built aircraft carrier in February 1929. Launched in February 1933, she was commissioned as the USS *Ranger*. Displacing over 15,500 tons, *Ranger* could carry 150 aircraft. The ship would see service in the Atlantic during World War II, the only large fleet carrier assigned to this theater of operations.

Developments in naval aviation continued to gather pace throughout the decade. In June 1926 Congress authorized the expansion of the naval air service to a force of 1,000 aircraft within five years. This large peacetime increase, however, still represented 1,100 planes fewer than the Navy had had at the end of World War I. However, the big question that dominated political discussions regarding the future of the Navy was exactly how many ships it was going to have. Since the presidency of Theodore Roosevelt (1901–1909) during the first decade of the century, ambitious plans had been drawn up to create a two-ocean navy, with one fleet in the Atlantic and the other in the Pacific. However, Congress had always refused to fully fund the creation of the fleets.

Postwar constraints

There had been a massive buildup of naval strength after the United States entered World War I. Prior to April 1917 there had been 64,777 men on the roll and 197 commissioned ships. By November 1918 there were 497,000 serving officers and men and 2,003 commissioned ships, making the U.S. Navy the third-largest in the world. After the war there was a rapid decrease in manpower and the number of commissioned ships. Although President Harding wanted the Navy to retain about 80,000 men, pressure from Congress to reduce military spending meant that these plans were shelved.

There were also financial constraints on the construction of new ships. Harding had wanted two fleets with 16 battleships each. This had been the minimum authorized by Congress in 1916, but it was an undertaking that Congress never fulfilled. Appropriations became even more difficult to obtain after the onset of the Great Depression in 1929. In February 1929 President Coolidge's administration (1923–1929) secured a bill authorizing the construction of 15 new cruisers within three years at a cost of $27 million. By 1933 only eight had been completed. This is perhaps one of the reasons why naval aviation developed so rapidly during the interwar years: Planes and a few aircraft carriers were cheaper to supply than heavily armored warships.

During the early years of the decade there was still money enough to build battleships and lay plans for the much-vaunted two-ocean navy. In 1921, during President Harding's administration, the battleships *California* and *West Virginia* entered service. Twenty years later both would be severely damaged and the USS *Arizona* sunk during the Japanese air raid on Pearl Harbor on December 7, 1941.

The *California* was the first battleship in the Navy to be built on the West Coast. Its construction there marked a growing awareness that the main threat the Navy would have to face in coming decades would be in the Pacific, and that the source of that threat would be Japan and its Imperial Navy. Other practical steps in preparation for this possible conflict included converting heavy cruisers from coal to fuel oil, which gave these warships greater range and speed, which were essential requirements for operations in the Pacific.

There were also changes at an organizational level. In 1922 President Harding reorganized the Navy and established the United States Fleet. The most powerful division of this new force would be known as the Battle Fleet and would be permanently based in the Pacific. To support the Battle Fleet, new shore installations and fuel-oil depots were established along the West Coast. Meanwhile the forward base in Hawaii, Pearl Harbor on Oahu, which had been in use since 1908, was expanded to allow it to become the starting point of any future operations by the fleet in the western Pacific.

A view of Pearl Harbor on Oahu, Hawaii, in 1923. Pearl Harbor became the base for the U.S. Battle Fleet in the Pacific. The Japanese attack on the base on December 7, 1941, led to the United States entering World War II.

The focus of these operations would be the islands of the Philippines, America's possession in Southeast Asia. Under the strategy developed by naval planners in 1911, known as War Plan Orange, if the Philippines came under attack from Japan, the most likely aggressor in the region, then the U.S. Battle Fleet would sail out to defeat the Japanese Imperial Navy in one great naval engagement.

The problem was that War Plan Orange had been rendered obsolete by the terms of the 1919 Versailles Treaty that ended World War I and gave Japan a greatly increased presence in the Pacific (*see box on p. 75*). In an effort to modify U.S. foreign policy accordingly, President Harding's secretary of state, Charles E. Hughes, called an international naval conference in Washington, D.C., in November 1921. What Hughes wanted from the major naval powers of the world—Great Britain, Japan, France, and Italy—was an international agreement on disarmament. The conference would agree on the numbers of battleships each nation could keep as well as establishing a temporary halt to all battleship construction, after which new vessels would be limited in size and firepower.

The Washington Naval Conference was a major event in the growing trend towards pacifism that spread across the United States in the years following World War I and won huge popular support. Every member of President Harding's Cabinet was present at the opening ceremony on November 12, together with the justices of the U.S. Supreme Court, a large number of senators, and reporters from newspapers all over the country. Harding himself gave the opening address: "A world staggering with debt needs its burdens lifted," he said. "Humanity which has been shocked by wanton destruction would minimize the agencies of that destruction.... I can speak only for our United States. One hundred millions frankly want less of armament and none of war."

U.S. voluntary disarmament

Hughes began the conference with a straightforward proposal to scrap 30 of the U.S. Navy's principal warships, some 845,000 tons of shipping. This was voluntary disarmament on such a huge scale that it took the international

Members of the International Conference on Naval Limitation in Washington, D.C., gather for a group photograph on November 10, 1921.

delegates completely by surprise. The ambition of the American vision shocked them. "Mr. Secretary Hughes sank in thirty-five minutes more ships than all the admirals in the world have destroyed in a cycle of centuries," reported the correspondent of the London *Times* newspaper. Under Hughes's proposal the U.S. offer would be matched by a reduction in the British fleet of 500,000 tons and a reduction of 450,000 tons in the size of Japan's fleet.

For the next three months the conference haggled over the relative sizes of each nation's navy and precisely how many tons of shipping each of them was willing to give up. Senior U.S. Navy officers were unhappy and thought that Hughes was giving away too much. Ideally they would have wanted equal strength with Britain and at least a 2-to-1 superiority over Japan. Harding forced them to accept a limit to the Navy's capital ships of just over 500,000 tons, a restriction the naval officers believed to be far too low, particularly with regard to their potential needs in the Pacific.

RECONNAISSANCE AIRCRAFT

As well as developing the aircraft carrier in order to bring large numbers of combat warplanes into its fleet operations, the U.S. Navy also investigated ways in which reconnaissance aircraft could operate from big-gun capital vessels such as battleships and cruisers. Experiments in May 1922 on the battleship *Maryland* using a VE-7 fighter and a compressed-air catapult were a success, but attempts the following year to launch an aircraft off a submarine proved less practical. In November 1923 the submarine S-1 hosted a series of trials undertaken by the crew of the *Langley* to discover whether a Martin MS-1 seaplane could be stowed aboard a submarine in pieces, reassembled on deck, and launched at sea. The experiments were a success, but the idea was taken no further.

THE PACIFIC

As a consequence of the Treaty of Versailles in 1919, Japan was allowed to take possession of three strategically important island chains in the central Pacific—the Carolines, the Marshalls, and the Marianas—that lay on the U.S. Battle Fleet's route to the Philippines. Tensions between Tokyo and Washington, D.C., increased as a result of their disagreement over the future of China. Throughout the 1920s China descended into anarchy and chaos. At the end of the decade Japan intervened militarily and grabbed various slices of territory in the north of the country. There were further annexations in the 1930s. The United States could do little to prevent these developments, but was gravely concerned about them because China was one of its most important trading partners. U.S. Navy gunboats were dispatched to patrol the major rivers of China to protect American business interests, but short of war with Japan—for which the U.S. Navy was not prepared—the United States was powerless to prevent Japanese expansionism.

This map shows how the mandates granted to Japan in 1919 gave the nation great strategic influence in the Pacific.

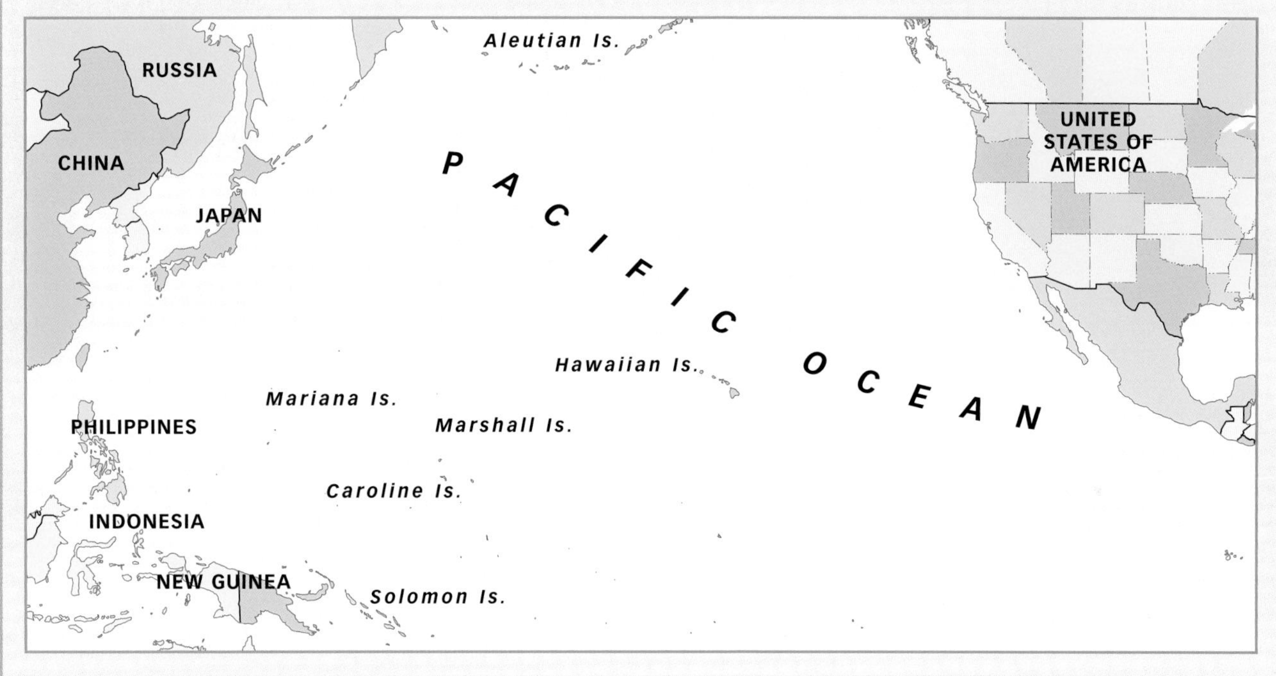

The Washington Conference concluded with the signing of the Five Power Naval Limitation Treaty in February 1922. The delegates agreed that there would be no building of capital ships for a period of 10 years, after which the size of battleships would be restricted to 35,000 tons and their armament limited to 16-in. guns. The treaty also limited the size of cruisers to 10,000 tons and carriers to 27,000 tons.

The treaty was hailed as a great step toward world peace. Hughes himself told conference delegates that their work was "taking perhaps the greatest step forward in history to establish the reign of peace." The fact that the world was fighting another world war within 20 years proves that he was being overoptimistic.

Failure of the treaty

In reality the delegates signed up to the Naval Treaty because it was politically expedient. Despite the fact that the United States, Britain, and Japan were all giving undertakings to their admirals that battlefleets would be modernized, by the time of the Washington Conference none of them could actually afford to fulfill their promises. By the beginning of the 1930s, in fact, the U.S. Navy was so starved of resources that the number of ships in commission was actually lower than the figure allowed by the treaty. The Japanese, however, had made sure that they held to the limits they were allowed, and by 1939 the Imperial fleet had naval superiority in the Pacific. President Franklin D. Roosevelt (1933–1945) would have to rush to address this problem in July 1940 with the Two Oceans Navy Bill, which finally gave the U.S. Navy the resources to build its fleets in the Atlantic and the Pacific. Part of the 1940 bill authorized the building of the four Iowa Class battleships (the first of the four was *USS Iowa*). These were the last and largest battleships ever built by the United States.

SEE ALSO:

Army • China • Japan • Versailles Treaty • Washington Naval Conference • World War I

NEWBERY AWARD AND CHILDREN'S LITERATURE

In the second half of the 19th century children's writing in the United States blossomed. The foundation in 1921 of the Newbery Award, the world's first literary prize specifically awarded to a children's book, signaled the growing importance of children's writers and publishers.

Authors such as Mark Twain (1835–1910) and Louisa May Alcott (1832–1888) forged a truly American children's literature that broke free both from the British models and the preaching, Sunday-school tone that had dominated children's books until then. Near-universal literacy, along with the rapid development of both the publishing industry and the public library system, nurtured successive generations of children who enthusiastically sought out, bought, and read juvenile books.

Recognizing a children's literature

The foundation—in 1921—of the United States', and indeed the world's, first literary prize specifically awarded to a children's book signaled the growing confidence and buoyancy of children's writers and publishers in the period.

The prize was the idea of the publisher Frederic G. Melcher and was named in honor of the 18th-century British bookseller and writer John Newbery (1713–1767), whose own works—including *A Little Pretty Pocket-Book* (1744)—had asserted the literary value of a distinct children's literature. The Newbery Award was imbued with much the same spirit—its aim was "to emphasize to the public that contributions to the literature for children deserve similar recognition to [adult] poetry, plays, or novels," as well as "to encourage original creative work in the field of books for children."

A list of the Newbery medal winners (*see box opposite*) and of the runners-up—the so-called "Honor Books"—during the 1920s gives an insight into the kinds of books children were reading at the time—or, at least, into the kind of books that adults thought they should be reading. The list is very diverse and includes educational books, adventure stories, historical fictions, and retellings of traditional tales, as well as picture books and animal stories. Few of the authors—with the possible exception of the British-born writer Hugh Lofting (*see box below*)—are widely read today. The twenties were more notable for the development of genres and ideas than for great authors.

Serious adventures

Before World War I (1914–1918) much of the historical fiction written for children was very romantic—the past was little more than a colorful backdrop for an exciting adventure story. During the 1920s, however, novels became much more realistic and serious in tone, as writers showed a deeper concern for

HUGH LOFTING

Perhaps the most enduring and best-loved character of 1920s children's literature is Dr. Dolittle, the eccentric doctor from Puddleby-in-the-Marsh who learns to speak the language of animals from his parrot. Dr. Dolittle was the creation of the British-born author Hugh Lofting (1886–1947). He studied civil engineering in England, and his work took him to Africa, the Caribbean, and Canada. In 1912 he decided to become a writer and moved to New York City. Lofting invented Dr. Dolittle when writing to his children from the trenches during World War I. In 1920 the first book of his series, *The Story of Dr. Dolittle,* appeared and was an immediate success. Until 1927 Lofting wrote a book a year, illustrated by himself, devoted to the doctor's adventures with his animal friends, such as Jip and Too-Too. The second novel in the series, the 1922 *Voyages of Doctor Dolittle*, won the Newbery Medal in the following year. Lofting began to tire of his hero and tried to get rid of him by sending him to the moon, but popular demand forced him to write *Dr. Dolittle's Return* in 1933. The last of the series took Lofting 13 years to write and was published after his death. Lofting wrote other books in which the doctor did not appear, but they were less successful.

1920S NEWBERY MEDAL WINNERS

1922 ***The Story of Mankind*, Hendrik Willem Van Loon**

1923 ***The Voyages of Doctor Dolittle*, Hugh Lofting**

1924 ***The Dark Frigate*, Charles Hawes**

1925 ***Tales from Silver Lands*, Charles Finger**

1926 ***Shen of the Sea*, Arthur Bowie Chrisman**

1927 ***Smoky, the Cowhorse*, Will James**

1928 ***Gay Neck, the Story of a Pigeon*, Dhan Gopal Mukerji**

1929 ***The Trumpeter of Krakow*, Eric P. Kelly**

Hendrik Willem Van Loon (1882–1944) in the year he won the Newbery Medal.

rooting their characters in their historical period. James Boyd's (1888–1944) 1925 novel *Drums* was originally written for adults but in 1927 was republished as an illustrated "boy's" book. The novel told the story of young Johnny Fraser, the son of Scottish immigrants, who goes off to fight in the American Revolution. At one level it is an exciting adventure story, but it also shows Boyd's concern for democratic principles. A similar combination of seriousness, meticulous historical detail, and adventure is found in the 1929 Newbery Medal winner *The Trumpeter of Krakow* by Eric Philbrook Kelly (1884–1960), which told the moving story of a Polish family during the 15th century.

Newbery Medal winner *Smoky the Cowhorse* (1926) was a pure adventure story written and illustrated by the former cowboy Will James (Ernest DuFault; 1892–1942). The novel related the touching story of a good-natured "mouse-colored" horse—from his birth in the wild, through his capture and work in the rodeo and on the range, to his happy old age.

Boys or girls

Many children's novels of this period were exclusively aimed at either boys or girls and offered somewhat stereotypical, conservative models for children to aspire to. *Smoky* was for boys who dreamed of running away to the West and living the mythical, romantic life of the cowboy. By contrast, Rachel Fields's (1894–1942) charming *Hitty, Her First Hundred Years* (1929) was distinctly for girls. Hitty is a wooden doll who relates the story of her travels from owner to owner around the world, always pining for her native Maine.

Picture books and poetry

For younger readers there were picture books—a genre that flourished during the twenties as color printing became ever cheaper and more sophisticated. Some of the most innovative picture books were produced by the Minnesota-born Wanda Hazel Gág (1893–1946), who often collaborated with her brother Howard. Her illustrations, as seen in her first children's book, *Millions of Cats* (1928), moved away from the ornate, fairytale images typical of many earlier children's illustrators to a bolder, graphic, and humorous style that was more closely related to the way children actually look at the world. *Millions of Cats* was a Newbery Honor Book in the year of its publication.

There was little notable poetry written for children during the 1920s. The exception is Elizabeth Madox Robert's (1886–1941) collection *Under the Tree* (1923), in which she evoked her childhood in the mountains of Kentucky in a sequence of simple, crystalline poems she called "butterbeans."

A conservative outlook?

It is easy to criticize 1920s children's literature as essentially conservative, reflecting the interests and norms of the white, Protestant culture of the period. Racial stereotypes (from Red Indians to faithful black servants) abounded, as did gender stereotypes. The exception was Dhan Gopal Mukerji (1890–1936)—the only Indian to win a Newbery Medal—whose 1928 winner told the story of an Indian Army pigeon during World War I.

However, what really sets many of the best books of the period apart is a new determination to appeal to children directly as intelligent, discerning readers, and to experiment with styles and genres in a fresh and vigorous way. It was this originality and freshness that the Newbery Award sought—and still seeks—to recognize.

SEE ALSO:

Books & Publishing • Literature • Poetry

NEWS AND CURRENT AFFAIRS

In the opening decades of the 20th century Americans looked to newspapers to keep themselves abreast of the news. By the late 1920s, however, the primacy of the press as the source of news and current affairs was being challenged by a revolutionary new medium—the radio.

While most newspapers and magazines were aimed at and read by a narrow section of the population living in a particular location—New York Democrats, for instance, or Chicago Poles—radio could, at least potentially, be broadcast coast to coast and listened to by the entire nation. The era of the "mass media" had been born.

Selling the news

There was an enormous diversity of newspapers and magazines available in 1920s America. In smaller towns most people were still content to read the weekly community paper, with its mix of local and national news; a few, however, would have taken one of the regional urban dailies or a weekly magazine—perhaps a compendium made up of syndicated stories from newspapers across the country or one of the popular new magazines such as *Time* (*see box on p. 82*) or *Reader's Digest*.

In the cities there was much more choice: usually two or three competing dailies, each of which might appear in anything up to six or seven editions, as well as a host of smaller papers and magazines. There were weekly papers, Sunday papers with supplements, morning papers, afternoon papers, and evening papers, papers for ethnic and religious communities, sports papers, and papers and magazines for women.

New York City had the most developed press in the United States. In the city there were more than a dozen dailies, each of which was aimed at a particular ethnic or sociopolitical community. The *New York World*, for instance, was aimed at supporters of the Democratic Party and

WOMEN MAKING THE NEWS

Journalism—often considered a male preserve—was increasingly opening its doors to women. Women had been involved in newspaper work since at least the beginning of the 19th century, but they were largely confined to reporting social news and other "soft" stories, and consequently came to be pejoratively classed as "sob sisters." Pioneering female journalists like Ida Tarbell (1857–1944), famous for her exposé of corruption in the Standard Oil Company, were the exception, not the norm.

During the 1920s, however, women successfully fought to gain a wider role on the newsroom floor. Maurine Watkins's (1896–1969) sensationalized reports on crime for the *Chicago Tribune*, for instance, habitually made the front page, while the Atlanta-born journalist Julia Collier Harris (1885–1967) fought a dogged and intelligent campaign against racial violence in the pages of the *Columbus Enquirer Sun*.

Ida Tarbell in 1922. Her series of articles on Standard Oil, written for McClure's Magazine *and later published as a book, helped develop and define investigative, exposé journalism.*

ist 7, 1920
Price 15 Cents
Subscription Price $7.00 a
Leslie's
Illustrated
wspaper
OFFICIAL
BALLOT
AUG
7
1920
JAMES MONTGOMERY FLAGG
What Will She Do With It?
Mixing With Americans
IV: What a Spirit Did for Kansas City
By CHARLES PHELPS CUSHING
A Mexican Misadventurer
By
TIMOTHY GILMAN TURNER

The cover of *Leslie's* in 1920. Founded in 1855 by publisher Frank Leslie (1821–1880), it was the first successful American weekly to combine pictures and news. After his death his wife Miriam took over his publishing business. The magazine closed in 1922.

the *Herald Tribune* at Republican supporters, while the highly respected *New York Times*, which claimed an independent stance, was read by the liberal middle classes. Downmarket tabloids such as the *Evening Graphic* and *Daily News* catered to the poorly educated mass of Italian, Irish, and Jewish immigrants. There were also several Yiddish and African American papers.

Diversity

The richness and diversity of the American press reflected the complex ethnic, political, and social makeup of the United States itself. During the 19th century immigrants had set up newspapers as one way of cementing their new communities and expressing their continued sense of ethnic identity and their commitment to the mother country (*see box on p. 85*). A free and vigorous press, as many commentators recognized, was one of the lynchpins of democracy.

However, the United States' highly decentralized and fragmented press meant it was a very rare newspaper or magazine indeed that was read widely and by all levels of society. During the early 20th century the ideal of a true mass-readership was the dream of many entrepreneurs—from liberal idealists such as Edward W. Scripps (1854–1926) to more commercially aggressive publishing magnates such as William Randolph Hearst, who pioneered a more provocative and dramatic form of publishing known as "yellow journalism" (*see box on p. 80*).

The changing face of the press

The U.S. press of the 1920s was changing, however. For one thing, there were fewer papers than in previous decades, although their numbers remained very high. Between 1909 and 1910 the number of newspapers published had peaked at around 2,600 dailies and 14,000 weeklies, but thereafter began to fall rapidly. By 1907, for instance, when the new state of Oklahoma was formed, more than 1,500 different newspapers had appeared in the territory; by 1926 only 51 daily and 354 weekly newspapers continued publication, and only nine cities were able to boast more than one paper. The limited appeal of many prewar newspapers meant that they proved economically unviable in the changed world of the twenties.

There were also changes in the pattern of newspaper ownership—partly in response to the need to make the newspaper industry profitable and partly to fulfill the perceived need for a mass-market press. At the end of the 19th century rich and powerful press barons, or magnates, began to build up large chains of newspapers. The Illinois publisher Edward W. Scripps, for example, either set up or bought up some 34 papers across 15 states, including titles such as the *San*

WILLIAM RANDOLPH HEARST

By the 1920s California-born newspaperman William Randolph Hearst (1863–1951) had already long been closely identified with a sensationalized, dramatic style of newspaper journalism.

Back in the 1890s Hearst's newspapers—which included the *San Francisco Examiner* and the *New York Morning Journal*—had helped forge what became known as "yellow journalism" by publishing sensationalized exposés of alleged political corruption and exaggerated or even fabricated accounts of events, together with brash, provocative headlines and dramatic photographs. In 1898 Hearst whipped up public feeling by publishing images of Spanish concentration camps on Cuba and a series of articles goading the U.S. government into war with Spain. Critics accused him of inciting war as a way of boosting the *Journal*'s sales.

Hearst was a politician as well as a newspaper magnate and had no qualms about using his papers to further his political career or to promote his often extremist beliefs. From 1903 to 1907 he was a member of the House of Representatives as a Democrat from New York and even had designs on the presidency—an ambition brought to an end when he failed to win either the mayorship or governorship of New York. In the 1930s Hearst supported the cause of Nazi Germany and was stridently anticommunist, going so far as to brand President Franklin D. Roosevelt a communist.

In 1941 film director Orson Welles made a thinly disguised and deeply unflattering film about Hearst's life—*Citizen Kane*.

This drawing (1896) by Homer Davenport shows Hearst with his legs crossed; his left shoe is labeled The Examiner, *his right shoe is labeled* The Journal. *These two papers were the beginning of Hearst's media empire.*

Frank Munsey, seen here in 1925, was a great advocate of newspaper consolidation and was said to have bought and sold more newspapers than anyone in American publishing. His papers included the *Baltimore News* (1908) and the *New York Star* (1891).

Diego Sun, *Seattle Star*, and the *Washington Daily News*. He also founded his own international news service, the United Press Association, and the Newspaper Enterprise Association, which supplied his papers with features, cartoons, and illustrations. William Randolph Hearst (*see box opposite*), meanwhile, had set up an extensive empire that at its peak in 1935 included 28 major newspapers, 14 local papers, and 18 magazines, along with several radio stations, movie companies, and news services. He used some of his vast fortune to build an extravagant castle at San Simeon, California, which he filled with antiques and works of art.

The power of the barons

The press barons usually kept a firm hold on the editorial policy of their newspapers and used them as a platform to promote their political and social views. Scripps, for example, was an ardent supporter of labor and openly used his papers to support liberal causes. Hearst also started off as a supporter of labor. Later, by contrast, he became fiercely conservative and famously claimed that one of his newspapers—the *Morning Journal*—had sent the United States to war against Spain in 1898. "How Do You Like the Journal's War?" was the triumphant front-page headline that followed. For politicians the power of the press magnates to influence public opinion became a troubling concern; President Theodore Roosevelt (1858–1919), for one, found Hearst "sinister" and "evil."

Chains, including those run by Scripps, Hearst, and Frank A. Munsey (1854–1925), continued to be an important force in the 1920s, but in reality the role of the all-powerful editor–proprietor was to some degree already a thing of the past. On the one hand, newspaper chains were already beginning to fall into the hands of powerful corporations—a trend that was to accelerate over subsequent decades—while, on the other hand, the editorial departments of many newspapers were increasingly asserting their professional independence from newspaper owners.

Despite the decreasing numbers of newspapers, the competition for readers remained strong in the 1920s—partly for the very reason that the papers that did survive into this period were the most vigorous. During the twenties some 500 cities across the United States had two or more competing daily newspapers, and "circulation wars" reached legendary proportions, especially in the great press cities of New York, Chicago, and San Francisco. This was the tough, rough world immortalized in Ben Hecht and Charles MacArthur's 1928 play about Chicago journalists and editors prepared to do anything for a good story—*The Front Page* (later made into several films, including the 1940 *His Girl Friday*).

In many ways the 1920s were the period when many of the features associated with modern journalism were forged: not just the clichés such as the hard-boiled, hard-drinking reporter and the unscrupulous editor, but also more serious ethical and professional issues, such as journalistic independence and the ideal of objectivity.

TIME

The 1920s was an innovative period for magazine publishing, and the decade saw the foundation of what proved to be long-lived news and current-affairs magazines—*Time*, founded by Henry Robinson Luce (1898–1967) and Briton Hadden (1898–1929) on March 3, 1923.

Luce and Hadden's idea for their new magazine was simple but original—to provide people with good-quality weekly summaries of news in a clear and informative way. "In an age when people are bombarded by information ...," Luce declared in 1923, "*Time* is dedicated to keeping busy men and women well informed by making information more readily accessible." The magazine was just 32 pages long and cost 15 cents—a reasonable price at the time. An important feature was the striking front cover, which was usually a photograph of a personality—the man or woman "of the moment." The formula was a huge success, and by 1927 *Time* was selling more than 175,000 copies a week.

Time had many critics, however. Many people saw the magazine simply as a mouthpiece for Luce, especially after he took over the editorship of the magazine when Hadden died unexpectedly in 1929. Luce was a vociferous Republican and internationalist, as well as being stridently anticommunist. He believed that objective reporting was impossible and encouraged his reporters and journalists to follow his views in their unsigned articles. Others were critical of the magazine's peculiar, adjective-laden writing style, which was meant to make the article easy to read and digest. The New York drama critic Wolcott Gibbs, parodied the style,"Backward ran sentences until reeled the mind. Where it would end, knows God."

Jazz journalism

The 1920s are particularly known for the development of the tabloid press and the sensational kind of news reporting later dubbed "jazz journalism." In 1919 editor Joseph Medill Patterson (1879–1946) founded America's first tabloid, the *Illustrated Daily News*, soon to be rechristened the *New York Daily News*. The paper took its inspiration from the successful British tabloid newspaper the *Daily Mirror*, the creation of the influential British press baron Alfred Harmsworth (1865–1922).

Like the *Daily Mirror*, the *Daily News* was about half the size of an ordinary newspaper and was made up of bold headlines, brief, simplified news stories, and big, brash photographs. But it was the subject matter, rather than the format, that really gave the *Daily News* its flavor. Its pages were filled with sensationalized stories of sex, crime, and scandal. The paper proved hugely successful, especially among the poorly educated immigrant communities of New York, and by 1924 the *Daily News* had became the United States' most widely circulated newspaper.

Other editors were quick to found or develop rival tabloids—most notably Hearst's *Mirror* and a new paper begun by Bernarr Macfadden (1868–1955), the *Evening Graphic*, both also based in New York. In order to attract readers, all three papers strove to outbid each other in the luridness and sordidness of their stories, and they had no qualms about exaggerating, distorting, or manipulating "the facts" to do so. The *Graphic*, for example, invented the composograph—a forged photograph fabricated by pasting the faces of celebrities onto staged scenes using models. One of the most famous composographs was a front-page picture of the silent-movie star Rudolph Valentino (1895–1926) dying in the hospital. The composographs were blatant lies, but readers did not seem to mind very much. After Valentino's death a further front-page composograph showed him in heaven meeting the opera star Enrico Caruso (1873–1921).

The tabloids also sought to make news as well as to report it. In the late 1920s many reporters began to investigate murders and other crimes, pushing for trials and whipping up public hysteria against the alleged perpetrators. In 1928 Ruth Snyder was bought to trial, charged with the murder of her husband, a magazine editor. The New York tabloid press was virulent in its hatred for this strong-minded woman, whom they dubbed "the Bloody Blonde." It came as no surprise when the jury found Snyder guilty after only an hour and a half's deliberation, and she was sentenced to death by electrocution. The *Daily News* went on to cover Snyder's execution, sending a photographer to take a secret photograph of Snyder during her execution by using a tiny camera strapped to his ankle. The resulting touched-up front-page photograph, with the simple headline "DEAD," boosted the *Daily News* circulation by 750,000 copies.

The spread of jazz journalism

Jazz journalism was not confined to the tabloids, but in some degree or other came to characterize a great deal of the press during the 1920s. After World War I (1914–1918) many people in the United States wanted relief from hard-hitting or disturbing news—they wanted to be entertained, not just informed—and the circulation wars meant that many editors and journalists were only too eager to pander to their desire.

There was an undertone of hysteria about some of the newspaper reporting of this period—whether about rising crime, the threat of Bolshevism or, in the later 1920s, even the threat of witchcraft and occultism. In 1928–1929, for example, the *New York World*, as well as numerous magazines such as *Fortune*, the *North American*, and the *Nation*, avidly reported the details of the Hex Trial. At one minute past midnight in November 1928 three men (two of them teenagers) murdered Nelson D. Rehmeyer. Their confessions left no doubt that their belief in witchcraft had led to the murder. They said that Rehmeyer had hexed them and that they were justified in killing him because he refused to give up a lock of hair and his copy of the witches' bible, both of which were needed to remove the curse. The reporting portrayed the Pennsylvania community where Rehmeyer had lived as "backward" and "medieval," and even compared the state to the island of Haiti.

Another feature, which has since become endemic to much contemporary media, was an obsession with celebrities. Well-known figures, such as matinee idol Rudolph Valentino and baseball player Babe Ruth, were the subject of features, interviews, reports, and photographs—sometimes by invitation, but just as often as the result of unscrupulous and intrusive journalistic practice. In a period enamored with consumerism, fashion, and entertainment, the press by turns glamorized and vilified the icons of the age.

A responsible press

The irresponsibility and frivolity of jazz journalism was not by any means characteristic of all 1920s news reporting. Long-established newspapers, such as the *New York Times*, continued to offer readers balanced and well-researched stories, and were widely respected.

Although there was far less of the great campaigning journalism (pejoratively described as "muckraking" by some commentators) of the prewar years, many journalists were still ready to make a stand for what they believed in—with serious investigations of issues such as racial violence and segregation, criminal gangs, and exploitation of the poor. There was also a vibrant progressive and left-wing press—including journals such as the *New Republic* (1914) and the *New Masses* (1924)—as well as more radical organs such as New York's communist newspaper the *Daily Worker* (1924) and its magazine the *Liberator*. Journalists were also developing a new sense of professionalism. Previously journalists had had—as a group—a poor reputation; in 1919 one commentator had even compared journalism to a brothel. During the 1920s, however, more and more journalists started out in the job armed with a college degree, and some had trained in the schools of journalism that were being founded across the country.

In addition to the professionalization of journalism there was an ongoing discussion about what constituted good news reporting. Before World War I a good newspaper was generally thought to be one that simply reported "the facts"; in the 1920s, however, a new ideal of objectivity arose. This ideal had much less to do with lack of bias (something, it was realized, journalists could never actually achieve) than with a scientific method of gathering news—as, for example, in the meticulous checking of sources. Objectivity became a watchword of the press in later decades.

There was a wider debate, too, about the purpose of news. The philosopher John Dewey (1859–1952) argued that the media played an important role in enabling citizens to take part in key national debates. Writer and columnist Walter Lippman (1889–1974) of the *New York World* argued that journalism could, at its best, provide the necessary context for democracy, but feared that people were often too caught up in their everyday lives and prejudices to use the news to good effect.

Broadcasting to the nation

At first newspapers did not feel threatened by the rapid development of radio broadcasting that took place in the United States during the 1920s. After radio was freed from government restrictions at the

"All the News That's Fit to Print."

The New York Times.

COOLIDGE DOES NOT CHOOSE TO RUN IN 1928; STARTLES PARTY WITH 12-WORD MESSAGE; SOME DOUBTERS, OTHERS SEE FIELD OPEN

NEW SACCO TRIAL INDICATED AS STEP FULLER WILL TAKE

Governor Is Expected to Call for Reprieve of Men and Action by the Legislature.

POLITICAL ISSUE IS RAISED

Move Would Be 'Expedient,' but Observers Say Executive Feels It Is Right.

PAIR ENTER DEATH HOUSE

Newly Found Vanzetti Alibi Is Presented as Fuller Interviews Last Witnesses.

Sept. 19 to Be French Holiday In Honor of American Legion

JAPANESE OFFER NEW NAVAL PLAN

Suggestion That May Save Conference Is Wired to Washington and London.

MAINTAINS STATUS QUO

PARTY HERE IS AMAZED

State Organization in Consternation at Coolidge Statement.

IS FINAL, HILLES THINKS

Leaders Expect Effort to Force Renomination by a Popular Demand.

DR. BUTLER LAUDS ACTION

Says President Has Done Wise and Patriotic Act—Ex-Senator Butler Is Silent.

Smith Is Silent on Coolidge, But Democrats See His Gain

COOLIDGE'S ACTION PLEASES CORN BELT

Iowa Leaders in Farm Legislation Agitation Think It Will Aid Their Cause.

BOOM IN LOWDEN'S STOCK

LEADERS ARE CAUTIOUS

Vice President Dawes Says Public Will Regret the Decision.

LONGWORTH KEEPS SILENT

Ex-Governor Lowden Repeats That No One Can Run Away From the Presidency.

HOOVER TO "THINK IT OVER"

Borah Accepts Announcement as Final—West Did It, Says Brookhart.

CALVIN COOLIDGE.
"I Do Not Choose to Run for President in Nineteen Twenty-eight."

Washington Sees 1928 Field Open; Some Talk of Drafting Coolidge

PRESIDENT ACTED ALONE

His Close Friends Were Unaware of His Stand on Another Term.

CALLS IN NEWSPAPER MEN

President Hands Out Typed Slip in School Room, and Declines to Comment.

DRAMATIC SURPRISE STAGED

Statement Is Issued on the Eve of Coolidge's Fourth Anniversary as President.

A *New York Times* front page of 1927 breaks the news about Calvin Coolidge's decision not to run for president. The paper was established in 1851, and by the 1920s it had built a reputation for excellence in all types of news.

end of World War I, some of the largest newspapers, such as Scripps' *Detroit News*, set up their own small radio stations, although mainly with the intention of advertising the newspaper itself rather than broadcasting news.

Already, however, many commentators in the press had seen the potential of radio, both as a way of bringing people the news and as an eventual threat to newspapers. On June 8, 1919, the *San Francisco Chronicle* had a report entitled "When the President at the Phone May Speak to All the People," in which the writer bore witness to the "astonishing advance of wireless by which a single voice may actually be heard in every corner of the country." In June the following year the specialist journal *Electrical Experimenter* reported on a proposed news service by telephone in an article called "'Newsophone' to Supplant Newspapers." The article looked forward to international broadcasting by radio—to "radio distribution of news by central news agencies in the larger cities to thousands of radio stations in all parts of the world" so that "anyone can simply 'listen in' on their pocket wireless set." In 1922 an article in *Popular Radio* was entitled "The Newspaper That Comes through Your Walls."

Newspapers were able to discount such predictions in the early 1920s because of the chaos and amateurism that were the hallmarks of the very early days in radio broadcasting. Early commercial stations—such as those run by Westinghouse in East Pittsburgh, Pennsylvania (1920), Newark, New Jersey (1921), Springfield, Massachusetts (1921), and Chicago (1921)—were at this stage still experimenting with the medium's possibilities, and most of their somewhat haphazard programming focused on light entertainment rather than on news and current affairs.

There were some notable exceptions. For example, East Pittsburgh station KDKA's first day of public broadcasting included news of the 1920 presidential election returns. This groundbreaking event seems hugely momentous with hindsight and, without a doubt, holds a special place in radio history; but at the time it was hardly noticed at all, save for a brief article in the *Electrical Review* entitled "Send Election Results by Wireless Telephone." The world of radio was advancing and changing so quickly that its potential seemed at once both fantastically huge to those with vision and still peripheral to the majority of people.

Network news

Radio broadcasting matured very rapidly, in part because of the huge interest and excitement it generated among an American public in love with all things new and in part because big business quickly recognized its huge economic potential, especially in terms of airtime sold to advertisers. In 1920 there were about a million homes with a radio; by 1926 there were 5.5 million—approximately 20 percent of all U.S. homes. The number of stations also boomed.

The newspaper chains provided a model for the growth of radio networks, such as those developed by American Telephone & Telegraph (AT&T) and the Radio Corporation of America (RCA), which were soon locked in fierce competition for

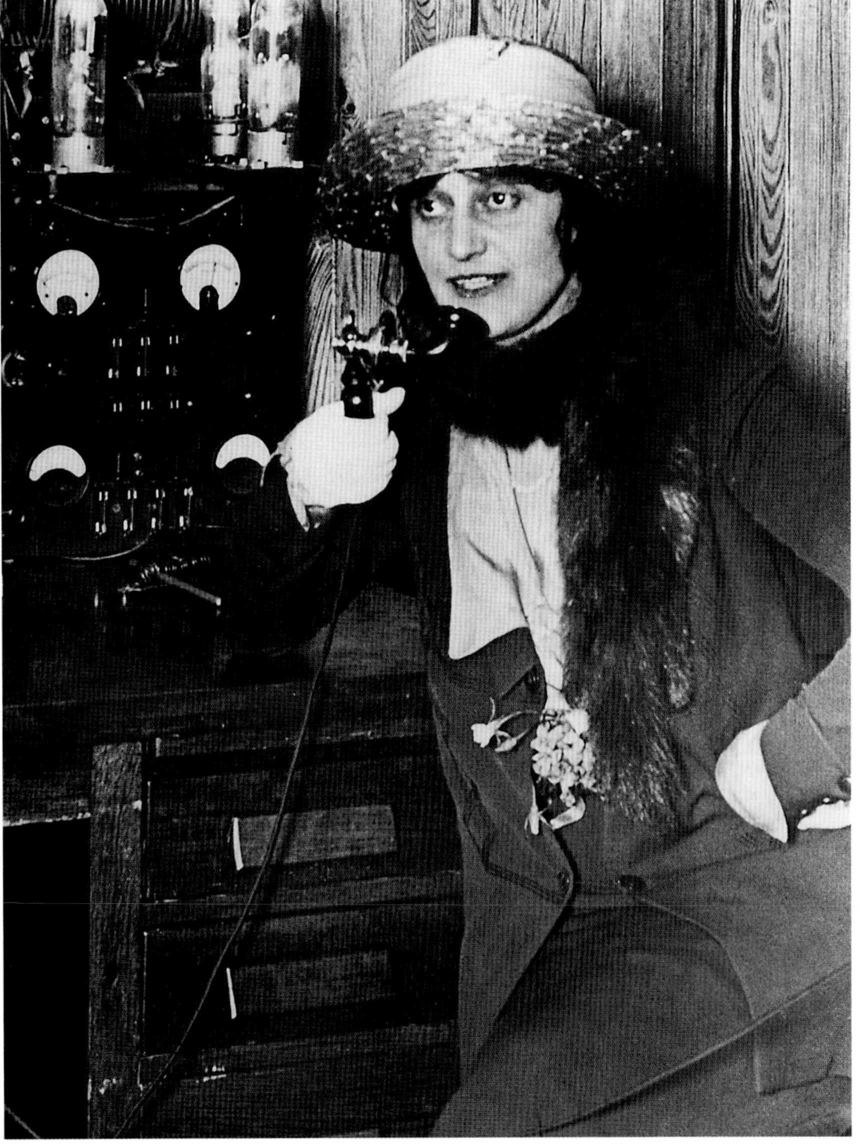

Singer Alma Gluck (1884–1938) makes her first radio broadcast on the *Atlanta Journal*'s new station in 1922. WSB was the first station in the South, the first to adopt a slogan, and one of the first to transmit programs to schools.

ETHNIC NEWSPAPERS

During the 19th century immigrants set up newspapers as a way of bringing together their new communities, maintaining ties with their country of origin, and transmitting their culture to the next generation. By the turn of the century many newcomers found more newspapers printed in their language in the United States than in their homeland. By 1873, for example, there were 530 German-language papers, many of them dailies. Anti-German feeling during World War I, however, forced many of them to close.

During the 1920s there was a marked decline in the numbers of ethnic papers, partly because of increasing pressure to Americanize, partly because isolation often led to an archaic use of the home language, and partly because the next generation was more comfortable reading English.

Typesetters at work on a Chinese newspaper in San Francisco in 1929—their job was to quickly locate some 12,000 separate pieces of Chinese type.

listeners and advertisers. In 1926 RCA bought up several AT&T stations to form the National Broadcasting Company (NBC) and with it the first permanent network, NBC Red (1926). The Columbia Broadcasting System (CBS) network went on air late in 1926. NBC Blue was founded in 1927 and specialized in culture and news. The first nationwide, coast-to-coast network broadcast in 1928 was a current-affairs item—a political rally broadcast from Madison Square Garden.

Both the network and other radio programming offered mainly light entertainment, such as the hugely popular "song and patter" shows. The networks did, however, broadcast weekly news programs, which invariably featured political news from Washington. They also broadcast major events, such as the 1927 ceremony marking Charles A. Lindbergh's (1902–1974) return home after the first solo, nonstop transatlantic flight, which was listened to by millions of rapt Americans. Such broadcasts were often subsequently released to the public as commemorative phonograph recordings.

The radio news programs largely depended on newspapers for their source of news. By 1928, however, the newspaper industry somewhat belatedly realized the threat posed by radio as a rival, rather than an additional, source of news and began to stop sharing reports with the networks. Radio stations had to begin the expensive task of gathering news for themselves—the news war between print and the air waves had begun.

SEE ALSO:

Communications • Magazines & Magazine Publishing • National Broadcasting Company • Photography • Radio & Radio Industry • Snyder, Ruth, Trial of

THE NEW YORKER

First published in 1925, *The New Yorker* is a weekly magazine that has had an important influence on the quality of writing and humor in the United States since its inception. Its founder and first editor was Harold Ross (1892–1951).

Harold Wallace Ross, the founder and editor of *The New Yorker* magazine, made his name in journalism while serving with the U.S. Army in France in World War I (1914–1918). In 1918 he became editor of *The Stars and Stripes*, the American forces' newspaper in France. By the end of the war he was described as "the most famous private in the army."

Returning to New York, in September 1923, Ross and his first wife Jane Grant went to live in a house at 412 West 47th Street in the area of Manhattan then known as Hell's Kitchen. Among the many frequent visitors to their chaotic menage, which became known as Wit's End, was the theater critic Alexander Woollcott, and it was through him that Ross became a member of the Round Table, the group of wits who met daily for lunch on weekdays at the Algonquin Hotel on 44th Street. Two years later Ross launched his new magazine, which though primarily literary, covered a whole range of artistic and political subjects. The first offices of *The New Yorker* were on nearby West 46th Street, but it was at the Ross family home that most of the serious editorial work was done.

The founder and editor of *The New Yorker*, Harold Ross, in Connecticut in 1925. Ross was born in Aspen, Colorado, and by the time he was 20 he had already worked as a reputable journalist in San Francisco, Panama, Atlanta, and New Orleans.

The launch

The first issue was published on February 21, 1925. Commercially, *The New Yorker* could scarcely have been launched at a better time. In 1925 radio and television had not yet become established, while new printing technology and low postage rates enabled magazines to make their publishers a fortune. However, what really set the magazine apart was the outstanding quality of its content and production. It was glossy and well written, and pioneered innovations in comedy and art. It covered current affairs as well as foreign reportage and in-depth biography. From the start *The New Yorker* established an exceptionally high standard of reporting—especially in its famous biographical "Profiles" and its letters from Paris and London by Janet Flanner and

CARTOONS

Besides the promotion of many of the leading writers of the period *The New Yorker* did a great deal to pioneer the work of cartoonists. In an era when photography was yet to become the preferred visual medium for magazines, illustration was the key form of visual representation. In the 1920s comic magazines flowered, and *The New Yorker* in particular embraced cartoons as a way of satirizing the various different classes of New York. The magazine introduced a more sophisticated form of cartoon—the one-line joke that used a single image (previously cartoons had tended to use several images). *The New Yorker's* cartoonists became experts in portraying social comment. They dealt with many areas of social behavior and class that had not been approached before, such as the nightlife of speakeasies, office politics among managers, commercial sports, and young women's social habits.

Some of the greatest cartoonists who worked for *The New Yorker* included James Thurber, Helen Hokinson, Charles Addams, and Peter Arno. James Thurber (1894–1961) was both a writer and a cartoonist. His cartoon characters included the angry wife, the put-upon husband, and a series of animals who acted as silent witnesses to the scenes. Today he is best remembered for creating Walter Mitty, a character from one of his short stories "The Secret Life of Walter Mitty" (1942). Helen Hokinson (1893–1949) drew naive young women who were obsessed with hats, dieting, and the pursuit of culture, while Peter Arno (1904–1968) used the city's aristocracy as his subject matter. Charles Addams (1912–1988), who started drawing for the magazine in 1933, specialized in macabre figures. In the 1960s his characters were turned into the TV series *The Addams Family*; two movies followed—*The Addams Family* (1991) and *Addams Family Values* (1993).

Mollie Panter Downes—and virtually invented the one-line-caption cartoon, featuring the drawings of Charles Addams, Peter Arno, Helen Hokinson, William Steig, Saul Steinberg, and James Thurber (*see box above*). In addition to Woollcott the magazine's leading writers included Robert Benchley, Ring Lardner, A.J. Liebling, Ogden Nash, John O'Hara, Dorothy Parker, Vladimir Nabokov, Rebecca West, H.L. Mencken, and E.B. White, all of whose reputations were cemented by the publication.

Publishing giant

The ringmaster of this great highbrow circus was Ross himself. Ross ran the magazine for 25 years until his death in 1951, and he used it to promote the work of a great many up-and-coming young writers and artists. However, his true character has to some extent been obscured by the large number of stories that have been told and written about him. One of the best accounts of him is in *The Years with Ross* (1951); but the author, James Thurber, like many other contributors to *The New Yorker*, was often more concerned with making wisecracks than with achieving biographical objectivity. Most literary depictions of Ross characterized him rather than described him. With that caveat in mind, Ross was commonly portrayed as something of a philistine, an uncouth provincial (he had been born and bred in Aspen, Colorado). The playwright Ben Hecht remarked that Ross "looked like a resident of the Ozarks and talked like a saloon brawler." Ross's supposed lack of culture was used to explain his obsessive attention to editorial detail—it has even been claimed that he read Fowler's *Modern English Usage* for light entertainment.

Yet there is a comparable body of evidence in support of the view that Ross's ignorance was affectation. He is said to have told Robert Benchley, "I don't want you to think I'm not inarticulate," and there were times when he used his rusticity (assumed or genuine) as an editorial device. For example, when he asked a contributor: "Is *Moby Dick* the whale or the man?" he was probably not revealing his ignorance of the work of Herman Melville but demanding clearer writing. He was described by many as a voracious reader and a closet intellectual who had a near perfect ear for language and wrote in what Rebecca West called a "hard, clear, classical American style."

Little can be said with certainty about the founder of *The New Yorker* other than that he was a fascinating bundle of contradictions. Of one thing, however, there is no doubt—as an editor, Ross pulled off the hardest trick of all: to keep good writers working for little or no pay. As Liebling joked: "Ross would no more have thought of offering his contributors money than of offering a horse an ice-cream soda." He achieved this by making *The New Yorker* the place to be published. When E.B. White (1899–1985) tried to resign, Ross told him, "You can't quit: this isn't a magazine, it's a movement."

In his editorial capacity Ross was greatly aided by Katharine Angell, who joined *The New Yorker* in 1925 six months after its launch and began reading unsolicited manuscripts for two hours a day. She soon became a full-time editor and the shaper of the magazine's advertising policy. In 1929 she left her first husband and married the young writer she had recommended Ross hire: E.B. White. Later Ross appointed her the publication's first head of fiction. Thurber called Katharine Angell White, as she became known, "the fountain and shrine of *The New Yorker*."

Today *The New Yorker* continues to attract great writers and artists, and remains one of the United States' most influential magazines.

SEE ALSO:

Books & Publishing • Magazines & Magazine Publishing • Poetry • Round Table • Thurber, James

NICARAGUA

The 1920s were a turbulent period in the relationship between the United States and the Central American republic of Nicaragua. Nicaragua was dogged by political unrest, and substantial U.S. economic and military involvement in the country became increasingly unpopular.

The origins of the troubled relationship between the United States and Nicaragua can be traced back to 1912. In that year the United States had backed a revolt to oust José Zelaya (1853–1919) after he ordered the execution of two North American adventurers; Zelaya had been president of Nicaragua since 1893. The country then became a protectorate of the United States and an American-approved politician, Adolfo Díaz (1874–1964), was installed as president. With an economic crisis looming as creditors called in loans that they had made to the government, and facing the threat of civil war, Díaz asked for U.S. military assistance from President William H. Taft (1909–1913) to protect U.S. economic interests. Taft readily dispatched Marines to Nicaragua.

Emiliano Chamorro around 1913. As president from 1917 to 1920, Chamorro followed the pro-American policies of his predecessor, Díaz. However, he lost U.S. support in 1926 when he seized the presidency from Carlos Solórzano.

A dominant presence

Much to the irritation of Nicaragua's Central American neighbors, Díaz soon signed a treaty with the United States. Faced with a near-bankrupt government, he agreed to allow the United States to build a second canal across the Central American isthmus—the first, the Panama Canal, was nearing completion—for a payment of $3 million and a guarantee of Nicaraguan independence. In exchange Díaz gave the United States a long-term lease on the Corn Islands in the Caribbean Sea and allowed U.S. naval concessions on both the Caribbean and Pacific coasts of his country. Nicaragua's closest neighbors were annoyed that Nicaragua granted land to their mighty northern neighbor. Further, with a U.S. military presence on its soil, Nicaragua's independence was now in question.

As well as the physical presence of U.S. Marines on Nicaraguan territory, the country's economy also came under American control. There had been U.S. intervention in Nicaraguan financial affairs since 1911. A U.S. appointee collected Nicaraguan customs taxes, which were

THE NATIONAL GUARD

During the 1920s the U.S. government was determined to withdraw its Marines from Nicaragua, but doing so proved very difficult. Different Nicaraguan presidents sought the protection of the U.S. Marines to keep peace and themselves in power. To satisfy all parties, the Americans devised a plan whereby the Marines would be replaced by an American-trained Nicaraguan National Guard.

Plans for the creation of a National Guard started in February 1923. The U.S. State Department wanted a constabulary made up of no more than 23 officers and 392 men under its supervision, which was intended to replace all Nicaragua's armed forces and police.

When the creation of a new National Guard was approved by the Nicaraguan Congress in May 1925, it was of a Nicaraguan-controlled force to be trained by American soldiers. The first attempt at organizing a National Guard was difficult. The United States wanted the Guard to be nonpolitical, but it soon became apparent that this was impossible. Different political factions in Nicaragua were determined to take control of the National Guard, recognizing that it would give them virtual authority in the country. When Chamorro seized power, he relied on the National Guard to keep him in power and sent them with the regular army to put down the Liberal uprisings.

When Adolfo Díaz replaced Chamorro as president in November 1926, he asked the U.S. government for help reorganizing the new Guardia Nacional de Nicaragua, as the organization was now known. The American government, eager to ensure that the 1928 election was fair, agreed to send Marines to work with the Guardia until new recruits could be trained.

The trainee guardsmen were paid $12 a month and received a uniform and medical expenses. They were given comprehensive training by U.S. Marines, who in a short time turned the force into a disciplined and efficient unit. The National Guard replaced both the army and the police force in Nicaragua. Its commander, General Anastasio Somoza (1896–1956), would later become Nicaragua's president and install a family dictatorship that lasted until the Nicaraguan Revolution of 1979.

paid directly to U.S. banks. Now, in order to reorganize Nicaragua's debts, American bankers took direct command of the country's finances, taking control of the national bank and the railroad system as security. The $3 million payment for the canal was repatriated to the New York banks that held Nicaragua's debt.

By the start of the 1920s Nicaragua was effectively controlled by the United States. The year 1920 was an election year in Nicaragua. The outgoing president, Emiliano Chamorro (1871–1966), known as the "General," was prohibited by the Nicaraguan constitution from running for a second term. However, he wanted to stay in power. To ensure that he continued to control the country, Chamorro nominated as his successor his uncle, Diego Manuel Chamorro (1881–1923). He appointed himself to the office of Nicaraguan minister to the United States, thereby ensuring his control of the country from Washington, D.C., while his uncle, under his direction, controlled everyday affairs in Managua, the Nicaraguan capital.

A printed portrait of Adolfo Díaz who was twice president of Nicaragua, from 1911 to 1916 and from 1926 to 1928. He relied heavily on U.S. support to remain in power and made many unpopular concessions to the United States.

The growth of anti-American feeling

As the decade got underway, opposition grew to the American military presence and to the economic subservience of Nicaragua to the United States. With U.S. Marines camped at Campo de Marte in sight of the National Palace in the capital, their presence was a highly visible reminder of foreign dominance. As early as 1921 there were clashes between the Marines and the Nicaraguan police, which resulted in the U.S. government paying compensation and apologizing for the behavior of the Marines.

In 1923 Nicaragua was plunged into crisis with the unexpected death of the president on October 19. His deputy, Bartolome Martinez (1860–1936), assumed the office, but Emiliano Chamorro wanted the presidency for himself. In order to ensure that the upcoming 1924 presidential election was fair, some Nicaraguans called for the U.S. Marines to stay and oversee the polls. However, the U.S. government wanted to withdraw its troops as part of President Warren G. Harding's (1921–1923) new

AUGUSTO CÉSAR SANDINO

After the 1979 Nicaraguan Revolution, in which the U.S.-supported Somoza dynasty was swept from power by the Sandinista rebels, the name Sandino—from which Sandinista is taken—became familiar across the United States. Augusto César Sandino (1893–1934) was a rebel leader in the late 1920s and early 1930s who fought against the power of the United States in his country. His technique of low-level fighting in the mountains and forests of Nicaragua was later followed by Fidel Castro (1926–) and Che Guevara (1928–1967) in the Cuban Revolution (1959) and by the Vietnamese in the sixties.

Sandino was born the illegitimate son of a landowner and a peasant girl on May 18, 1893. He grew up surrounded by books, even adopting the name César as a mark of his love of classical literature. Sandino worked in Central America before going to Mexico, where he was inspired by the Mexican Revolution and nationalist cause.

As a young man Sandino worked for the United Fruit Company and other U.S.-owned companies, notably mines, across Central America. On his return to Nicaragua he raised a force of 29 armed men and started to fight against American imperialism. After he refused to sign the peace accord negotiated by his leader General Moncada and U.S. Special Envoy Stimson in May 1927, Sandino conducted a guerrilla war against the National Guard and the U.S. presence. He was helped by sympathetic local people and peasants who fed him and hid him for six years. The Marines were unable to find Sandino, but he got close enough to U.S. Marine camps to photograph them and then sent the photographs to the U.S. headquarters to taunt the Americans.

After the withdrawal of Marines in 1933 and the inauguration of Juan Bautista Sacasa as president, Sandino was invited to meet with General Anastasio Somoza, head of the National Guard, for a peace conference. After his arrival in Managua for the conference he was seized and, against the wishes of the United States, executed on February 21, 1934, by the National Guard.

Sandino's exploits against the United States made him one of Latin America's greatest 20th-century heroes and an inspiration to revolutionaries.

Augusto César Sandino, pictured around January 1928.

laissez-faire, or noninterventionist, approach to foreign policy. Washington thought that the best solution to Nicaragua's electoral difficulties was a coalition government. It forced Chamorro to accept a fellow Conservative, Carlos Solórzano, as president, supported by members of the rival Liberal Party. President Solórzano's first request, on assuming office in 1925, was that the U.S. Marines stay in Nicaragua.

The U.S. government, eager to stick to its pledge to remove the Marines and believing that all was well with the coalition, withdrew its troops in 1925 after agreeing to the creation of a new nonpartisan American-trained force, the National Guard (*see box on p. 89*). Emiliano Chamorro, angry at his exclusion from the government, took control of the National Guard and forced

Solórzano to remove all the Liberal members of the government. In January 1926 Chamorro, acting without the backing of the United States, seized the presidency for himself. The United States reacted with horror, accurately predicting a Liberal revolution. When a Liberal revolution broke out on May 2, 1926, Chamorro used the National Guard to suppress the uprising.

Unrest and civil war

Chamorro had not counted on the resourcefulness of the vice president, Juan Bautista Sacasa (1879–1946), who had sought the backing of the Mexican government of Plutarco Elías Calles (1924–1928). Calles provided weapons for the Liberal forces; faced with such strong opposition, Chamorro had little choice but to back down. The United States was alarmed at Mexico's intervention and worried that Nicaragua would go the same way as Mexico, which had had a nationalistic revolution. The U.S. refused to recognize Chamorro's government, and he was forced to resign in favor of ex-president Adolfo Díaz. Díaz immediately asked for direct U.S. military protection. President Calvin Coolidge (1923–1929) refused but recognized that some intervention was necessary.

Between the fall of 1926 and May 1927 Nicaragua was convulsed by civil war. The U.S. Marines returned in January 1927 in increased numbers. The larger force ensured Díaz stayed in power. However, the United States government did not want direct conflict with the Liberal rebels, who were led by Mexican-supported General José María Moncada (1871–1945). To avoid direct conflict, President Coolidge sent his special envoy Henry Stimson (1867–1950) to negotiate a truce. Sacasa and Moncada could see that Washington was in a strong position to put down their rebellion but would accept their victory in the next presidential election in 1928.

Under these terms Moncada signed an agreement with Stimson known as the Pact of Espino Negro, on May 20, 1927. In 1928 Moncada was duly elected president in voting overseen by U.S. Marines. However, events were complicated by the failure of one of Moncada's generals, Augusto César Sandino, to sign the Espino Negro Pact. For the next six years Sandino led a low-level guerrilla campaign against both the U.S. Marines and the National Guard (*see box opposite*). Sandino's nationalist mission to expel the "Yankee" gained worldwide attention.

Sandino's guerrilla campaign dominated the end of the decade. The U.S. continued to help fund the National Guard, while U.S. Marines were actively involved in the hunt for Sandino. American involvement in the killing of Nicaraguans made the United States and President Moncada very unpopular among the Nicaraguan people, but Moncada did not want the Marines to leave because he depended on them for his own safety.

However, as Marines died in service and costs escalated, the U.S. involvement in Nicaragua became increasingly unpopular back home. In 1931 Stimson announced that the Marines would be withdrawn. He instructed Moncada to hold an election in 1932, which was supervised by the remaining 400 Marines. Juan Bautista Sacasa was elected president, and American troops finally left Nicaragua on January 2, 1933.

SEE ALSO:

Central America • Foreign Policy, U.S. • Latin America • Mexico

A U.S. Marine patrol and reconnaissance airplane in Nicaragua in 1928. From late 1927 Marines became increasingly involved in rooting out Augusto César Sandino's rebels in the remote northern region of the country.

NIGHTCLUBS

Nightclubs flourished in the twenties and epitomized the fast-living, partying lifestyle often associated with the era. They attracted people in search of drink, dancing, music, and a good time: They were the home of jazz, and they were often controlled by organized crime.

The Prohibition era created the nightclub phenomenon. When the Eighteenth Amendment went into effect in 1920, it made the manufacture, transportation, and sale of alcohol illegal. However, it did not make the consumption of alcohol illegal, and it did little to lessen people's desire to drink—if anything, Prohibition increased people's desire to drink by making it more glamorous. Illicit bars, or speakeasies, soon proliferated. During the twenties there were an estimated 20,000 to 100,000 in New York City alone, and competition between them was fierce. It was not long before proprietors began to add additional inducements to their customers in the form of entertainment, and soon the stakes were raised. Entertainers and musicians became the main attractions for drinkers, and the nightclub era was born.

The promise of a good time

From modest single-roomed bars with a small stage to ritzy palaces of glass, chrome, and gilt, nightclubs promised their patrons a good time. Waiters in tuxedos carrying cocktail-laden trays wove their way between closely packed tables. Cigarette girls, wearing short skirts and carrying trays of cigarettes and cigars, strolled among the patrons selling their wares. Even the hat-check girls in the cloakrooms were an alluring promise of the good times to come. Well-supplied with cocktails and cigarettes, the audience was promised a rich array of entertainment: hot jazz bands, crooners, witty masters of ceremonies, and chorus lines of scantily dressed girls. They could take to the dance floor themselves, or they could sit comfortably and watch the flamboyant dancers while sipping an ice-cold dry martini—the cocktail that came to symbolize the era.

Above all, nightclubs were about jazz music. Nightclubs were the only places that hired black musicians. White youths from all social classes were drawn to jazz and to the seductive new dances—from the turkey trot to the Charleston—that went with it. On Chicago's South Side, for example, clubs called "black and tans" catered to a mixed clientele. While black performers dominated the stage, the dance floor was alive with both white and black patrons, all of whom wanted to be part of the hottest scene in town. Black and tans were one of the few places in Chicago where blacks and whites mixed. This heady cocktail of interracial mixing, new-found physical freedom, and a widespread belief that jazz music and dancing were sexually stimulating fueled the passions of antijazz campaigners. In the words of Ann Shaw Faulkner, president of the General Federation of Women's Clubs: "Jazz was originally the accompaniment of the voodoo dance, stimulating half-crazed barbarians to the vilest of deeds ...."

Nightclubs and organized crime

During the Prohibition era the production and sale of alcohol quickly fell into the hands of criminals and fueled a huge growth in organized crime. Nightclub-owners were forced to reach various accommodations with mobsters, as well as making "payoffs" to corrupt city officials to buy their silence.

The British-born gangster Owen "Owney" Madden was one of many criminals who thrived on the illicit trade in

NIGHTCLUB CELEBRITY

Mary "Texas" Guinan (1884–1933) was the most famous nightclub hostess of the twenties. She had started out her stage career as a chorus-line performer. She then went to Hollywood, where she made a number of movies starring as a self-reliant, gun-slinging Texan. In 1922 she returned to New York and was hired as a singer at the nightclub in the Beaux Arts hotel. Her witty, self-assertive style soon led her into the role of "master of ceremonies," and throughout the 1920s she became the "queen of the nightclubs," moving from club to club as they were successively shut down by the authorities. Although Guinan was arrested several times for operating a speakeasy, she was never convicted, and her ownership was never proved. She capitalized on the notoriety generated by club closures and her arrests, and in 1926, while the clubs with which she was associated were routinely being raided, she earned $700,000 in 10 months. The following year she appeared as the hostess in a Broadway review named *Padlocks* (1927). She was uniquely skilled at establishing a rapport with the audience and enjoyed trading insults, jokes, and one-liners with them. She became celebrated for her trademark greeting "Hello, sucker!" Guinan died in Canada exactly one month before Prohibition was repealed.

Mary "Texas" Guinan, whose flamboyant embrace of the role of hostess in many of New York's nightclubs—coupled with her not infrequent arrests—made her one of the most notorious and popular figures of the Prohibition era.

drink and racketeering, and who branched out into the nightclub business. He started his own brewery and supplied alcohol to many of the clubs and speakeasies in New York's notorious Hell's Kitchen district. In 1922 he bought the Club Deluxe, a failing nightclub on 142nd Street and Lenox Avenue in East Harlem, Manhattan. He reopened it in 1923 as the Cotton Club, and it soon became one of the most popular nightspots in the city. The club operated a strict whites-only policy, although the performers and most of the waiters were black. The Cotton Club was the venue for many of the country's top jazz, blues, and tap performers. Don Redman (1900–1964) and Coleman Hawkins (1904–1969) were among the musicians who played at the club's opening night. Celebrated jazz musician Duke Ellington (1899–1974) was the in-house performer for many years; and when he left, Cab Calloway (1907–1994) took over. Tap-dancer Bill "Bojangles" Robinson (1878–1949) and blues singer Lena Horne (1917–) both began their careers in the Cotton Club. But patrons were always reminded of the club's gangland roots when they were greeted by the terrifying head doorman, George Dean DeMange, or "Big Frenchie," Madden's chief "enforcer."

Many other nightclubs opened on 133rd Street in Harlem. They served vaudeville-style black entertainment, jazz, big bands, and blues to the white patrons who flooded into Harlem from downtown Manhattan. Alcohol sales and consumption climbed rapidly, and the mob's power grew.

SEE ALSO:

Charleston • Cotton Club • Dance • Ellington, Duke • Jazz • Organized Crime • Prohibition

NORMALCY

Promoted by President Warren G. Harding, normalcy became the watchword of the Republican administrations of the twenties. It implied a return to conservative values and a broadly noninterventionist style of government in both national and international affairs.

The election of 1920 came to hinge on a single word, and an unusual word at that. Warren G. Harding (1865–1923), a Republican senator from Ohio, sought the presidency that year, and he used a May 1920 speech in Boston to summarize his campaign theme. Harding declared: "America's present need is not heroics, but healing; not nostrums, but normalcy; not revolution, but restoration; not agitation, but adjustment; not surgery, but serenity; not the dramatic, but the dispassionate; not experiment, but equipoise; not submergence in internationality, but sustainment in triumphant nationality."

Harding and normalcy

The word "normalcy" came to stand for all that Harding promised. However, it had hardly ever been used in the English language before Harding's speech—the word first appeared in 1857 as an algebraic term in a dictionary of mathematics. Harding's use of the word "normalcy" was as brilliant as it was unorthodox. With his theme of a return to normalcy, Harding won the Republican nomination for president in 1920. He faced Democrat James M. Cox (1870–1957), a supporter of the outgoing president, Woodrow Wilson (1913–1921), and the League of Nations. Harding crushed Cox in the popular vote and in the electoral college, and the Republican Party amassed a huge majority in Congress.

Although, after his death, his legacy became mired in scandal, Harding's emphasis on normalcy set the tone for the politics of the 1920s. The conservative wing of the Republican Party rallied behind Harding's promise to return the United States to normalcy, and the Republicans maintained their position as the dominant political party throughout the 1920s even after Harding himself passed from the scene.

What was normalcy?

The very vagueness of the concept was the key to its popularity. The definition of "normalcy" in the *Merriam-Webster's Dictionary* is "the state of being normal." In other words, it meant conforming to a standard, of being "regular" or "usual." Instead of using the term "normality," which was already in widespread use at the time, Harding deliberately chose a word that evoked the past. In this sense Harding's emphasis on normalcy was an endorsement of classic conservatism, especially the conservative commitment to defend the status quo. He was appealing to conservative Americans at a time when they were nostalgic for a time before mechanized wars, revolutionary politics, and women's rights.

Harding intended to contrast his promised normalcy with a state of "irregular" and "unusual" conditions. In the May 1920 speech Harding offered "normalcy" instead of "nostrums" (defined as "quack remedies" or "a pet scheme for bringing about some political reform"). He was offering normalcy as an alternative to progressivism and the idealism of Woodrow Wilson. Wilson's ambitious social reforms and even more ambitious role for the United States in world affairs were the "nostrums" that Harding rejected. In the same normalcy speech Harding explicitly rejected "heroism" in favor of "healing." The implication was that American involvement in World War I (1914–1918) may have been a mistake, and certainly that America should steer clear of Wilson's beloved League of Nations.

More broadly Harding placed his concept of normalcy in opposition to the general state of upheaval that pervaded America in the late 1910s. The upheaval included the progressivism of Wilson—and perhaps that of Theodore Roosevelt (1901–1909) before him—the push for woman suffrage, the onset of Prohibition, the Red Scare, and above all else the brief but traumatic American participation in World War I and the tremendous social and economic changes that it brought.

By the time of the 1920 presidential election many Americans were weary of these upheavals. Other developments, such as the rise of anti-immigrant sentiment among many white Protestant Americans, also meant that there was a strong reactionary movement at the time. There was also a strong belief among many Americans in isolationism in foreign policy. Harding, therefore, stressed that normalcy would end the changes and return America to the way it used to be. He was rewarded with the biggest majority in the history of American presidential elections up to that time.

The appeal of normalcy began with its promise of peace and tranquillity, a pause after a storm of change. However, as a practical matter, the promise of normalcy is only appealing if one believes that the regular or usual condition is a good one. If the normal condition is perceived to be bad, then normalcy is not a good thing. Normalcy also ran a risk: It was a very vague term, and its lack of definition meant that it was all things to all peoples. As a result, many people were bound to be disappointed by what Harding did. The other problem with normalcy is that it evoked an idealized America that, in fact, never really existed.

Harding may have been a conservative in the sense of preserving the regular or usual condition, but he was not a reactionary, meaning one who is committed to turn back the clock to erase changes. This characteristic was another crucial dimension in the popularity of normalcy. Although the idea of returning to normalcy could have been interpreted as an all-out attack on the reforms of the 1910s, Harding instead pursued only an end to further reform.

Harding's inconsistencies in his implementation of normalcy were obvious from his policies. Harding would refuse to join the League of Nations, and he would decline to enact any further progressive reforms. He introduced quota laws to stem immigration and positively embraced the deeply controversial prohibition of alcohol. But he also declined the opportunity to tear down the major progressive accomplishments of the previous generation: woman suffrage, the Federal Reserve, antitrust laws, and Civil Service reforms. Although one interpretation of normalcy was as a cry to "bring back the good old days," Harding was wise enough not to embark on a reactionary crusade.

Harding died in office in 1923. He was hailed as a great president and a great man upon his death, one whose passing was mourned by the entire nation. Only after his death was Harding's reputation destroyed by a series of scandals that had bubbled beneath the surface of his placid presidency. Harding's secretary of the interior and his attorney general were discredited after the famous Teapot Dome scandal, after they sold government-owned lands for great personal profit. Harding himself was revealed to have had an affair with a young woman, Nan Britton, with whom he had a daughter: Britton wrote a book, *The President's Daughter*, after Harding died.

A photograph of Warren G. Harding (left) and his running mate for the 1920 election, Calvin Coolidge (right), taken in June of that year. The presidencies of both men were based on their concept of normalcy.

Who Says a Watched Pot Never Boils?

A cartoon by W.T. Enright satirizes the Teapot Dome scandal, from a February 1924 issue of *Judge* magazine. Harding's administration, so closely identified at the time with "normalcy," was later found to be riddled with corruption.

Calvin Coolidge and normalcy

Harding's successor as president, Calvin Coolidge (1923–1929), had his own interpretation of normalcy. Campaigning as Harding's running mate in 1920, Coolidge declared that the election of the Harding–Coolidge ticket would mark "the end of a period which has seemed to substitute words for things." A man of notoriously few words himself, Coolidge (even more than Harding) saw normalcy as meaning a government that did little to interfere with business or with the economic life of the country.

Upon Harding's death in 1923 Coolidge ascended to the presidency, where he had the good fortune to preside over one of the greatest economic booms in the country's history. Following a severe recession in the early 1920s, the economy roared back to life. Transport and communication industries thrived. The industrial and financial sectors grew at an astonishing rate, bringing both real, tangible economic prosperity and the illusion that the prosperity was even more widespread and more enduring than it actually was. Only agriculture was left out of the great boom.

The somewhat abstract numbers represented by the stock market and economic growth charts were complemented by a rapid diffusion of consumer technologies. Through the course of the 1920s the automobile, the radio, electric appliances, interurban rail, and even the airplane became commonplace in homes or cities. The material progress of the decade was the kind of development that promised to transform daily life.

President Coolidge was able to bask in the glow of the prosperity that coincided with his time in office in the 1920s. Coolidge's philosophy of limited government intervention and faith in the private sector may not have caused, or even much contributed to, the economic and technological boom of the twenties. However, much of the nation believed, as Coolidge did, that material improvement and limited government were the normal condition of American life.

Normalcy and the end of prosperity

To Coolidge normalcy certainly meant progress, although not in the direction of the social and political reforms so beloved by Wilson and the progressives. Within a year of the end of Coolidge's term in office, however, the normalcy of the 1920s came to a bitter end: The October 1929 stock market crash heralded the onset of the Great Depression, the worst and longest economic crisis the country had ever confronted. To millions of unemployed, impoverished, and hungry Americans normalcy would mean something very different in the 1930s.

SEE ALSO:

Conservatism • Coolidge, Calvin • Harding, Warren G. • Progressivism • Teapot Dome Scandal • Wilson, Woodrow

OFF-BROADWAY

Off-Broadway describes a range of theater productions staged in New York as alternatives to the mainstream commercial shows of Broadway. This type of theater developed in the 1910s and 1920s, when it became the main setting for new, avant-garde plays and productions.

Off-Broadway productions include revivals and classics, new European and American plays, and experimental forms of production. The term was first coined by the critic Burns Mantle (1873–1948) in 1935 to describe semiprofessional or amateur theater in New York, although the term was not recognized as a distinct category until after World War II (1939–1945).

Mainstream theater

The origins of commercial mainstream theater lie in the late 19th century, when it became more economical for companies to make long runs of a single play and send it on tour than to produce a series of new plays. These companies were controlled by the Theatrical Syndicate, which came to dominate all theatrical production in the United States at the end of the 1800s and beginning of the 1900s.

While the monopoly of the Theatrical Syndicate was overturned in 1915, the commercialization of productions continued. Melodramas were the most common type of play. By 1912 there were 8,000 theaters in the United States. Economic prosperity and the increase in the middle-class urban population in the 1920s created a demand for a greater variety of theatrical entertainment.

Little theaters

The origins of Off-Broadway theater lay in "little theaters," a term used to describe the smaller theater companies that flourished in the United States in the 1910s and 1920s. The name came from the Little Theater in Chicago, founded in 1911; the models were European art theaters such as the Théâtre Libre in Paris, the Freie Bühne in Berlin, the Independent Theatre in London, and the Moscow Art Theater. Constance D'Arcy Mackay (about 1887–1966), a writer for and about nonprofessional theater, surveyed this type of theater in her book *The Little Theater in the United States* (1917). She described 63 theaters across the country: Some were a form of community entertainment, others had more serious intellectual and aesthetic aims, but the key to their success was that they were small. Some little theaters lasted only through the 1920s, others became professional groups, while many lived on as community theaters.

A new tradition

Three of these small theaters, all in New York City, are considered to have introduced modernism to American theater: the Neighborhood Playhouse, the Washington Square Players, and the Provincetown Players. The Provincetown Players and the Washington Square Players originated among the intellectuals and artists who gathered around the Liberal Club in Greenwich Village, the center of bohemian life in New York. The Neighborhood Playhouse had a humble beginning in a social center on the Lower East Side of Manhattan as a philanthropic project initiated by the sisters Alice and Irene Lewisohn.

By 1912 the Neighborhood Playhouse had organized one-act plays. In 1915 it established a new small theater of 390 seats at 466 Grand Street, where it presented short plays by John Galsworthy, Anton Chekhov, and George Bernard Shaw. In 1920 the Neighborhood Playhouse became the professional Neighborhood Playhouse Acting Company; its first play was Galsworthy's *The Mob*. When the company closed in 1927, it had staged 43 productions, notably *The Little Clay Cat* (1924), based on a Native American fable, and *The Dybbuk* (1925), a Yiddish drama by S. Ansky.

The Washington Square Players was founded in 1914. In the following year they rented the Bandbox Theater on East 57th Street and staged short European plays such as Maurice Maeterlinck's *Interior* and works by members of the company such as Lawrence Langner's *Licensed* and Edward Goodman's *Eugenically Speaking*. The Players were funded by a system of membership and subscription tickets; by 1925 they had 25,000 subscribers, and by 1930, 70,000 throughout the United States. They moved to the Comedy Theater in 1916 and continued staging plays of "artistic merit," mostly by American writers but also by Chekhov, Maeterlinck, Shaw, and Oscar Wilde. The Players remained an amateur organization until the company was disbanded in 1918. The following year they reorganized as a professional theater company, the Theater Guild, and continued the policy of staging plays by new European writers—such as Shaw, Ferenc Molnár, Leonid Andreyev, and Luigi Pirandello. U.S. works included Elmer Rice's *The Adding Machine* (1923) and Eugene O'Neill's *Strange Interlude* (1928). A new theater, the 900-seat Guild, was built on 52nd Street in 1924. The Theater Guild expanded its activity, founding an acting school between 1927 and 1930 and sending productions on tour.

The Provincetown Players was founded by some of the original members of the Washington Square Players, including Eugene O'Neill (1888–1953), Susan Glaspell (1882–1948), and George Cram Cook (1873–1924). They opened with O'Neill's *Bound East for Cardiff* in a makeshift theater on an old wharf in

An undated portrait of Edna Ferber (1887–1968). Ferber began to write plays in the early 1920s. Although some were staged, she did not achieve real success until she began working with George S. Kaufman (1889–1961).

Provincetown, Massachusetts, on July 18, 1916. In the winter of 1916 they moved to a small theater in Greenwich Village. They mounted plays of high dramatic standards and in six seasons staged over 90 new plays by emerging talents such as O'Neill, Glaspell, Edna St. Vincent Millay, and Edna Ferber. They launched not only writers but also actors, directors, and designers. Under the direction of O'Neill, theater designer Robert Edmund Jones (1887–1954), and critic Kenneth McGowan the company became more professional in the mid-1920s. However, it remained committed to staging quality drama such as O'Neill's *All God's Chillun Got Wings* (1923) and *Desire under the Elms* (1924), and Paul Green's *In Abraham's Bosom* (1926). The Provincetown Players was dissolved just before the stock market crash in 1929.

Off-Broadway established

As Broadway became increasingly conservative in the years after World War II (1939–1945), performing mostly musicals and comedies, it became difficult for new playwrights, actors, directors, and producers to break into theater. During the 1940s Off-Broadway began to be the main producer of serious drama; in 1949 the Off-Broadway Theater League limited the size and location of Off-Broadway theaters so as not to compete with Broadway. As Off-Broadway became a contractual rather than an artistic definition, it became mainstream and generated a need for a new noncommercial and experimental theater, which came to be called off-Off-Broadway. Graduates of the new postwar theater departments in universities and colleges, too numerous be absorbed into the professional theater, created an "academic" theater. A new term, "alternative theater," came into existence in the 1960s.

SEE ALSO:

Broadway • Greenwich Village • Millay, Edna St. Vincent • Modernism • Musicals & Musical Theater • O'Neill, Eugene • Theater

OHIO GANG

The so-called Ohio Gang was a group of corrupt politicians who achieved positions of high public office during the presidency of Warren G. Harding. The scandals in which they were embroiled were exposed after Harding's death in 1923 and brought infamy to his administration.

Presidents often reward political friends and backers with government jobs of one kind and another. It is part and parcel of the extensive patronage at their disposal. In collecting his friends around him and making them gifts of high office, President Warren G. Harding (1921–1923) was no exception. However, some of those friends and acquaintances from the president's days in Ohio state politics abused the positions they were given, treating their offices as personal gold mines. Nicknamed the Ohio Gang, they turned the federal government into a machine for making money.

Most of the gang were old poker-playing and golf-playing friends of the president, men whom Harding wanted around him—despite the burdens of office, Harding did not give up his twice-weekly card sessions or his twice-weekly rounds of golf. The big names in the gang were the president's campaign manager, Harry Daugherty (1860–1941), who became attorney general; Charles Forbes, head of the Veterans' Bureau; Thomas Miller, head of the Alien Property Bureau; and Albert Fall (1861–1944), plucked from the Senate to be secretary of the interior.

The scandals

The most notorious scandal associated with the Ohio Gang was that of Teapot Dome, which was never far from the headlines in the second half of the twenties. Teapot Dome in Wyoming and

Harry Daugherty leaves the White House after a meeting with President Calvin Coolidge on August 13, 1923. Regarded as the leader of the Ohio Gang, Daugherty was removed from office by the new president in March 1924.

HARRY DAUGHERTY AND THE "LOVE NEST"

Harry Daugherty was a successful corporate lawyer in Ohio, a slick operator, and a man with political ambitions. When he first met Harding in the late 1890s, Daugherty was struck by his good looks and sonorous voice, and is said to have exclaimed, "Gee, what a president he'd make." He became the strategist behind Harding's political career. Republicans and press warned Harding against appointing him to the cabinet. "Harry Daugherty has been my best friend from the beginning of this whole thing," Harding said. "I have told him that he can have any place in the Cabinet he wants, outside of Secretary of State. He tells me that he wants to be Attorney General and by God he will be Attorney General."

In Washington, D.C., Daugherty lived openly with a man, Jess Smith, in an apartment at the Ward Park Hotel. They also kept a house on H Street that became known as the "Love Nest." It was one block from the White House and two blocks from the Justice Department. Congressmen, Ohio friends, lobbyists, and men looking for government jobs were frequent visitors, as was the president himself. Smith—who had no official appointment in the government but was given an office in the Justice Department and wrote his letters on the attorney general's letterhead—boasted that the house cost $50,000 a year to maintain. When Daugherty arrived in Washington in 1921, he was $17,000 in debt. Within two years he had deposited more than $75,000 in his brother's bank account, in addition to bonds worth $40,000 and 200 shares in an aircraft company that had profited by $3.5 million from a government overpayment. Daugherty avoided criminal prosecution by burning bank records and getting rid of government files. However, he was dismissed as attorney general by President Calvin Coolidge (1923–1929) in March 1924 for obstructing investigation into the Justice Department.

Elk Hills in California were public lands with oil reserves set aside for the use of the Navy. In his role as secretary of the interior Albert Fall engineered responsibility for the reserves and promptly leased them to private oil companies, from whom he received gifts and loans of some $400,000. Protected for a while by Daugherty, Fall was eventually scrutinized by a Senate investigation. A series of criminal and civil cases against the men involved in the oil deals lasted throughout the twenties. In 1929 Fall was found guilty of bribery; he was fined $100,000 and sentenced to one year in prison, earning for himself the distinction of being the first member of an American cabinet ever to go to prison for crimes committed while in office.

The tip of the iceberg

Teapot Dome was not the only Ohio Gang scandal. Harding's last months as president were dogged by his knowledge of corruption in the Veterans' Bureau. The bureau had been set up in 1921 to oversee the welfare of soldiers who had returned from World War I (1914–1918) and had as its director Harding's friend Charles Forbes. Forbes went on to misappropriate at least $200 million of government funds while selling surplus government war stocks, making a tidy sum for himself from fraudulent construction contracts and the sale of government medical supplies. Harding allowed Forbes to flee to Europe; shortly afterward Charles F. Cramer, attorney for the bureau, committed suicide. In 1925 Forbes was found guilty of bribery and corruption; he was fined $10,000 and sentenced to two years in jail.

There was more wrongdoing in the Alien Property Bureau, which was responsible for administering the return of property confiscated during the war. In processing a claim for the return of assets to the American Metal Company, bureau chief Thomas Miller made $50,000 for himself, $112,000 for a Republican national committeeman, and $224,000 for Jess Smith, Daugherty's close friend and right-hand man. In 1927 Miller was convicted of conspiracy to defraud the government and sentenced to 18 months in prison.

Jess Smith lived with Daugherty and was the liaison between the Justice Department and the gang's downtown Washington headquarters on H Street (*see box above*). The attorney general was himself tainted by scandal when Smith was exposed, along with Justice Department officials, for selling pardons and immunity from prosecution. Smith's death in 1923 was apparently suicide, but there were suspicious circumstances—although he seemed to have shot himself, the gun was in his right hand and the bullet hole was in his left temple.

The gang's contempt for the law was evident in its exploitation of the Eighteenth Amendment, which banned the manufacture, transportation, and sale of alcohol. Howard Mannington, a Republican who had served on the Ohio Railroad Commission, had no official position in the government. He told friends that he was in Washington "to help the attorney general." In fact, he was the go-between who handed out "permits" to local "agents" who sold them to bootleggers for $15—one permit bought a bootlegger 3 gallons of liquor. Mannington took a cut of each permit sale for himself. Under the Prohibition Commissioner appointed by Harding—Ray Haynes, once the mayor of Hillsboro, Ohio—Prohibition officers found it so easy to make money from bribes that their federal office became known as the nation's "finest school for bootleggers."

While Harding was not personally involved in the Ohio Gang, his lax administration allowed it to flourish. As he became aware of the corruption, his health declined. After his death the scandals brought lasting disgrace to his presidency.

SEE ALSO:

Election of 1920 • FBI • Harding, Warren G. • Teapot Dome Scandal

Georgia O'KEEFFE (1887–1986)

Georgia O'Keeffe was one of the most renowned and successful American artists of the 20th century. Her evocative paintings of city skylines and skyscrapers from the 1920s remain iconic images of the era.

Georgia O'Keeffe produced some of the most distinctive and best-known American paintings of the 20th century. In the 1920s she was one of the most significant members of the circle of avant-garde artists associated with the photographer and champion of modern art Alfred Stieglitz (1864–1946), whom she married in 1924. Always highly original, she was nonetheless influenced by the paintings and photographs of other members of Stieglitz's circle. Like them, she explored abstract qualities—particularly the expressive potential of color and form—while basing her paintings on subjects that ranged from flowers to skyscrapers.

Georgia O'Keeffe was born near Sun Prairie, Wisconsin. She studied at the Art Institute of Chicago (1904–1905) and the Art Students League of New York (1907–1908). From 1909 she had a number of jobs working as a freelance artist and teacher while intermittently pursuing her own studies. Her break came when Stieglitz included some of her work in two group shows at his 291 gallery in New York in 1916, then gave her a solo show the following year. In 1918 she moved to New York and lived with Stieglitz, beginning a personal and professional relationship that would last some 30 years.

O'Keeffe worked in a broad range of media, from charcoal, watercolor, and pastel to oil. She developed a carefully modulated style of subtly blended brush work, strong color, and broad forms through which she aimed to convey an essence or spirituality that went beyond the physical appearance of objects. In this blending of realism and abstraction she was influenced by the U.S. painter Arthur Dove, and like him she produced many meditations on landscape, including the watercolor *Light Coming on the Plains III* (1917) and the more vigorously structured oil *Blue and Green Music* (1919).

A photograph from 1950 of the artist Georgia O'Keeffe taken by Carl Van Vechten. After O'Keeffe settled in New Mexico in 1946, the desert landscape of the Southwest became a central theme in her painting.

However, O'Keeffe's most popular works from the twenties are her flower paintings. Influenced by the photographs of Paul Strand and Imogen Cunningham among others, she created huge images of flowers, often in extreme closeup. Removed from their context and proper scale, these images of calla lilies, irises, and roses often appear almost completely abstract, although with their delicate folds, hollows, and protuberant stamens many appear to have a sexual meaning. In common with other artists associated with Stieglitz, such as Charles Sheeler (1883–1965) and Charles Demuth (1883–1935), O'Keeffe also painted the massive structures that were transforming the city skyline in the twenties. In works such as *Radiator Building, Night, New York, 1927* (1927) and *The Shelton Hotel, New York, No. 1* (1926) she produced some of the most iconic images of the era's skyscrapers.

From 1929 O'Keeffe made regular visits to the artists' colony in Taos, New Mexico, at the invitation of art patron Mabel Dodge Luhan (1879–1962). From then on desert landscape became a central theme in O'Keeffe's art. Stieglitz died in 1946, and three years later O'Keeffe settled in New Mexico. She remained a prolific painter until 1971, when she became partially blind. Her highly original work and achievement as a woman, in an era when women had only just won the right to vote, made her one of the most popular artists of the 20th century.

SEE ALSO:

Art • Design • Modernism • Painting • Photography • Stieglitz, Alfred

OLYMPIC GAMES

The United States dominated the summer Olympic Games during the 1920s. American sportsmen and women won 247 medals out of a total of 986 in all three games—the Belgium Olympics in 1920, the Paris Olympics in 1924, and the Amsterdam Olympics in 1928.

The modern Olympic Games, which began in 1896 but were not held in 1916 owing to World War I (1914–1918), were awarded to Antwerp in 1920 in recognition of the heroism of the Belgian people and the devastation of Belgium by the German armed forces. The Olympic movement was controlled by Allied countries, and the defeated Central Powers—Germany, Austria, Hungary, Bulgaria, and Turkey—were not invited to take part. Russia, caught up in an ideological conflict with the capitalist West, did not send competitors.

Throughout the 1920s the Olympics remained chiefly a competition for North America, Europe, and the dominions of the British Empire (Canada, Australia, New Zealand, and South Africa). There were exceptions, but not very successful ones. From Asia Japan won two gold medals, four silver, and two bronze over the decade; India won one gold. From Latin America Argentina won three golds, three silver, and one bronze (all in 1928); Uruguay won two golds; Brazil one gold, a silver, and a bronze; and Haiti one silver and a bronze. From Africa (excluding South Africa) Egypt won two golds, a silver, and a bronze (all in 1928). In 1928 the Philippines won a bronze.

The shattered European economy meant that the 1920 Olympics were a low-key affair. They were not impressively organized, nor was the level of competition much admired. The games grew in strength thereafter. Paris in 1924 attracted just under 3,000 competitors from 44 countries (easily surpassing the 1920 entry of 29), and four years later the "Geneva spirit" of reconciliation in international diplomacy was extended to sports. Germany and the other defeated nations of 1918 returned to the Olympic fold. The impact was immediate. At Amsterdam in 1928 Germany finished

One of the first photographs of the Olympic track games in 1924 shows U.S. runner Jackson V. Sholz of New York Athletic Club on his way to winning his heat in the 200 meters in Colombes Stadium in Paris.

THE FLYING FINNS

The last cross-country Olympic race was run at Paris in 1924. It ended in a repeat victory for the matchless Finnish runner Paavo Nurmi (1897–1973), who finished a minute and a half ahead of his compatriot, Vilho Eino "Ville" Ritola (1896–1982). However, the event was a disaster. It took place in sweltering heat on a difficult course that included sections of stone paths overrun with knee-high thistles. Of the 38 runners who started, only 15 completed the course. Nurmi entered the stadium for the final lap looking entirely fresh. In 1924 he won five gold medals. Two days before the cross-country he had astonished everyone by winning both the 1,500 meters and the 5,000 meters—races that were separated by less than two hours. He was also on the Finnish teams that won gold in the 3,000 meters and cross-country team events. Nurmi's performance, which overshadowed Ritola's feat of winning four golds—the 10,000 meters, the 3,000-meter steeplechase, and the two team events—in addition to two silvers, remains the single most impressive achievement in Olympic history. In his overall Olympic career Nurmi, who won the steeplechase once and the 10,000 meters twice, won nine gold medals and three silver. He held 25 world records at various distances, including the record for the mile, which he held from 1923 to 1931. He remains one of the great legends. Ritola won five golds and three silvers, and was twice the record holder at 10,000 meters. Although he never received the fame of Nurmi, he is still considered one of the greats of middle-distance running. Finnish athletes also won the marathon in 1920 and 1924 and the steeplechase in 1924 and 1928, achieving a clean sweep.

The final of the 3,000-meter steeplechase in 1924 in Paris; Ville Ritola is in second place, Paavo Nurmi in sixth. Ritola went on to win the race, while Nurmi took the silver.

U.S. MEDAL HAUL, SUMMER OLYMPICS, 1920–1928

[Figure skating and ice hockey were included in the 1920 games at Antwerp]

Events	Medals Available	Medals Won G	S	B	Total
MEN					
Track	107	13	11	9	33
Field*	90	16	15	14	45
Boxing	72	5	4	4	13
Cross-country	8	0	1	1	2
Cycling	42	0	0	0	0
Diving	24	6	5	4	15
Fencing	36	0	0	2	2
Figure skating**	3	0	0	0	0
Football (Soccer)	3	0	0	0	0
Gymnastics	49	0	0	0	0
Hockey (field)	2	0	0	0	0
Hockey (ice)**	1	0	1	0	1
Modern pentathlon	9	0	0	0	0
Polo	2	0	1	1	2
Rowing	19	7	3	4	14
Rugby	2	2	0	0	2
Shooting	96	18	6	8	32
Swimming	48	13	6	5	24
Tennis	12	2	0	0	2
Tug of war	1	0	0	0	0
Walk	9	0	1	1	2
Water polo	3	0	0	1	1
Weightlifting	45	0	0	0	0
Wrestling (freestyle)	57	6	4	3	13
Wrestling (Gr-Rom)	51	0	0	0	0
Yachting	60	0	0	0	0
*including pentathlon and decathlon		** included in the Antwerp summer games			
Totals	851	88	58	57	203
WOMEN					
Track	7	1	1	0	2
Field	6	0	1	1	2
Diving	18	5	5	3	13
Fencing	6	0	0	0	0
Figure skating	3	0	1	0	1
Gymnastics	1	0	0	0	0
Swimming	33	10	6	6	22
Tennis*	18	2	1	0	3
*including mixed doubles	*mixed events				
Totals	92	18	15	10	43
MEN & WOMEN					
Equestrian	38	0	0	1	1
Figure skating (pairs)	3	0	0	0	0
Totals	43	0	0	1	1
GRAND TOTALS	**986**	**106**	**73**	**68**	**247**

second in the medal table, behind the United States and ahead of America's chief rivals in 1920 and 1924, Finland and Sweden. In 1924 the winter Olympics made their debut, and in 1928 women were allowed to take part in track and field events for the first time. The games were open only to amateurs, as they remained until 1988, and the only controversy arose when some British commentators accused the United States of getting around the amateur rule by providing college sports scholarships.

Growing interest

St. Louis had hosted the games in 1904, but distance from Europe in the days before television meant that the Olympics made little impact on the American people as a whole. Indeed, there were American and European voices calling for the games to be brought to an end. With the exception of Johnny Weissmuller (1904–1984), no American Olympian of the 1920s became a national hero—and he did so only after embarking on a film career as Tarzan in 1932. Yet the United States dominated the Olympics in the 1920s to a degree that it was never able to achieve again. The nation won at least twice as many gold medals as any other country at all three games and overall nearly as many medals as the rest of the world together.

American superiority on the track was demonstrated by the relay teams, who won gold in the 4 x 100-meter relay three times and in the 4 x 400-meters in 1924 and 1928. The star of the 1920 team was Charles Paddock (1900–1943), a flamboyant eccentric loved by photographers for his habit of jumping high into the air about four meters out from the finishing tape. He just missed bringing off the sprint double, being beaten into second place in the 200 meters by his compatriot, Allen Woodring. No other country could match the American hurdlers. Daniel Kinsey won gold in 1924 in the 110-meter event and American athletes won silver and bronze in 1920 and 1928. In the 400-meter hurdles the United States followed a clean sweep of the medals in 1920 with gold and silver in 1924 and silver and bronze in 1928.

Beyond the sprint distances the United States faded. Raymond Barbuti won the 400 meters in 1928, but no American won the 800 meters, 1,500 meters, 5,000 meters, 10,000 meters, marathon, or steeplechase. The distance races belonged to the great Finnish runners, Paavo Nurmi and Ville Ritola (*see box on p. 103*). The 1920s thus set a pattern that has been maintained ever since: America powerful in the sprints and comparatively disappointing in middle-distance and distance events.

In field events Americans won exactly half the medals on offer over the three Olympics of the decade—the gold and silver in the high jump on each occasion, all but one of the bronzes in the pole vault, and two golds in the long jump, shot put, discus, and hammer. Harold Osborn (1899–1975) achieved a rare double, winning the high jump and the decathlon in 1924. In 1920 Frank Foss won the pole vault by by 39.37cm (15½ in), the biggest margin in Olympic history. The long-jumper, William DeHart Hubbard (1903–1976), a student at the University of Michigan, became the first black athlete to win an individual Olympic gold, in 1924, and the runner-up, Edward Gourdin of the United States, was also an African American. Hubbard may have been lucky. Robert LeGendre, who had failed to be selected for the American long-jump team, set a world record in the event of 7.76 meters while competing in the pentathlon the day before Hubbard won his medal with a leap 32 centimeters shorter. In each of the games the discus was a battle between the United States and Finland. Americans won three golds and two bronzes in the event, Finnish athletes one gold and three silvers. "Bud" Houser, who won gold in 1924 and 1928, also won the shot in Paris—the last competitor to achieve that double.

WINTER GAMES MEDAL TOTALS

1924 Chamonix

	G	S	B
Norway	4	7	6
Finland	4	3	3
Austria	2	1	0
USA	1	2	1
Switzerland	1	0	1
Canada	1	0	0
Sweden	1	0	0
Great Britain	0	1	2
Belgium	0	0	1
France	0	0	1

1928 St. Moritz

	G	S	B
Norway	6	4	5
USA	2	2	2
Sweden	2	2	1
Finland	2	1	1
Canada	1	0	0
France	1	0	0
Austria	0	3	1
Belgium	0	0	1
Czechoslovakia	0	0	1
Germany	0	0	1
Great Britain	0	0	1

Women athletes

Before 1928 women had competed in a number of Olympic events—archery, fencing, figure skating, golf, swimming, tennis, and yachting. The first American woman to win an Olympic title was Margaret Abbott, in golf at the Paris games of 1900. Not until the Amsterdam games were women allowed onto the main stage to compete in five events—the 100 meters, the 800 meters, the 4 x 100-meter relay, the high jump, and the discus. The 100 meters, the first ever Olympic track event for women, was hardly auspicious. There were only six competitors, three of them from Canada, and two of the six were disqualified for false starts. The winner, Elizabeth Robinson of the United States in a time of 12.2 seconds, had raced competitively only three times before.

The major talking point of the 1928 games was the women's 800-meter race, at the end of which several of the runners collapsed in exhaustion. Antifeminists seized on the opportunity handed to them and had the event banned. A limit of 200 meters was put on women's events. The president of the International Olympic Committee, the Comte de Baillet-Latour, went so far as to call for a return to all-male Olympics. He failed. In 1932 two new women's events—the 80-meter hurdles and the javelin—were added to the Olympic program.

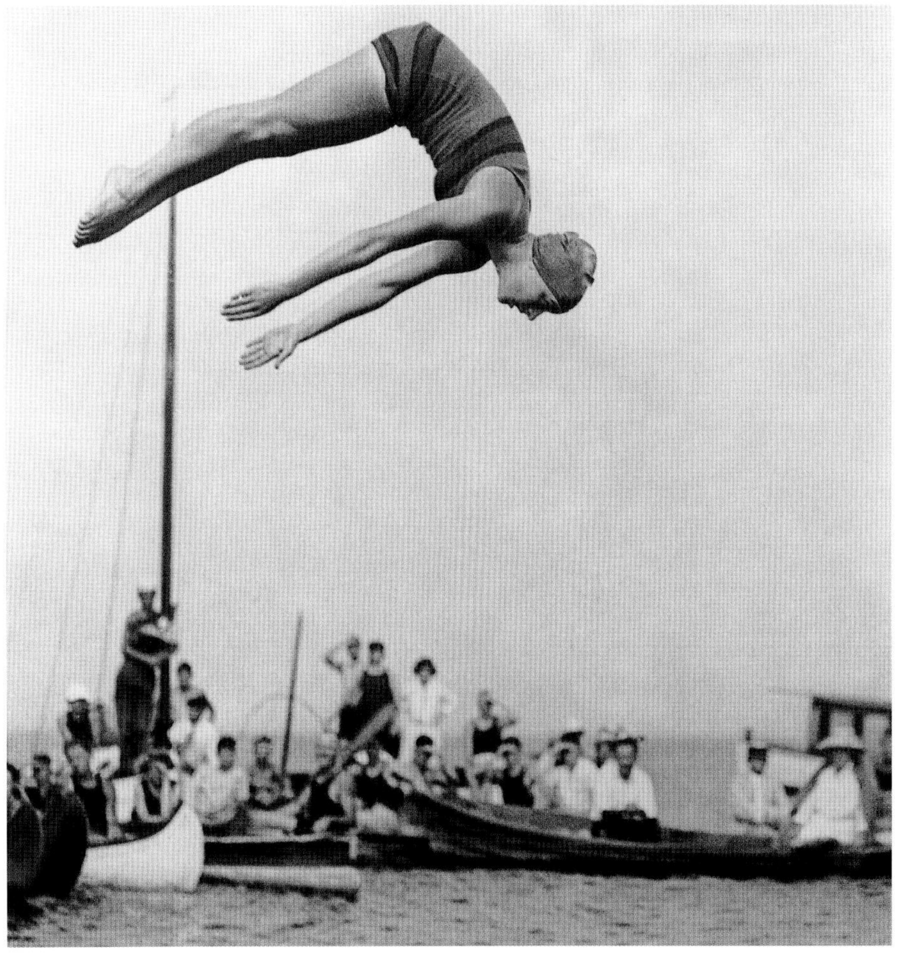

Aileen Riggin, the Olympic diving champion, at the aquatic carnival of the Huguenot Boat Club in New Rochelle, New York, in 1922. She won the gold medal in springboard diving at the 1920 Olympics aged just 14.

In the pool American men and women were dominant, winning 82 medals against the rest of the world's total of 89. In 1920 the women swept all the medals in the individual events and took gold in the relay. The men, too, finished one-two-three in the blue-ribbon event, the 100-meter freestyle, in 1920 and 1924, and in the backstroke in 1924 and 1928. Johnny Weissmuller, who took gold in the 100 meters in 1924, did the 100-meter and 400-meter freestyle double in 1928. America's women swimmers and divers did remarkably well in 1924, despite being handicapped by their own Olympic committee. Fearful of their charges' moral welfare in a city as notorious as Paris, the committee housed the girls a long distance from the city, making them travel five to six hours to and from the pool each day. Americans won the gold medal in six of the seven events in the pool and swept the board in the two freestyles, the relay, and the springboard diving. Some of the competitors were very young. In 1920 Aileen Riggin (1906–2002), only 4 ft. 7 in. (1.3m) tall and weighing 65 lb. (29kg), won the springboard event at the age of 14, and the silver medal went to another 14-year-old American, Helen Wainwright. Gertrude Ederle (1906–2003), who two years later was to become the first woman to swim the English Channel—infuriating male chauvinists by breaking the record by about two hours—won bronze in Paris in the 100-meter and 400-meter freestyle.

American prowess also came to the fore in shooting; in boxing and rowing Americans could be said to have done no more than hold their own. The featherweight, John Fields, in 1924 became the only boxer under the age of 17 ever to win an Olympic title. Two names appear in the rowing record books with interest added to them by hindsight. John B. Kelly (1889–1960), a Philadelphia industrialist and the father of the actress Grace Kelly, won the single and double sculls in 1920 and the double sculls in 1924. Benjamin Spock (1903–1998), then at Yale, who went on to become the guru of child-rearing in the 1950s and 1960s, rowed in the gold-medal coxed eights for the United States in 1924.

Winter Olympics

Figure skating was scheduled as part of the 1900 summer games in Paris. The competitions never took place, but the campaign for winter sports to be given Olympic status continued, and in 1920 figure skating and ice hockey were included in the summer games at Antwerp. In 1924 an international winter "Sports Week" at Chamonix in France was so successful that it was retroactively recognized as the first winter Olympics (*see box on p. 105*). Four years later St. Moritz, Switzerland, hosted the games, setting a precedent afterward followed for the winter and summer games to be held in different countries (the first North American winter games were at Lake Placid, New York, in 1932). The ice hockey competition was badly one-sided. Canada played eight games in winning the gold in 1924 and 1928, scoring 148 goals and giving up only six. The 33–0 pasting of Switzerland in 1924 remains the largest margin of victory ever. The American Beatrice Loughran won silver in the figure skating in 1924 and bronze in 1928, the year that Norwegian Sonja Henje won the first of three consecutive Olympic titles. Henje was then just 18 years old—she went on to become a leading Hollywood actress in the late 1930s and early 1940s under the name Sonja Henie.

SEE ALSO:

Boxing • Hockey • Sports • Sports, Professionalism & • Tennis • Weissmuller, Johnny

Eugene O'NEILL (1888–1953)

Eugene O'Neill is widely regarded as the founder of modern American drama. Before him most American plays were melodramas or farces, emphasizing plot; O'Neill put characterization rather than action at the heart of the play.

Eugene Gladstone O'Neill was born in New York City on October 16, 1888. His father, James O'Neill, was a matinee idol who starred in *The Count of Monte Cristo*. His acting commitments meant that Eugene's early life was spent living in hotels since the family had no permanent home other than a summer cottage in New London, Connecticut. Eugene's elder brother became an actor, while his younger brother died in infancy. O'Neill's difficult family life provided him with the material for some of his greatest plays.

Before the 1920s O'Neill's life was a mess. He drank heavily, drifting from one unskilled job to another. Following an unsuccessful suicide attempt in 1912, O'Neill spent six months in a sanatorium, where he read widely. By the time he left, he had resolved to become a playwright.

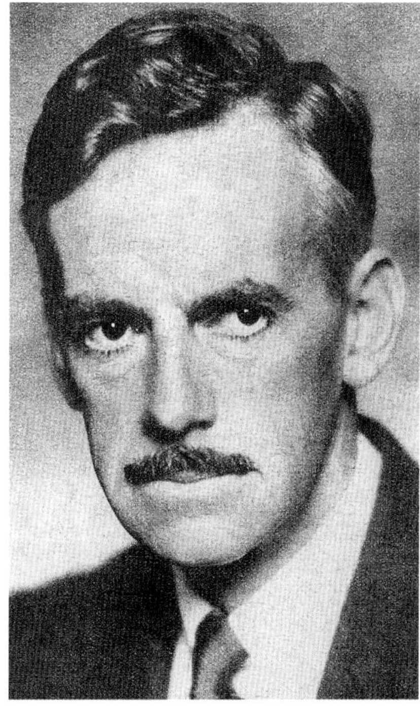

An undated photograph of Eugene O'Neill. Although his plays were rooted in the tradition of the ancient Greek tragedies, his subjects—prostitutes, derelicts, the struggle between God and man—were new to the American stage.

Writing career

O'Neill began with a number of one-act plays that were performed by an experimental theater group based first in Provincetown, Massachusetts, and then in Greenwich Village, New York. In 1918 O'Neill wrote his first four-act play, *Beyond the Horizon*. A tragedy set on a New England farm, the play was a critical and popular success when it appeared on Broadway and won O'Neill the first of his four Pulitzer Prizes in 1920.

Very prolific, O'Neill often wrote several plays at the same time. He continually experimented with different techniques and approaches, not all of which were successful. *The Emperor Jones* (1920) was the first American play to adopt expressionistic techniques in its treatment of race and the legacy of slavery. O'Neill won his second Pulitzer Prize for two plays, *Anna Christie* (1921), which became an instant popular success, and *The Hairy Ape* (1922), about a steamship stoker.

In 1923 O'Neill was awarded the gold medal from the National Institute of Arts and Letters. With a couple of friends he took over the running of two Greenwich Village theaters, putting on experimental work, much of it foreign, that was rarely staged. The same year his morphine-addicted mother died, and his brother returned to drinking. Those family tragedies formed the basis for *Long Day's Journey into Night* (1941).

In 1924 O'Neill moved to Bermuda with his second wife, Agnes Boulton. His only daughter, Oona, was born in 1925. (She later married Charlie Chaplin.) O'Neill already had two sons, one by his first marriage and the second, Shane, by Agnes. After a period of psychoanalysis O'Neill decided to quit drinking because of its negative influence on his writing.

He continued writing lengthy plays, including an ambitious eight-act play, *Marco's Millions* (1925–1928), that retold the adventures of the medieval explorer Marco Polo in China. Shortened to three acts, it was a popular success, as was the nine-act drama *Strange Interlude* (1928), which recounted the events of a woman's life. Running for more than 400 performances, *Strange Interlude* was one of the most successful productions of the twenties and won O'Neill his third Pulitzer Prize. The published text was a bestseller, selling over 100,000 copies.

In 1929 O'Neill divorced Agnes and married the actress Carlotta Monterey. She took care of him for the rest of his life and allowed him to concentrate on his writing. Some of his greatest tragedies were written in the early 1930s, as well as his only comedy, *Ah, Wilderness!* (1933). In 1936 O'Neill was awarded the Nobel Prize in Literature, the only American playwright to be so honored.

Increasing ill health forced O'Neill to stop writing in 1947. Unable to work, he longed for death, which finally came on November 27, 1953.

SEE ALSO:

Greenwich Village • Literature • Off-Broadway • Pulitzer Prize • Theater

OPERA

Opera had been popular in the United States since the 18th century, with companies performing works by great European composers. Patronized by the wealthy, it continued to flourish in the twenties, although it was not until the thirties that a truly American idiom developed.

Opera is a type of drama in which all or most characters sing and act, and in which music constitutes a principal element. It is one of the most complex art forms, requiring composers, librettists (who write the texts), directors, stage designers, and impresarios (who produce or sponsor performances). Opera flourished in the United States during the 18th and 19th centuries.

During the early 18th century English ballad opera, characterized by often satirical stories with spoken dialogue and catchy tunes, became popular. It was followed by French opera at the end of the 18th century, Italian opera in the mid-19th century, and German opera at the end of the 19th century. In the United States in the 19th century there was also a desire to create distinctly national traditions in the arts. To this end composers wrote operas on American themes while retaining romantic European styles. Their works include John Philip Sousa's *El capitán* (1896), Victor Herbert's *Natoma* (1911), Arthur Nevin's *Poia* (1910), and Paul Hastings Allen's *The Last of the Mohicans* (1916). While English ballad opera later developed into the Broadway and Hollywood musical, European opera became associated with the social elite.

American institutions

The founding of the Metropolitan Opera House in New York City in 1883 by a group of wealthy business families, including the Astors and Vanderbilts, brought major changes to opera in the United States. With a secure financial base the Metropolitan Opera could set new standards for productions, but its most successful were the established Italian and German classics, especially the "music drama" of the German composer Richard Wagner. Although the Metropolitan Opera had premiered works by the American composers Victor Herbert (1859–1924) and Walter Damrosch (1862–1950) before 1920, it did not present another American opera until 1927, when it staged *The King's Henchman* by Deems Taylor (1885–1966), with a libretto by the poet Edna St. Vincent Millay. The Academy of Music, which had been founded in New York City in 1847, ceased to stage operas almost as soon as it opened. The Manhattan Opera Company, directed by Oscar Hammerstein (1846–1919), ran for only four years from 1906, when it introduced new works by contemporary French composers such as *Thaïs* by Jules-Emile-Frédéric Massenet in 1907 and *Pelléas et Mélisande* by Claude Debussy in 1908.

The Chicago Opera House, also known as the Auditorium, was designed by the city's leading architect, Louis Sullivan (1856–1924), and opened in 1889. It

The Chicago Civic Opera House pictured shortly after its opening on October 5, 1929. The huge throne-shaped building included office space to help finance the opera. However, as the Depression set in, the opera was forced to close.

A scene from the Theater Guild's production of George Gershwin's *Porgy and Bess*, which opened in 1935. Sometimes known as the "American Folk Opera," *Porgy and Bess* is regarded as a uniquely American variant of opera.

depended on touring companies, which, between 1889 and 1909, performed some 79 operas, most of which were old favorites. The Chicago Grand Opera became its first resident company from 1910. One of the most interesting opera companies in America during the 1920s, the Chicago Grand Opera commissioned *The Love for Three Oranges* (1919) from the Russian composer Sergei Prokofiev (1891–1953), which it premiered in 1921. The soprano Mary Garden (1874–1967) was one of the singing stars who worked with the company in the twenties—she ran it for the 1921–1922 season. The company was reorganized as the Chicago Civic Opera and moved to a specially built theater, the Civic Opera House, in 1929. It opened just days before the stock market crash of October 1929 and was forced to close temporarily in 1932. Other companies that flourished in the 1920s were the Summer Opera Association in Cincinnati, founded in 1920; the San Francisco Opera, founded in 1923; and the Rochester American Opera Company, formed out of the Opera Department of the Eastman School of Music in 1922.

American opera

During the 1920s there was enthusiasm and hopes for "the Great American Opera," but operas that captured specifically American themes in an American idiom did not appear until the 1930s. Most works were in romantic European styles, such as *Rose Marie* (1924) and *The Vagabond King* (1925) by Rudolf Friml and *The Student Prince* (1924), *The Desert Song* (1926), and *The New Moon* (1926) by Sigmund Romberg, or Indian-themed operas such as *The Flaming Arrow* (1922) by Mary Carr Moore.

Virgil Thomson's *Four Saints in Three Acts* (1934), with a libretto by the writer Gertrude Stein, is considered the first genuinely American opera. It was premiered at the Hartford Athenaeum, Connecticut, in 1934 with an all-Negro cast; it moved to Broadway and later to the Chicago Opera House. Virgil Thomson (1896–1989) was a pupil of renowned teacher Nadia Boulanger in Paris; he was inspired by revivalist hymns and successfully incorporated English speech into the musical structure. Marc Blitzstein (1905–1964) was also a pupil of Boulanger; he wrote his own libretto for *The Cradle Will Rock* (1937), in which he introduced ethnic speech and popular music into a story of labor unrest. George Antheil (1900–1959) was a radical composer who wrote *Ballet mécanique* for airplane propellers and car horns in 1927; he searched for "an authentic American style" in his political satire *Transatlantic*, which was performed in Frankfurt in 1930 but did not have an American premiere until 50 years later.

The most successful early American opera was *Porgy and Bess* (1935) by George Gershwin (1898–1937), with a libretto by Dubose Heyward based on his novel *Porgy* (1925). Gershwin, best known for his musicals, experimented with combining jazz and classical music during the 1920s in works such as *Rhapsody in Blue* (1924): *Porgy and Bess* was inspired by jazz and Negro spirituals. It opened in 1935 at the Theater Guild in New York and had 124 performances on Broadway. Although not without its critics, *Porgy and Bess* entered the opera repertoire. Several later musicals have also been described as operas by some critics: Richard Rodgers's *Oklahoma* (1943), Kurt Weill's *Street Scene* (1947), and Leonard Bernstein's *West Side Story* (1957).

While the new mediums of radio, phonograph recordings, and film were a threat to opera during the 1920s, they also helped disseminate it to a wider audience. Deems Taylor's *The King's Henchman* was the first opera to be broadcast on the newly opened CBS network in 1927, leading to the *Saturday Opera*, which has been broadcast continuously since 1931; the first opera to be televised was Verdi's *Otello* in 1948.

SEE ALSO:

Classical Music • Gershwin, George & Ira • Musicals & Musical Theater • Popular Music • Radio & Radio Industry

ORGANIZED CRIME

Prohibition in 1920 made it a crime to produce or sell alcohol, but not to drink it. The people best placed to satisfy the vast public demand for alcohol were those who were already outside the law. Prohibition thus led to a rapid growth of organized crime.

The passage of the Volstead Act in 1919 led to the start of Prohibition the following year and thereby created the largest market for illegal goods that the world had ever seen. Legitimate business concerns could no longer trade in alcohol, but demand for liquor was still great throughout the United States. America's criminals saw an unparalleled business opportunity: They quickly set about filling the gap in the market and exploiting it to the full.

To this end they set up and ran illicit breweries, distilleries, distribution networks, smuggling rings, and clandestine bars known as speakeasies. Recognizing that they could achieve more through cooperation than even the biggest gangs would be able to manage alone, they entered an era of unprecedented cooperation in order to achieve economies of scale—they stopped being disparate groups of hoodlums and turned themselves into businesses.

Although organized crime grew and consolidated during Prohibition, it was not a creation of the 1920s. Since the start of the 20th century ambitious gangsters had developed citywide, or even interstate, criminal networks. One of the earliest and most successful of these gang bosses was Italian immigrant James "Big Jim" Colosimo. Based in Chicago, Colosimo made a fortune from running more than 200 brothels across the Midwest. To keep his business—known as "the Outfit"—supplied with women, he helped establish

At the start of Prohibition federal authorities confiscated vast quantities of liquor and stored them in secured buildings such as this. People who still wanted alcohol were forced to make it themselves or buy it from criminals.

RACKETS

In October 1929 *Harper's Monthly Magazine* published an article by John Gunther that explained the etymology of the word "racket" and described some of the effects that the practice had had on U.S. society:

"The word 'racket' originated in Chicago six or seven years ago. In the neighborhood of 12th and Halstead Streets, in the district of 'alky' peddlers, thugs, and hoodlums, a group of satellites grew up, hanging on the outskirts of the great 'mobs'—the O'Bannion 'mob,' the Genna 'mob,' the Capone 'mob.' These satellites were not often actual killers. They were parasites. With gangster protection, they went into 'business.' At first the word describing them was 'racketer.' In the newspaper stories during 1923 and 1924 the word grew to 'racketeer.' Probably it first referred to the hullabaloo in the 'joints' where gangsters assembled. 'How's the racket?' became, 'What's your racket?'

"Rackets are, of course, as old as the hills. This decade holds no monopoly on extortion. But extortion has rarely reached such a point of development as distinguishes the Chicago rackets today. "

Prohibition was certainly one of the causes. Traffic in alcohol enormously increased the wealth of hoodlums, who became extravagant spendthrifts—leading gangsters of the twenties were buried in silver coffins. The traffic in illegal liquor increased not only the number of professional criminals, but also their power, ruthlessness, and immunity to law, as police and politicians bought into or were paid off by gangs.

Prohibition turned criminals into celebrities. Here Chicago Cub Gabby Hartnett autographs a young fan's baseball while exchanging a few words with the boy's father, Al Capone.

"DUTCH" SCHULTZ

Born in New York in 1902, Arthur Flegenheimer took the name "Dutch" Schultz when he came to prominence as a gangster in the twenties. He began his criminal career as a burglar, but diversified during Prohibition into bootlegging and ownership of breweries and speakeasies and later into protection rackets. His gang fought turf wars in the Bronx and Manhattan. In 1933 Schultz was charged with income-tax fraud after investigation by New York special prosecutor Thomas E. Dewey. Although he was acquitted, in 1935, Schultz tried to enlist the support of rival gangs in a plot to kill Dewey. Instead, they decided to kill "Dutch" himself. Schultz was gunned down in a Newark restaurant on October 23, 1935.

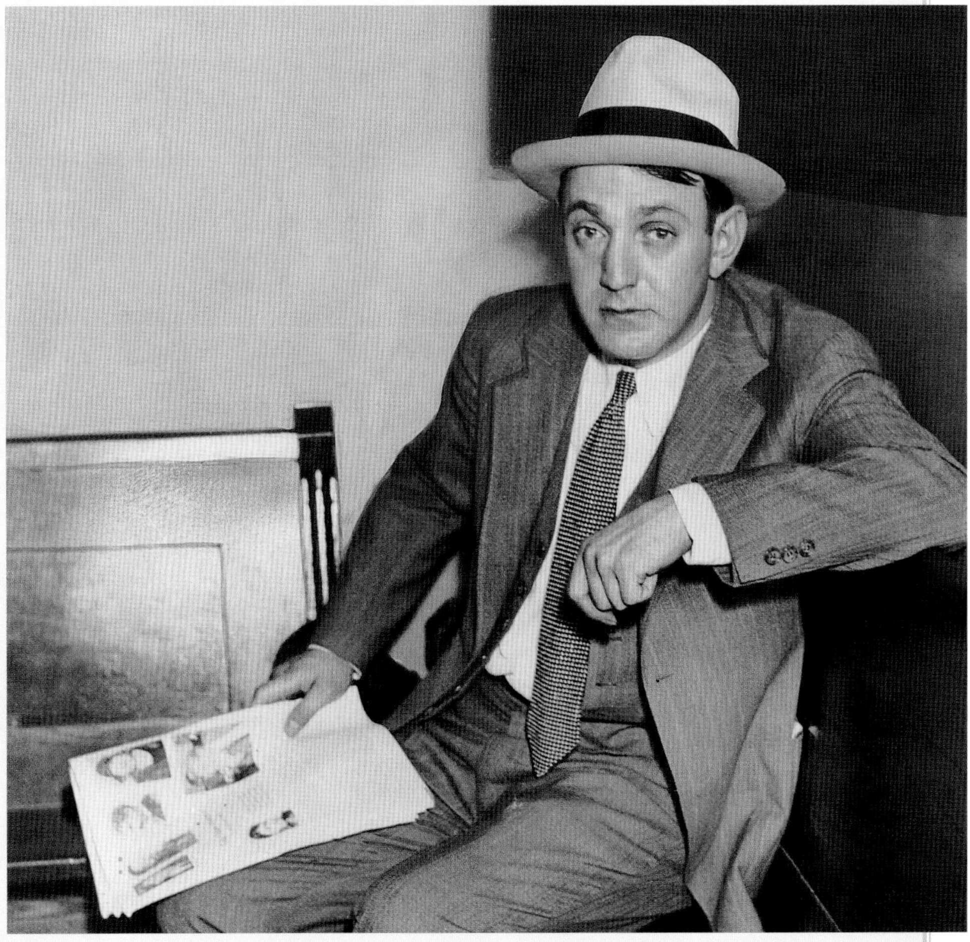

"Dutch"Schultz awaits the verdict in an income-tax fraud case brought against him.

Chicago's White Slave Ring, for which young girls were kidnapped, beaten, raped, and brutalized into prostitution. Colosimo would then sell them to pimps for up to $400.

During the same period gangsters from south Italy—mainly Naples and Sicily—began branching out from New York and Brooklyn, where they had originally settled, to establish themselves in Chicago and other Midwest cities. Many used the cover of the Unione Siciliana. Founded as a charitable organization to help Sicilian immigrants, by 1910 the Unione had been infiltrated by criminals and was being exploited for nefarious ends. In the twenties the Unione Siciliana became one of the main fronts behind which the Sicilian Mafia established itself across the United States. One of the Mafia's first U.S. organizations was the Black Hand Gang. Founded in Manhattan in the late 1890s, the Black Hand specialized in counterfeiting and extortion. Another criminal society from Italy was the Camorra, which had originated in Naples. By 1916 the Camorra extended its influence along much of the U.S. eastern seaboard, although in the twenties it was largely eclipsed by the Mafia.

Other ethnic gangs

Both the Black Hand and the Camorra drew their membership from Italian immigrants and depended for their survival on the close-knit nature of their community. Italians were not the only ethnic group to embrace organized crime, however. There were many Irish and Jewish gangs. The most notorious of the latter was led by Edward "Monk" Eastman. At the height of its influence the Eastman Gang had some 1,200 members and dominated the crime and street life of Manhattan's Lower East Side. The Eastmans were so powerful that in 1903 they were able to start one of the biggest gun battles in New York history without fear of arrest. A rival gang, the Five Points, had held up a gambling hall run by the Eastmans. A gunfight ensued and spread along 2 miles of Rivington Street. For an hour the battle went on, intensifying after the Gophers, a prominent Irish gang, joined in and 500 police arrived to restore order. The Rivington Street battle left three dead and seven wounded.

The gangs could not have got away with such behavior without the protection of corrupt New York politicians: There had been collusion between City Hall and the underworld since the 19th century. The gangs used threats and inducements to mobilize electoral support in their neighborhoods for the most malleable candidates; once elected, the politicians returned the favor by guaranteeing the gangs protection from the law.

City politicians became accustomed to taking bribes; so, too, did many civic officials and policemen. At the start of Prohibition, when the gangs began to make huge profits, the politicians running Chicago and New York, the two largest U.S. cities, were happy to take an even bigger share of the spoils. While they welcomed the material benefits, however, they failed to foresee that by accepting them they would increase the power of the gangs. By the mid-1920s the criminals had earned so much from bootlegging and become so well connected through superficially legitimate front organizations such as the Unione Siciliana that they were no longer just hoodlums holding sway over a few city blocks but bigtime mobsters who controlled whole districts and even, in some cases, entire cities.

Many of the politicians and police officers who should have been in a position to uphold the law and limit the growth of crime were fatally compromised by their own corruption and powerless to control the criminals. The gang leaders soon began to use their freedom to legitimize themselves and their business activities.

Racketeers

From the mid-1920s the campaign to repeal the Eighteenth Amendment and end Prohibition gathered popular support and political momentum. Many gangsters who had grown rich on bootleg liquor now realized that Prohibition could not last forever, and that they would have to diversify to survive. In order to do this, they began to use their wealth and aptitude for violence to move in on legitimate businesses. The "rackets," as they became known, were a form of extortion (*see box on p. 111*). Mobsters infiltrated existing trade associations and labor unions or founded new ones, and threatened members, who paid the gangsters protection money. In order to recoup their losses, the unions increased the cost of membership. Competitors outside the racket were either shut down by violence or intimidated into joining. The rackets became so successful that by 1929 Chicago alone had up to 90 in operation. Antiracketeering groups estimated that the extortioners cost the people of Chicago up to $136 million a year. Few industries or services in the city were free from interference. One of the biggest rackets controlled the city's laundries and made the mobsters $20,000 a week. Three separate mobs ran the laundries as well as their retailers and the delivery drivers. The gangsters' hold was so strong that when an independent group tried to set up business in 1928, they could do so only under the protection of crime boss Al Capone and his new enterprise, Sanitary Cleaning Shops Inc.

The violence of the gangs

Criminal gangs could not control their organizations without violence. The mobs relied on thuggery and intimidation to hold onto their rackets and keep their share of the bootleg market. If threats, beatings, or mutilations failed to work, then they resorted to contract killings. According to contemporary accounts in the twenties, the going rate for a "hit," or a "one-way ride"—both euphemisms for murder—could be as little as $50. The higher the public profile of the target, the more expensive the cost of the killing: The life of a journalist might be worth $1,000, while the cost of murdering a businessman or a city official might be as much as

Vincent "Mad Dog" Coll attracts a crowd of spectators as he is brought in for questioning by New York City police. Coll was hired by Salvatore Maranzano to kill Lucky Luciano, but killed Maranzano instead. He was never charged.

JOHNNY TORRIO

Johnny Torrio came to New York from Naples, Italy, in 1884 at age two. In 1904 he became leader of the James Street Boys, whom he amalgamated with the Five Points Gang. In 1909 "Big Jim" Colosimo hired him to run his brothels and gambling operations in Chicago. Ten years later Torrio brought his old friend Al Capone from New York to manage one of the brothels and, in 1920, had either him or Frankie Yale murder Colosimo. Torrio took over Colosimo's empire and during Prohibition expanded it into bootlegging and casinos. In 1925 Torrio handed over the business to Capone and invested in real estate. Torrio was a director of the national crime syndicate formed in 1934 by Lucky Luciano. In 1941 Torrio semiretired. He died of a heart attack in the chair of a New York barbershop in 1957.

$10,000. Everyone had a price. The mobs running racketeering operations also specialized in destroying property. Businesses unwilling to sign up to this extortion had their properties destroyed by arson attacks. The mobs also used bombs. In Chicago throughout the twenties there were on average 50 bombings a year; the number peaked in 1928, when there were 116 reported bomb attacks. A "black-powder" (gunpowder) bomb cost around $100, while $1,000 could provide a gangster with a bomb made of dynamite.

Gangland attacks were often carried out in broad daylight, and no matter how public they were, law officers seemed either unwilling or unable to stop them. One of the most dramatic incidents took place on September 20, 1926, during one of the frequent "wars" between the Outfit, now run by Al Capone, and the Northsiders. Outside Capone's headquarters at the Hawthorne Hotel in Cicero, Illinois, a small town outside Chicago, a convoy of eight limousines slowly drew up, and gunmen inside unleashed more than 1,000 rounds of machine-gun fire into the hotel, killing Capone's bodyguard and blinding an innocent bystander.

Political power

The gangsters, spotting another weakness in society they could exploit, became hungry for political power. On Chicago's North Side officials and aldermen of the 42nd and 43rd Wards were appointed and controlled by Dion O'Bannion, boss of the Northsiders. There were still superficially democratic elections, but for years O'Bannion got the result he wanted by intimidating opposition candidates and fixing the vote. A popular song of the period featured the lyric: "Who holds the 42nd and 43rd Wards?/O'Bannion in his pistol pockets."

Gradually gangster control of politics extended beyond Chicago's city limits. In 1924, when the election of a new mayor of Chicago heralded a crackdown by the police department, Johnny Torrio (*see box above*), boss of the Outfit and the man who would eventually hand over the gang to Al Capone, moved his operation out of downtown and took over Cicero. To do that, Torrio fixed the town's mayoral

"LUCKY" LUCIANO

Salvatore Lucania (1897–1962) immigrated with his parents from Sicily to New York in 1906. He was a criminal from a young age—his early specialties included shoplifting, mugging, and extortion—and in 1916 he spent six months in jail for selling heroin. In 1925 he became chief lieutenant to rising crime boss Joe Masseria. The nickname "Lucky"—originally acquired from his skill at cards—was reinforced after he became one of the very few gangsters to survive a "one-way ride." In October 1929 he was bundled into a car by four men who beat him, stabbed him with an ice pick, cut his throat, and left him for dead on a Staten Island beach. Shortly after recovering from this attack, he changed his name to Luciano. In 1931 Luciano organized the killing of Masseria and shortly afterward emerged as the top syndicate leader in the United States, with more power than any boss before him.

Lucky Luciano in 1935, around the time he was convicted of extortion and sent to prison; he was released in 1945.

election, putting 250 thugs on the streets to intimidate voters and thus make sure that his candidate won.

Syndication

It was Torrio who, in 1921, first had the idea of consolidating this power by organizing Chicago's gangs into a crime syndicate. His objective was to put an end to intergang warfare and increase profits by dividing up Chicago among the gangs and assigning to each a clearly demarcated territory. Torrio was in a strong position to do this because his Outfit was the oldest and most powerful gang in the city, having been founded by "Big Jim" Colosimo decades earlier to run vice operations. Torrio, Colosimo's lieutenant, had taken over after his boss had been gunned down in his own cafe in May 1921. It was a killing that Torrio had set up.

Under Torrio's plan for the syndicate the city was to be divided into eight territories. The largest would belong to the Outfit and would include the downtown area and the South Side. O'Bannion's gang would take the North Side, while the six Italian Genna Brothers would control Little Italy and Southwest Chicago. Other gangs would run the West Side, the docklands, and the suburbs. There would not be a single block in or around Chicago where crime was not run by a member of the syndicate.

Torrio made it clear, however, that the syndicate would be his organization. As the city boss, he expected the gangs to pay him a fee for their territories and a percentage of all their earnings. Anyone who objected would be faced with war. This was organization by force, and at first all the gangs agreed. Yet getting violent criminals to cooperate, even when to do so was in their best interests, proved impossible. There was too much money in bootlegging, and the gangs were greedy: they were always finding new reasons to eliminate competitors.

In May 1924, for example, O'Bannion's mob hijacked 2,000 barrels of whiskey, with a value of $1 million, from one of Torrio's warehouses, while the Genna Brothers moved into the North Side, undercutting the price of O'Bannion's bootleg liquor with their own. On November 10, 1924 Dion O'Bannion was shot dead inside Schofield's Flower Shop by three men who had arrived, they said, to pick up flowers for a funeral. The Gennas were implicated in the killing, but that did not stop the Northsiders from targeting Johnny Torrio, seriously wounding the Outfit's boss in a drive-by shooting a month later.

The Northsiders' new boss, Earl "Hymie" Weiss, and his lieutenant, George "Bugs" Moran, were held responsible for the Torrio shooting. Weiss was machine-gunned to death on the steps of the Holy Name Cathedral in reprisal on October 11, 1926, after which an uneasy calm settled over Chicago.

For a while Moran, now the boss of the Northsiders, kept the peace. In 1928, however, a dispute between the Outfit's new head, Al Capone, and the local leadership of the Mafia front, the Unione Siciliana, led Moran to take advantage and assist in the killing of two of Capone's close allies. This was to result in February 1929 in Capone's order to finish Moran and the Northsiders for good. What followed became known as the Saint Valentine's Day Massacre (*see box on p. 116*), the most famous gangland bloodbath of all time.

In the presence of the world's press Chicago police officers stage a reenactment of the 1929 St. Valentine's Day massacre for the benefit of a coroner's jury.

Mafia

By 1928 the Mafia had ousted New York's Irish and Jewish gangs and taken control of the city's underworld. Their success sparked a power struggle at the top of the mob that culminated in what became known as the Castellammarese War. At that time one of the leaders of the New York Mafia was Joe "the Boss" Masseria. His position was threatened by younger mobsters from the Castellammarese region of Sicily led by Salvatore Maranzano. Maranzano wanted to extend the Mafia's influence across the United States. Disagreement over the future direction of the organization led to a split that degenerated into a four-year war. The Castellammarese War caused the murders of at least 60 mobsters across the country. It ended only when Masseria himself was shot dead in a Coney Island restaurant in April 1931. The execution was set up by Charlie "Lucky" Luciano (*see box on p. 114*), a former associate of Masseria who changed sides to support Manzano.

After Masseria's death Manzano took over the leadership of the Mafia in New York and seized the opportunity to stamp his mark on the organization. His ambition was to take control of the entire setup and become the "*capo di tutti capi*" ("boss of all bosses"). To this end, in the summer of 1931 he called a special meeting in New York of Mafia bosses from all over the United States. Some 500 mobsters are believed to have gathered to hear Manzano's new plan. He proposed the establishment of five "families," each with its own boss, or *capo*, who would report directly to him. Like Johnny Torrio's earlier scheme in Chicago, the new syndicate was to be founded on mutual security, a greater assured share of the profits, and certain retribution and war if anyone stepped out of line.

THE ST. VALENTINE'S DAY MASSACRE

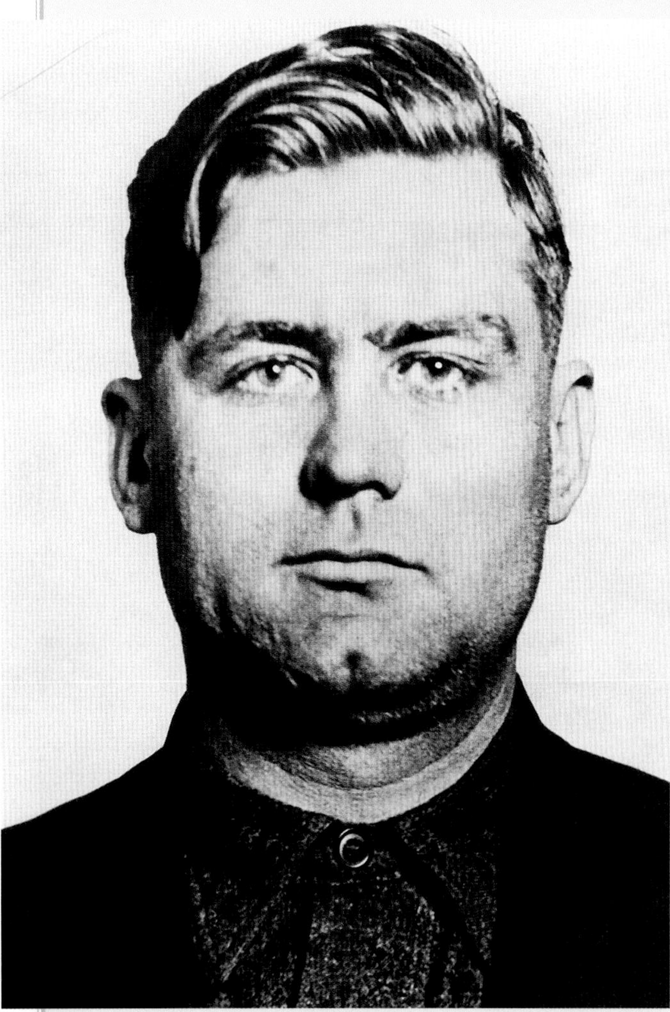

After the death of his leading henchmen "Bugs" Moran lost much of his power as a gangleader and drifted into bank robbery. He died in prison in 1957.

On the morning of February 14, St. Valentine's Day, 1929, seven unarmed men—six of them members of "Bugs" Moran's gang—were shot dead in cold blood against the back wall of the former S-M-C Garage building at 2122 North Clark Street, Chicago. Even in a city used to brutality—there had been nearly 400 gang-related killings the previous year—the massacre on Clark Street caused shock and outrage. The authorities were particularly worried that eyewitnesses reported seeing two policemen enter the building immediately before the shootings. The killers had vanished, however, and the identity of the man who had ordered the "hit" remained a mystery, although Moran, himself an intended victim, was in no doubt and told the press: "Only Capone kills guys like that."

The men who carried out the St. Valentine's Day massacre were never identified or caught, although they were thought to have been recruited from Detroit, St. Louis, and other Midwestern cities in order to avoid connecting Capone with the killings. Capone remained the chief suspect, however. The day after the massacre Chicago police commissioner William Russell told the *New York Times*: "It's a war to the finish. I've never known of a challenge like this—the killers dressed as policemen—but now the challenge has been accepted. We're going to make this the knell of gangdom in Chicago." Russell had taken bribes from gangsters, so his words were greeted with skepticism. More dangerous for Capone was a deputation of Chicago businessmen who went to President Herbert Hoover demanding federal action. As a result, Prohibition enforcement agent Eliot Ness was dispatched to Chicago, where he led a campaign to bring Capone to trial. In 1931 it succeeded: Capone was sentenced to 11 years in jail. Although he was convicted of income-tax evasion, rather than any of the gangland crimes for which he was widely held to be responsible, the authorities had achieved their main objective of getting Capone off the streets.

The people of Chicago turn out to watch the funeral of gangster Angelo Genna, murdered by "Bugs" Moran in 1925. The cortege included a brass band and 30 carloads of flowers.

Manzano became *capo di tutti capi* after the New York meeting, but his hold on power did not last the year. "Lucky" Luciano discovered that Manzano was going to secure his position by ordering the deaths of many of those who had helped him to power. Realizing his life was in the balance, Luciano acted first. Four of his men, posing as tax inspectors, called at Manzano's office on September 10, 1931. They disarmed his bodyguards, walked in on Manzano, and shot him to death. This was the first of 40 gangland killings across the United States that day. By September 11 few of Manzano's allies were left alive.

Luciano had removed the immediate threat to himself, but the Five Families remained, and in the 1930s they became the center of a national crime syndicate run not by a single all-powerful boss—their business interests were now too big and too diverse for that—but by "the Commission," a joint grouping established by Luciano after Manzano's death of all the leading Mafia organizations.

SEE ALSO:

Capone, Al • Crime & Punishment • Law & Order • Politics, Local • Prohibition • St.Valentine's Day Massacre

PAINTING

In the 1920s painting in the United States started to embrace urbanization, representing scenes of city life and modern architecture. Other developments, particularly in photography, also influenced a new generation of painters, such as Georgia O'Keeffe and Charles Sheeler.

Painting in 1920s America drew on and expressed many recent developments and changes in art and society, as well as the long-standing desire to create an American style. Most painting of the era was representational, with a basis in the physical appearances of the world, as opposed to the abstract qualities of color, form, and line that were being explored by avant-garde artists in Europe.

However, the paintings that became most closely associated with the decade in America are urban and industrial scenes in a highly polished style that became known as "precisionist." The photographer, gallery owner, and advocate of modern art Alfred Stieglitz (1864–1946) was the driving force behind this U.S. modernism, and the painters Charles Sheeler (1883–1965), Georgia O'Keeffe (1887–1986), and Charles Demuth (1883–1935) were its greatest exponents.

Dempsey and Firpo by George Bellows, painted in 1924. Bellows specialized in portraying scenes from everyday life and used dark tones and a limited range of colors to mirror the tough conditions of urban America in the 1920s.

STUART DAVIS

Stuart Davis (1894–1964) continued to experiment with avant-garde ideas and abstraction when most other modernist painters returned to representational art after World War I (1914–1918). He was born in Philadelphia, Pennsylvania. His mother was a sculptor, and his father was the art director of a Philadelphia newspaper that often gave work to a number of the Ashcan artists early in their careers. After his family moved to New York, Davis studied painting under Robert Henri, on his example devoting himself to dark, realistic depictions of city life.

The Armory Show (*see box on p. 120*) was a revelation to Davis. He himself had five watercolors included in the exhibition, but what struck him most was the daring new European art on show, particularly the paintings of Paul Gauguin, Vincent Van Gogh, Henri Matisse, and the cubists. From this time onward, Davis dedicated himself to exploring the formal qualities of painting while trying to create a specifically American art. Attracted to cubist paintings and collages that incorporated lettering, he produced paintings such as *Lucky Strike* (1921) and *Sweet Caporal* (1922) that look like collages and incorporate the packaging and ads that proliferated in the consumer boom of twenties America. In 1927 he embarked on a series of his most radically abstract works. *Egg Beater No. I* (1927) is typical, the result of much reworking to pare down a still life to what appears to be an arrangement of flat, abstract shapes, rather like paper cutouts. He continued to develop this style after a trip to Paris in 1928. In *Swing Landscape* (1938), a mural commissioned by the Federal Art Project, he produced an exuberant, brightly colored work that combines imagery of the port of New York with the visual equivalent of the vibrancy and fun of jazz. Davis was an important link between early American modernism and modern art movements after World War II, particularly abstract expressionism and pop art.

American style and subject matter

Ever since the American Revolution (1775–1783) writers and artists had aimed to create work that defined and celebrated the values of their new nation. Benjamin West (1738–1820) had already mythologized the history of America in paintings that drew on the traditions of Western art but updated them. From the early 19th century painters in particular looked to the continent's vast expanses of untamed wilderness to find a specifically American subject. Painters such as Thomas Cole (1801–1848), Asher B. Durand (1796–1886), Albert Bierstadt (1830–1902), and Frederick Edwin Church (1826–1900) celebrated awe-inspiring scenery that offered the promise of cultivation and prosperity while also embodying God's presence. Others, such as George Caleb Bingham (1811–1879), Winslow Homer (1836–1910), and Frederic Remington (1861–1909), celebrated the lives of ordinary Americans from fur traders to cowboys, encapsulating in these subjects the pioneering spirit that underlay the new nation. The National Academy of Design (established in 1824) provided a national framework for art education and exhibitions, and the American-Art Union (created in 1844) supported a national art, based on a genuinely American subject matter and a straightforward, realistic style—free from the complex literary and historical allusions typical of academic European painting.

In the early years of the 20th century the quest for an authentically American style led some artists to turn their attention to the nation's burgeoning cities. Rapid industrialization in the second half of the 19th century had seen the economy shift away from agriculture as cities expanded and immigrants poured in to work in factories. New York in particular rose to prominence in the nation's economic and cultural life. Painters such as Robert Henri (1865–1929), George Luks (1867–1933), John Sloan (1871–1951), and George Bellows (1882–1925) began to portray the lives of its working-class masses. They depicted crowded streets, markets, tenements, bars, and boxing matches in vigorously executed paintings whose dark tones and limited range of colors often mirrored the grime of the city. Following an exhibition of such artists at the Macbeth Gallery in New York in 1908, conservative critics referred to them disparagingly as the Ashcan school, the Black Gang, and the Apostles of the Ugly. Their gritty realism and subject matter challenged traditional ideas of art as a vehicle for beauty. Their paintings reported rather than celebrated life in America. In their challenge to convention and the introduction of the city as subject matter the so-called Ashcan artists set the scene for developments in the twenties.

Modern style and abstraction

Painting in the early decades of the 20th century was also inspired by stylistic developments taking place in Europe, particularly Paris. Toward the end of the 19th century, prompted in part by the rise of photography, some avant-garde European artists and writers had begun to question the nature of painting: Should it seek to imitate the appearance of the world—as Western art had since the Renaissance—or should it explore the formal elements of the painting itself: color, line, and form? A shift in emphasis from representational to formal abstract values is seen from the 1880s in the paintings of Paul Cézanne (1839–1906), Paul Gauguin (1848–1903), Vincent Van Gogh (1853–1890), and Georges Seurat (1859–1891)—artists now termed post-impressionists. In the early 20th century Henri Matisse (1869–1954) and a group of painters known as the fauves ("wild beasts") exploited the abstract qualities of color, while Georges Braque (1882–1963) and Pablo Picasso (1881–1973) explored new ideas about pictorial space and structure in a style known as cubism.

THE ARMORY SHOW

The Armory Show (1913), or International Exhibition of Modern Art, was the single most significant event in the development of modern art in the United States. It was organized by the newly formed Association of American Painters and Sculptors, whose president, Arthur B. Davies (1862–1928), was largely responsible for its conception and the selection of exhibits. It was staged first in the huge 69th Infantry Regiment Armory in New York City before touring to Chicago and Boston. With around 1,300 exhibits, the show was divided into two parts, one presenting recent and contemporary American art, the other charting the emergence of modern art in Europe. The American section included the work of the Ashcan school as well as Marsden Hartley, John Marin, Charles Sheeler, Joseph Stella, and two American artists working in Paris, Stanton Macdonald Wright and Morgan Russell. However, much of their work looked conservative alongside the daring formal experiments of the European artists on show. About a third of the exhibits were European, tracing developments mainly in French art from the mid-19th century, including work by Eugène Delacroix (1798–1863), the impressionists, postimpressionists, fauves, and cubists.

Most critics and reviewers were shocked and indignant at the work they saw—particularly the European work—outraged at paintings and sculpture that rebelled against accepted ideas of what constituted art. A cubist painting by Marcel Duchamp, *Nude Descending a Staircase, No. 2*, was singled out for particular vilification and was popularly described as "an explosion in a shingle factory." The barrage of hostile newspaper reviews helped attract visitors to the show: Around a quarter of a million people paid to see it. While most of the public concurred with the critics' judgment, a few new collectors came forward to buy works. This fact, combined with the show's notoriety, prepared the ground for the exploration of abstract art later in the century.

The Armory Show in New York presented work by American artists as well as emerging modern art from Europe. This photograph shows the European section.

In the 1910s the progressive ideas and work of these avant-garde European artists influenced American painters who were attracted to Europe to study or live. Arthur Dove (1880–1946), Marsden Hartley (1877–1943), Max Weber (1881–1961), John Marin (1870–1953), and Joseph Stella (1877–1946) were among the most significant of these artists. Dove visited Paris between 1907 and 1909, and back in the United States he became the first American painter to produce abstract paintings. In tune with the traditional reverence of landscape his images drew on and evoked the natural world. Their colors, forms, and lines were inspired by natural objects and scenes but were transformed into abstract arrangements intended to convey the sentiment or mood of nature. Hartley and Weber worked in different directions toward abstraction.

John Marin and Joseph Stella applied the formal experimentation they saw in avant-garde European paintings to representations of the New York cityscape. In watercolors such as *Movement, Fifth Avenue* (1912) Marin conveyed New York's frantic pace and towering buildings using disjointed strokes of color to impart a sense of energy and vitality. Stella's work is more robust but responds to similar stimuli. His *Battle of Lights, Coney Island, Mardi Gras* (1913–1914) is a riot of color and swirling fragmented forms that convey the chaos and exuberance of the famous pleasure park. Both men were inspired by the French painter Robert Delaunay's (1885–1941) experiments in pure color, which showed fragmented views of the Eiffel Tower, and by futurism, an art movement that had originated in Italy in 1909 and aimed to express the modern world by glorifying the machine and the beauty of speed.

Stieglitz and modernism

Of key importance in the promotion of young painters—and of modern art in general—was the wealthy gallery owner and photographer Alfred Stieglitz. In the first three decades of the 20th century he was the driving force behind modernism in America. In 1908 he held the first exhibitions of modern European painting in the United States at his 291 gallery in New York, and in 1909 he organized an exhibition that showcased the paintings of Dove, Weber, Hartley, and Marin among others. However, the event that had the most impact in bringing modern art to the public was the Armory Show of 1913 (*see box opposite*).

By 1917, the year in which the United States entered World War I (1914–1918), the already small market for avant-garde art in the United States had dried up. When the conflict ended, American artists, unlike their European counterparts, returned to predominantly representational art—a notable exception being Stuart Davis (*see box on p. 119*). On one level this trend reflected a general return to conservative values—the "normalcy" stressed by Warren G. Harding in his 1920 presidential campaign. Abstraction had not gained as strong a following in the United States as it had in Europe. Some conservative critics condemned it as alien and anti-American, equating it to the immigrants from southern and eastern Europe who were pouring into the country and—as many people saw it—threatening traditional American values.

Stella began the twenties with *The Voice of the City of New York Interpreted: The Bridge* (1920–1922), a dramatic and somber evocation of Brooklyn Bridge, a feat of engineering that he saw as "the shrine containing all the efforts of the new civilization of America." The equation of

An undated photograph of the American abstract painter Max Weber, who, like many of his contemporaries, was particularly attracted by the progressive ideas and work of avant-garde European artists of the period.

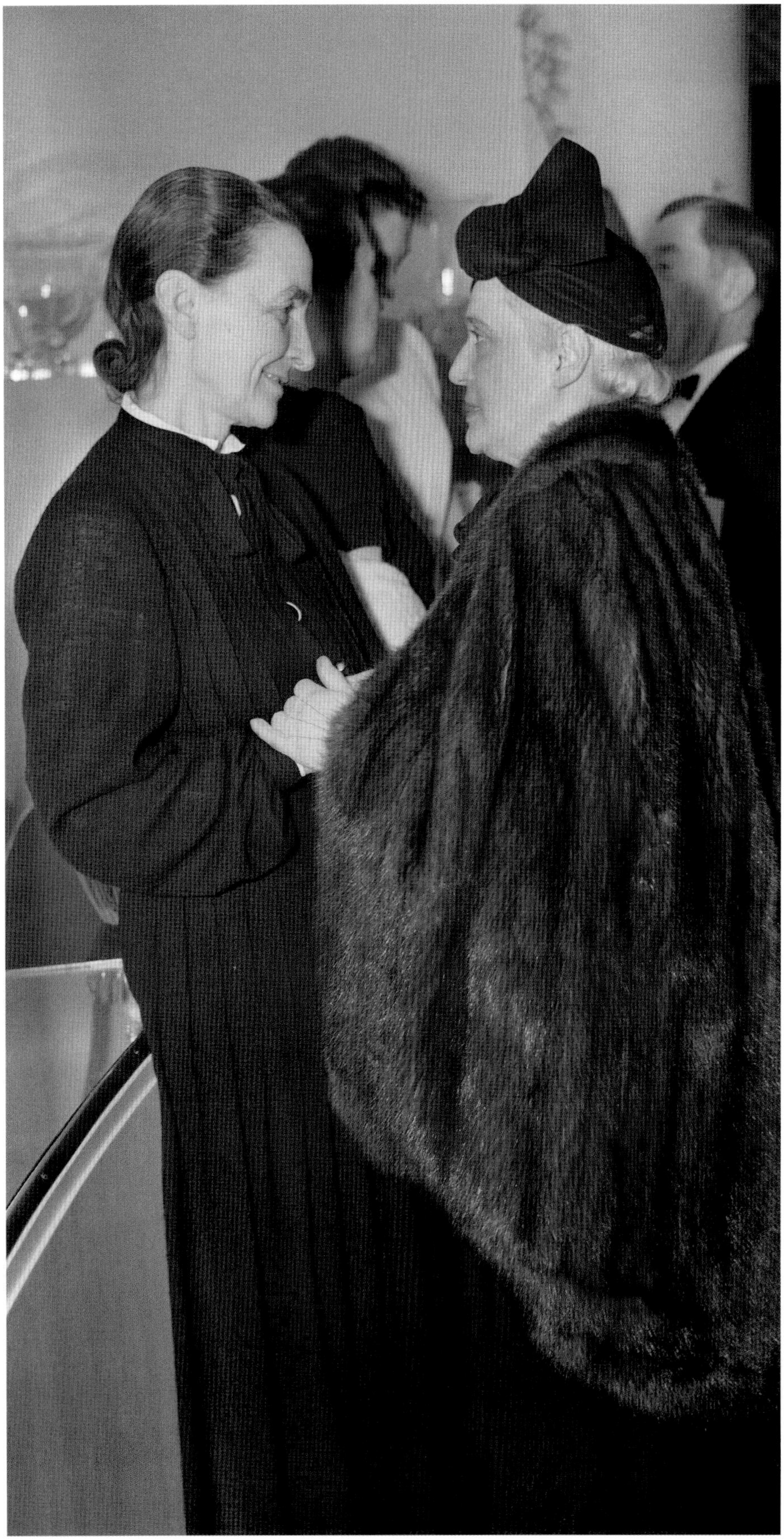

modernity and progress with the machine age was not only an aesthetic idea: It was a reality visible in everyday life. Henry Ford's mass-production lines were making his Model T car available to growing numbers of Americans, manufacturers churned out domestic appliances, the radio brought the world into people's homes, railroads crisscrossed the nation, and airplanes were taking to the skies. In urban architecture modernism was clearly the inspiration of numerous skyscrapers, most famously the Chrysler Building in New York City, which was ornamented with automobile motifs.

Precisionism

Painters such as Charles Sheeler, Georgia O'Keeffe, and Charles Demuth reflected these new realities in their paintings, many of which showed urban and industrial scenes. Unlike the Ashcan artists, they did not paint the bustling life of the city but instead chose towering urban and industrial structures devoid of human presence as their subject matter. Centered around Stieglitz, these progressive artists were not part of a formal group, although similarities in their subject matter and style led some critics to group them together under the label "precisionist"—a term first coined by Sheeler to describe his own work. Their paintings share a smooth, precise style in which paint is applied evenly without visible brush strokes, and in which forms are clearly delineated; often they show brightly lit scenes—all qualities that again set them apart from the Ashcan artists. The style has similarities to graphic art—the illusionistic style used in ads and magazine illustrations—and particularly to photography, which Stieglitz promoted as an art form in its own right.

The link between photography and art is clearly demonstrated in the work of

Georgia O'Keeffe (left) greets one of her collectors, Mrs. Chester Dale, at a preview of an exhibition in New York in 1940. O'Keeffe's own work was greatly influenced by the photography and the ideas of her husband Alfred Stieglitz.

ART AND THE HARLEM RENAISSANCE

In the 1920s black Americans were still largely excluded from political, economic, and cultural institutions. However, the decade witnessed the growth of a new confidence and racial pride among African Americans, which was manifested in a flowering of black creativity centered in the Harlem district of New York City. Many leading black activists, writers, and thinkers, including W.E.B. Dubois (1868–1963), James Weldon Johnson (1871–1938), and Alain Locke (1886–1954), viewed art and culture as essential elements in the promotion of black American identity and the struggle for equality. While the Harlem Renaissance is primarily associated with literature, a number of painters were also linked with the movement, including Jacob Lawrence (1917–2000) and William H. Johnson (1901–1970). Their work appeared as illustrations in journals, magazines, and books, and was also encouraged by award and exhibition programs organized by the William E. Harmon Foundation, a philanthropic organization set up in New York to promote black art. Throughout the twenties, however, black artists and subject matter remained marginalized.

One black painter who set the scene for a sympathetic portrayal of black American life, cutting through the stereotypical images promoted in white culture, was Henry Ossawa Tanner (1859–1937). Tanner had trained at the Pennsylvania Academy of Art under the realist painter Thomas Eakins and continued his studies in Paris, France. Although primarily known for his religious paintings, for which he received international acclaim, in the early 1890s he turned to black American everyday life for his subject matter, producing a number of sensitive studies such as *The Banjo Lesson* (1893).

Of the several artists associated with the Harlem Renaissance, including Palmer Hayden (1890–1973) and Archibald J. Motley, Jr. (1891–1981), Aaron Douglas (1899–1979) is the most significant. After finishing his bachelor's degree at the University of Nebraska in 1922, Douglas taught art for a year before moving to Harlem, where he studied with the German painter and illustrator Winold Reiss (1887–1953). Reiss was interested in Native Americans and African Americans, and portrayed both in his art. In 1924 he produced a series of portraits of key figures in the Harlem Renaissance for *Survey Graphic* magazine and in 1925, with Aaron Douglas, provided illustrations for Alain Locke's anthology of black writing, *The New Negro*.

Douglas was influenced by Reiss's graphic style, in which forms are reduced to flat silhouettes and fragmented shapes, vaguely in the manner of cubism, to create a sense of energy and movement. Douglas developed a similar pared-down style that drew on both African art and modernism to create images expressing the black struggle for political and creative freedom. In his mural *Harriet Tubman* (1931) he used a series of clearly defined silhouettes colored in subtle tones of blue and green to portray the escaped slave of the title as she frees and casts aside the shackles of other slaves. Circular and diagonal rays of light cast a veil-like covering over the image in a manner reminiscent of Charles Demuth's precisionist paintings.

Sheeler, who worked as both a painter and a photographer. His *Church Street, El* (1920), an abstracted aerial view of soaring city buildings, is based on a still from an experimental film (*Mannahatta*, 1921), which he made with the photographer Paul Strand. The painting is semiabstract, reducing the scene to largely unmodulated blocks of brown, ocher, and black. However, through the course of the twenties Sheeler developed a more meticulously detailed style. *Upper Dock* (1929) and *American Landscape* (1930) are typical of his meticulously rendered, brightly lit scenes, which emphasize the geometric structures, underlying factories, and machinery—and often exude a sense of isolation and bleakness. Similar formal qualities can be seen in his photographs, such as the series commissioned from the Ford Motor Company showing their car plant at Dearborn, Michigan (1927).

O'Keeffe's work was also influenced by photography. She lived with Stieglitz from 1918 and married him in 1924; and although she was an exceptionally original artist, she was profoundly affected by his ideas. The extreme closeup format of her flower paintings reflects the influence of photography. So too does the low viewpoint of raking cityscapes such as *Street, New York, 1* (1926) and *The Shelton with Sunspots* (1926); the latter also exploits the glare produced when a camera is pointed into the sun, the suffused white paint, rich yellow blobs, and stylized clouds creating a vaporous film through which the towering skyscraper emerges.

O'Keeffe's works are far more than photography-inspired presentations of their subjects. The extreme closeup views, carefully modulated brushwork, saturated tones and colors, and broad forms confer a semiabstract, poetic quality to her paintings. Early on she was influenced by Arthur Dove, and his ideas on abstraction and symbolism permeate her canvases. Although O'Keeffe created such iconic images of New York skyscrapers as *The Radiator Building—Night, New York, 1927* (1927), she also painted natural landscapes. The best known were produced after 1929 in New Mexico, but she was always drawn to the subject from her earliest, semiabstract watercolors of the late 1910s. In the 1920s her flower paintings were her most popular meditations on nature. Her images of calla lilies, irises, roses, and poppies often blur the conventional distinctions between representation and abstraction, and with their protuberant stamens and soft, enveloping forms, many appear redolent with sexual imagery—an interpretation promoted by Stieglitz but denied by O'Keeffe.

Another leading American exponent of precisionism was painter and illustrator Charles Demuth. He had visited Paris several times in the early 20th century and became particularly interested in cubism. He transmuted the fractured forms of the style in the cityscapes he executed once back in America. In particular, he depicted the industrial structures of Lancaster, Pennsylvania, his home city. With a spare, refined style he conferred a dignity and timelessness to the factories, grain elevators, and water towers he portrayed. *My Egypt* (1927) presents a frontal view of a massive grain elevator, its forms—the silos, chimney, and funnels—flattened and intersected by diagonal shafts, as if of sunlight. The resulting faceted, geometrical shapes and the cool palette of blues, grays, and browns encapsulate Demuth's lyrical reworking of the tenets of cubism.

Demuth also created a series of highly personal "poster portraits," pictures composed of words and motifs associated with the person represented. *The Figure Five in Gold* (1928) is the best known, a tribute to Demuth's friend, the poet William Carlos Williams, based on his poem of the same name. Marsden Hartley had produced similar works in the 1910s, for example, *Iron Cross* (1915), a symbolic tribute to the German officer with whom he was in love. But where Hartley's images were forceful combinations of strident, contrasting colors and tones with freely painted forms, Demuth's were more measured and meticulously worked, with memories of cubism.

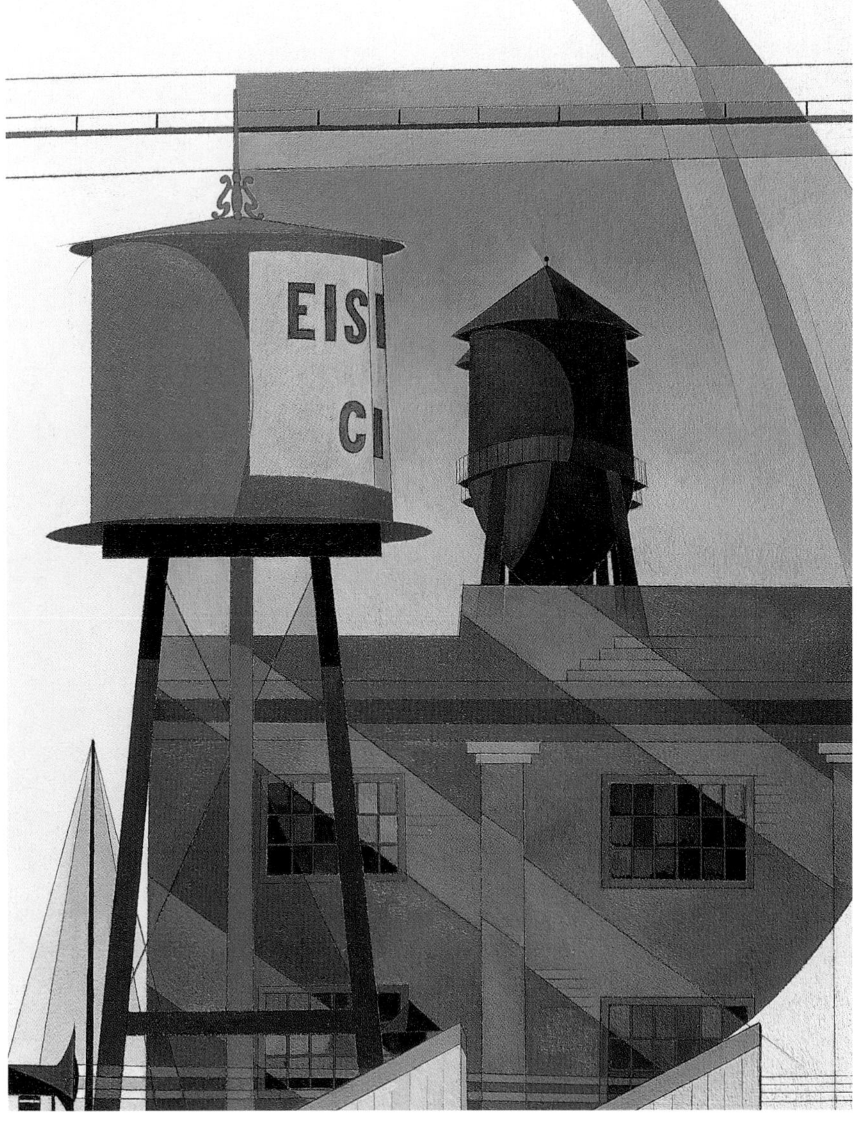

Buildings Abstraction, Lancaster **by Charles Demuth from 1931. Demuth was influenced by cubism and adopted fractured forms when painting American cityscapes. Typically he painted elevators, factories, and water towers.**

American scene painting

Toward the end of the twenties a number of artists began to look to different sources for a genuinely American art. Reacting against the brand of modernism promoted by Stieglitz, some painters demanded a return to a realistic style uninfluenced by modern European art, one that drew on everyday American life for its subject matter. This trend, later labeled American scene painting, encompassed a number of unconnected artists. They included Thomas Hart Benton (1889–1975), Grant Wood (1892–1942), and John Steuart Curry (1897–1946), each of whom came to concentrate in the twenties on scenes of rural life in the different regions of the Midwest from which they came. In work tinged with nostalgia these regionalists—as they came to be known—celebrated ways of life and values that they considered fundamental to American identity. In some senses theirs was an idealized view of the past rather than a realistic record of the present; although a significant proportion of the population still lived in the countryside, farming was in severe recession in the twenties. Benton's *The Lord Is My Shepherd* (1926), Curry's *Baptism in Kansas* (1928), and Wood's iconic *American Gothic* (1930) all in their different ways express reverence and nostalgia for the values and rituals of the hardy rural communities that had shaped the nation's history before industrialization and mass immigration.

Edward Hopper (1882–1967) is another artist who is often described as an American scene painter—a label to which he objected because it grouped him with the regionalists, who presented, he thought, a caricatured view of the United

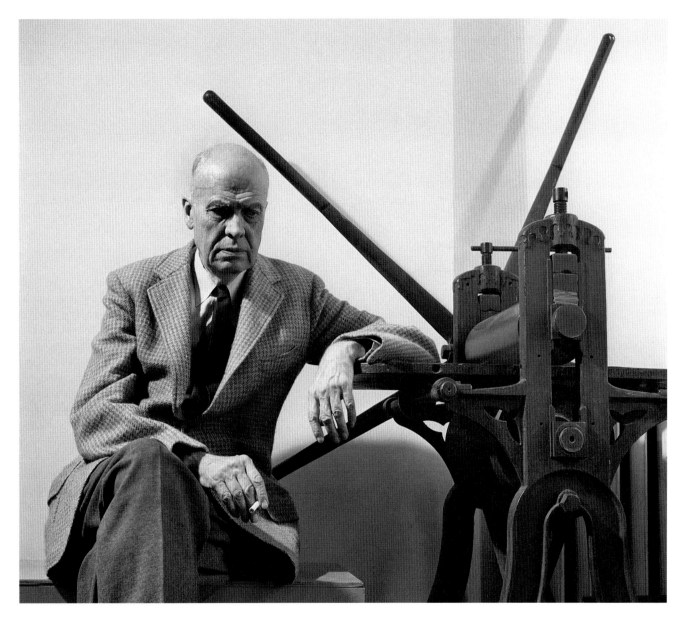

The painter Edward Hopper sitting by a printing press in his Greenwich Village studio in about 1955. Hopper's paintings of solitary figures sitting in bars and cafes are some of the most enduring images from 1920s and 1930s America.

States. Hopper had trained under Robert Henri, and something of his teacher's emphasis on realism pervades his unidealized presentation of the loneliness and isolation of life in small towns and cities across the nation. In paintings such as *Sunday* (1926), *Automat* (1927), and *Chop Suey* (1929) Hopper explores motifs and themes that defined his output. Solitary figures sit lost in introspection, interacting with neither their surroundings nor their fellow human beings.

The work of the regionalists was vigorously promoted during the years of the Great Depression. The artists' patriotic, nostalgic image of American identity provided solace in a time of deep uncertainty and was embraced under the Federal Art Project (1935–1943) of President Franklin D. Roosevelt's New Deal. In the long run, however, it was Hopper's bleak meditations on the isolation of human existence that came to define the disillusionment of the thirties. It took time for the abstract tendencies first experimented with in the 1910s and 1920s to supplant the strong realist tradition in American painting, but the seeds had been sown. In 1929 New York's Museum of Modern Art was founded. However, it was not until the late 1940s that abstraction replaced realism as the dominant trend in American painting, when abstract expressionism made New York the center of the art world.

SEE ALSO:

Art • Harlem Renaissance • Modernism • Photography • O'Keeffe, Georgia • Sculpture • Stieglitz, Alfred

A. Mitchell PALMER (1872–1936)

Politician Alexander Mitchell Palmer might well have become the Democratic presidential nominee in 1920 had he not launched an unprecedented campaign against left-wing organizations and political radicals—the so-called "Palmer Raids."

Palmer was President Woodrow Wilson's (1913–1921) last attorney general. He stands as an example of how quickly the shifting tides of the political current can undo a man's reputation and ruin a once-promising career. Originally the darling of the Democrats and of organized labor, Palmer was odds-on favorite to succeed Woodrow Wilson as the party's next presidential candidate. As a result of his central role in the Red Scare of 1919, however, workers' organizations turned against him, and in 1920 he found that his political career was over.

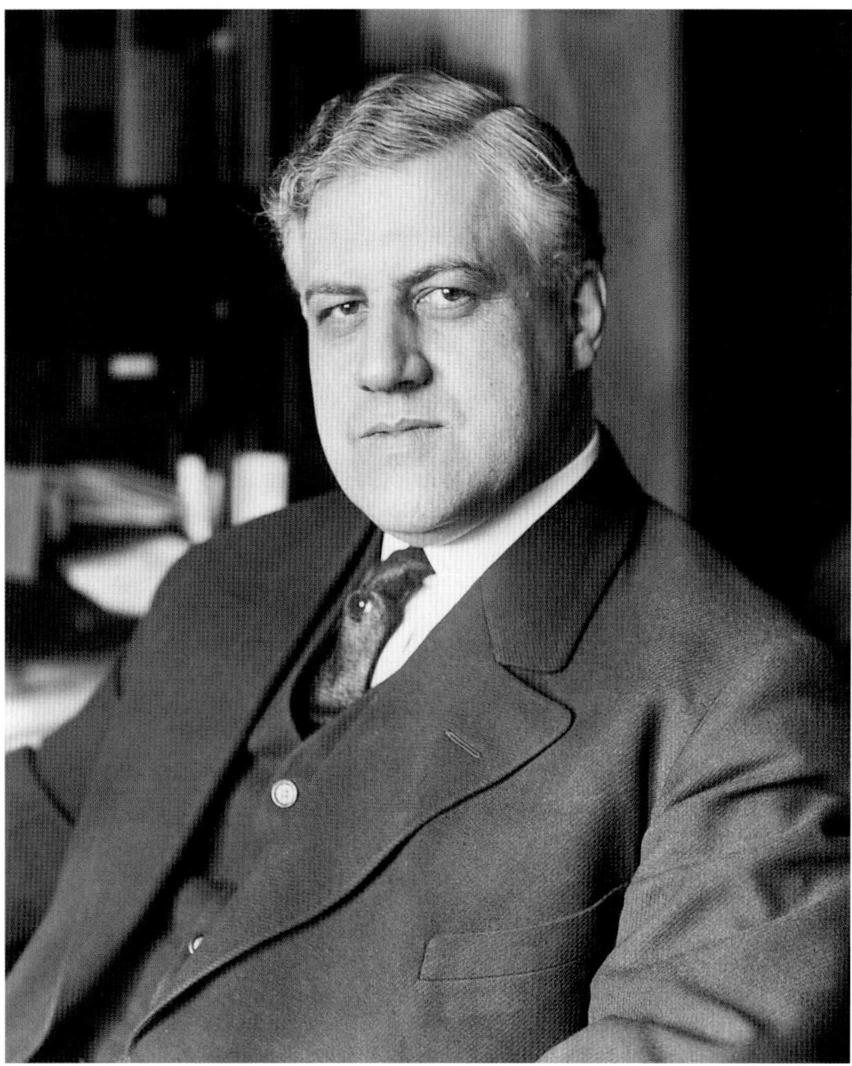

Palmer was born into a well-off Quaker family that ran a lumber business and had long been active in the Pennsylvania Democratic Party. He earned a law degree in 1891, practiced for a while, married into a banking family, and entered politics in 1908, when he was elected in a steel and coal district of Pennsylvania by the highest majority ever recorded in the district. Eloquent, easy-going, and politically smart, he rose quickly in the Democratic Party. He joined Wilson's campaign team in 1912, and the president-elect, apparently not knowing that Palmer was a Pacifist Quaker, invited him to be secretary of war. Palmer turned the invitation down and was appointed chairman of the Executive Committee of the Democratic National Committee.

The appointment to so powerful a position was the mark of how quickly Palmer had won high standing in the Democratic Party. But it was in Congress that he made his national reputation. He supported woman suffrage, and his voting record on labor issues was approved by the American Federation of Labor. Had his bill of 1915 to protect child labor succeeded, it would have been a milestone

A photograph of Palmer from about 1913. During World War I President Wilson put him in charge of controlling the assets of foreign-owned companies, especially German firms, that had operations in the United States.

"PALMER RAIDS"

The "Palmer Raids" lasted from fall 1919 until 1920. In 1919 there were a series of social conflicts, including workers strikes, riots in Chicago, and the introduction of Prohibition. In the summer of the same year there were bombings in eight cities. One of these bombs exploded outside the house of the attorney general, A. Mitchell Palmer, who immediately accused radical groups, such as anarchists, of being responsible. Although it still remains unclear who was responsible for the bomb, it sparked off a severe backlash against radical political and worker organizations. Palmer did much to help encourage the Red Scare and later wrote, "Like a prairie-fire, the blaze of revolution was ... eating its way into the homes of the American workman ... burning up the foundations of society."

Palmer recruited the future head of the FBI, J. Edgar Hoover, as his special assistant and launched the first raids on November 7, 1919—the second anniversary of the Bolshevik Revolution. Large numbers of people were seized, and many were deported to Russia. The following year organizations such as the Industrial Workers of the World (IWW) were raided and ransacked. On January 2 some 5,000 people were arrested in 30 cities and held without trial. Although the vast majority were set free, many critics considered the arrests unconstitutional and unjustified.

in American constitutional and commercial history. It proposed to ban interstate commerce in manufactured goods or mined products in which child labor had been involved. Congress passed it by a large majority. However, the Keating–Owen Child Labor Act was declared unconstitutional by the U.S. Supreme Court in 1918: There were fears that changing the rules of interstate commerce would open the door to federal intervention in the whole economy.

Labor turns against Palmer

In 1916 Palmer ran for the Senate in Pennsylvania. The state was a Republican stronghold, so predictably he lost heavily to the right-wing Republican incumbent, Boies Penrose (1860–1921). Blue-collar voters flocked to Penrose, opening a breach between Palmer and labor that was never to be closed. Excluded from Congress, Palmer acted during World War I (1914–1918) as the Alien Property Custodian, in which capacity he was given charge of the management, that is to say, the confiscation, of foreign-owned companies, a large and miscellaneous group of predominantly German concerns. Palmer established and administered more than 32,000 trusts with an aggregate value of $502 million. Although the whole business gave rise to much fraud, Palmer himself was blameless of illegal activity.

Palmer's last public office was as attorney general from 1919 until 1921, when amid a postwar price rise and a sharp fall in standards of living the United States was plunged into an epidemic of strikes and a resurgence of radical political activity that gave rise to fears of a Bolshevist takeover. After a bomb exploded outside his home and a Senate resolution demanded action against radicals by the attorney general, Palmer used existing wartime powers to quash a strike by the United Mine Workers and, acting on information of a communist conspiracy supplied to him by his special assistant, J. Edgar Hoover (1895–1972), he succumbed to the Red Scare.

Only a few weeks earlier Palmer had been resisting voices in Congress asking for the Espionage Act's curbs on dissent to be extended into peacetime. However, the "Palmer Raids" (*see box above*) on private dwellings and communist headquarters in the fall of 1919 rounded up more than 3,000 suspected communists, anarchists, and "undesirable aliens." When about 250 of them were deported, there was widespread rejoicing, even though they were expelled without due process of law in violation of their constitutional rights.

Woodrow Wilson, absent in Versailles, France, and debilitated by a stroke, had left Palmer to deal with the law-and-order emergency on his own. By the middle of 1920, when the hysteria had settled down, lawyers such as Charles Evans Hughes (U.S. secretary of state 1921–1925) and Roscoe Pound, the dean of the Harvard Law School, were turning on Palmer and vilifying him for his disregard of civil liberties. Public opinion shifted against him, too. *Life* magazine attacked Palmer for arresting too many innocent people and holding them in custody for many months. "Order without Liberty is no slogan at all for the people of these States," it intoned. "So inquisitors and deporters are now moving unobtrusively toward the back benches, and it is time they did."

No doubt Palmer had hoped to make political capital from his hard line against radicals. He undoubtedly had ambitions to become president in 1920 and knew that taking a tough position against radical organizations would made him popular. However, his position worked against him in the long run since it alienated many liberal journalists, lawyers, and politicians. Although he arrived at the Democratic convention in the summer of 1920 with more delegates in his pocket than any other candidate, his reputation was besmirched. The antipathy of organized labor scuttled his presidential chance, and his public career ended in disappointment and defeat. He remained a loyal and hard-working Democrat. His final service to the party was as chief writer for Democratic candidate Franklin D. Roosevelt in the 1932 presidential election.

SEE ALSO:

Anarchism • Democratic Party • FBI • Hoover, J. Edgar • Labor Movement • Political Radicalism • Red Scare • World War I

PAN-AMERICANISM

The United States had strong links with many Latin American countries during the twenties. Pan-Americanism—the promotion of the relationship between America and Latin America—took the form of meetings held in different American capital cities at irregular intervals.

As the 20th century unfolded, the Monroe Doctrine of 1823 continued to dominate American political thought. The Monroe Doctrine had been a declaration of American foreign policy. Originally the doctrine concerned outside interference in the Western Hemisphere. It asserted American protection over this region of the world, and its essence was a "hands-off" warning to European powers. However, as time passed, the doctrine also came to cover events within Latin America—disputes between nations or civil disturbance within them—and to justify the United States' acting as the policeman of the whole region. Latin America was looked on as the United States' own backyard, and the Roosevelt Corollary (1902) to the doctrine argued that it was the United States' right to interfere anywhere in the hemisphere to protect "civilizing influences."

The fledgling League of Nations did not presume to challenge the American position. In 1920 Peru took a boundary dispute with Chile over the provinces of Tacna and Arica to the league for arbitration. Wary of treading on American toes, the league persuaded Peru to withdraw its appeal. Again in 1921, when the United States mediated a territorial dispute between Costa Rica and Panama in Costa Rica's favor, Panama's appeal to the league fell on deaf ears.

Pan-Americanism—a movement for cooperation and partnership among all the nations of Latin America—developed to a great degree in opposition to the Monroe Doctrine. Pan-Americanism promoted the idea of equality and fraternity of nations. It drew strength from the resentment felt throughout Latin America toward American presumption in thinking that the United States should exercise overlordship over the whole of the Western Hemisphere. Latin American countries also longed for greater economic independence from the United States, whose business corporations invested heavily in Latin America and expected to have a say in the running of its economies and governments. Latin Americans protested loudly that the principles of 1823 were a

A cartoon entitled "Opportunity Knocks" from 1915 shows a female figure labeled "Pan-America" knocking on Mexico's door. A pot, in pieces, lies next to the door, symbolizing the state of Mexico at the time.

President Coolidge (center) shortly before leaving for the Pan-American Conference in Havana, Cuba, in 1928. At the conference the United States continued to insist on the right of intervention in Latin America.

hangover from the past and constituted an affront to the sovereign dignity of independent states.

The first Pan-American Conferences in 1889 and 1901 showed little eagerness for friendship with the United States, and suspicions rose during the first two decades of the 20th century. At the same time, the idea grew that the United States should be brought within the Pan-American movement and the Monroe Doctrine either dropped or reformulated as a set of international principles. President Woodrow Wilson (1913–1921) envisioned a Pan-American pact that would guarantee the territorial integrity and republican form of government of every nation. In 1915 the idea was explored with the three great South American powers—Argentina, Brazil, and Chile—but the Chilean government, engaged in a border dispute with Peru, was distinctly cool to the idea, and it came to nothing. The 1914 occupation of Veracruz by U.S. marines and the invasion of Mexico in 1916 by U.S. General Pershing's (1860–1948) troops in search of the revolutionary leader Pancho Villa (1878–1923) hardly improved matters. Nor did President Wilson's statement to a Pan-American Scientific Congress at Washington in 1916 that the Monroe Doctrine "has always been maintained and always will be maintained."

The 1923 Pan-American conference at Santiago, Chile, was generally hostile toward the United States. A proposal from Uruguay for an American League of Nations—the U.S. Senate had just for the second time rejected the League of Nations—aimed to extend the Monroe Doctrine to include the United States within its framework. In other words, American aggression could be dealt with by the intervention of other American nations. The idea was completely unacceptable to the United States, and the head of the American delegation at the conference reasserted that the principles of the Monroe Doctrine were "essentially national," that is, preserving the freedom of action of the United States. The Uruguayan proposal was dropped.

In speeches delivered later in the year at Minneapolis and Philadelphia, Charles Evans Hughes (1862–1948), the U.S. secretary of state, sought to be conciliatory, saying that the United States had no wish to exercise a protectorate over the Latin American states nor to assert an "overlordship." However, he repeated that the United States reserved to itself the "definition, interpretation and application" of the Monroe Doctrine, and that in the exercise of its principles it must have "an unhampered discretion." Hughes did not come near renouncing the right of intervention.

When Nicaragua was torn apart by civil war between the fall of 1926 and May 1927, U.S. Marines were sent to protect American business interests against a possible left-wing coup. In his message to Congress in 1927 President Calvin Coolidge (1923–1929) proclaimed the necessity of confronting the menace of Bolshevism in the Caribbean.

In 1927 the Pan-American Union's Commission of Jurists, which met at Rio de Janeiro, drew up a code of international law and issued a declaration that "no state could interfere in the internal affairs of another." That provoked heated debate at the sixth Pan-American conference of 1928 in Havana. To dampen irritation, both the U.S. and Latin American delegations avoided references to the Monroe Doctrine. Once again the U.S. delegation, led by Charles Evans Hughes, insisted on the right of intervention as falling within the principles of international law. Only Cuba saw any merit in the U.S. position. The conference broke up without agreement, and the decade ended as it had begun, with Pan-American unity still a dream and Latin American hostility toward the United States undiminished.

SEE ALSO:

Central America • Coolidge, Calvin • Foreign Policy, U.S. • Hughes, Charles Evans • Isolationism • Latin America • League of Nations • Mexico • Nicaragua • Wilson, Woodrow

PARIS

During the twenties Paris became the adopted home of many American expatriates, including several famous artists, photographers, musicians, performers, and writers.

At the start of the decade the French capital had been the world's leading city of exile for three-quarters of a century. The city first acquired its reputation as a haven for repressed and persecuted people of any nationality during the reign of Louis-Philippe (1830–1848), who allowed greater freedom for publishing and political activity than most other continental European ruler of the time. The simultaneous rise of bourgeois capitalism

Sylvia Beach watches the composer George Antheil climb up to the first floor window of her bookshop Shakespeare and Company at 12 rue de l'Odeon. She published the first edition of James Joyce's *Ulysses*.

BLACK AMERICANS IN PARIS

The expatriate population of Paris in the 1920s contained a large number of African Americans, including many ex-servicemen who had no compelling reason to return to their prewar occupations. Whereas at home many of them had been treated little better than slaves, in Paris they enjoyed greatly superior social conditions and had much better prospects for work. They were welcomed and feted, particularly for their music—it was they who were the prime movers of the Jazz Age—and also for their general contribution to the culture. Their impact on white Parisian society was immense. Josephine Baker (1906–1975) captivated Paris audiences with her dance routine in *La Revue Nègre*, an American jazz production that opened in 1925. Avant-garde artists courted her and other black personalities such as Henry Crowder and Langston Hughes for their style, vitality, and "otherness." Brancusi, Giacometti, Leger, Man Ray, and Picasso all collected African sculptures and wore tribal jewelry and clothes. More importantly, they adopted African forms in their work, and through them African styles soon influenced a much larger audience. A passion for African culture swept through Paris, and African forms influenced the commercially successful art deco style.

helped Paris become a safe haven for artists, intellectuals, and rebels. The bohemian counterculture thus created continued to thrive into the 20th century, and as Paris increasingly became a focal point of style and fashion, its popularity for expatriates kept on growing.

Postwar Paris

After 1918 Paris was quick to cast off the gloom of World War I and launch itself into a period of celebration and creativity that lasted throughout the twenties. The city became a magnet for former U.S. servicemen, many of whom took up permanent residence there at the end of the hostilities. They were soon joined by numerous of their compatriots who felt disquiet at the growing insularity and puritanism of their homeland, where a return to conservative values, or "normalcy," was being promoted by politicians. Prohibition in 1920 drove many Americans to Paris, where alcohol was legally available, and the general cost of living was much lower than in the United States—in 1925 one U.S. dollar was worth 22 French francs. High-speed steamships made international travel a practical proposition, and young and wealthy people grabbed the chance to cross the Atlantic Ocean. Once they had oriented themselves in Europe, many of them decided that Paris, even more than London, was the place to be.

Among the leading American male writers who settled or spent extended periods in the French capital were E. E. Cummings (1894–1962), F. Scott Fitzgerald (1896–1940), Ezra Pound (1885–1972), and Ernest Hemingway (1899–1961), who all arrived in the city in 1921, and Henry Miller (1891–1980), who moved there in 1930. Also resident for a time was Ford Madox Ford (1873–1939). They shared the city with several American women of letters. The most influential of these was Gertrude Stein (1874–1946), who had lived there since 1903. Of the others the most successful eventually were the novelist Djuna Barnes (1892–1982) and the diarist Anaïs Nin (1903–1977). Also in Paris from 1921 was Man Ray (1890–1976)—an innovative American painter and photographer who was a pioneer of the Dada, surrealist, and abstract art movements.

Meeting places

Many of these artists frequented the same haunts and knew each other at least as acquaintances. One of the meeting places was Shakespeare and Company, a bookshop on the left bank of the Seine River opened in 1919 by American Sylvia Beach. Another was Stein's home at 27 rue de Fleuris, where she kept her celebrated art collection. More popular than either, however, were Le Coupole, La Rotonde, Le Selecte, and above all, Le Dôme—late-night bars in Montparnasse, the area of the city in which many Americans made their homes. There they mixed not only with each other but also with artists of numerous other nationalities. Many, of course, were French: They included the prolific and versatile novelist, poet, playwright, painter, designer, and filmmaker Jean Cocteau (1889–1963); the painters Georges Braque (1882–1963), Fernand Leger (1881–1955), and Henri Matisse (1869–1954); and the classical composers Darius Milhaud (1892–1974) and Erik Satie (1866–1925). Among the noted foreigners living in Paris during the twenties were great painters and sculptors—the Romanian Constantin Brancusi (1876–1957), the Swiss Alberto Giacometti (1901–1966), the Italian Amedeo Modigliani (1884–1920), and the Spaniard Pablo Picasso (1881–1973). Also domiciled in the city were two brilliant Russian exiles—impresario Sergei Diaghilev (1872–1929), creator of the Ballets Russes, and composer Igor Stravinsky (1882–1971).

The fires of creative energy that had illuminated Paris from 1920 were doused by the Wall Street stock market crash in late 1929. The ensuing global financial crisis forced many expatriate residents of the city, particularly the Americans, to return to their native countries. Some, including Henry Miller, stayed behind, but for them life was never the same again. The joyous sense of release that had been so widely felt in Paris after World War I gave way to gloom and foreboding as it became clear that another war on a global scale was inevitable.

SEE ALSO:

Baker, Josephine • Black Americans • Expatriates • Jazz • Lost Generation • World War I

Dorothy PARKER (1893–1967)

Dorothy Parker was one of the most influential and important writers of the era. Renowned for her wit and merciless prose style, she worked as a theater critic and short-story writer in New York and was a contributor to *Vanity Fair*, *The New Yorker*, and the *Saturday Evening Post*.

Dorothy Parker was a literary talent of many skills. A wit, poet, and short-story writer, she was also a magazine drama critic for many years and a committed political activist. Some of her funniest lines, such as "Brevity is the soul of lingerie," entered popular American currency. During the 1920s she was the undisputed wit of New York and the city's number one satirist.

She was born Dorothy Rothschild, the youngest of three siblings, on August 22, 1893, in West End, New Jersey. Her father was Jewish and her mother Presbyterian. Her mother died shortly after her birth, and her father remarried a devout Roman Catholic. Parker's childhood was extremely unhappy. After attending Miss Dana's School in New Jersey, her stepmother sent her to a Roman Catholic convent school. In 1911 she moved to New York, supporting herself by playing the piano at night in a dance school. In 1912 her brother died on the *Titanic*, and a year later her father died.

Parker's ambition, however, was to be a writer, and after her first poem was accepted for publication in *Vanity Fair* in 1915, she landed a job writing captions for *Vogue* magazine. Her pithy captions were too caustic for a fashion magazine, and she moved to *Vanity Fair*. There she wrote articles, captions, and verse. In May 1917 she married Edwin Pond Parker II, a Wall Street businessman. The marriage was not a success, and they separated after World War I (1914–1918), divorcing much later in 1928. Eager to get rid of her maiden name, Dorothy kept her married name of Parker for the rest of her life.

In 1917 she became drama critic on *Vanity Fair*, succeeding the British comic writer P.G. Wodehouse. There she met the humorist Robert Benchley and the critic Robert Sherwood, with whom she formed the Round Table, a literary lunch set who met daily on weekdays at the Algonquin Hotel in New York. Her reviews were merciless, and in 1920 she was fired from the job for being too rude.

Parker wrote for many magazines during the 1920s. By 1922 she was writing a comic page for the *Saturday Evening Post*: "Short Turns and Encores." She became the theater critic for *Ainslee's* magazine in 1920, a position she held until 1933. Her reputation as a wit and humorist was cemented by the reporting of her witty comments by one of her fellow lunch companions at the Algonquin, Franklin P. Adams (F.P.A.) in his newspaper column. Parker's early reputation owed as much to Adams as it did to her own writing. As she established her reputation as a humorist, Parker started to write more seriously.

Literary career

Her first short story, "Such a Pretty Little Picture," inspired by the marriage of her friend Robert Benchley, appeared in the magazine *Smart Set* in December 1922. Parker, meanwhile, was estranged from her husband. Her life became one of hard drinking and partying. She spent much of the decade in an alcoholic haze, falling for unsuitable men. She also suffered from depression, partly a result of her growing awareness of the sharp social differences between the classes. She attempted suicide several times.

In 1926 she published her first collection of poetry, *Enough Rope*. The book, with its themes of love, loneliness, and death and the difficult position of women, was a great popular success. In her second volume, *Sunset Gun* (1928), the same themes reappear more intensely.

PARKER'S SOCIAL CONSCIENCE

Dorothy Parker championed many causes in her life. One of her writing's major underlying themes is the position of women and their dependence on men. The theme is dealt with in many of her short stories. She made oppression—be it of women, African Americans, servants—her special subject. She showed, through satire, how upper-class women were unable to change the position society has given them.

Parker took up the cause of the Italian anarchists Sacco and Vanzetti, who were tried and convicted of murder under dubious circumstances. Parker was arrested in Boston for marching in their support. Their execution only added to her feelings of depression. In the late 1930s she traveled to Spain to support the Loyalist cause in the Spanish Civil War (1936–1939) and later said that it was the single action in her life of which she was most proud. Her political activism continued during World War II (1939–1945).

Later Parker became a strong supporter of Martin Luther King, Jr., and the civil rights movement. She willed her estate to King. Following his death, it was passed on to the National Association for the Advancement of Colored People (NAACP).

Dorothy Parker and her second husband, the actor and author Alan Campbell, collaborate on a dramatization of Parker's story "One Hour Late" for Paramount in 1934.

The years between 1926 and 1936 were Parker's most productive. She started to publish stories in *The Bookman*, *Scribners*, and *The New Yorker* from the middle of the 1920s and continued to do so for the next 20 years. Further volumes of poetry followed, in 1931 and 1936, with *Death and Taxes* and *Not So Deep As a Well*. In 1929 she won the prestigious O. Henry Award for the year's best fiction for "Big Blonde"—the semi-autobiographical short story about Hazel Morse, an ageing alcoholic, who is overly dependent on men and tries unsuccessfully to kill herself.

In 1927 Parker joined *The New Yorker* as a book reviewer. She had been one of the founding members of the magazine and initially published her reviews under the pseudonym "Constant Reader." She used her reviews to champion writers such as Ernest Hemingway (1899–1961), whose spare style she adopted in her own fiction.

In 1931 she signed a three-month contract with the film production company MGM to write screenplays and moved to Hollywood. She spent the next two decades in Hollywood with her second husband, Alan Campbell, whom she married in 1933 and with whom she had a tempestuous relationship until his death in 1963. In 1937 they won an Academy Award for their joint screenplay of *A Star Is Born*. Parker herself is also credited with 15 other screenplays.

Parker spent the last two years of her life in New York City, living alone in the Volney Hotel, where she died of a heart attack. Although her body was discovered on June 7, 1967, the precise date of her death remains unknown. Her ashes are now housed at the NAACP's headquarters (*see box opposite*).

SEE ALSO:

Books & Publishing • Hollywood • Literature • *New Yorker* • Round Table • Sacco & Vanzetti

PETROLEUM INDUSTRY

In the 1920s millions of automobiles were manufactured by Ford and other firms, while hundreds of thousands of people turned to oil-burning furnaces to heat their homes and businesses. As a result, there was an enormous increase in the demand for petroleum.

As people took to the road in their Model T Fords, a change came over the landscape. Oil companies dotted the streets and highways of the nation with distinctive brightly colored service stations. Texaco came up with glass boxes underneath overhanging roofs. Gulf combined curved glass with horizontal strips and fins. Standard Oil's porcelain panels in red, white, and blue were even included in the International Style exhibition at the Museum of Modern Art in New York in 1932.

Those new service stations were the visible evidence of a booming petroleum industry. In 1918 the United States was the world's largest source of crude petroleum, accounting for about two-thirds of the global total. Even though world production more than doubled in the 1920s, the United States still commanded two-thirds of the total at the end of the decade. Domestic crude oil production in 1919 was 378 million barrels; by 1929 it had reached one billion barrels. That record of expansion was almost matched by the manufacture of refined oil, or gasoline.

Crude oil deposits were located in 25 states. The discovery of vast fields in the Southwest before World War I (1914–1918) led to oil booms in Texas and Oklahoma in the 1920s. Seven times more barrels were produced in the South in 1927 than in 1910. California, too, was a major producer. Eventually the petroleum explosion was to produce a huge transfer of population and wealth to the "sunshine states," with a corresponding shift in political influence. In the 1920s its main effect was to make possible the rise in conspicuous consumption for which the decade is best remembered. Automobile production grew by 156 percent between 1919 and 1929—a record of expansion unmatched by any other industry except for the manufacture of certain domestic appliances. Oil (kerosene) boilers, costly but clean and efficient, signaled the end of coal furnaces. In 1926 the leading makers installed 73,000 of them in American homes. Three years later the number had risen to 550,00 and, in addition, 220,000 were sold to public buildings such as shops, hotels, and theaters.

Innovations

High demand produced a wide array of technological innovations. In many oil fields seismic and magnetic methods of prospecting replaced the use of the torsion balance. Pipes for transporting the oil came to be welded, rather than screwed together, and to be made from high-carbon steel of great tensile strength. The result was thinner pipes able to withstand high pumping pressure. Corrosion was significantly reduced by the introduction of improved asphaltic coatings. The result of those and other improvements was that 20,000 new miles (32,190km) of pipeline were laid down in the 1920s—an increase of 80 percent—at a greatly reduced cost. Perhaps the most significant technological advance, affecting the manufacture of gasoline for automobiles, was the introduction of stabilizers (*see box below*).

STABILIZERS

Extraction processes yielded a crude natural petroleum with a heavy presence of low-boiling constituents, such as butane and propane. Those "impurities," especially propane, raised the vapor pressure of refined gasoline to so high a level as to cause large losses in handling and shipping. In addition, because they were highly volatile elements, they produced a "gassy" gasoline for automobiles that tended to cause carburetor troubles and was dangerous to use in the form of liquefied petroleum (bottled) gas for cooking.

Therefore, what was needed was a way of removing all of the propane and some of the butane from petroleum without the loss of salable gasoline—a process that was called "stabilizing." In 1922 J.A. Rafferty of Carbide and Carbon Chemical Company invented a rectifying column for a phased distillation of petroleum that separated the dangerous elements from the "good" gasoline. At the same time Shell came up with its own stabilizing mechanism, the De Brey process, which used a similar column.

An oil well in Oklahoma in about 1922. In the 1920s world oil production more than doubled, with the United States accounting for two-thirds of the total. The introduction of the mass-market automobile helped increase demand.

So great was the impact of petroleum on American life that there was great public concern about the future availability of the resource. Many people demanded regulation to conserve a nonrenewable fuel, and in 1924 President Coolidge (1923–1929) established the Federal Oil Conservation Board. Fears that petroleum deposits would soon be exhausted were premature, but the board called for greater imports to sustain American fields into the future. There was also disquiet about wastage in production, the environmental effects of the industry, and price instability. However, even though the government itself owned vast oil lands, Republican administrations, true to their general economic principles, chose not to regulate the industry. The Federal Oil Conservation Board was left to concern itself chiefly with the technical means of crude oil production.

Ownership of the petroleum industry was concentrated in very few hands. In 1911 the Supreme Court had ruled that Standard Oil was a combination in restraint of trade and ordered that it be dissolved. All that happened was that the parent company was required to dispose of its own stockholdings and distribute them to its stockholders in its subsidiary companies. Widespread stockholding was supposed to create a "community of interest" trust. It did nothing to break up Standard Oil. When, in 1924, Standard Oil was convicted under the antitrust laws, the U.S. Supreme Court overturned the decision. At the end of the decade 20 companies controlled 60 percent of crude-oil production.

SEE ALSO:

Automobile Industry • Latin America • Rockefeller, John D., Jr. • Suburbs & Suburbanization • Trusts

PHOTOGRAPHY

The 1920s were an immensely creative period in the history of photography. Under the leadership of men such as Alfred Stieglitz the medium was established as an art form, while photographers such as Edward Steichen created iconic images of fashion and celebrities in popular magazines.

Photography sprang from the new technologies of industrialization in the first half of the 19th century. Early forms of photography were developed almost simultaneously in England by William Henry Fox Talbot in 1835 and in France by Louis-Jacques-Mandé Daguerre in 1839. The inventor Joseph Saxton (1799–1873) took the earliest American daguerreotype soon after the process became public in 1839. Photography expanded rapidly in the United States, both in the quantity of photographs produced—by 1850 there were 50 studios in New York City—and in the development of associated technologies. Some of the most notable improvements were made by the inventor and industrialist George Eastman (1854–1932), including flexible film negatives (rather than rigid plates) in 1883, the roll-film system in 1885, and the portable Kodak camera in 1888. With the slogan "You press the button, we do the rest," Eastman Kodak tapped an enormous amateur market and launched popular photography.

Recording the nation

Such was the novelty of a process that enabled people to capture images of the world around them that soon thousands of photographs were being taken; photography was seen as a truthful revelation of the world. Portraiture was an early subject: Mathew Brady (about 1823–1896) photographed illustrious Americans from 1845. With the technology perfected, the idea of recording the world was extended to current events. Images of war marked an important stage in the acceptance of photography as documentation; they revealed the medium's capacity to extract specific and meaningful moments from the stream of time. Photographers such as Timothy H. O'Sullivan (about 1840–1882), Alexander Gardner (1821–1882), and Andrew J. Russell (1830–1902) published almost 8,000 images of the Civil War (1861–1865).

Early photography in the United States played an important role in the survey of the Western frontiers from the 1860s. Photographers accompanied teams of surveyors, and their photographs of the beauties of the natural world were instrumental in the campaign for conservation. Carleton E. Watkins (1829–1916) first recorded Yosemite in 1861, which led to it becoming a protected area in 1864; his *Yosemite Book* was published in 1868. William Henry Jackson's (1843–1942) photographs of Yellowstone convinced Congress to establish it as a National Park in 1872. Timothy H. O'Sullivan published photographs of the West and Southwest in the mid-1870s.

Photography in the United States also developed as a social tool. In the West the subject was the lives of the endangered Native population: William Henry Jackson made a photographic album, *Portraits of American Indians* (1877), and Adam Clark Vroman (1856–1916) and Edward S. Curtis (1868–1952) compiled *The North American Indian*, consisting of 20 volumes published between 1907 and 1930. In the East photographers were drawn to the living conditions of the working poor. Jacob A. Riis (1849–1914) and later Lewis W. Hine (1874–1940) saw photography as a means to raise public awareness of unjust social conditions and to foster social reform. Riis's book *How the Other Half Lives* (1890) was the first American photographic social document. Hine documented the working and living conditions of children from the 1900s for the National Child Labor Committee. In 1905 he began a series of images of immigrants arriving at Ellis Island, New York. In the 1920s he documented industrial workers, and in the 1930s he worked for the Farm Security Administration.

Photography was also enormously popular. There were photographic studios in most towns, and their archives, where they have survived, form an invaluable resource for social history. The enormous demand for professional photography meant that many photographers who aspired to fine art could earn a living.

Pictorialism

Changes in materials and processes in the 1890s simplified the use of cameras, and photography became a widespread activity accessible to many. In part as a reaction to this trend, some professionals made a conscious effort to elevate photography to the realms of art. An early attempt to equate photography to art was the pictorialist movement of the late 19th century, which first emerged in England and influenced American photographers such as Clarence H. White (1871–1925), Gertrude Käsebier (1852–1934), and Alfred Stieglitz (1864–1946). Pictorialists tried to avoid the technical appearance of commercial photography and emphasized picturesque qualities. They usually made prints on gum-bichromate paper, which gave the appearance of a lithograph (a type of art print), and the subjects were those of high art—portraits, still lifes, landscapes, and nudes. The pictorialists split into two groups: those searching for an artistic aesthetic and those who defended commercial practice. They had a huge influence in Hollywood, where their emphasis on soft-focus images established a convention for female beauty.

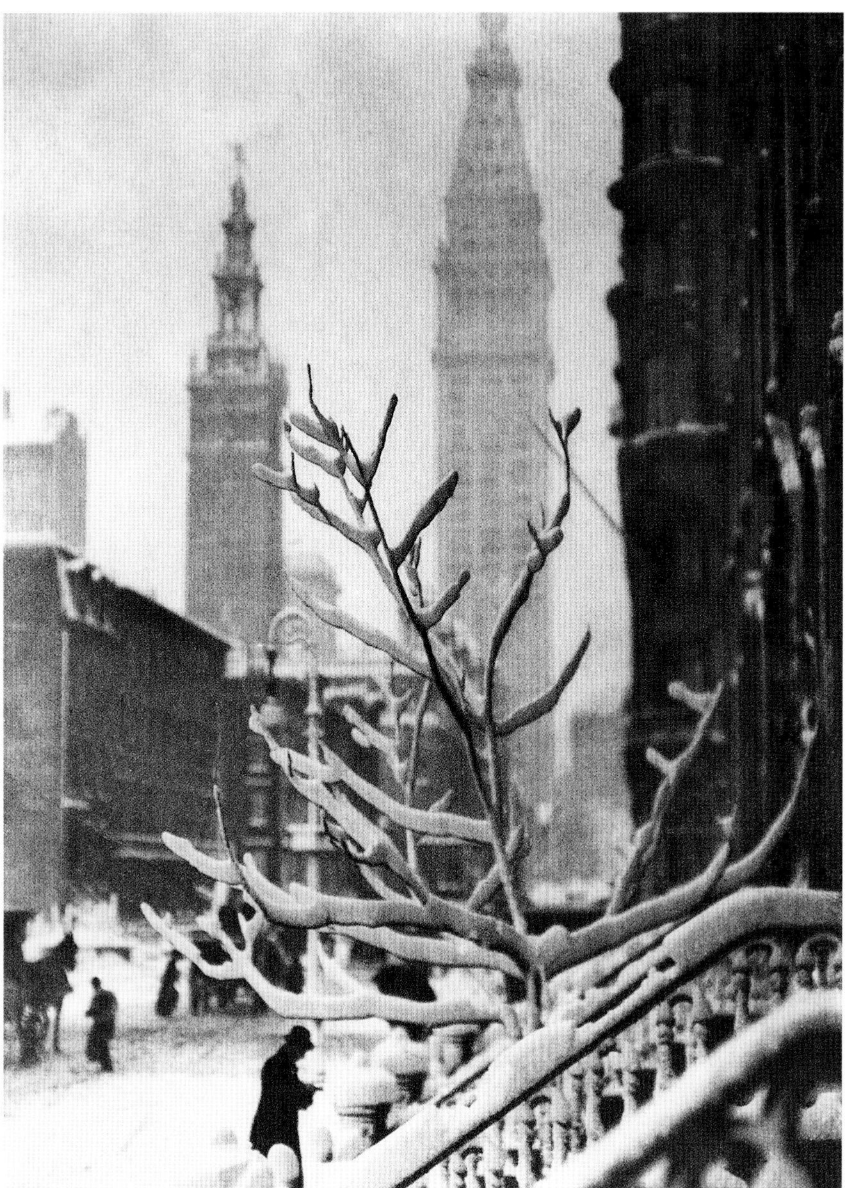

A photograph of New York City in the snow by Alfred Stieglitz. The image was reproduced in the March 1914 edition of Stieglitz's magazine *Camera Work*. America's rapidly growing cities were popular subjects for photographers.

Alfred Stieglitz became the main exponent of the pure artistic trend that grew out of pictorialism. Stieglitz was born in Hoboken, New Jersey, in 1864; he moved to New York City in 1890. He joined the Society of Amateur Photographers in 1891 and in 1896 helped form the Camera Club of New York, which is still in operation today. In 1902 Stieglitz and Edward Steichen (1879–1973) founded the influential Photo-Secession group, which promoted photography as an art form. Stieglitz disseminated his ideas on photography and modern art in his magazine *Camera Work*, and his gallery 291—which took its name from its address, 291 Fifth Avenue—became a center of intellectual life in New York. He closed 291 and *Camera Work* in 1917, when the United States entered World War I (1914–1918).

Straight photography

The activism of Stieglitz and the movement for photography as art helped promote photography as a whole, so that in the 1920s it entered a productive period as both a utilitarian and an artistic medium. Experimentation with different techniques, styles, and approaches was supported by developments in both the visual arts and printing technology, particularly photogravure. In this process images are transferred from film and etched into a metal plate from which prints can be made; improvements in photogravure affected fashion magazines in particular. The major achievement of photographers in the 1920s was "straight photography," in which supposedly unmanipulated prints fully exploited the technical possibilities of the medium—sharp focus, great depth of field (meaning that objects both near to and far from the camera lens are in focus), and broad tonal range. Photographers who favored this approach used large-format cameras such as the Graflex 8 x 10 inch plate camera and 5 x 8 inch half-plate camera (*see box on p. 141*). The large size of the negative gave unprecedented detail but required contact printing—printing directly from the negative without using an enlarger—which meant that correcting exposure or composition during printing was limited. Straight photography was the dominant trend in America in the 1920s.

There were two centers of photography in the United States during the 1920s, the first based around Stieglitz in New York and the second in San Francisco. Stieglitz had renounced pictorialism in favor of straight photography in the 1910s. From 1917 he developed this approach in portraits of the artist Georgia O'Keeffe (whom he married in 1924), studies of New York, and cloud series entitled *Equivalents*. He began to use platinum paper, which gave a highly defined and tonally rich print, and then, when this material became too expensive, silver paper. From 1929 he ran a new gallery, An American Place at 509 Madison Avenue, where he promoted the work of American photographers.

The East Coast photographers

With Stieglitz, Edward Steichen was a founder member of the Photo-Secession and played an important role in the life and design of its galleries, programs, and

Edward Steichen, *Greta Garbo*, 1928. As chief of photography on *Vogue* and *Vanity Fair* magazines from 1923 to 1938, Steichen produced some of the most influential images of fashion and movie icons in the twenties and thirties.

publications. Steichen was born in Luxembourg in 1879 and emigrated to the United States in 1882. He was influenced by the work of Clarence H. White, who saw Steichen's work in 1899 and introduced him to Stieglitz. His work from that time was highly pictorial, such as *Little Round Mirror* (1902), a nude in soft focus printed on gum-bichromate paper. After helping Stieglitz found the Photo-Secession in 1902, Steichen went to Paris, where he met the American writer Gertrude Stein (1874–1946) and became part of avant-garde circles in the city. He introduced many of the artists he met there to Stieglitz, who showed their work at the 291 gallery. The French publisher Lucien Vogel, who founded the fashion magazine *La Gazette du Bon Ton*, encouraged Steichen to take up fashion photography.

Steichen returned to New York on the eve of World War I intending to become a photojournalist, but was appointed head of photography for the American Expeditionary Forces Air Service in 1917. The freelance fashion photography he also undertook in New York led to his appointment in 1923 as chief of photography for Condé Nast Publications, which published the fashion magazines *Vogue* and *Vanity Fair*. His photograph of the actress Gloria Swanson, taken the following year, showed his new expertise in sharp-focus photography; he shot her face through a veil, which adds a layer of graphic interest to the portrait. Steichen's relationship with Stieglitz became strained over issues concerning his commercial work. Stieglitz disapproved of such photography, whereas Steichen believed it could be raised to the level of art. In 1929 Steichen co-organized the American section of the *Film und Foto* exhibition in Stuttgart, Germany, with fellow photographer Edward Weston (1886–1958). He became director of the photography department at the Museum of Modern Art, New York, in 1947, a position he held until 1962. In this role he organized more than 50 shows, including one of the most popular exhibitions in the history of photography, *The Family of Man* (1955).

Paul Strand

Paul Strand (1890–1976) was another influential photographer in the circle around Stieglitz. He was born in New York and studied with Lewis Hine in 1908. His early work was quite pictorial, but he came to know Stieglitz and the work of the Photo-Secession and soon realized the power of abstract imagery possible in photography. By 1915 he had made several photographs with abstract composition and lighting. The most famous of them is *Wall Street* (1915), a diagonal view along the edge of a building that emphasizes its scale and dramatizes its enormous black windows, lit by a low, raking light. Stieglitz devoted the last edition of *Camera Work* to Strand in 1917. During the 1920s Strand continued to photograph the "modern life" of New York, such as *Truckman's House, New York* (1920), and he is today regarded as one of the major forces in photographic modernism. However, he devoted himself increasingly to cinema; with Charles Sheeler he made the avant-garde film *Mannahatta* (1921), showing the colossal scale and animation of New York. During World War I he had become interested in political issues and after the war supported himself mainly as a freelance film photographer, working in Mexico from 1933 to 1934. In 1936 he shot *The Plow That Broke the Plains*. The documentary, which soon became a classic, showed the farming practices that had led to the Dust Bowl of the thirties. In 1937 he founded the Frontier Films cooperative in New York. He returned to still photography in 1943.

Charles Sheeler (1883–1965) was born in Philadelphia and studied to be a painter. He was a leading exponent of precisionism, a style of painting characterized by its smooth finish, meticulous delineation, emphasis on geometric forms, and subject matter of urban and industrial scenes. Sheeler trained as a commercial photographer to support himself as a painter but, encouraged by Stieglitz, came to consider photography an equally valid artistic medium. His first photographs were of ordinary architecture and early industrial artifacts in Bucks County, Pennsylvania, in 1917. Sheeler began to work as a fashion photographer for *Vogue* and *Vanity Fair* in 1923, and in 1927 was commissioned by the Ford Motor Company to photograph its River Rouge automobile factory. The resulting photographs, which presented the buildings as collections of pure abstract geometries, brought Sheeler enormous fame.

Walker Evans

Another New York photographer who achieved recognition a little later had a different outlook. Walker Evans (1903–1975) was born in St. Louis but moved to New York as a child. He studied in Paris for a year in 1926 with the intention of becoming a writer but, unable to support himself with his pen, took up photography instead in 1928. His friendship with Lincoln Kirstein (1907–1996), a director of the Museum of Modern Art in New York, brought him several commissions. In 1933 Kirstein commissioned the exhibition *Walker Evans: Photographs of 19th-Century Houses* and donated it to the museum. Evans's photographs of Victorian architecture and those of the rural South during the Depression, made for the Farm Security Administration, remain his best work. They include his collaboration with the author James Agee (1909–1955), *Let Us Now Praise Famous Men*, published in 1941, and *American*

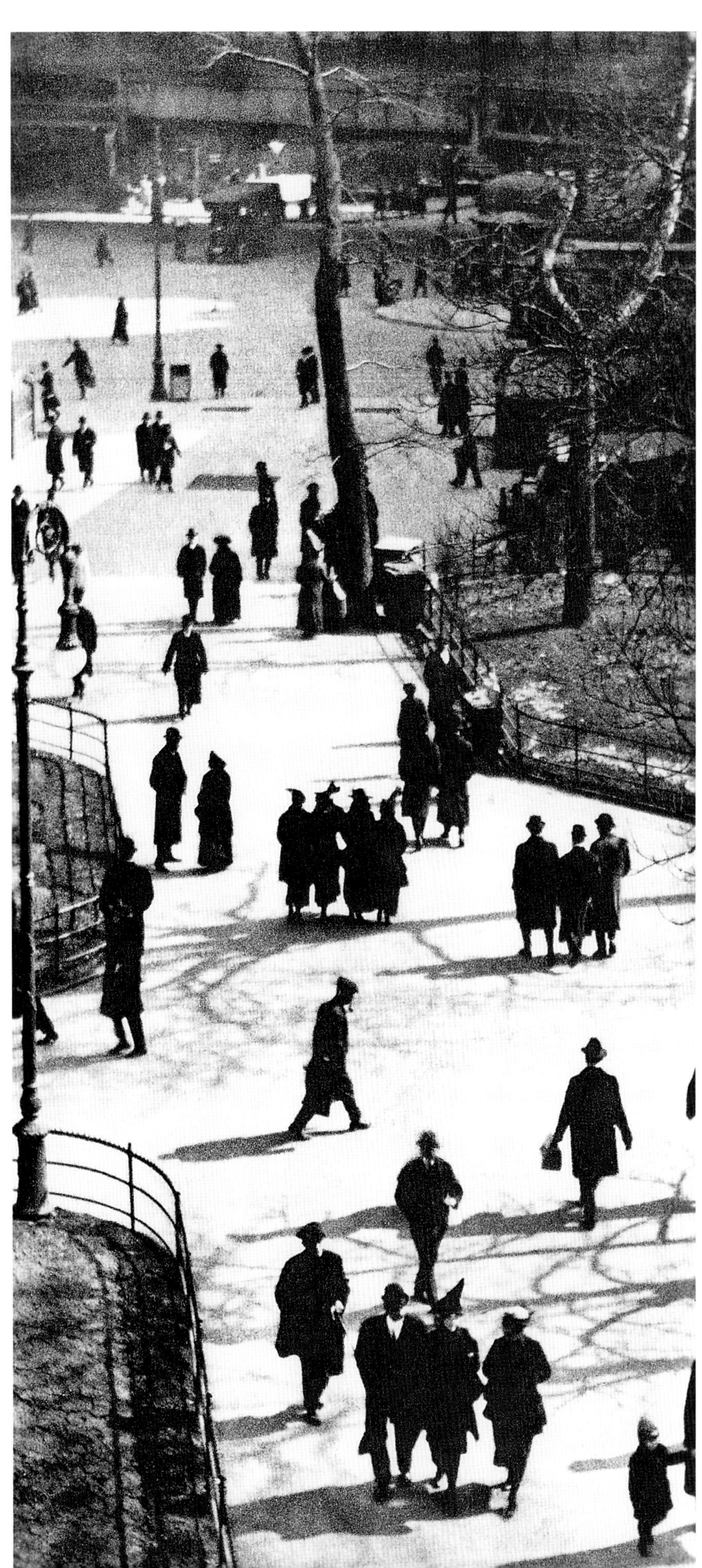

Paul Strand, *City Hall Park, New York*, 1916. The high viewpoint and narrow format focus attention on the abstract patterns underlying an everyday scene, a characteristic theme in Strand's work.

Photographs, published in 1938 by the Museum of Modern Art. Evans's vision of the United States was of a nation caught between dreams of the future and a more prosaic present, of struggles for survival and the persistence of human spirit in the face of relentless decay.

The West Coast photographers

Edward Weston was as important for photography on the West Coast as Stieglitz was on the East. He was not only an important photographer in his own right but was an inspiration and mentor for numerous other photographers. He was born in Chicago and moved to Los Angeles in 1906. He started taking photographs in 1902 and studied photography at the Illinois Institute of Photography in 1908. He returned to Los Angeles in 1909 and by 1912 had started his own successful studio, taking on another photographer, Margrethe Mather, as partner in 1917. Weston started as a pictorialist, but the cosmopolitan Mather introduced him to more artistic ideas about photography.

Weston underwent a transformation in 1922. On a trip to Ohio and New York he made his first industrial landscape photograph: the stacks and pipes of *Armco Steel, Ohio*. In New York he met Stieglitz, who encouraged him and introduced him to Sheeler and Strand. On his return to Los Angeles Weston decided to move to Mexico with Tina Modotti (*see box on p. 142*), whom he had first met around 1919. Mexico was then undergoing an artistic revolution following 10 years of civil war, and artists were highly valued: Weston became friends with the Mexican painters Diego Rivera (1886–1957) and José Clemente Orozco (1883–1949), who held his work in high esteem. He also began taking portraits with the newly introduced Series B Graflex, a large-format, single-lens reflex camera which allowed tight closeups (*see box opposite*). His portraits and numerous images of Tina Modotti opened up new possibilities for the expressive use of photography. He also began to take highly erotic nude photographs, including *Tina Modotti on the Roof* (1924).

Weston returned to Los Angeles in 1926, where he met the Canadian artist Henrietta Shore (1880–1963) the following year. She worked in the precisionist manner, often depicting shells and plants. Weston immediately began a series of shells and bell peppers, such as *Pepper No. 30* (1930). In 1929 he moved to Carmel, California, and began to take photographs of the landscape there and in Point Lobos. The same year he co-organized the American section of the *Film und Foto* exhibition in Stuttgart with Edward Steichen. During the 1930s Weston made some of his most famous works, such as *Dunes, Oceano* (1934), and *Nude on Dunes, Oceano* (1936), in which both the landscape and the female form are treated as sensual and erotic objects. In 1933 he produced photographs for the WPA's Federal Art Project in Mexico and California. In 1937 he traveled throughout California and the West on a Guggenheim Fellowship, the first to be awarded to a photographer, and in 1941 throughout the South and East.

Weston, along with Ansel Adams (1902–1984) and Imogen Cunningham (*see box on p. 142*), was one of the principal members of the "f.64" group. Formed in 1932, this informal association of California photographers was dedicated to the advancement of sharply defined—rather than pictorialist—prints and took its name from the minimum f-stop of a

This photograph, entitled *Edward Weston and Margrethe Mather*, was taken by Imogen Cunningham in 1923. Weston and Mather collaborated for 10 years on a wide range of innovative photography techniques.

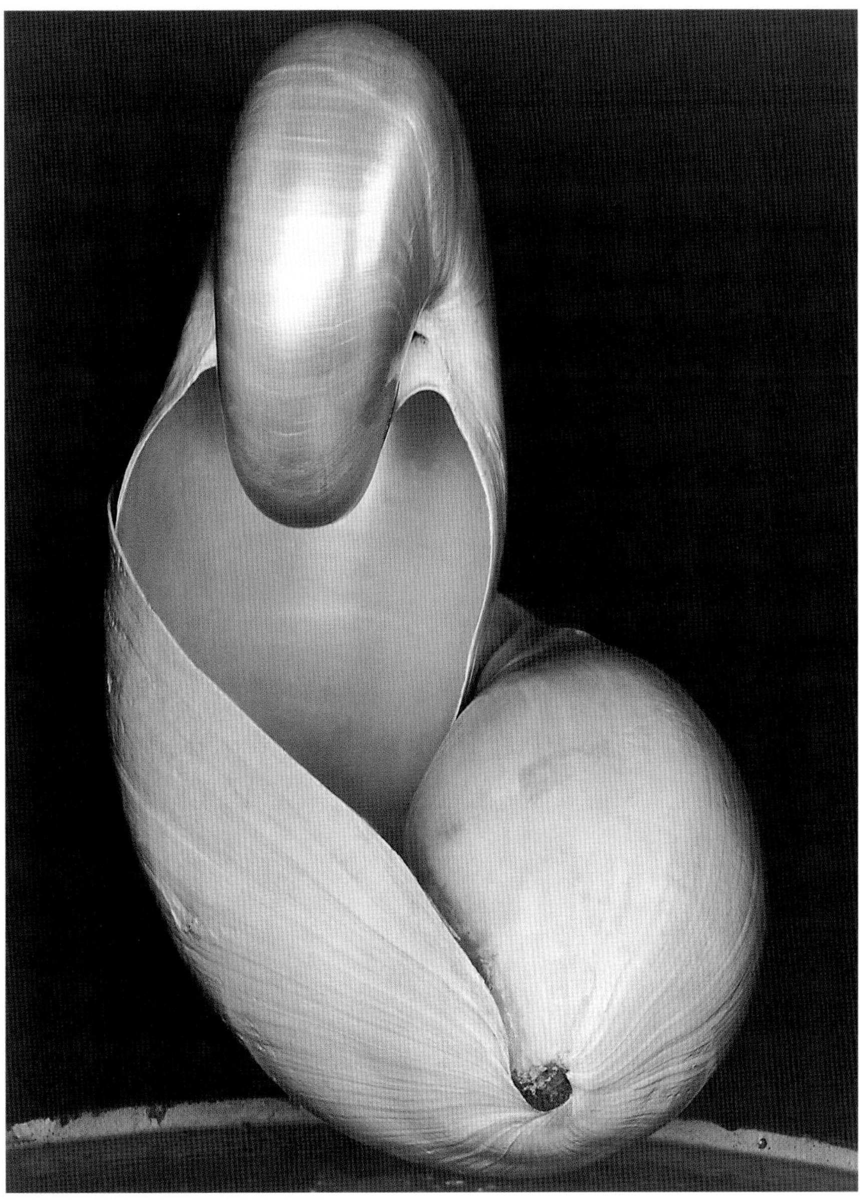

Edward Weston, *Two Shells*, 1927. This photograph belongs to a series of images of shells and peppers in which Weston explored the beauty of natural objects through careful composition and subtleties of light, tone, and texture.

large-format camera lens—f-stops are the different aperture sizes that, with the shutter speed, determine the film's exposure; f64 gives the maximum definition and depth of field.

Ansel Adams

Ansel Adams was born in San Francisco; he took his first pictures with a Box Brownie in 1916 while on vacation in Yosemite National Park. From 1920 to 1927 he worked as a guide for the Sierra Club in Yosemite. In 1927 he took one of his most famous images: *Monolith, The Face of Half Dome, Yosemite National Park*, which led to his first published portfolio, *Parmellian Prints of the High Sierras* (1927), and then to *Taos Pueblo* (1930). In *Monolith* Adams's vision of photography and the American landscape was already fully formed: The sublime scale of nature is celebrated in an image composed with meticulous attention to light, composition, and exposure. In 1930 Adams met Paul Strand and decided to devote himself to photography. He met Stieglitz in 1933 and exhibited at his gallery in 1936. In 1940 he helped establish the department of photography

THE GRAFLEX CAMERA

The Graflex cameras epitomized early 20th-century American camera design and remained in production, with various improvements, for almost 75 years. The original Graflex was made by Folmer & Schwing in New York in 1902; it was a large-format, single-lens reflex camera with a cloth focal plane shutter, folding viewing hood, removable back for film plates, and interchangeable lenses. Graflex was bought by Eastman Kodak in 1905 and moved to Rochester, but became independent again in 1926. The Series B, introduced in 1925 and produced until 1948, became the favorite camera of portrait photographers—Edward Weston used one. In 1926 Graflex developed a folding camera with rangefinder focusing and both a focal plane and leaf shutters, called the Speed Graphic; a cheaper version, lacking the focal plane shutter, was marketed as the Crown in 1947. The Speed Graphic became the preferred camera of news photographers—it was used by the New York crime photographer Weegee (1899–1968) in the 1940s. The leaf shutter, although it made the lens more expensive, was better suited to flash photography. The peak of Graflex production was during World War II (1939–1945), when the company made 350,000 cameras of all types. Graflex continued to market the Speed Graphic until 1968 and the Crown until 1973. They suffered competition from more versatile large-format view cameras, the medium-format Rolliflex twin-lens reflex (1929), Hasselblad single-lens reflex (1959), and the 35mm Nikon single-lens reflex (1948).

at the Museum of Modern Art. He was on the board of directors of the Sierra Club from 1936 to 1971. Other influential photographers based in the West include Imogen Cunningham and Dorothea Lange (*see box below*).

Americans in Paris

So strong was the "straight" aesthetic that photographers who wanted to explore other preoccupations moved to Paris. Man Ray (1890–1976) was born Emmanuel Rudnitsky in Philadelphia and moved to New York as a child. He studied at the New York Academy of Art and became a painter and sculptor. Throughout the 1910s he was involved in various avant-garde movements and was a frequent visitor to the 291 Gallery, where Stieglitz introduced him to photography. In order to participate more fully in surrealist circles, he moved to Paris in 1921. He supported himself by fashion photography for *Harper's Bazaar*, *Vu*, and *Vogue*. At the same, time he experimented with "cameraless" pictures, which he called "rayographs." The technique involved placing three-dimensional opaque and translucent objects directly on light-sensitive paper, which was then exposed to light and developed. He also made "cine-rayographs" such as *Le Retour à la raison* (1923) and *L'Étoile de mer* (1928). He was one of the first photographers to utilize solarization, a technique in which an undeveloped print is exposed to bright light before being developed normally. The process reverses some of the tones and produces ghostly images—effects that appealed to the surrealists.

Another American to live and establish a successful photographic studio in Paris was Berenice Abbott (*see box below*). In addition to her own work, which remains highly regarded, she is known for almost singlehandedly preserving and promoting the work of the Parisian photographer Eugène Atget (*see box opposite*).

WOMEN PHOTOGRAPHERS

Commentators have often overlooked the work of women photographers in the 1920s, concentrating instead on the output of their male counterparts. However, women were active and successful in the discipline, producing innovative, incisive, and technically advanced work.

One of the leading photographers of the period was Imogen Cunningham (1883–1976). Her early work was pictorialist in style. From 1907 to 1909 she worked as an assistant to Edward S. Curtis in Seattle, and in 1909 she studied photography for a year at the Technische Hochschule in Dresden, Germany. On her return she opened a portrait studio in Seattle. In the 1920s, having moved to San Francisco, she began to favor a more sharp-focus style. She photographed landscapes, such as Point Lobos, and plants, such as lilies and magnolias, which were to be her most famous works. She often worked in closeup, emphasizing the formal qualities of her subjects—their surface textures, shapes, and patterns—to produce images of great purity, which often bordered on the abstract. She exhibited at the *Film und Foto* exhibition in Stuttgart and with Ansel Adams, Edward Weston, and others formed the informal "f.64" group of photographers in 1932.

Another talented woman photographer working in the West, known almost solely for her relationship with Weston—he later called her "the first important person" in his life—was Margrethe Mather. They met in 1913, had a brief love affair, and developed a close working relationship. Mather's creativity and strong sense of composition and style greatly influenced Weston. However, by 1923 Weston was involved with another woman, who was to become much more well known: Tina Modotti (1896–1942). Modotti was working as a film actress when she met Weston in 1919 and two years later began modeling for him. Inspired by Weston, she determined to become a professional photographer and began working as his assistant. The pair left to work in Mexico in 1923. Modotti soon developed an assured modernist style that emphasized clarity and the formal qualities of the subject and the print. She was a sensitive photographer of people, from leading political figures and artists to ordinary citizens. She became increasingly involved with contemporary Mexican art and was a contributing editor and photographer for *Mexican Folkways* magazine. In 1927 she joined the Communist Party, and her work became more sociopolitical. Believing that Mexico's government had failed to deliver promised reforms, she became increasingly involved with political activism. Her activism led to her deportation in 1929. Modotti then worked as a member of the International Red Aid in Berlin, Moscow, Paris, and Spain during the Spanish Civil War. She returned to Mexico in 1939.

Another successful woman photographer working in the twenties, albeit mostly in Paris, was Berenice Abbott (1898–1991). She had left America for Europe in 1921 and from 1924 to 1926 worked as an assistant to Man Ray in Paris. She developed her own photography, meanwhile, and took portraits of artistic and literary celebrities such as Jean Cocteau, André Gide, and James Joyce. She recognized the importance of Parisian photographer Eugene Atget early on and was instrumental in promoting his work (*see box opposite*). In 1929 she returned to New York and, inspired by the work of Atget, began documenting the rapidly changing city. In 1935 she secured funding for her project from the Federal Art Project. The photographs were published in her book *Changing New York* in 1939.

The twenties were a formative period for several women photographers who went on to produce outstanding work in the 1930s. They include Dorothea Lange (1895–1965), famous for her images of the suffering and dignity of migratory farm workers during the Great Depression, and the renowned photojournalist Margaret Bourke-White (1906–1971).

EUGÈNE ATGET

The work of French photographer Eugène Atget (1856–1927) had a major influence on American practitioners of the art. Atget was born in Libourne, France, and worked as sailor and actor until he decided to become a photographer in 1899. His subjects were street scenes and interiors in Paris, almost always without people.He was unselfconscious in approach and never quite understood the acclaim that greeted his work. In two series of photographs, *Arts in Old Paris* and *Picturesque Paris*, completed by 1920, and two unfinished series, *Arts and Crafts in Old Paris* and *Art in Districts around Paris*, Atget recorded scenes that appeared to contain multiple, sometimes contradictory, meanings. Old buildings were overlaid with contemporary signs; contemporary uses were often at odds with the original functions of buildings. "Old Paris" was rapidly disappearing under the new wave of industrialization and urban expansion at the time.

Man Ray, an American photographer working in Paris, introduced Atget's work to the surrealist group, who regarded the Frenchman's unselfconscious observations of urban life as the apotheosis of surrealism. Some of Atget's images were featured in the magazine *La Révolution Surréaliste* in 1926, and others appeared in the *Film und Foto* exhibition in Stuttgart, Germany, in 1929. Atget died in poverty in 1927. After his death the American photographer Berenice Abbott purchased a large number of his negatives and prints, and vigorously promoted his work. In 1968 she donated her collection to the Museum of Modern Art, New York.

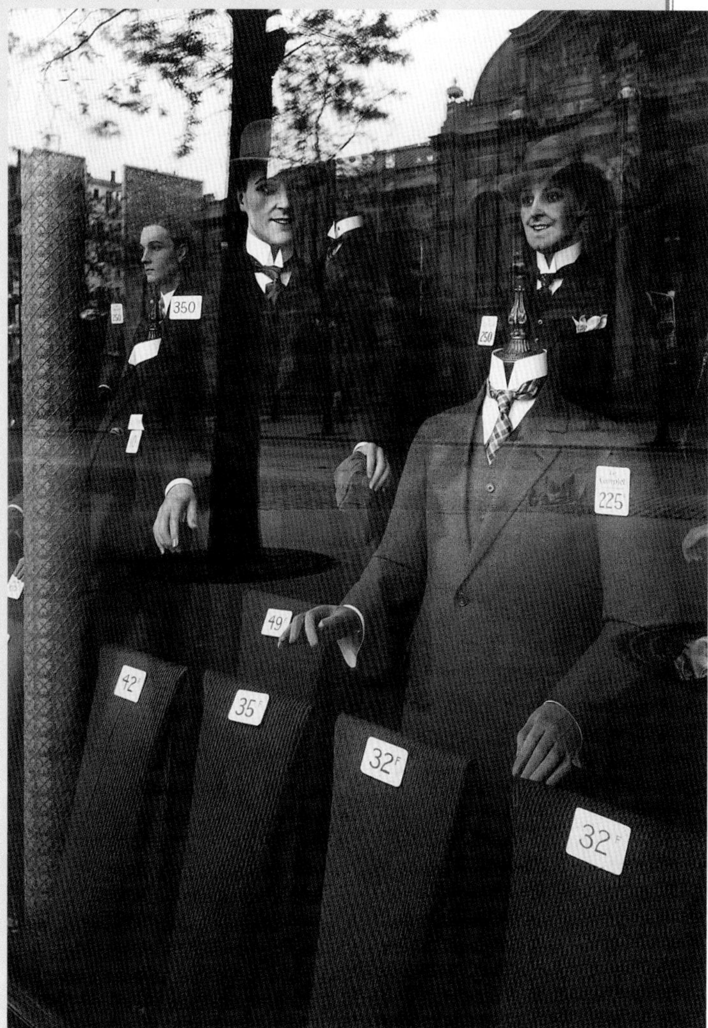

Men's Fashions *by Eugène Atget.*

By 1929 photography was closely associated with developments in modern art and was recognized as an art form in its own right. It could not be isolated from popular culture, however. Edward Steichen, Charles Sheeler, and Man Ray made significant contributions to fashion photography. Ralph Steiner (1899–1986), who worked in Paris with Man Ray and Abbott, blurred the line between high and low culture with an advertisement for Camel cigarettes in 1923. Reproductions of Ansel Adams's prints continue to sell in huge quantities, and his awe-inspiring photographs of the Sierra Nevada and Yosemite Valley have become iconic images of the American West. However, Adams's legacy has also had negative effects. His codification of exposure and development known as the "Zone System" spawned many imitators and was used to justify technical accomplishment at the expense of artistic vision.

After the 1929 stock market crash many photographers began to regard landscape as a trivial subject and turned instead to documentary photography, which they saw as more relevant to contemporary society. The first exhibition of work by the French photographer Henri Cartier-Bresson (1908–2004) was held in New York in 1933. The immediacy of his photographs, taken with a 35mm Leica, challenged the supremacy of large-format cameras. Many American photographers, including Dorothea Lange and Margaret Bourke-White, became known for their political projects, such as studies of the privations of the Great Depression. Meanwhile others, such as Walker Evans, remained largely "straight" but started to include a greater breadth of political vision in their work. In 1936 the news magazine *Life* began publication, and its worldwide success contributed to the popularity of documentary photography.

SEE ALSO:

Eastman, George • Hine, Lewis W. • Magazines & Magazine Publishing • Modernism • Steichen, Edward • Stieglitz, Alfred

PHYSICS

The 1920s were a very important period for the development of physics, in particular, atomic and quantum physics. The United States was at the forefront of the atomic and nuclear experimentation being developed by scientists such as Compton, Davisson, and Einstein.

The 1920s were an extremely important decade in 20th-century physics: Scientists translated their experiments with atoms into quantum theory, there was intense debate about the theories of the German-born American physicist Albert Einstein (1879–1955), and rocket propulsion was developed by the American engineer Robert Hutchings Goddard (1882–1945).

The quantum revolution

Near the end of the 19th century scientists were starting to believe that physics was almost complete. The American physicist Albert Abraham Michelson (1852–1931) summarized the mood in a typically overoptimistic statement of the time: "Our future discoveries must be looked for in the sixth decimal place." But this situation was about to change radically.

At the start of the 20th century scientists had a reasonable understanding of matter. They believed that all common substances are made from atoms chemically combined into various compounds and molecules. Chemists had found about 90 types of atoms of pure elements such as hydrogen, oxygen, and gold. The chemical and physical properties of these elements displayed certain patterns—for example, the second, 10th, and 18th heaviest atoms (helium, neon, and argon) were inert gases, whereas the third, 11th, and 19th (lithium, sodium, and potassium) were highly reactive metals. Scientists summarized this behavior in a chart called the periodic table of the elements.

By the 1920s scientists' understanding of the atom had increased enormously. The new science of atomic physics, spearheaded by New Zealand-born British physicist Ernest Rutherford (1871–1937), was providing a wealth of information about the fundamental makeup of matter. In 1911 Rutherford showed that an atom contains a small, dense nucleus around which electrons revolve. This nucleus has a positive electric charge to which the negatively charged electrons are attracted. The positive and negative charges balance each other out, making the atom electrically neutral.

However, Rutherford's theory of atoms seemed to have flaws. The laws of electromagnetism predict that an electron orbiting a nucleus should radiate energy and fall into the center of the atom. Yet atoms appeared stable, and their electrons had precise energies. Furthermore, both Albert Einstein and the German physicist Max Planck (1858–1947) had explained certain anomalies in the behavior of light by suggesting that radiation comes in discrete packets of energy. Such radiation quanta, however, had no explanation in known physics. The solution to these problems came in the form of quantum theory, and it would revolutionize humankind's view of the physical world.

A quantum leap

The discovery of quantum theory is considered by many people to be the most important event in 20th-century science. Quantum theory enabled the development of new technologies, such as the atom bomb, lasers, nuclear power, superconductors, and solid-state electronics for computer chips. The main causes of the quantum revolution were a combination of insightful theoretical work in Europe backed up by crucial experiments in the United States. European universities contained a new generation of young, mathematically gifted academics brought up on the revolutionary theories of Einstein. Meanwhile, laboratories and universities throughout the U.S. had plentiful private funding available for industrial and experimental research.

AMERICAN NOBEL PRIZES FOR PHYSICS

Since 1901 the Nobel Prize for physics has been the highest public accolade that any physicist can receive. The Nobel Prizes were founded by the Swedish inventor Alfred Bernhard Nobel (1833–1896) in response to the wartime horrors of his own invention, dynamite. In the first few decades of the 20th century two American physicists won Nobel Prizes for outstanding contributions to physics made during the 1920s.

1927: Arthur Holly Compton for "his discovery of the effect named after him." In 1922 Compton showed that light acts like a particle when it scatters off electrons in metals.

1937: Clinton Joseph Davisson for his "experimental [1927] discovery of the diffraction of electrons by crystals." Davisson's discovery provided the first evidence that electrons could sometimes act in a wavelike manner.

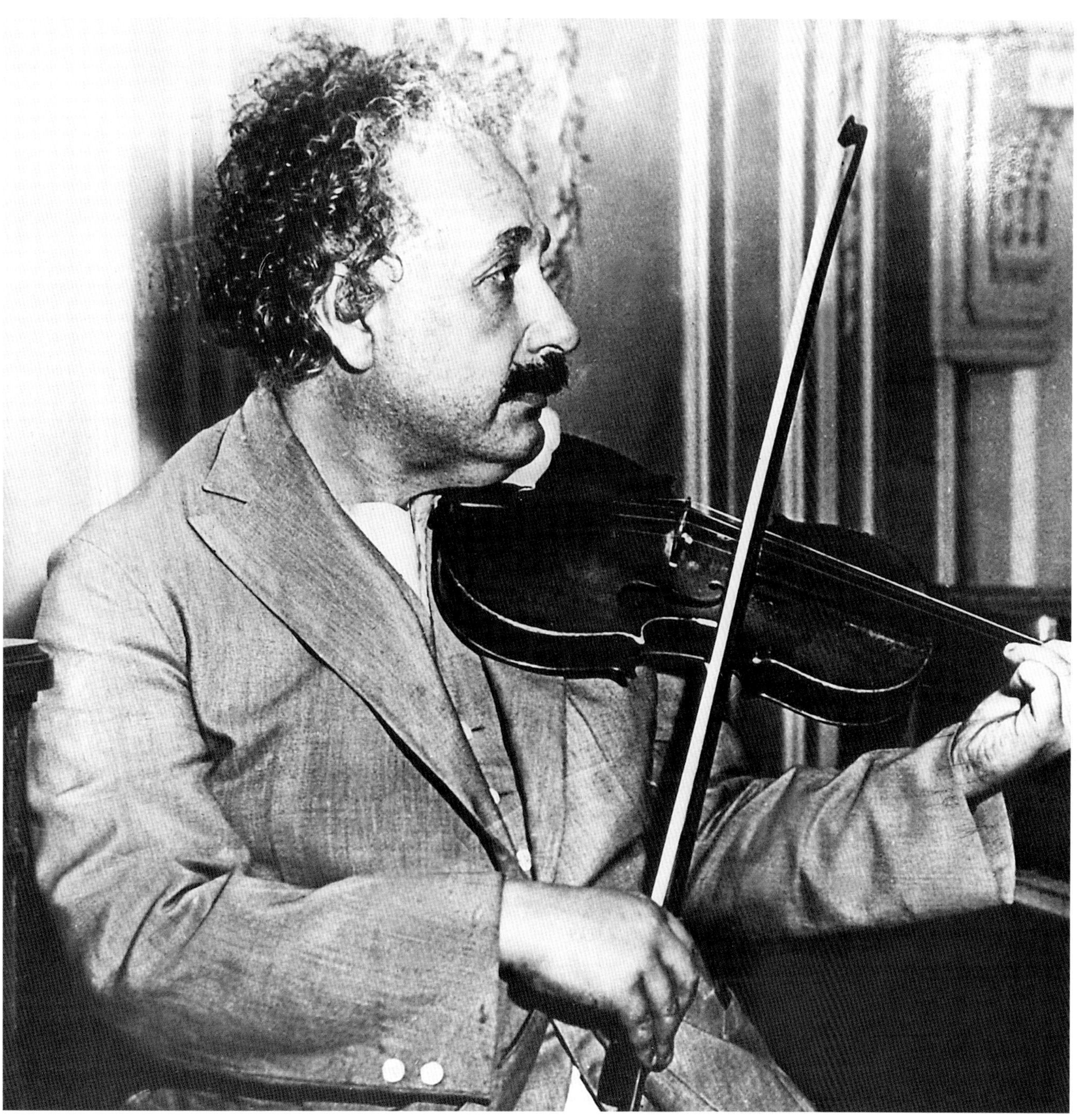

This undated photograph shows Albert Einstein playing the violin. Einstein was born in Germany in 1879 but immigrated to America in 1933 to escape the horrors of the Nazi regime. He became an American citizen in 1940.

In 1913 the Danish physicist Niels Bohr (1885–1962) laid the groundwork for quantum physics. Seeking to show how Rutherford's picture of electrons orbiting a nucleus was consistent with Planck and Einstein's light quanta, Bohr proposed the first quantum theory of the atom. In his atomic model electrons rotate around the nucleus in distinct energy levels, releasing or absorbing packets of radiation energy when they jump between levels. This theory worked well for hydrogen, which has just a nucleus and one electron, giving the correct answers for its radiation energies. However, the theory failed for more complex atoms such as helium. Bohr's model seemed to capture some part of nature yet was incomplete and simplistic. Further progress in quantum physics had to wait several years as Europe entered World War I (1914–1918).

Waves and particles

The next major event in quantum theory came in 1922, when the American physicist Arthur Holly Compton (1892–1962) discovered how light scatters off electrons in atoms. While working at

Washington University, St. Louis, he found that high-energy X-rays appeared to behave like particles rather than waves when they hit electrons. This effect agreed with the idea that quantum packets of radiation energy were in fact particles, which Compton named "photons." Physicists were now becoming familiar with one of the main ideas behind quantum theory: that light could sometimes behave like a wave—for example, when traveling through a medium—and at other times act like a particle. Somehow quantum physics had to combine these two, apparently contradictory, notions.

In 1924, the French theoretician Louis Victor de Broglie (1892–1987) added the next piece to the puzzle. If light—an electromagnetic wave—can also act like a particle, he proposed that particles such as electrons could also act like waves. This wave-particle duality paved the way for the wave equation for matter in quantum physics, a theory proposed by the Austrian physicist Erwin Schrödinger (1887–1961). In 1925 Schrödinger solved his wave equation for electrons orbiting the hydrogen atom and found answers similar to Bohr's atomic model; furthermore, the extension of his results to the helium atom also agreed with experimental evidence.

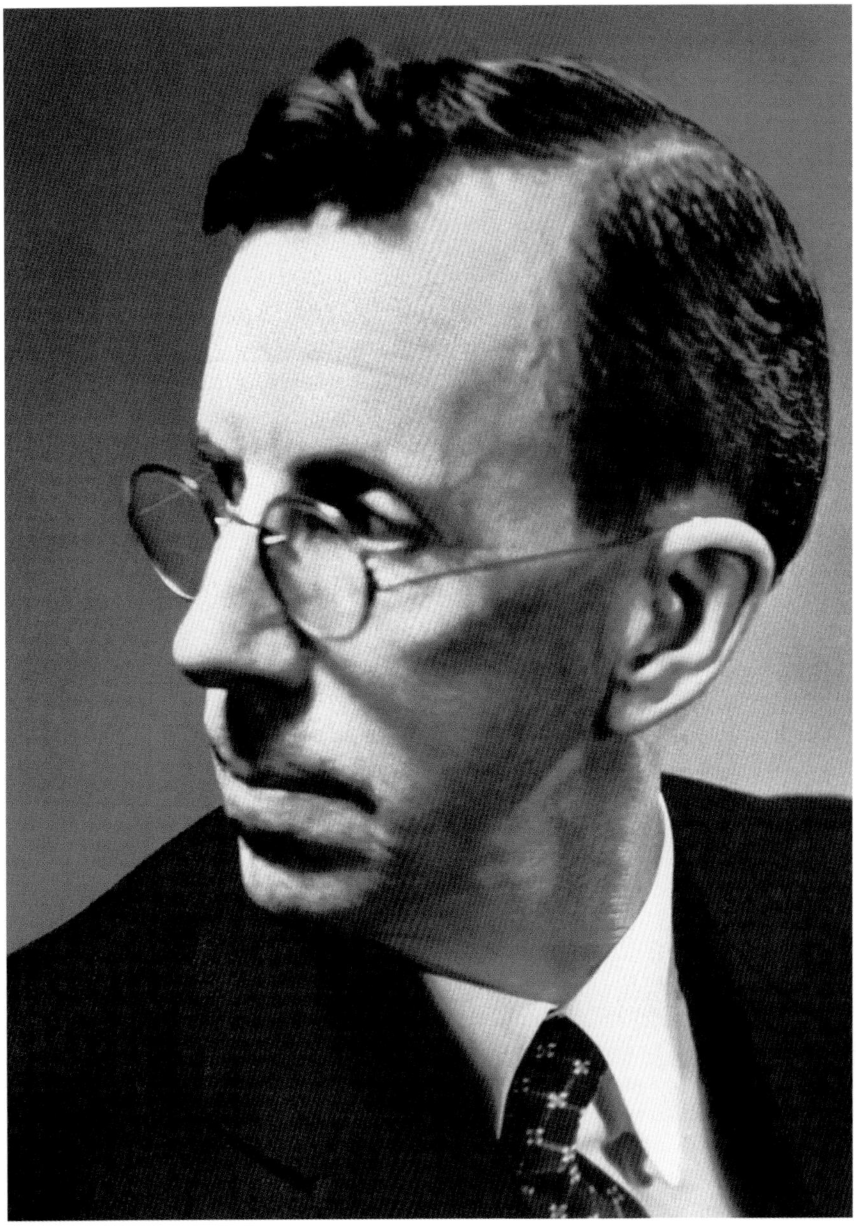

Direct experimental validation of de Broglie's ideas was provided in 1927 by American physicist Clinton Joseph Davisson (1881–1958) and his assistant Lester Germer (1896–1971). Davisson was born in Bloomington, Illinois, where he went to public school and gained a scholarship to study physics and mathematics at the University of Chicago. After being recommended by the American physicist Robert Andrews Millikan (1868–1953), Davisson worked as a researcher at several institutions. Finally, in 1918 he settled at the Bell Telephone Laboratories in New York, where he spent most of his career and did his best work.

In 1927 Davisson and Germer found that a metallic crystal diffracts electrons in a way that is similar to light and other electromagnetic waves. Therefore electrons could sometimes behave like waves and at other times act like particles, just like light. Quantum physics was now on a firm footing. Davisson received the 1937 Nobel Prize in physics for this important discovery (*see box on p. 144*).

In the following years no fundamental flaws have been found in the basic principles of quantum physics. Scientists have discovered phenomena inside the atom and described the basic constituents of its nucleus, but all new physics has remained within the original framework set in the 1920s. Quantum physics has completely changed scientists' view of the world. The wave-particle duality of all matter, from atomic nuclei to subatomic particles, means that it is distributed throughout space, disappearing from one place and reappearing at another as it changes energy and interacts.

Particle accelerators

Toward the end of the 1920s the American physicist Ernest Orlando Lawrence (1901–1958) was thinking about the

A portrait of Clinton Joseph Davisson from 1937, the year he won the Nobel Prize for Physics for his discovery of the diffraction of electrons in crystals—that electrons could sometimes behave like waves.

An early cyclotron designed by Ernest Lawrence and Milton Livingston in 1932. The cyclotron accelerated particles in a spiral pattern within a pair of semicylinders mounted in a vacuum between the poles of an electromagnet.

future of atomic and nuclear physics. While working at the University of California in Berkeley in 1929, Lawrence conceived the cyclotron—a circular device in which charged particles such as electrons and atomic nuclei are accelerated to extremely high velocities and then collided. The cyclotron works by having two hollow D-shaped electromagnets, called dees, that guide the charged particles in semicircular paths; between the dees is a slight gap over which a strong electric field is applied to accelerate the particles. Thus the particles circle around the cyclotron, gaining higher and higher speeds.

Such particle accelerators became the main instruments for 20th-century research in nuclear and particle physics. Most major discoveries, such as the various subatomic particles and the creation of new atomic elements, used devices based on Lawrence's original cyclotron. The instrument used to electromagnetically separate uranium-235 for making an atomic bomb was of a similar design.

Lawrence's first cyclotron, which was built by his student, the American physicist Milton Stanley Livingston (1905–1986), was a few meters across and applied about 13,000 volts of electricity. Modern particle accelerators, such as the Tevatron at the Fermi National Accelerator Laboratory (Fermilab) in Illinois, are several miles in diameter and operate at one trillion volts. The Lawrence Berkeley Radiation Laboratory in California, which Lawrence founded, is named in his honor.

Einstein's theory of relativity

Physics underwent another massive upheaval in the first two decades of the 20th century with the theories of German-born U.S. physicist Albert Einstein. In 1905 Einstein published his special theory of relativity. Then, in 1916, Einstein overturned several centuries of physics when he published his general theory of relativity. In this theory Einstein suggested that gravity—the force that makes objects fall to the earth and planets orbit the sun—is caused by mass distorting space and time. Therefore a satellite appears to have a circular orbit because space is bent, but actually the satellite travels in a straight line. In 1919 the British astronomer Sir Arthur Stanley Eddington (1882–1944) confirmed Einstein's theory by studying a solar eclipse. Eddington found that the positions of stars near the sun were distorted in exactly the way predicted by general relativity.

At the start of the 1920s the world was still reeling from Einstein's discoveries. Einstein embarked on a lecture tour of the United States in 1921, visiting many of the major universities such as Princeton and New York University. He spoke to packed auditoriums and lecture halls, and his actions were reported widely in the American press. From the 1920s onward Einstein spent a large amount of his life in the United States working on his unified theory of gravity and electromagnetism. His efforts were to prove in vain; the problem remains unsolved today.

Around the same time as Einstein was touring the United States, the American astronomer Edwin Powell Hubble (1889–1953) made several important discoveries about the cosmos while working at Mount Wilson Observatory, California. Between 1922 and 1924 he showed that the universe contains galaxies other than our own vast star system, the Milky Way. Then in 1927 he discovered that these galaxies are moving away from the Milky Way—in other words, the universe is expanding. The Hubble Space Telescope is named for Hubble in honor of his outstanding contribution to astronomy,

Hubble's discovery had a direct effect on general relativity. When Einstein came up with his general theory of relativity, a mathematical solution to the equations he derived suggested that the universe was either expanding or contracting. Like most astronomers of his day, Einstein assumed that the universe was static, so he added a cosmological constant to balance the equations and allow for a stable universe. Hubble's discovery meant that Einstein's original equations had been correct—there was no need for the cosmological constant. Russian-born American physicist George Gamow (1904–1968) later referred to the introduction of the cosmological constant as "Einstein's greatest blunder."

However, the most recent evidence suggests that Einstein was right after all. There does seem to be some unknown force, or cosmological constant, working against gravity's contracting force. Astrophysicists have now produced evidence for a "dark energy" that is pushing the universe apart—faster and faster. This concept agrees with previous suggestions that the mysterious repulsive force is causing the expansion of the universe to accelerate rather than slow down. The new research also suggests that ordinary matter—matter that people can see around them—accounts for just 4 percent of the universe. Dark matter—a different type of matter that cannot be perceived directly even if a light is shined on it—makes up about 21 percent of everything. Dark energy accounts for the remaining 75 percent of the universe.

This new evidence agrees with earlier conclusions that beginning about 6 billion years ago, the expansion of the universe began to pick up speed. That was not what scientists had expected for the last 70 years. Rather, after Hubble's 1929 discovery that the universe is expanding, most scientists believed that as momentum from the big bang decreased under gravity's resistance, the expansion of the universe would slow down. Some believed that it would eventually stop, and the galaxies would fall back to a central point in a big crunch. Instead, scientists now think that dark energy is apparently causing the galaxies to move apart faster and faster. These new observations agree with the concept of a cosmological constant first proposed by Einstein as a force that countered the attractive force of gravity.

The birth of rocket science

The American physicist Robert Hutchings Goddard is widely acknowledged as the father of modern rocketry. Although scientists such as the Russian Konstantin Tsiolkovsky (1857–1935) and the German Hermann Oberth (1894–1989) were working on the theory and practice of rocket flight, none could match Goddard's expertise.

Goddard developed the theory of rocket propulsion in his spare time, while working as a physics tutor at Clark University in Worcester, Massachusetts. In 1919 he published what was to become a classic scientific paper on rocket science, *A Method of Reaching Extreme Altitudes*, in which he conceived of a rocket reaching the moon. Over the years 1920 to 1926 Goddard designed, tested, and built a rocket powered by liquid fuel, a mixture of gasoline and liquid oxygen. On March 16, 1926, Goddard successfully sent his rocket on its first flight at his aunt's farm in Auburn, Massachusetts. The rocket flew for 2.5 seconds and climbed to 41 feet (12.5m). Three years later Goddard

COSMIC RAYS

At the start of the 20th century scientists were beginning to understand that the earth is being bombarded by high-energy radiation from outer space called cosmic rays. Austrian-born American physicist Victor Franz Hess (1883–1964) discovered this radiation between 1911 and 1912. By placing detectors in balloons, Hess showed that radiation became stronger at higher altitudes and therefore was likely to come from outside the earth's atmosphere.

Throughout the 1920s Robert Millikan pursued the main research into cosmic radiation. At the time he was the most famous scientist in the United States and had achieved a Nobel Prize in physics for an ingenious measurement of the charge of an electron. Millikan's experiments confirmed Hess's original discovery, which many scientists doubted at the time, and greatly developed the technology of cosmic radiation measurement. Millikan also thought of the name "cosmic rays."

Most of Millikan's work on cosmic rays was done at the Norman Bridge Laboratory of Physics at the California Institute of Technology (Caltech) in Pasadena, California, where he was appointed director in 1921. As chairman of the executive council until he retired in 1945, Millikan turned the Norman Bridge Laboratory into one of the foremost physics research centers in the world.

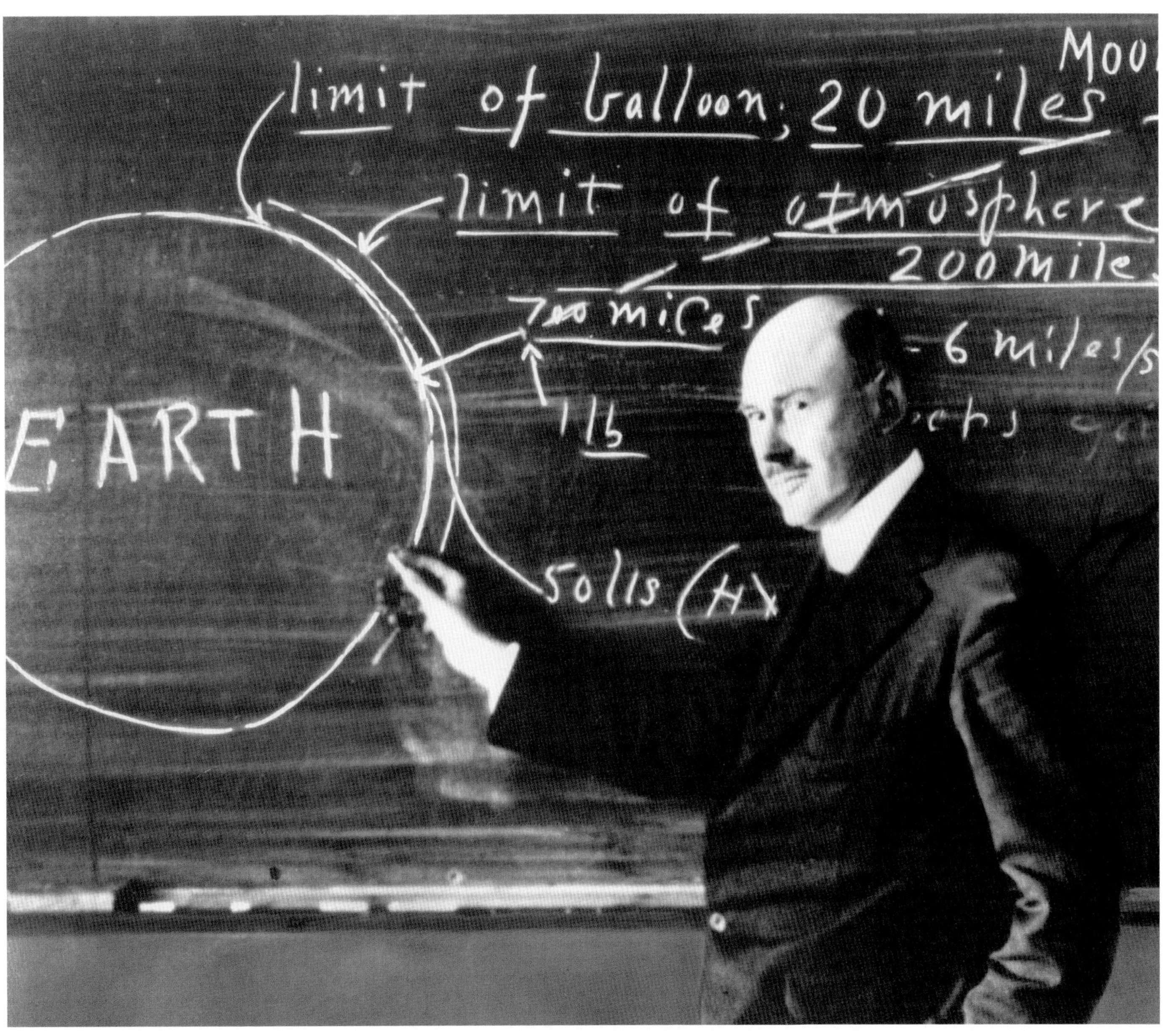

Dr. Robert H. Goddard at Clark University in Worcester, Massachusetts, in 1924, where he taught physics. As early as 1920 he asserted that rockets would one day be used to send payloads to the moon.

launched the first scientific payload—a barometer, thermometer, and a camera—in a rocket flight.

In 1929, after receiving unwanted media attention from a noisy test flight, Goddard attracted financial support through a petition by the American aviator Charles A. Lindbergh (1902–1974) to the Guggenheim Foundation Fund for the Promotion of Aeronautics. The funding meant that Goddard could move to Mescalero Ranch in Roswell, New Mexico, where he created rockets that could reach higher altitudes. The rockets Goddard built at Roswell later proved instrumental to the development of the Saturn moon rockets launched by the National Aeronautics and Space Administration (NASA) in the 1960s.

During his lifetime Goddard's work was largely dismissed. His experiments often involved loud explosions and drew large crowds, and the American press ridiculed him as an eccentric lunatic. Recognition for his considerable achievements came many years after his death in 1945, when the U.S. government awarded Goddard's relatives millions of dollars for the patents he had taken out on his inventions. In 1959 NASA opened the Goddard Space Flight Center in Greenbelt, Maryland, named in his honor.

SEE ALSO:

Astronomy • Compton, Arthur H. • Goddard, Robert H. • Hubble, Edwin P. • Lawrence, Ernest O. • Millikan, Robert A.

Mary PICKFORD (1893–1979)

Mary Pickford grew up in poverty. She went on to become the nation's favorite child actor, America's most successful female star, one of the richest and most powerful film producers in Hollywood, and a pioneer of early cinema.

"America's sweetheart," as Mary Pickford was affectionately known for her long, blonde curls, cute smile, and sunny disposition, became Hollywood's greatest female star by the 1920s. Her natural screen presence and mastery of mime set her apart from her peers in the silent film industry. After she cofounded her own movie distribution business, United Artists Corporation, she also became the richest and most powerful woman in the growing movie industry.

Pickford was born Gladys Mary Smith in Toronto, Canada, on April 8, 1893. The eldest of three children, Gladys, her siblings, and mother were left in dire financial straits when her father was killed. To ease their financial situation, their mother agreed to the children appearing on stage. Gladys made her stage debut, aged five, in *The Silver King*.

Between 1898 and 1907 the family earned barely enough money to survive despite appearing in several New York City productions. Gladys, who received only six months of formal education, taught herself to read as she toured with various theatrical companies. In 1907 Gladys Smith became Mary Pickford when she won a leading role in *The Warrens of Virginia*. The play, her debut on Broadway, was a hit, running for two years. When the play finished, Pickford was out of work. Her mother suggested she look for work at one of New York's movie companies. From 1909 to 1912 she appeared in countless films (*see box below*).

On her return to Broadway in 1912 she starred in *A Good Little Devil*. The show was a great success because audiences were prepared to pay to see their favorite movie star in the flesh. The rights to the play were bought by Adolph Zukor, head of Famous Players, later Paramount Pictures. Pickford played her role for the camera, earning $500 a week. Over the next five years from 1913 to 1918 she starred in *Hearts Adrift* (1914), *Tess of the Storm County* (1914), and *Rebecca of Sunnybrook Farm* (1917).

Her move to superstar status came with Tess. She played a little girl with a sweet, sunny disposition. The public loved "Little Mary" or "America's sweetheart." Fully aware of her popularity, Pickford not only earned more and more money but was also able to choose her scripts, cameramen, and directors. In 1916 she founded the Mary Pickford Corporation as part of Paramount Pictures and became the first actress to produce her own films. By 1917 she was earning more than $1 million a year. For the public Pickford's characters were never more than 16. Films such as *The Poor Little Rich Girl* (1917) and *Pollyanna* (1920) captured an intoxicating mixture of innocence and purity.

Marriage to Douglas Fairbanks

By the start of 1920 Pickford was the most popular actress in the country, rivaled in popularity only by Charlie Chaplin (1889–1977). That year she married another Hollywood great, Douglas Fairbanks Sr. (1883–1939). The couple had fallen in love in 1917 when both were married to other people—Pickford had married silent-film actor Owen Moore (1886–1939) in 1911. Fearing public disapproval if they divorced, they waited and then married in 1920. The public went crazy with excitement. They became the most popular couple in the country, and their Holly-

"THE GIRL WITH THE CURLS"

When Pickford left the stage to work for the Biograph Studio under D.W. Griffith in 1909, many thought it was a bad career move because moving pictures had no future.

Griffith spotted Pickford's star potential, and she debuted in *Her First Biscuits* in 1909. Silent movies were churned out, and Pickford appeared weekly in a different picture. Between 1909 and 1912 she appeared in almost 150 films, making 43 in 1911 alone. Since it was not the custom to name the actors and actresses, Pickford became known among picture audiences as "the girl with the curls."

The silent film suited Pickford's acting style. The characters she portrayed captured an idealized, rural America with its values of simplicity, innocence, and hard work.

By 1910 Pickford's salary had increased from $5 a week to $150, and she was fast becoming one of the industry's first stars. Despite starring in more hits, including *The New York Hat* (1912), Pickford, by now an established star, wanted to return to the stage. By the time she left Biograph in 1912, Pickford had redefined film acting. She would go on to become Hollywood's biggest female star.

A poster from 1921 for Mary Pickford's film *Through the Back Door*. Throughout the 1920s Pickford played little girl roles in nearly all her films. She finally gave up playing young girls in 1928 when she was already over 30.

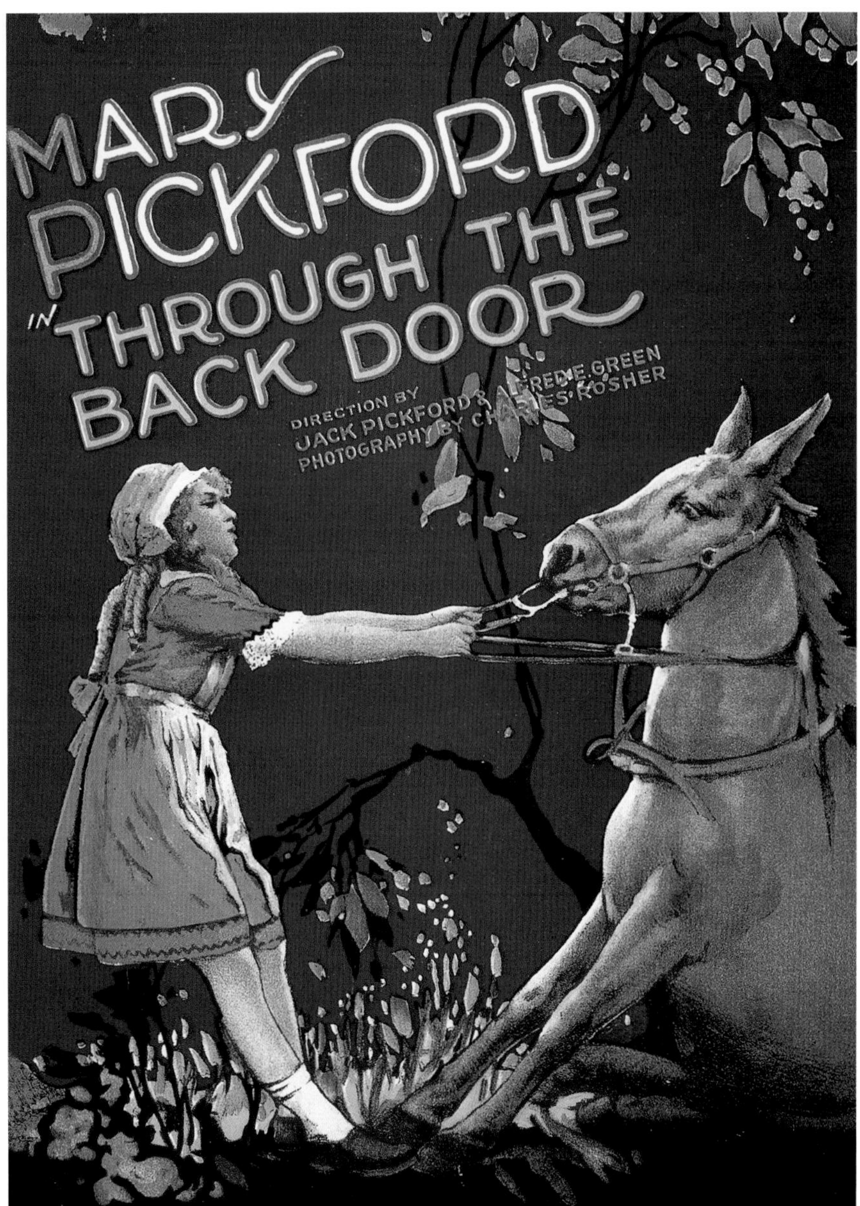

wood mansion, Pickfair, became the social center of the Hollywood film industry.

Pickford continued to star in films that she also produced throughout the decade. *Pollyanna*, made for United Artists in 1920—the company Pickford formed along with her husband, Charlie Chaplin, and D.W. Griffith (1875–1948)—was a huge success. The following year *Little Lord Fauntleroy* appeared. Pickford played both Fauntleroy and his mother. The film included advanced double-exposure techniques for a scene when Pickford, as the mother, kisses Pickford the son. Pickford's popularity endured, and she became an international celebrity. When she and Fairbanks visited the Soviet Union in 1926, hundreds of thousands of fans lined Moscow's streets to see her.

Later years

As Pickford grew older and approached 30, she no longer wanted to appear as a prepubescent girl. Her attempts at playing more mature women were not well received. Pressure from her fans led to her playing a young girl again in the 1925 hit *Little Annie Rooney*. Following the death of her mother, to whom she was very close, in 1928, Pickford cut off her curls, bobbed her hair, and never again played a young girl.

In 1929 Pickford made her first talkie, *Coquette*. She played a Southern belle and won the Academy Award for best actress. The same year she and Fairbanks appeared together for the only time in *The Taming of the Shrew*. The movie was not a success, and the cracks in Pickford's and Fairbanks's marriage were apparent. The couple divorced in 1936, and Pickford married for a third and final time. Her third husband was actor and bandleader Charles "Buddy" Rogers (1904–1999).

In 1933 Pickford retired from the movies after her 194th film. She knew that her fans wanted her to continue playing the role of a sweet, young girl, but she was no longer prepared to satisfy them. In the second half of 1936 Pickford became the first vice president of United Artists, and in 1937 she started her own cosmetics company, Mary Pickford Cosmetics.

By now one of the richest people in Hollywood, Mary Pickford increasingly became a recluse at Pickfair. She faded from the public's attention for the remainder of her life, due in no small measure to her refusal to let her films be shown on television. Instead, she donated most of her films to the American Film Institute. The only place where her films can now be shown is at the Library of Congress in Washington, D.C.

Pickford's last public appearance was in 1976 when she appeared on film at Pickfair to thank the Academy of Motion Picture Arts and Sciences for an honorary Oscar. She died on May 29, 1979, in Santa Monica, California.

SEE ALSO:

Broadway • Chaplin, Charlie • Griffith, D.W. • Hollywood • Movie Industry

POETRY

The United States produced a wide range of poets in the twenties. Many were traditional versifiers, while some wrote experimental work that broke away from the established conventions of the 19th and early 20th centuries. The period was dominated by three literary giants—Ezra Pound and T.S. Eliot, who both worked in Europe, and William Carlos Williams.

American poets of the twenties made strenuous efforts to find original modes of expression. That in itself was nothing new. In every age emerging artists deliberately attempt to break free from the influence of the previous generation and find fresh ways of describing the world and human experience. They do this partly as an act of self-assertion, partly in order to avoid imitation and pastiche.

The poet from whose shadow American poets of the twenties most wanted to emerge was Walt Whitman (1819–1892). His incantatory style, without regular meter or rhyme, had generated numerous imitators since the publication of *Leaves of Grass* in 1855. Few, however, were of the first rank, and their quality was steadily diminishing—a truly new voice was a long time coming, and many writers of the late 19th century were either incapable of finding their own distinctive voice or else failed to realize that Whitman was unique and inimitable.

Pound and imagism

While the influence of Whitman remained powerful—many would say oppressive—at the start of the twenties, it was by then finally in decline. The reaction against his style had been led by Ezra Pound (1885–1972). In 1912 Pound had founded imagism, a movement that flourished until about 1918. Its aim had been to revitalize the language of poetry; its methods were to remove every word that could possibly be judged superfluous and to develop a rhythm that was musical but not metronomically regular. Pound's poetry before 1920 was characterized by tight, often elliptical expressions and crystalline images. It also reflected his interest in Chinese ideograms (a symbol used in writing to represent a thing or idea, rather than a specific word) and the Japanese haiku (a traditional verse form expressing a single emotion or idea in which 17 syllables are arranged in lines of 5, 7, and 5 syllables). Some of Pound's short poems, such as "In a Station of the Metro" (1913), were attempts to epitomize the theory of imagism in a few lines:

"The apparition of these faces in the crowd;
Petals on a wet, black bough."

EMILY DICKINSON

Although Emily Dickinson (1830–1886) was a contemporary of Walt Whitman, it was not until the twenties that she received public acknowledgment, mainly through the efforts of critic and poet Conrad Aiken.

Dickinson began writing in about 1858. Her poems were unconventional in form, consisting of irregular rhythms adapted from the meters of hymns, slant rhymes, and eccentric phrasing and syntax. The poems were also deceptive in tone: Beneath their superficial simplicity of language and theme—she dealt principally with death, eternity, and the inner life—lay an almost unparalleled emotional intensity and candor. Unknown at the start of the twenties, by the end of the decade Dickinson was widely acclaimed as the greatest female poet since Sappho (sixth century B.C.).

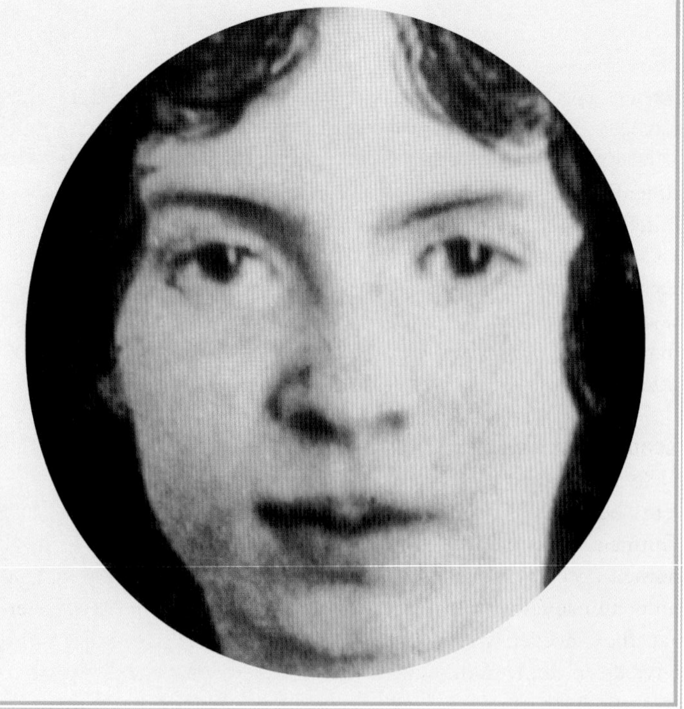

Emily Dickinson in about 1850. This portrait is the only one accepted as authentic by historians.

Archibald MacLeish in the 1940s. Three times a Pulitzer Prize winner for poetry, MacLeish wrote verse that reflected a concern with national and social issues. Before becoming known as a poet, he practiced law.

Pound's most controversial work was *Cantos*, the first installment of which appeared in 1925. By the time he finally set it aside in 1959, it had stretched to 800 pages and 10 volumes. The epic attempts to explain the history, economics, and culture not just of America but of the world. This aim was overambitious, and the work contains passages of impenetrable obscurity. Yet *Cantos* is not entirely a failure: It also features some of the greatest work on which Pound's lasting reputation is based.

Perhaps even more significant than Pound's own poetry was his work as an editor and nurturer of talent. The most important of his many discoveries was T.S. Eliot (1888–1965), who announced himself in 1915 with "The Love Song of J. Alfred Prufrock." The poem was first published in *Poetry* magazine, of which Pound, then based in London, England, was foreign editor. When Eliot produced his masterpiece in 1922, *The Waste Land*, he dedicated it to Pound, whom he described as *il miglior fabbro* (the better maker).

Poetry: A Magazine of Verse was founded in 1912 by poet Harriet Monroe (*see box on p. 156*). It became one of the most influential journals ever to appear in the United States. Although Monroe herself was not an innovative poet, *Poetry* magazine provided an outlet for all the major poets of the twenties, many of whom might not have become known without the opportunity it offered.

Escape from tradition

While American poets of the twenties were belatedly laying the ghost of Whitman, they were still haunted by another specter that they found even harder to exorcise. That was the feeling that they needed to escape from the conventions and traditions of British literature. As the poet Wallace Stevens put it: "We live in two different physical worlds, and it is not nonsense to think that that matters." Although the English-born W.H. Auden would later assert that "there is scarcely one American poet, from [William Cullen] Bryant [1794–1878] on, who can be mistaken for an Englishman," that was not how Americans themselves saw their literary history. Their sense of cultural inferiority was a double bind: The harder they tried to escape the influence of England, the more they found themselves sounding like Whitman, who had himself set out to create poetry that would

William Carlos Williams in 1963. His poetry was a celebration of things rather than ideas. His early poems were imagist, but later he became a major modernist writer, helping create a new American voice.

reflect the American melting pot of races and nationalities, the democratic aspirations of the people, and the physical vastness of the United States.

Black poets were also struggling to escape European literary influences and to find their own unique voice. They began to experiment by combining European literary techniques with African American themes. The cultural movement known as the Harlem Renaissance provided a stimulating environment for a new generation of black poets such as Langston Hughes (1902–1967), Countee Cullen (1903–1946), and Claude McKay (1890–1948).

Pound and Eliot

Even the greatest of the rebels were not immune to this English influence. Pound's *Hugh Selwyn Mauberley* (1920)—a semi-autobiographical sequence of poems describing a young American poet's attempts to influence the English literary tradition—was imagist in intention but contained rhythms of chanting that were unmistakably Whitmanesque.

The most extreme case was that of T.S. Eliot, who became a strange midatlantic hybrid. Although Missouri-born and Harvard-educated, his scholarly poetic diction was strongly influenced by the work of the 17th-century metaphysical poets—above all John Donne—and his work revealed a mind-set that was classical, reactionary, and thus essentially English. Unlike the work of almost all his North American contemporaries, Eliot's verse betrays virtually no internal signs of having been written by a native American. Eliot settled in England and in 1927 ritualistically severed his American roots by becoming a British subject.

Being not meaning

If any group of artists can truly be said to have a single aim, that of the American poets of the twenties is well summed up

THE SYNTHETIC POET

While it is often convenient to pigeonhole the poets of the twenties into one of two categories—avant-garde to describe the likes of Ezra Pound, traditionalist as a label for Robert Frost—most of them wrote in more than one manner, and such labels are of limited use. Few, however, had a foot as firmly in both camps as Carl Sandburg (1878–1967). Although Sandburg dabbled in concrete poetry (*see p. 157*), his work remained strongly influenced by Walt Whitman. An unlikely combination, perhaps, but an effective and successful one: Sandburg was always a distinctive and original voice. His early collection *Chicago Poems* (1916) was metrically irregular, using unrhymed lines of varying length, and shocked the public through its use of street slang.

Sandburg also wrote children's books, such as *Rootabaga Stories* (1922), topical books such as *The Chicago Race Riots* (1919), which were based on his observations as a newspaper reporter, and a series of celebrated biographies of Abraham Lincoln. *The American Songbag* (1927) was a collection of the folk songs he used in his public performances as a singer and reader of his poems. Sandburg's evocations of American urban and rural life, his compassion for the working class, and his love of nature all influenced American literature.

by Archibald MacLeish (1892–1982), the author of four books of verse, who asserted that "a poem must not mean but be." If the work that best fits this description is *The Waste Land*, the poet who adopted it most consistently as his watchword was Conrad Aiken (1889–1973). Aiken sought to strip verse of its intellectual content and thereby achieve "absolute" poetry, in which the poet uses words with the same detachment as a musical composer employs notes or chords. His early poetry, which shows the influence of Eliot (who was his classmate at Harvard), John Masefield, Edgar Lee Masters, Edgar Allan Poe, and the imagists, is largely narrative verse, but these poems foreshadow the mature Aiken in the role of poet as musician.

The musical quality of Aiken's poetry is evident in his best-known lyric, "Morning Song from Senlin," contained in *The Charnel Rose* (1918). Aiken's *Selected Poems* (1929), which won the Pulitzer Prize for poetry, were an attempt to create a musical structure with words while exploring the human psyche. As a critic, Aiken helped establish Emily Dickinson's reputation by editing and writing an introduction to her *Selected Poems* (1924) (*see box on p. 152*).

Hilda Doolittle (known as H.D.) in 1960. Her early poems, with their spare, elegant lyrics, vivid imagery, and short lines, were strongly imagist, but later H.D. became an important modernist writer.

HARRIET MONROE

Harriet Monroe was born in 1860 in Chicago, Illinois, and educated privately, first in her native city and later in Washington, D.C. Her efforts to become a poet were encouraged by Robert Louis Stevenson, with whom she corresponded for several years. In 1888 a sonnet entitled "With Shelley's Poems" became her first published work, appearing in *Century* magazine. On the strength of that she was picked in 1892 to write "Columbian Ode," which was recited at the opening of the following year's world's fair in Chicago.

In 1896 Monroe published a biography of her late brother-in-law, the architect John Wellborn Root. Her "Cantata," a specially commissioned celebration of the history of Chicago, was sung at the dedication of the Auditorium Building in 1889.

By the start of the 20th century Moore's verse appeared regularly in national magazines, and she also worked as an art and drama critic for Chicago newspapers. Her subsequent books of poetry included *After All* (1900), *The Passing Show: Five Modern Plays in Verse* (1903), *The Dance of the Seasons* (1911), and *The Difference and Other Poems* (1924).

Harriet Monroe's output was prolific, but her verse is generally second-rate. Her real achievement was *Poetry: A Magazine of Verse*, which she founded in Chicago in 1912 and edited until her death, in Arequipa, Peru, in 1936. The monthly periodical brought a range of new poets to the attention of a wider public than they would ever otherwise have reached. Many of the early contributors were American—most notably Carl Sandburg, Vachel Lindsay (1879–1931), and Edgar Lee Masters (1869–1950)—but up to a third were British and Irish, including Rupert Brooke, James Joyce, Edward Thomas, and W.B. Yeats.

Poetry was highly regarded by writers and critics, but most other people were baffled by its contents: Pound and Eliot were too avant-garde for a readership brought up on Longfellow and Whitman. Thus its circulation was never great, and it always struggled financially. That it survived at all was due in large measure to philanthropic patronage. *Poetry* is still published today from offices in the Newberry Library on Chicago's North Side. Its extensive archive is now housed in the Lilly Library at Indiana University.

A portrait of Harriet Monroe. She was a minor poet herself but a leading judge of the poetry of others. She lived a solitary life and never married. Her main recreation was mountaineering, and it was during a trip to the Andes that she died, aged 75.

Frost and H.D.

In addition to Eliot, Ezra Pound either discovered or cultivated several other writers, including the poets Robert Frost (1874–1963) and Hilda Doolittle (1886–1961). Frost—who was in his forties by the time Pound brought him to the world's attention—was an important poet who pioneered new interplays between rhythm and meter and brought to poetry the vocabulary and inflections of contemporary everyday speech. Yet although to that extent he was an innovator, he was primarily an old-fashioned pastoral poet of the New England countryside. For the most part he stuck rigidly to traditional forms and once remarked that he would as soon play tennis without a net as write free verse, a form that was popularized in the twenties by several other poets including Carl Sandburg (*see box on p. 155*).

The other famous New England poet of the period was Edwin Arlington Robinson (1869–1935). He was not noted for his technical experimentation—he found conventional verse forms such as ballads, blank verse, and sonnets perfectly adequate for his purposes—but despite or possibly because of this he won both critical and popular acclaim, winning three Pulitzer Prizes for *Collected Poems* (1921), *The Man Who Died Twice* (1924), and *Tristram* (1927). His most widely read short poems, "Richard Cory" and "Miniver Cheevy," are both about unhappy and disappointed individuals.

Known as H.D., Hilda Doolittle came under Pound's influence after she moved to England in 1911. Her best-known works—including "Heat" and "Oread"—contain the precise images, economical language, and freedom of form that characterize imagism. Like others involved in that movement, H.D. passed through this developmental period to find a new style, utilizing classical Greek myths and exploring archetypes. Her collections of poetry include *Sea Garden* (1916), *Collected Poems* (1925, 1940), *The Walls Do Not Fall* (1944), and *Helen in Egypt* (1961).

Doctor of poetry

If Ezra Pound laid the foundations of American poetry of the interwar years, it was his close friend William Carlos Williams (1883–1963) who built the greatest edifice on them. Williams published his first book, *Poems*, in 1909, three years after graduating from the University of Pennsylvania Medical School—he remained a practicing doctor all his life. His importance as a poet lies partly in his insistence that American art be based on American experience and partly in the direct way he found of expressing timeless truths in verse that was almost completely without verbal ornament. To Williams innovation was the only accurate gauge of a writer's merit: Imagery was flimflam.

Pound had called on poets to "make it new," and Williams continuously sought to follow that injunction in his own writing, which included *The Tempers* (1913), *Al Que Quiere!* (1917), the prose poem *Kora in Hell: Improvisations* (1920), and *Spring and All* (1923). He followed these volumes with *In the American Grain* (1925), which dealt with the myths and cultural history of his native land. Williams's poems are filled with people and their speaking voices, but they also contain close observations of nature and thus exemplify a method that Williams termed "objectivist." As he himself later put it in the epic poem *Paterson*, there can be "no ideas but in things."

Other leading figures

E.E. Cummings (1894–1962) was a poet whose unique use of typography, punctuation, and vocabulary—some of his poems contain forceful and, for the period, notably frank language—was highly influential in the development of modern poetry. He was also a painter, novelist, and playwright. He adopted lower-case letters in printed versions of his own name—e. e. cummings—after a printer's error in *Eight Harvard Poets* (1917). His later unconventional use of typography and punctuation was, however, premeditated. He used capitalization only for emphasis, not simply to indicate proper nouns and the beginnings of sentences, and invented numerous new phrases such as "non-sufficiently inunderstood."

Cummings also used typographical design and spacing on the page to create images. This was a modern form of concrete poetry, an old device in which the poem is printed in a particular shape or pattern. A famous example of the genre is "The Altar" by the 17th-century English poet George Herbert, in which the words on the page are arranged so that they resemble the object described.

Many of the other major American poets of the twenties were similar to Robert Frost inasmuch as they were too idiosyncratic to have established schools or traditions. That was particularly true of Wallace Stevens (1879–1955), whose first published poems appeared in *Poetry* magazine in 1914. He was an insurance salesman whose elusive and unconventional poems are philosophical meditations on the nature of appearance and reality and the significance of belief. *Harmonium* (1923), the only volume that he published in the twenties, is deliberately timeless and lacking in a sense of place.

The most famous work by Stephen Vincent Benet (1898–1943) is *John Brown's Body* (1928), which won the 1929 Pulitzer Prize for poetry. Over 300 pages long, the poem covers the Civil War from Brown's raid at Harpers Ferry to peace at Appomattox. It is not a eulogy of Brown but an epic narrative that pays tribute to the fruitful diversity on which the modern United States is built. It contains invented stories of men from all parts of America and from many walks of life—from cabinet officers to frontiersmen—in contexts that range from wartime heroism to domestic routine. Benet's historical perspective, based on wide reading, is not especially profound, but neither is it simplistic or partisan. Benet had a remarkable gift for clear and rapid narration and could bring scenes vividly to life by the skillful use of image and metaphor.

Harold Hart Crane (1899–1932) became known for complex and carefully crafted verse. The first of the two volumes of poetry published in his lifetime, *White Buildings* (1926), attracted the favorable attention of critics. Crane is best known for *The Bridge* (1930), an ambitious epic in which he attempted to encompass the totality of American visions and myths. The title refers to New York's Brooklyn Bridge, which Crane turns into a unifying link between nature (the water below) and civilization (the surrounding metropolis). With this as its central symbol, the poem moves back and forth in time and place through the American experience. *The Bridge* won the annual Poetry Award in 1930, and some critics still rank Crane second only to Eliot among early 20th-century poets. Crane was a fervent interpreter of his own work, writing numerous letters to friends in which he painstakingly explained phrases such as "adagios of islands."

Marianne Moore (1887–1972) wrote witty, ironic verse that is often complex in technique but conservative in content. Long sentences seem to break arbitrarily at line endings, but Moore always observed a strict syllabic measure. She quoted extensively in her work, surrounding her borrowings with quotation marks and identifying sources in footnotes. Her two collections of the twenties were *Poems* (1921) and *Marriage* (1923).

Edna St. Vincent Millay (1892–1950) was conservative in her use of form and technique, but her outspoken attitudes and liberated views made her the embodiment of the New Woman. The frank love poetry of her 1920 collection *A Few Figs from Thistles* shocked many critics. She was the first woman to win the Pulitzer Prize for poetry in 1923 with *The Harp Weaver and Other Poems*.

SEE ALSO:

Black Writers • Cummings, E.E. • Frost, Robert • Harlem Renaissance • Hughes, Langston • Literature • Lost Generation • Millay, Edna St. Vincent • Modernism • Paris • Pound, Ezra

POLITICAL RADICALISM

Radicalism is a political stance advocating fundamental changes in the existing political, economic, and social order. In the United States in the 1920s it was a strong movement, but it never became politically powerful, principally because the U.S. electoral system is inimical to third parties.

Although many international observers predicted that the social conditions arising from industrialization and urbanization in the United States would lead, as they had in Europe, to the emergence of radical socialist politics, left-wing parties were never more than a minor influence. There were numerous reasons for that. The two-party system and the lack of any kind of proportional representation made it difficult for a third party to gain electoral success. Because parties that came in second in an election got nothing, a vote for a third party was even more likely to be wasted. The labor movement as a whole, meanwhile, was reluctant to support any specific workers' party for fear of alienating its Republican and Democratic members. For many Americans, too, socialism and communism were closely associated with foreign influence—particularly after the Bolshevik Revolution in Russia in 1917—at a time when the United States was experiencing a general upswell in nativism, or suspicion of attitudes and values that were regarded as "un-American." Nativism sparked the Red Scare of 1919, during which numerous foreign radicals were rounded up and deported without trial.

Radical parties

However, despite concerted political opposition and popular hostility, a number of radical parties did emerge in the United States. They included the Socialist Labor Party, the Progressive Party, the Socialist Party, the National Labor Party, and the Communist Party, which from 1929 became known as the Communist Party–United States of America (CPUSA).

The Socialist Labor Party was founded in 1877 but was largely outmoded in 1901 when its "Kangaroo" wing joined the Social Democratic Party of Eugene V. Debs (1855–1926) to form the Socialist Party of America. In 1912 the Socialist Party won 6 percent of the vote in congressional elections but ended up without a single representative.

Debs, a former union leader, ran for president in five of the six elections between 1900 and 1920. He made his best showing in 1920, when he received almost one million votes but still finished last. He fought the entire 1920 campaign from a jail cell, where he was imprisoned for making a speech against U.S. involvement in World War I.

Russian revolutionary Leon Trotsky (1879–1940) lived briefly in the Bronx in 1917 and noted the conveniences enjoyed by American workers. One explanation of why a radical workers' party did not take hold in the United States was that many U.S. citizens enjoyed a comparatively high standard of living.

Socialist schism

At the end of World War I the Socialist Party was the major leftist U.S. political grouping, but it split after internal disagreements about the best way to achieve political objectives in the light of the Russian Revolution. Some members wanted to reject participation in the democratic system and follow the Bolshevik example of direct, violent action against the state. In 1919 these radicals quit the Socialist Party, but they then themselves split internally into two factions, the Communist Labor Party and the mostly Russian Communist Party. The latter was the more popular; but even its membership was never more than 10,000, and it had little electoral success. The party put up candidates in local elections during the 1920s, but no communist was ever elected to Congress or any state legislature. It was the subject of widespread suspicion because of its links with bolshevism and was shunned

WAR ON THE LEFT: THE ESPIONAGE AND SEDITION ACTS

"The seed of revolution is repression," said President Woodrow Wilson in 1919. Wilson's presidency, however, had seen two acts passed by Congress that were among the most repressive ever enacted by a U.S. government. They were used extensively to suppress left-wing political parties. Between them the Espionage Act of June 1917 and the Sedition Act of May 1918 broadened federal and judicial authority to become involved in the suppression of "anti-American" activities. They reflected the anti-German, anti-Bolshevik, and antipacifist prejudice generated by the U.S. declaration of war against Germany in April 1917. The first fixed a maximum penalty of $10,000 and 20 years in prison for anyone who interfered with the military draft or encouraged disloyalty. It also authorized the postmaster general to intercept materials he considered to be seditious. The second banned dissent; among its provisions it made it an offense to incite subordination, discourage recruitment into the armed forces, publish "any disloyal, profane, scurrilous or abusive language about the form of government," or bring the government "into contempt."

Hardest hit by the measures were the Industrial Workers of the World (IWW) and the Socialist Party. In 1918 almost one-third of the party's 5,000 local branches were suppressed, and its leading members, Eugene V. Debs and Victor Berger, were sent to prison, along with the secretary general, C.T. Schenck. Debs was convicted of encouraging draft-dodging and Berger and Schenck of denouncing the war. Elected to Congress in 1918 and 1920, Berger was twice refused admission to take his seat, and in New York five Socialist members were expelled from the state legislature in 1919.

by parties that were wary of being damned by association. In 1922, for example, communists were barred from the convention called by the Conference for Progressive Political Action, and the socialists supported the ban.

Limited appeal

The electoral appeal of socialism, although greater than that of communism, remained strictly limited. In Milwaukee, Wisconsin, Emil Seidel (1864–1947) became the first socialist mayor of a major U.S. city in 1910. Party leader Victor Berger (1860–1929), with the backing of labor unions, especially the garment workers and the brewers, was elected to Congress in five consecutive elections from 1918 to 1926. Daniel Hoan (1881–1961) became Milwaukee mayor in 1916 and remained in office until 1940. He was followed in 1948 by Frank Zeidler (1912–).The only other member of the party to make it to Congress was Meyer London (1871–1926) of New York. In the 1912 elections 1,200 Socialists were elected to state and local offices, but the party struggled to attract members—just 109,000 in 1920—in the face of government repression and the inherent problems facing all third parties.

Labor parties also found their progress restricted. The most important of them, the Minnesota Farmer–Labor Party (MFLP), was formed in 1916 during the buildup to U.S. entry into World War I. It was an amalgam of the state branch of the national Non-Partisan League (NPL), the Minnesota Socialist Party, and the Minnesota state Federation of Labor, which soon formally voted an ongoing affiliation with the party under the name of the Farmer–Labor Association.

The MFLP grew rapidly until the mid-1920s. At its peak in 1922–1923 it had both the state's U.S. senators, together with three representatives, 24 state senators, and 46 members of the state legislature. MFLP leader Floyd B. Olson (1891–1936) served three terms as governor from 1930. In 1924 the MFLP played a key role in the presidential candidacy of Robert La Follette (1855–1925). But in the late twenties the MFLP faltered, losing attractive candidates, voter enthusiasm, and, eventually and crucially, the formal support of the state Federation of Labor.

Another labor grouping, the Chicago Farmer–Labor Party (CFLP), was formed in 1920 through the merger of the Labor Party of Illinois with sister labor parties and progressives who had left the Republican party in 1912. However, the CFLP never joined forces with the MFLP, and that was symptomatic of one of the key problems of American radicalism: the difficulty its supporters found in forming alliances. La Follette was concerned about what he regarded as the socialism of the CFLP, and so he declined an invitation to be its presidential candidate in 1920. When he ran four years later, it was as the candidate of the League for Progressive Political Action (the Progressives), a party that was never socialist despite advocating reform in business legislation. He lost the election but polled 4.8 million votes, one-sixth of the total, including many former supporters of the CFLP.

False socialist dawn

In the twenties the Socialist Party won elections in Minneapolis, New York City, and Reading, Pennsylvania, but such breakthroughs were few. In Milwaukee the party gradually declined, although as late as 1926 it won 45 percent of the seats on the city council. Even in their heyday Milwaukee Socialists were unable, owing to restrictions on the power of city hall, to implement much of their program, which included free medical care and extensive public ownership. As a socialist mayor of Minneapolis said, "Socialism cannot be put into effect in any one city."

SEE ALSO:

Debs, Eugene V. • Labor Movement • La Follette, Robert • Politics & Government • Progressivism • Red Scare

POLITICS AND GOVERNMENT

The politics of the 1920s were in many respects a reaction to the progressivism of the 1910s and the upheavals of World War I. The Republican governments of Warren G. Harding, Calvin Coolidge, and Herbert Hoover embraced a return to "normalcy," conservatism, and nonintervention.

American politics began the 1920s in a waning storm of change and reform, and ended the decade just as another storm of change and reform was on the horizon. For much of the mid-twenties a sense of "normalcy" seemed to prevail; beneath the surface, however, the American political system was adjusting to many fundamental changes and was preparing for many more.

Woodrow Wilson: the postwar years

From 1917 to 1919 U.S. society and politics were dramatically altered by the nation's belated but intense participation in World War I (1914–1918). The federal government grew dramatically during the war, supervising the creation of an army of four million men and controlling the economic and political activity of a nation at war. President Woodrow Wilson (1913–1921), reelected by a narrow margin in 1916 on the campaign claim that "he kept us out of war," embraced what he perceived to be the need for the United States to provide a beacon for democracy around the world.

Wilson's idealistic illusions died a hard death in the years following the end of the war in 1918. Wilson traveled to France to the peace conference at Versailles, where the victorious Allies met to reshape the world. However, he left the conference bitterly disappointed, since the British, French, and Italian delegations seemed more interested in settling old scores and pursuing their own national interests than in a "world made safe for democracy."

Despite Wilson's disillusionment, the Versailles Treaty crafted by the Allies contained at least one of his most treasured goals: the creation of a League of Nations, a body in which each nation would have a vote and in which each nation would pledge to protect others against attack. It was the league that made the treaty worth signing in Wilson's mind. He embarked on a nationwide

President Woodrow Wilson pictured around 1916, the year in which he was reelected to a second term in office. Wilson's idealism for the postwar peace settlements was largely rejected in both the United States and Europe.

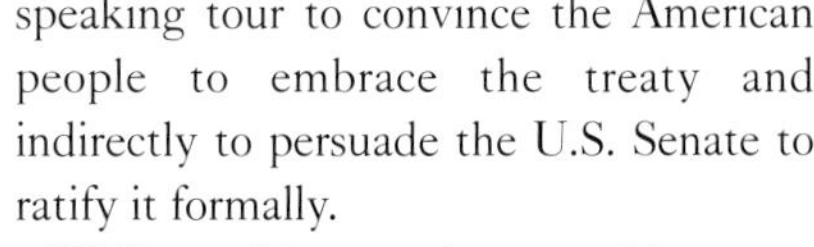

speaking tour to convince the American people to embrace the treaty and indirectly to persuade the U.S. Senate to ratify it formally.

While on his marathon speaking tour, Wilson suffered a serious stroke that left him incapacitated for months and seriously impaired for the rest of his presidency. His wife Edith served ably to conceal the severity of the president's illness and to aid him in his daily duties, working in many ways as the first female chief of staff. All of Wilson's efforts and sufferings were in vain: The Senate refused to ratify the Treaty of Versailles or the League of Nations. The United States later agreed to a separate peace treaty with Germany in 1923.

The communist threat

Another unsettled issue from the war vexed America at the dawn of the twenties. The Allies at Versailles no longer included Russia, which had fought Germany with such fervor until 1917 but left the war on the fall of the czar and the communist takeover. The revolutionary leaders Vladimir Ilich Lenin (1870–1924) and Leon Trotsky (1879–1940) made it clear that they had no intention of limiting their communist movement to the old Russian Empire. The new communist government wanted world revolution, and many people in the United States took the perceived threat very seriously.

American society had long had a small but active radical strand, and the waves of

Women demonstrate in support of Prohibition around 1920. With slogans such as "character in candidates" and "law makers must not be law breakers," they urge politicians to adhere to the new law, which was widely flouted.

immigration in the early 20th century brought in a number of committed European socialists and anarchists. They included the anarchists Sacco and Vanzetti, whose trial for murder riveted the nation in the 1920s. However, there was very little evidence of a genuine threat to the U.S. government from these groups or of a grand Soviet conspiracy of any kind operating on American soil.

Nevertheless, the specter of a communist coup in the United States was powerful enough to enable the passage of a number of state and federal laws intended to stifle radical dissent, frequently at the cost of individual rights (*see box on p. 166*). By 1919 fear of communism had grown into the full-fledged Red Scare, a nationwide crackdown on subversive groups led by Attorney General A. Mitchell Palmer (1872–1936). On January 2, 1920, some 5,000 "radicals" were arrested in over 30 cities across the United States in one of the largest mass arrests in the nation's history. The spread of communism fell far short of American shores in the 1920s—the only country successfully "recruited" by Lenin and Trotsky in the decade was Russia's neighbor Mongolia. However, Palmer's reaction to the small radical movements in the United States did little to enhance U.S. security and much to damage freedom of expression and political diversity in the country.

The Versailles Treaty and the Red Scare were among several significant ongoing issues to feature in U.S. politics as the twenties dawned. Two more were embodied in amendments passed to the U.S. Constitution in the wake of World War I; both reshaped politics in the 1920s. The Eighteenth Amendment, ratified in 1919, prohibited the manufacture, transportation, and sale of alcohol, and the Nineteenth Amendment, ratified in 1920, extended the right to vote to women nationwide, although many states had allowed women to vote in state-level elections for years. Both Prohibition and woman suffrage were the culmination of decades of work, often by reformers who

THE FIRST FEMALE GOVERNORS

The Nineteenth Amendment of the U.S. Constitution, ratified in 1920, gave full rights to women to vote in elections and to run for public office. Five years later the first female state governor was inaugurated. She was Nellie Ross (1876–1977), a Democrat who was elected as governor of Wyoming, the state that had been the first to give women the right to vote in state elections in 1887. In 1933 Ross became one of the first women to hold an important federal office when Franklin D. Roosevelt appointed her director of the U.S. Mint, a position she held until 1953.

A week after Governor Ross took office, Miriam "Ma" Ferguson (1875–1961) was inaugurated as governor of Texas, a state that had not led the way in the struggle for voting rights for women. Governor Ferguson had followed a path to office very different from that which the suffrage movement had imagined.

Miriam Ferguson first became involved in politics as a dutiful wife supporting the political career of her husband, James Ferguson (1871–1944), a very successful Texas politician who was twice elected governor in the 1910s. In his second term, however, James was hounded from office in a scandal involving allegations that he had taken bribes in return for state contracts and pardons from the state prison.

Capitalizing on her husband's enduring popularity with the voters, Miriam Ferguson ran for governor in 1924 and won, even though she had never held any elected office of any kind before. Indeed, at least part of her appeal was the belief of many voters that she would simply do as her husband advised her. James Ferguson would get to be governor again after all. The reality of Ma Ferguson's terms in office was more complicated. Miriam was a popular governor in her own right and a powerful symbol of the new rights of women in U.S. politics. However, she was dogged by the same allegations that had followed her husband: that she was corrupt in her treatment of pardons. Miriam Ferguson pardoned or paroled hundreds of convicted criminals each year, and in a state famous for its tough law-and-order reputation it was never clear whether the pardons reflected mercy or a bribe. Ma Ferguson lost her bid for her party's nomination in 1928. Her rival for the governor's job had the misfortune of being elected just in time to be in office for the first years of the Great Depression. Ma ran again in 1932, this time successfully, and continued her unusual political career well into the 1930s.

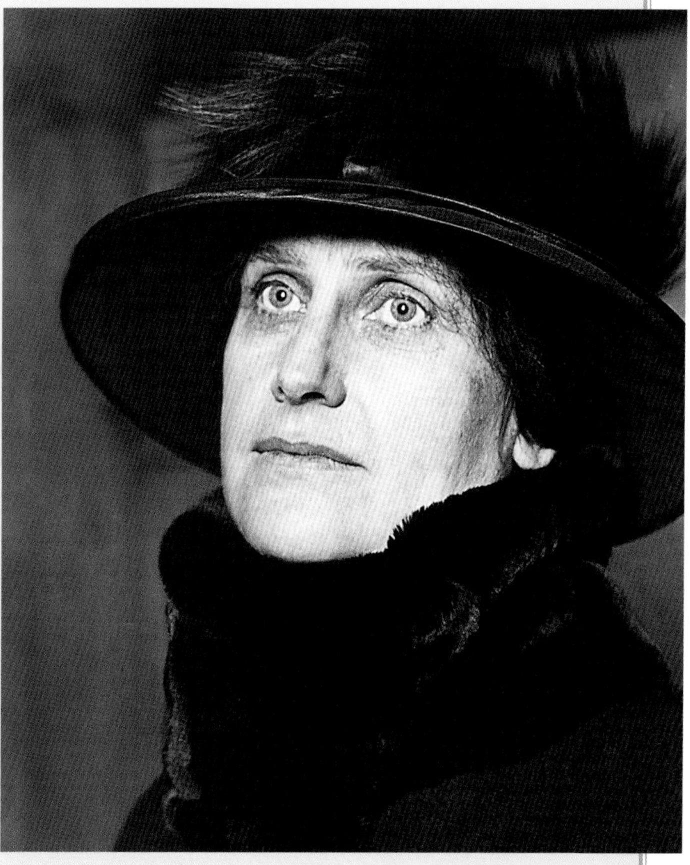

Nellie Ross photographed in March 1925, just before her inauguration as governor of Wyoming.

pursued both causes simultaneously, such as the Women's Christian Temperance Union. However, the upheaval accompanying World War I gave both causes a final, needed boost.

Prohibition

With Prohibition the country initiated a great experiment in social reform, which was celebrated by many supporters as a decisive blow against "Demon Rum" and all the social ills that accompanied alcohol, but which was just as hated by many other people on principle and violated by still more in practice. Prohibition was especially popular among Protestant Americans, especially in rural or small-town settings. To many Protestant Americans whose ancestors had immigrated to America generations before, the waves of Catholic immigrants from southern and eastern Europe presented a grave risk to the United States' social fabric and traditional values. Prohibition's supporters saw the banning of alcohol as a necessary part of channeling the behavior of recent immigrants away from crime and poverty and into work and thrift. Most immigrant groups opposed this kind of "help," seeing Prohibition as an illegitimate attack on individual freedom.

The issue of Prohibition tore away at American political institutions throughout the 1920s. On the one hand, so many millions of Americans wanted to drink alcohol, whether legal or not, that a huge illegal industry arose. Some of the production and distribution was run by organized crime, such as Al Capone's Chicago mob, and some by very disorganized crime, such as Southern rural "moonshiners" and "bootleggers." Huge amounts of money were funneled into efforts to keep this illegal industry in business, including bribing public officials to look the other way and intimidating or assassinating those who tried to enforce the law. Many citizens questioned whether the goals of Prohibition were worth the cost to the rule of law.

The issue of Prohibition also tore apart the Democratic Party, which was almost evenly divided between rural Protestant supporters of Prohibition (the "drys") and urban, largely Catholic opponents (the "wets"). No issue caused more battles among Democrats or more weakened the Democrats in competition with the Republicans, a solid majority of whom favored Prohibition. The Democrats' internal battles over Prohibition contributed to the almost complete collapse of the party in many regions of the country in the 1920s and to the very poor showings of Democratic presidential candidates in the 1920, 1924, and 1928 elections.

Woman suffrage

The final extension of women's right to vote and to run for office enshrined in the Nineteenth Amendment also represented a fundamental change in American politics in the 1920s. It was the largest single increase in the number of eligible voters in the nation's history. Within five years of its passage women had been elected to offices as high as state governor (*see box opposite*).

However, even though the number of potential voters dramatically increased, the percentage of those who actually turned out at elections to vote continued to fall. In the 1880 presidential election 79 percent of eligible voters voted, but by 1916 turnout had slipped to 62 percent. Only 49 percent of all eligible men and women voted in the 1920 presidential election, which was held just months after the ratification of the Nineteenth Amendment. That was the first time fewer than half the electorate had voted, and it happened right after the number of people eligible to vote had been doubled. In the 1924 election turnout slipped even further.

The total number of votes cast did increase through the 1920s. Many women exercised their newly guaranteed right, but many more chose not to, mirroring the decline in turnout among men. The Nineteenth Amendment did little to secure the vote for African American women who, like African American men, were largely prevented from voting by a combination of state-level laws and physical intimidation, despite supposed constitutional guarantees. Whatever the promise of political equality meant to women in the 1920s, there was precious little political equality for African Americans in the 1920s.

A poster produced by the League of Women Voters in the early 1920s to encourage women to use their vote. A mother accompanied by her daughter casts her vote, while a guardian figure points to the U.S. Capitol.

Democratic presidential candidate James Cox (left) and his running mate Franklin D. Roosevelt (right) on the campaign trail in Dayton, Ohio, in August 1920. They lost to Warren G. Harding in the November election.

Return to conservatism

The social and political upheavals of the late 1910s and early 1920s were soon followed by a conservative reaction. In the twenties the Republican Party rallied around an idea voiced by Senator Warren G. Harding (1865–1923) in May 1920: After so much change what America most needed was a return to "normalcy." The specifics of what normalcy meant were unclear; normalcy was not a word in common usage until Harding made it his own. Yet whatever it meant, the idea of normalcy brought strong Republican majorities in elections throughout the decade and became the inspiration for the dominant governing philosophy of the era.

Harding had entered politics after a successful career as a newspaper editor and publisher in his native Ohio. He was considered to be a popular speaker, good looking and magnetic, but perhaps a bit shallow. Harding's supporters in the conservative wing of the party outnumbered the old progressive wing, which had been badly wounded by the Roosevelt–Taft feud in 1912 (*see box opposite*). After a long fight at the 1920 national convention the Republicans nominated Harding as their presidential candidate. Harding's promise of normalcy implied a return to peace, prosperity, and limited government, and a sharp reduction in political reform and engagement in world affairs. Whatever normalcy was, it certainly was not progressivism or the League of Nations.

The Democratic Party in 1920 nominated as its presidential candidate James M. Cox (1870–1957), the mildly reformist governor of Ohio. Cox was a compromise choice, whose path to the nomination was even rockier than was

WILLIAM HOWARD TAFT

William Howard Taft (1857–1930) became the 27th president of the United States in 1909, succeeding his good friend Theodore Roosevelt (1858–1919) and winning a smashing victory in the 1908 election. However, over the course of his term in office Taft had a bitter falling out with Roosevelt. The feud split the Republican Party, and in 1912 Taft suffered the worst defeat ever experienced by an incumbent president. All along Taft had been reluctant to be president. Only the pleadings of Roosevelt had talked him into pursuing the presidency; his true love was the law. He had tearfully turned down an appointment to the U.S. Supreme Court while Roosevelt was president, out of his sense of duty that he should continue to serve in the Cabinet.

Taft got a second chance when President Harding chose him to be the new Chief Justice of the Supreme Court in June 1921. It was the first, and so far only, time a former president had been appointed as a federal judge. Uniquely among ex-presidents, Taft proved more successful and longer lasting in his postpresidential career. As president Taft had espoused conservative interpretations of the U.S. Constitution. As chief justice, however, he was not as rigidly conservative as many people predicted. Rather, Taft used his political and executive experience to help him become one of the most skillful organizers the Supreme Court had ever seen. Taft participated in many cases in the 1920s, including decisions that threw out antitrust and child labor laws. However, Taft sided with the court's progressives in supporting a state minimum wage law and in increasing the power of the presidency, an area of law in which he had gained bitter expertise. In the end President William Howard Taft had gotten exactly the job he wanted.

Former president William Howard Taft photographed around 1927, when he was chief justice of the Supreme Court, an office he held from 1921 to 1930.

GITLOW V. NEW YORK

The First Amendment to the U.S. Constitution protects freedom of speech and freedom of the press. However, for most of the country's history the Supreme Court held that the First Amendment limited only what the federal government could and could not do. If a state wished to limit an individual's freedom of speech, the state government was not bound by the U.S. Constitution, only by what the state's own constitution protected.

The Supreme Court changed its position on the First Amendment in 1925, in the case of *Gitlow v. New York*. Benjamin Gitlow (1891–1965) had been a member of the New York Socialist Party since 1909 and in 1918 had joined its radical wing. In 1919 the Socialist Party expelled this left-wing faction. With fellow radicals John Reed and James Larkin, Gitlow then founded the Communist Labor Party. In November 1919 he and James Larkin were arrested while distributing pamphlets that called for "revolutionary mass action" to overthrow the capitalist system, which Gitlow claimed was "in the process of disintegration and collapse."

The state of New York had passed a law during World War I that made it a crime to advocate the violent overthrow of the federal or state government. Gitlow was convicted, but appealed on the grounds that the state law violated his rights under the First Amendment. Attorneys for New York argued that the state government was not limited by the provisions of the U.S. Constitution, only by what the state's own constitution dictated. The New York state constitution gave no such wide-ranging protection for free speech.

The Supreme Court returned a split decision. The court let Gitlow's conviction stand but did make the claim that "We may and do assume that the freedom of speech and of the press ... are among the fundamental personal rights and 'liberties' protected ... from infringement by the States," under the due process clause of the Fourteenth Amendment.

So Gitlow did have a right to free speech, because the right of free speech is so critical to democracy that a claim of states' rights cannot trump it. However, Gitlow's right to free speech did not include the right to attempt to overthrow the government or cause others to make such an attempt. The Supreme Court extended First Amendment protection to cover actions of state governments, but made it very clear that the First Amendment rights themselves are not absolute.

In so doing, the Supreme Court began a process known as "nationalization" or "selective incorporation," under which, very gradually, most of the major rights in the U.S. Bill of Rights were enforced on state governments. Over time the Supreme Court came to recognize that the great importance of the right to an attorney, the freedom from unreasonable searches, and the prohibition on cruel and unusual punishment should be added to the list of provisions enforced on the states. However, to this day, the Supreme Court maintains that the Bill of Rights, as a whole, does not apply to state governments.

BENJAMIN GITLOW

Benjamin Gitlow was born in Elizabeth, New Jersey, on December 22, 1891. His political career dates from 1907, when he joined the Socialist Party. The following year he was elected delegate to its State Convention. During 1916 and 1917 he was active in the anti-war campaign, serving on the Executive Committee of the People's Council formed to prevent the entry of the United States into the World War. He was then elected to the New York State Ass bly, where he served for one term

In 1918 Gitlow allied himself the Left Wing of the Socialist Pa and became one of its leaders a with John Reed and James La With John Reed, he published edited the first left wing Socialist Communist papers in the Ur States: Revolutionary Age, Voic Labor and The Communist. In same year he helped to found Communist Labor Party. When was arrested in 1919 under the Cr nal Syndicalist Law, it was the case of its kind. His case was pealed to the United States Supr Court, and still serves as a prece for cases of this character. A three years in Sing Sing Prison was pardoned by Governor Al Sn While in prison, he was elected honorary member of the Mos Soviet. Twice, Gitlow ran as ca date for Vice-President of the Ur States, and once for Mayor of York, on the Communist ticket.

Gitlow was a member of the Po cal Committee of the American C munist Party and its all-powerful retariat of Three for a number years, was Secretary of the Part 1929, and a member of the Execu Committee of the Communist In national, and of the Red Internati of Trade Unions, as well as the l ing Presidium of both internation In these official capacities, he vis the Soviet Union in 1927, 1928 1929. In the latter year, he was pelled from the Communist Party the United States and the Commu International for defiance of Jos Stalin.

Benjamin Gitlow has now rea the conclusion that the present c in the Soviet Union and in the ternational Communist movemen crisis which is bringing about a r disintegration and collapse of Bol vism, dates from its assumptio power. In this book, "I CONFE Gitlow writes of his experience the course of more than thirty y in the Socialist and Communist m ments, and reveals the steps by w he arrived at this conclusion.

A newspaper report on Benjamin Gitlow. While in prison for breaking the New York State Criminal Anarchy Act, Gitlow ran as the Communist candidate for mayor of New York City and on his release for U.S. vice president in 1924 and 1928.

Harding's. Teamed with a dynamic young New Yorker named Franklin D. Roosevelt (1882–1945) as a running mate, Cox campaigned in strong support of the Versailles Treaty and the League of Nations. Despite a valiant effort from the Cox team, Harding won by a landslide in the electoral college and in the popular vote, while the Republicans also gained huge majorities in Congress.

The Harding administration

As the newly elected president, Harding registered two major accomplishments in his first year: the creation of the Bureau of the Budget and the Washington Conference for the Limitation of Armament. The Bureau of the Budget (known today as the Office of Management and Budget) gave the president a major tool in controlling federal spending and influencing national priorities more broadly. The Washington Naval Conference resulted in an agreement between Britain, Japan, France, Italy, and the United States to reduce the size of their navies. It was the first arms limitation treaty entered into by the United States, and it underscored Harding's desire to limit U.S. commitments and influence around the world; but ironically it also demonstrated that the U.S. could not just leave the world to get along on its own.

Harding remained personally popular throughout his time in office, but the country suffered a severe economic recession in 1920 and 1921, and the initial sluggishness of economic recovery hurt the Republican Party in the 1922 congressional elections. That November the Democrats cut into the Republican majorities in both the Senate and the House of Representatives.

Beneath the surface of Harding's personal popularity deep problems were growing in his administration. The most serious was the corruption of Harding's old

Calvin Coolidge poses on the White House lawn in February 1925. Coolidge succeeded to the presidency when Harding died in 1923 and was elected in 1924. He continued the conservative policies of his predecessor.

VICE PRESIDENT CHARLES DAWES

The Republican National Convention in 1924 had to choose a vice-presidential running mate for Calvin Coolidge, who had been elected as vice president in 1920, and who became president after the death of President Harding in 1923. The Republican convention delegates chose a man who was everyone's second choice, Charles Gates Dawes (1865–1951).

A very successful businessman before World War I, Dawes had served as a major in the Corps of Engineers during the war. He first gained fame in 1921, when he was called to testify before a congressional committee investigating misuse of funds during the war. Accused of having spent too much money while in charge of procuring horses for the Army in France, Dawes leapt to his feet and exclaimed, "Hell 'n Maria, we would have paid horse prices for sheep, if they could pull artillery." Dawes went on to defend his conduct, and the Army's, with a crowd-pleasing mix of patriotism and profanity.

The newly dubbed "Hell 'n' Maria" Dawes was then appointed to a series of important jobs in the Harding administration. He began as the first director of the Bureau of the Budget and was later given the task of restructuring the German war debt to the United States. The Dawes Plan (1924) for relieving the crushing German debt was a big success, economically and politically, and earned Charles Dawes a Nobel Peace Prize in 1925. From 1921 to 1925 Dawes also led a large citizens' group that actively opposed both labor unions and the Ku Klux Klan.

Dawes brought an impressive résumé to the job of vice president, but unfortunately for him, neither he nor the U.S. Constitution had much of an idea what the job of vice president involved. He irritated his boss, President Coolidge, by refusing to attend Cabinet meetings and by giving a major speech against the Senate's use of the filibuster (a tactic used by a minority of senators to delay or prevent parliamentary action by talking so long that the majority either grants concessions or withdraws the bill) on the same day as Coolidge's inaugural address.

One of the few responsibilities that the U.S. Constitution did give to the vice president was to be the presiding officer of the Senate. Dawes took this responsibility very seriously and was the last vice president to make an effort to preside over most Senate deliberations. However, Dawes found the debates boring and "rather irksome," and instead of becoming the Senate's true leader, he became a major irritant to most senators.

Dawes also picked a bad time to take an afternoon off. Miscalculating how long a day of recesses and debates would take, Dawes stole away from the Senate to take a quick nap at a nearby hotel. While he slept, the Senate took a vote on whether to confirm Coolidge's controversial choice for attorney general. The first vote ended in a tie. This result should have been a wonderful opportunity for Dawes. The only time a vice president may cast a vote in the Senate is to break a tie. While Senate staffers frantically tried to locate the absent and slumbering vice president, Coolidge's opponents in the Senate convinced a Democratic senator to change his vote. By the time Dawes could be informed of the need to break a tie, a second vote was underway, and Coolidge's nominee for attorney general lost by a single vote.

Dawes became the laughing-stock of the nation. To his credit, he bore this humiliation with great humor. Dawes enjoyed the spotlight whether he was playing the hero or the fool. When Dawes left office in 1929, a member of the Senate informed him that "The Senate got very tired of you at the beginning of your service." Dawes replied, "I should hate to think that the Senate was as tired of me at the beginning of my service as I am of the Senate at the end of it."Dawes went on to become U.S. ambassador to Great Britain and a talented composer.

Charles Dawes photographed at his desk in March 1925, shortly after his appointment as vice president to President Coolidge.

friends from Ohio, many of whom had received high-ranking positions in the executive branch. The worst offender was Secretary of the Interior Albert Fall (1861–1944), who arranged for the sale of government-owned oil fields to private companies, which in turn arranged for a substantial payoff for Secretary Fall. This affair, which came to be known as the Teapot Dome scandal for the name of one of the oil fields involved, came to encompass not only Fall's corruption but a whole network of bribery and corruption in the Harding administration.

The extent of the scandal was not yet clear in August of 1923, when Harding suffered a fatal stroke while on a vacation on the West Coast. The president's sudden death prompted a period of national mourning and grief. However, Harding's body had barely been laid to rest when the full fury of the Teapot Dome scandal broke. Almost overnight Harding's reputation plummeted. It was tarnished not just by the corruption of the president's close political friends but also by press investigations that purported to have uncovered extramarital affairs Harding had had, including one with a married woman and another with a much younger woman who admitted to romantic encounters with Harding in the White House itself. Harding's image was harmed so badly by these disclosures that historians ever since have almost unanimously ranked him as the worst president in American history.

The Coolidge administration

Harding's vice president, Calvin Coolidge (1872–1933), succeeded him in office in August 1923. Coolidge had risen slowly but steadily in his political career, beginning with election as a city council member in Northampton, Massachusetts, in 1900. In 1918 Coolidge won election as governor of Massachusetts, where press coverage of his handling of a police strike made him a popular national figure among Republicans. Coolidge also became famous for his legendary reluctance to give speeches or interviews, or even to engage in small talk.

"Silent Cal" had a sense of humor though. One of his favorite stories about himself involved a Washington party that he attended early in his term in office as president. Coolidge was standing alone at the party when he was approached by a Washington society wife who attempted to engage him in a friendly conversation. "Mr. President," the lady said, beaming, "I have a bet with my husband that I need you to settle. He bet me that I can't get you to say three words to me." Coolidge looked at her and thought for a moment, then replied: "You lose."

Coolidge's image of integrity and sternness made him a perfect successor to the disgraced Harding. As the sitting president, he was easily nominated as the Republican presidential candidate for the 1924 election, although Coolidge was disappointed in the convention's choice for his running mate (*see box opposite*). Coolidge also benefited immensely from the economic prosperity the country experienced in the mid-1920s. He forged a strong association in the public mind between the Republican Party, big business, the booming economy, and the spread of new technologies, such as radio and the airplane. "The chief business of America is business," Coolidge declared in 1924, and those Americans who enjoyed the full fruit of the 1920s economic boom wholeheartedly agreed.

However, for many Americans who did not fully share in the prosperity of the 1920s, Coolidge's faith in tax cuts, smaller government, and free enterprise was less convincing. Socialists, the labor movement, and farmers, in particular, were

THE FARMER–LABOR PARTY

The most famous third-party movement of the 1920s was the Progressive Party, which ran a strong presidential campaign under Wisconsin Senator Robert La Follette in 1924. However, a smaller third-party movement—the Farmer–Labor Party—proved much more enduring and, by that standard, more successful. Confusingly, during the twenties and thirties there were a number of different parties operating under the label of Farmer–Labor.

The most significant Farmer–Labor Party was formed in Minnesota in 1916 when state branches of the Non-Partisan League, the Socialist Party, and the Federation of Labor amalgated to form the Minnesota Farmer–Labor Party (MFLP). In 1922 MFLP candidate Henrik Shipstead (1881–1960) was elected to the U.S. Senate. In 1924 the MLFP chose to endorse La Follette rather than to run its own candidate. In the late twenties the party floundered and, vitally, lost the support of the state Federation of Labor. In 1930 the MFLP's gubernatorial candidate Floyd B. Olson (1891–1936) was elected and served as governor until his death in office.

Although the MFLP prospered during the thirties, the Democratic Party also revitalized itself and came to be seen as the nation's liberal party. The MFLP chose to join what it could not beat, merging with the Democratic Party in 1944. To this day the Minnesota Democratic–Farmer–Labor Party (DFL) remains one of the state's two major parties.

Another Farmer–Labor Party was formed at a labor convention in Chicago in 1920 when the Labor Party of Illinois amalgamated with sister labor parties and progressives who had left the Republican Party in 1912. The CFLP's semisocialist platform, which called for a variety of social and economic reforms, was intended to link together the interests of urban factory workers with the interests of small farmers in the Midwest and Great Plains. The CFLP did not affiliate with the MFLP. When La Follette turned down CFLP's invitation to run as their presidential nominee, they turned to Utah lawyer Parley P. Christensen (1869–1954). The party won 250,000 votes in 18 states in 1920 but lost its impetus and much of its support when La Follette ran in 1924.

searching for a new political home. In 1922 the Conference for Progressive Political Action (CPPA) was formed. On July 4, 1924, CPPA delegates selected Robert La Follette (1895–1953) of Wisconsin as the presidential candidate for a new Progressive Party. In contrast to Coolidge, La Follette called for increased federal efforts to break up monopolies, higher taxes on estates and inheritances, public ownership of railroads and utilities, and elections for federal judges.

While La Follette's wing challenged Coolidge's conservative Republicans, the Democratic Party tore itself apart in its 1924 convention. The Democrats were divided to their core over the issues of Prohibition and the Ku Klux Klan. The national convention debated a motion to denounce the Klan in its platform but, following heated argument, rejected the motion by an extremely narrow margin.

There was little more agreement on the presidential nominee. Al Smith (1873–1944), the anti-Prohibition and Catholic governor of New York, deadlocked with William McAdoo (1863–1941) of California, who garnered support from Southern and Western delegates. After over 100 separate rounds of balloting, the Democratic convention selected West Virginia attorney John W. Davis (1873–1955) as its nominee.

The 1924 election was a crushing victory for Coolidge. Davis won less than 30 percent of the overall vote and failed to win any states outside of the Democrats' bastion in the South. In many Western states Davis was barely on the ballot; the race there was between Coolidge and La Follette. The sheer magnitude of the Democrats' loss, coupled with the obvious divisions in the party, fed speculation that the Democrats would cease to be a major party at all.

La Follette polled 16.6 percent of the overall vote, winning his home state of Wisconsin and finishing ahead of the Democrat Davis in 11 states in the West and Midwest. In that sense the 1924 Progressive Party presidential ticket was one of the most successful third-party efforts in American history. At the local level, in many areas of the country a variety of groups loosely described as progressives were remaking city politics in the party's image.

However, the 1924 election marked the high point for the Progressive Party nationwide. The success of La Follette's 1924 campaign was not duplicated in later

Leaders of the Progressive Party confer about their presidential campaign in August 1924. Presidential candidate Robert La Follette is seated front left; Burton Wheeler, candidate for vice president, is seated in the center.

Herbert Hoover photographed around 1928, the year in which he was elected president. Once America's most popular statesman, he fell from public favor as he struggled unsuccessfully to pull the nation out of the Great Depression.

elections. Most Progressive Party voters drifted back to the Republicans or Democrats for the 1928 elections, and the New Deal in the 1930s cemented the allegiance of most Progressives to the Democrats. La Follette himself died in 1925, and the prospects for an enduring third party seemed to have died with him (*see box on p. 169*).

Coolidge was reelected with a mandate for more of the same, which he interpreted as a mandate not to do very much. Above all else, Coolidge's popularity was associated with the relative economic prosperity of the mid-1920s. Coolidge and most of his Republican supporters, notably Secretary of the Treasury Andrew Mellon (1855–1937), thought that the best way to ensure prosperity was for government to cut taxes and generally to stay out of the way of business. Although labor groups and farm groups actively organized to encourage a larger government role in the economy, a majority in Congress and a majority among the voters were behind Coolidge's laissez-faire policies.

The combination of a prosperous national economy and Coolidge's personal popularity seemed to make it certain that he would again be the Republican nominee in 1928. However, in August 1927 Coolidge stunned the nation. He handed members of the press a statement, typical in its brevity, declaring: "I do not choose to run for President in 1928." He never explained the decision.

Herbert Hoover

Coolidge's abdication threw the contest for the Republican nomination wide open. A favorite soon emerged, however, in the person of Herbert Hoover (1874–1964), who had been secretary of commerce under Coolidge and Harding. Hoover's résumé was as impressive as any presidential candidate before or since. A self-made man from Iowa, who studied engineering as one of the first graduates of Stanford University, Hoover made a fortune as a mining engineer, working extensively around the world, with spectacular success in Australia and China. He became an international hero for his tireless and resourceful relief efforts during World War I. Here his great practical intellect was turned away from mining and money and toward the immense challenges of feeding millions of

TIMELINE OF POLITICAL EVENTS IN THE 1920S

1920	**January**	part of 1919–1920 "Red Scare," about 5,000 so-called "radicals" in 30 cities arrested
	May	presidential candidate Warren Harding (R) calls for a return to "normalcy" in America
	November	Harding (R) defeats Cox (D) in presidential election; Republicans gain huge majority in Congress
1921	**May**	Tulsa, Oklahoma "race riot" leaves dozens of black residents dead
	June	President Harding nominates former President William Taft to be new chief justice of Supreme Court
1922	**February**	Five-Power Naval Treaty signed as a result of Washington Naval Conference; ties strength of U.S. Navy to that of Britain and Japan
	April	Senate investigation begins into what would become the Teapot Dome scandal; full extent of scandal not evident until 1924
	November	Republican majority shrinks considerably in 1922 congressional elections
1923	**May**	first issue of *Time* magazine introduced; would become nation's dominant news magazine
	August	President Harding dies in office; succeeded by Vice President Calvin Coolidge
1924	**November**	Coolidge (R) easily defeats Davis (D) and La Follette (Prog.) in presidential election; Republican majority in Congress increases slightly
1925	**February**	Nellie Ross of Wyoming inaugurated as the first female governor of a U.S. state
1926	**May**	Congress passes the Air Commerce Act, beginning the rise of the modern airline system
	November	Democrats cut into Republican majority in 1926 congressional elections
1927	**April**	Great Mississippi Flood strikes South and Midwest; major Army Corps of Engineers effort to prevent future floods begins
1928	**August**	U.S. signs Kellogg–Briand Pact, which attempts to make the waging of war against international law
	November	Herbert Hoover (R) defeats Al Smith (D) in presidential election; Republicans reclaim dominant majority in congressional elections
1929	**June**	President Hoover and Congress create federal Farm Board
	October	U.S. stock market crashes, losing the majority of its value in a week; Great Depression begins
	December	President Hoover assures Congress that the worst of the Depression is already over; instead, Great Depression would last another 10 years

The Democratic presidential candidate Al Smith and his team campaign in Chicago in 1928. Although Smith lost the election, he helped prepare the way for the later resurgence of the Democratic Party.

refugees in war-torn Europe, a task he accomplished primarily through private donations and diplomacy rather than through an official government agency. By 1920 Hoover was one of the most famous and celebrated private citizens in the country, known throughout the world as "the great humanitarian."

As secretary of commerce, Hoover was one of the most active members of the otherwise laissez-faire Harding and Coolidge administrations. He was involved with the creation and regulation of the radio and airline industries, and personally endorsed a number of the reforms favored by the La Follette faction. In many ways he was the perfect candidate to build even further on Coolidge's majority: a businessman and philanthropist who was personally venerated and who was moderately and inoffensively progressive. Hoover won the Republican nomination easily and looked to win the 1928 presidential election just as easily.

Al Smith and the 1928 election

To run against Hoover, the Democrats chose one of the runners-up from their last nomination battle: Al Smith of New York. In the years since the 1924 debacle the Democrats had begun to put the party back together again. The Democrats had made a modest comeback in the 1926 congressional elections, whittling down the Republican majority in the Senate to two. Smith's selection by the convention in Houston in 1928 was surprisingly quick; only one full round of balloting was required.

Smith's campaign leading up to the November 1928 election tried desperately to address the two issues that seemed likely to seal his defeat: Smith's long-standing opposition to Prohibition and his Catholicism. No Catholic had ever won, or even been nominated for, the presidency, and anti-Catholic feelings were pervasive in much of the country, especially in areas in which the Ku Klux Klan was strong. Hoover himself did not make an issue of Smith's religion; however, Hoover was certain to benefit from anti-Catholic voters in the Democratic heartland of the South.

The election was not close, but it was very significant. In his first election for any public office Hoover beat Smith in both the electoral college and the popular vote, winning old Democratic strongholds including Texas, Virginia, and Florida along the way. Smith won only eight states out of 48.

However, Smith's defeat had a silver lining for the Democrats. Smith carried all of the nation's 12 largest cities, where his urban Catholic background played to his advantage. Immigrants, ethnic minority voters, and poorer urban residents were energized by Smith's candidacy and would continue to vote Democratic in the 1930s and beyond. A split had appeared in U.S. politics between urban ethnic groups and rural WASPs.

Smith's decision to run for president in 1928 opened the door for Franklin D. Roosevelt to run for governor of New York. Roosevelt won Smith's old job and, as governor of the nation's most populous state, had a very prominent stage on which to develop his own hopes for the presidency. Roosevelt's later run of successful presidential elections owed a great deal to the opportunities and the new Democratic voters provided by Smith's 1928 campaign.

Hoover takes office

Herbert Hoover took office in 1929. Almost immediately he seemed to fall short of the expectations that his great résumé and landslide victory had raised. After a bitter fight within the Republican majority in Congress Hoover won passage of a federal Farm Board to run a new system of federal subsidies and regulations for American farmers, who had suffered terribly in the 1920s while the rest of the economy boomed. However, the vicious manner and the limited substance of Hoover's victory forever cost him many of his progressive supporters.

Hoover was struggling so badly early in his term of office that the fatal blow to his presidency at first seemed like an opportunity. In late October 1929 the stock market crashed. Over the course of a few days many of the economic gains and the economic illusions of the 1920s were wiped away. It was a financial emergency of the first order, and the bankers and financiers of America seemed powerless to stop the slide. For such a crisis a man as accomplished and brilliant as Herbert Hoover seemed to have been born.

Hoover and economic recession

No one blamed Hoover for the stock market crash, but everyone looked to him to do something about it. However, as a Republican, he was doctrinally opposed to federal interference in the economy. His first response to the Wall Street Crash was to attempt to restore investor confidence with a series of upbeat speeches. In December 1929 Hoover confidently declared to Congress that "the worst is over." In March 1930 he claimed to the press that "the worst effects of the crash upon unemployment will have passed in the next 60 days." In fact, however, the economy was constantly deteriorating, and the nation was steadily declining into the Great Depression.

As pressure mounted on the president, he was forced, despite his beliefs, to intervene. On Hoover's recommendation Congress established the Reconstruction Finance Corporation, approved January 22, 1932, with an initial working capital of $500 million. However, such experiments were not bold enough. By the end of Hoover's term in office in 1932 a quarter of American workers were unemployed, the nation's banking system had collapsed completely, the stock market had dropped to 11 percent of its 1929 levels, and the farm economy was in a shambles. Once known as "the great humanitarian," Hoover became associated with poverty and hopelessness.

Return of the Democrats

New York Governor Franklin D. Roosevelt defeated Hoover in 1932. As president, Roosevelt completed the reconstruction of the Democratic Party that Al Smith had begun in 1928. By 1936 Roosevelt's Democrats were even more dominant than Harding's Republicans had been in 1920. Roosevelt borrowed extensively from the ideas of the La Follette Progressives as well. Much of Roosevelt's New Deal of the 1930s could have been found in the proposals of La Follette and even Hoover in the 1920s. The reformers who had been exiled to the fringes of the political scene in the twenties dominated politics in the next decade.

SEE ALSO:

Agriculture • Business • Communism •Conservatism • Coolidge, Calvin • Democratic Party • Economy • Election of 1920 • Election of 1924 • Election of 1928 • Harding, Warren G. • Hoover, Herbert • Isolationism • Ku Klux Klan • Labor Movement • La Follette, Robert • Normalcy • Ohio Gang • Political Radicalism • Politics, Local • Progressivism • Prohibition • Protectionism • Red Scare • Republican Party • Roosevelt, Franklin D. • Smith, Al • Suffrage & Women's Rights • Supreme Court • Teapot Dome Scandal • Versailles Treaty • Wall Street Crash • Wilson, Woodrow

POLITICS, LOCAL

During the twenties two opposing models for local government came into flower: the political machine, which originally dated from the late 1800s, and the progressive model, which developed in the early decades of the 20th century to challenge the machines.

The 1920s marked the culmination of a long process in American history: the transition from a country that had been mostly rural, a nation of farmers and small towns, to a country that became majority urban, a nation that had more people living in big cities than on farms or in small towns. Technologies such as the automobile, the subway, and interurban rail reached maturity during the 1920s, making possible the growth of huge cities such as New York and Los Angeles and the development of the sprawling suburbs that surrounded them.

In contrast to the traditional farms and small towns, the settings of the big city and the suburb demanded a large and active local government, one that would pave the streets, employ a sizable police force, deliver water, pipe away sewage, and educate children in increasingly large schools. How well those services were provided became a major concern for urban citizens, and controlling the millions of dollars and thousands of jobs involved became an even greater concern for local politicians and political parties.

The machine model

The machine model of local government, although hardly new in the 1920s, initially benefited tremendously from the increasing urbanization of the country. To the famous and long-standing Tammany Hall machine of New York City the 1920s added the most powerful versions of the Pendergast machine in Kansas City, the Crump machine in Memphis, and the Kelly–Nash machine in Chicago, which was itself interrupted by the rival Chicago machine of William "Big Bill" Thompson (*see box on p. 176*).

A machine government was one that relied on service and favors, and that paid little attention to big ideas and moral issues in politics. The purpose of local government under a machine was to stay in power, and the best way to stay in power was to win the loyalty of the voters to the party machine and also to ensure

Tammany Hall, New York City, in 1914. In 1789 a soldier founded Tammany as a patriotic society named for a Native American chief. It developed first into a political club and then into a political machine. Its meeting place became known as Tammany Hall.

"BIG BILL" THOMPSON

The city of Chicago gained its reputation for wildness and corruption largely during the tenure of larger-than-life Mayor William "Big Bill" Hale Thompson (1867–1944). First elected mayor in 1915, Thompson was a Republican in a city more usually dominated by a Democratic party machine. "Big Bill" relied on an array of crowd-pleasing stunts, including a pledge to punch King George V of England should the British sovereign dare to set foot in Chicago.

Thompson ran City Hall into the 1920s. It was commonly believed that Thompson himself was run by the notorious Torrio/Capone gang, as the recipient of regular bribes and kickbacks from the Chicago mobsters. Although the alleged ties to Capone were never proven, Thompson did make a public spectacle of flouting Prohibition. "Big Bill" threatened to fire any Chicago cop who searched a citizen for a bottle of whiskey. Thompson's first tenure in office ended in 1923, when his popularity was briefly undermined by a failed libel suit and an investigation into fraud committed while in office.

Thompson won reelection to the mayor's office in 1927, campaigning on a pledge to reopen the taverns and bars of Chicago even as Prohibition continued on a national level. In his second term as mayor, however, Thompson was less able to rely on the support of Al Capone, who had moved his operation to the Illinois suburb of Cicero. In 1931 Thompson lost his bid for reelection. In 1936 he lost the race for governor, and in 1939 he lost his fifth bid for reelection as mayor. When he died shortly afterward, he was worth $2.1 million.

Mayor Thompson listens as Ruth Etting (1897–1978) sings his favorite song, "Big Bill the Builder," in 1928 in Chicago.

THE CONSUMATE CIVIC BOOSTER

Jesse Jones (1874–1956) rose from modest beginnings to become the most successful example of a "civic booster" in the history of Texas. Having made a huge fortune as a builder and banker in the 1900s and 1910s, Jones turned his business skills to use in enlarging and enriching his adopted hometown of Houston. Jones led a coalition of Houston businessmen in convincing the U.S. Congress and the Army Corps of Engineers to build a ship channel linking Houston to the Gulf of Mexico, thus transforming the landlocked city into one of the nation's largest deep-water ports.

Although he never sought local elected office, Jones functioned as a kind of political boss through the meetings he organized between Houston's business and civic leaders. Jones hosted these meetings, which were held in the plush Rice Hotel, which he had built and still owned. The assembled leaders discussed the most significant issues facing the community, planned for the city's commercial and territorial growth, and reached decisions that were then put into effect by the elected officials. To ensure that the decisions of the business elite were effectively communicated to the population at large, Jones relied on his ownership of and influence over the city's largest newspaper, the *Houston Chronicle*.

Jones explained the mingling of his political power and his private wealth by claiming that "enlightened self-interest" was his motivating principle. He believed that business leaders should think beyond narrow, short-term greed and instead should link their personal fortunes to the growth and health of the community. It was not just rhetoric: Jones established Houston's largest philanthropic foundation and spent World War I (1914–1918) in Washington, D.C., as the head of Red Cross relief efforts at the personal request of President Woodrow Wilson.

Jones's most significant act of "civic boosterism" took place in 1928, when he convinced the Democratic Party to hold its nominating convention in Houston. Jones believed that hosting a national party convention would bring the city nationwide prestige and fame, and cement fast-growing Houston's reputation as a "first-class" U.S. city. To convince the reluctant national Democratic leaders to award the convention to Houston, Jones wrote the party a personal check for $200,000 (over $2 million in 2004 values) and also personally promised to ensure the construction of a 25,000-seat convention hall. Starting from scratch only weeks before the convention, Jones had the arena ready just in time for the Democratic Party to award Al Smith its 1928 nomination.

the loyalty of the members of the machine to each other. The Tammany Hall machine in New York City, which originally developed in the 1830s, used its control of city contracts and city property to reward its loyal followers and to give nothing at all to its opponents.

Tammany leader George Washington Plunkitt (1842–1924), whose machine career lasted until his death, explained the Tammany method best: "I seen my opportunities ... and I took 'em." Such an opportunity might mean making money from inside information or using the control of the party's nomination to reward loyal "foot soldiers" and freeze out would-be reformers. Plunkitt publicly defended such corruption as "honest graft."

Machines could be of either party, although a majority were Democratic, at least in name. Philadelphia was dominated by a Republican machine, and during the twenties Chicago was hotly contested by rival Democratic and Republican machines.

Machine politicians sought office not to further the goals of a national party or a national movement but to gain control over the resources of the city government, which would then be used to keep the machine in power. If an immigrant arrived in the city with only the clothes on his back, the machine could arrange a place to live and a job in a factory. If a business feared that a building inspection might shut down its shop, a favorable inspection could be arranged. If a young man with little training or education wanted a job, then a career as a policeman, a highway engineer, or a building inspector was his for the asking.

In return the machine asked that all who received a favor do one in return. The machine used its control of the city payroll and city ordinances to do favors, and above all else, the machine needed to win elections in order to be able to stay in power and continue to do favors. To win, it needed money and it needed votes, and the machine asked a city's residents for both of these things. Alderman Joe McDonough, a Chicago machine politician of the late twenties, summed up his appeal in his popular campaign song:

Whataya gonna do for McDonough?
Whataya gonna do for YOU?
Are ya gonna carry your precinct?
Are ya gonna be true blue?
Whenever ya wanted a favor,
McDonough was ready to do.
Whataya gonna do for McDonough,
after what he done for you?

A political machine was corrupt to the core, and that corruption was the very glue that held the machine together and made it work as well as it did. To the existing mix of rapid growth and heavy immigration Prohibition added yet more opportunities for organized corruption, as local machine politicians accommodated gangsters and speakeasies—for a price.

The progressive model

The progressive movement arose in the early 1900s to combat the power and corruption of the machines. Although the progressive movement flamed out at the national level in the 1920s, it had a powerful impact in local politics, providing an alternative to machine politics in the big cities and coming to dominate completely the politics of the suburbs. At the local level the progressive movement did not align itself with either of the major national political parties. Indeed, many local progressives intended to destroy the party system rather than to control it. The progressives came in a number of variants: In the South and the Southwest the civic-booster version predominated, while in the West and the Midwest the technocratic vision was most common.

Civic-booster progressives

The civic-booster progressives believed that "government should run like a business." A growing city that employed thousands and provided services for hundreds of thousands should model itself on the pattern of a large corporation. Government should be run efficiently and cleanly, with decisions made not to provide favors but to encourage the growth and prosperity of the city as a whole, much as a corporate board of directors seeks to ensure the long-term health and wealth of a company. In fast-growing Southern and Southwestern cities, such as Houston, Dallas, San Antonio, and Phoenix, major local business leaders, such as Jesse Jones of Houston (*see box on p. 177*), cooperated with each other to dominate and influence local politics without ever bothering to run for elected office. Indeed "civic boosters" were often overtly contemptuous of elected office.

Technocratic progressives

The technocratic progressives shared the vision of local growth and wealth of the civic boosters but drew their inspiration from social science as much as from business. A "technocrat" was someone who had trained to perform a specific job and who received that job on the basis of expertise and merit. Take the corruption and the favors out of local politics, progressives believed, and let technocrats bring the benefits of efficiency and expertise to all the people (*see box opposite*).

The progressives placed great faith in reforms to the structure of city government. The major reforms on the progressive wish list for local politics usually included a short ballot, on which voters elected only a small number of offices directly, and a civil service system that handed out jobs on the basis of training and testing rather than party loyalty.

City managers

The ultimate local progressive reform was the city manager system, which began in the 1910s and grew rapidly in the 1920s. In a city manager system voters elected a city council whose job was to pass local

New York Mayor Fiorello La Guardia, Theodore Granik, the presenter of a weekly radio program for the discussion of national problems, and Al Smith, ex-governor of New York, in 1933.

THE RISE AND FALL OF A TECHNOCRAT

A young, penniless Irish immigrant, William Mulholland (1855–1935) arrived in the small, dusty outpost of Los Angeles, California, in 1877. Lacking any formal education, Mulholland was fortunate to find a job maintaining a ditch for the local water company. Mulholland worked his way up the company ladder until 1902, when the city government of Los Angeles bought the company and made Mulholland the chief engineer of the new Bureau of Water Supply.

Through a combination of natural engineering talent and ruthless business skills Mulholland achieved his goal: ensuring the city's growth and prosperity by ensuring a secure and plentiful water supply. His crowning achievement was the completion in 1913 of a 240-mile (386-km) aqueduct that drained water from the fertile Owens Valley in central California and delivered it, cleanly and cheaply, to parched southern California. The aqueduct was hailed as one of the great technological achievements of history, and Mulholland basked in the credit.

Mulholland ran the LA Department of Water and Power as his own personal kingdom, repeatedly refusing to run for higher elected office. "I'd rather give birth to a porcupine backwards than be mayor of Los Angeles," he once vowed. But mayors of Los Angeles were, in practice, much less powerful than William Mulholland.

Mulholland's reign as LA's most accomplished public official came to a tragic end in the late 1920s. Staying on the job well past retirement age, Mulholland improved his aqueduct with a series of reservoirs and dams, including one at San Francisquito Canyon, which he had personally designed in 1925. On March 12, 1928, small cracks appeared in the San Francisquito dam. Mulholland personally inspected it and declared it safe. Twelve hours later the dam collapsed completely, unleashing a terrible flood from the reservoir behind it. A wave 75 feet (23m) high and 2 miles (3.2km) wide swept away everything in its path, until finally emptying into the ocean 55 miles (88.5km) away. Five hundred people died.

Mulholland was found not guilty of manslaughter in a court of law but was convicted of arrogance and negligence in the court of public opinion. Once a hero, Mulholland resigned in disgrace and died a broken man a few years later. Owens Valley also paid a high price as its fertile lands dried out and its once prosperous farms lost their precious water supply.

laws and, most importantly, to hire a city manager—a person trained in running a city government who would be responsible for guiding the city's daily affairs the way a chief executive officer leads a company. Ideally, the city manager would be from a different city and have no history with the city he would be running. In that way a manager could run his new city free from any favors or past corruption. Ideally, too, the council that hired the manager would be elected by the city as a whole rather than by a small district or neighborhood and would be nonpartisan, with no party labels for voters to rely on.

It was impossible for a political machine to flourish in a city run by these "ideal" progressive principles. Over the course of the 1920s, 335 cities adopted the city manager system, which gradually replaced an earlier reform whereby the mayor and council were replaced by commissioners who each ran a specific department.

Machines continued to dominate in the largest cities, but by the end of the 1920s some enterprising political leaders, notably New York Governor Al Smith (1873–1944) and New York City Mayor Fiorello La Guardia (1882–1947), had begun to refine a mixture of machine and progressive techniques. Al Smith, in particular, pioneered a blend of competence and expertise in providing social services with the vote-getting methods of old Tammany Hall. Smith's efforts were successful in their own right and also served as an inspiration for much of President Franklin D. Roosevelt's New Deal in the 1930s.

Reformers or elitists?

Although the progressives relied on the rhetoric of fighting corruption and establishing businesslike efficiency in local government, many were also motivated by a distaste for democracy and a concern for their own economic self-interest. Civic boosters such as Jesse Jones despised the open corruption of the machines, but the wealth and finances of those same civic boosters were often intertwined with those of the cities they ran. While a George Washington Plunkitt might settle for small kickbacks and gifts, a Jesse Jones might make the equivalent of millions of dollars in his dealings with the city government.

The progressive preference for trained experts carried a bias in favor of wealth and privilege, and against democracy. Progressive reforms emphasized appointed offices rather than elected offices. This meant that fewer offices were controlled by voters through the ballot, and that those offices were often stripped of much of their powers. A city manager, for instance, was not under the control of a corrupt local machine, but nor was that manager under much control by voters. The very distance from local elections that made the city manager system efficient also made it antidemocratic.

Progressives of all types were usually white, Protestant, and of northern European ancestry, while the machines the progressives battled relied heavily on Catholic immigrants from eastern and southern Europe. In that sense the struggle between the corrupt machines and the efficient progressives was also a struggle between poorer immigrant communities and wealthier Protestants.

Machines often justified their existence by claiming that they provided assistance and opportunities for new immigrants. While there is little doubt that such claims

Ku Klux Klan members from Chicago, Illinois, gather around an altar in 1920. Rituals with religious and patriotic overtones were important to the Klan, which used them to bind its membership together.

were often exaggerated, there is no question that the progressive reformers sought to take power away from poorer and immigrant communities in favor of wealthier, better educated, native-born Americans.

Progressive reforms had the effect of concentrating power in the hands of those with wealth and education. They also had the effect of depressing voter turnout, particularly in contrast with the high levels of voter turnout encouraged by the machines. Historians dispute whether those results were merely side effects of the reforms, or whether they were intended all along.

Country vs. city

In rapidly shrinking rural America the political movements that spoke the loudest were less interested in political reform than in fighting the social changes that rural residents associated with the big cities. As historian Robert Wiebe stressed, the technological and economic changes that benefited the cities signaled doom for the "island communities" of rural America: small towns, spaced out only a few miles apart, that relied on the surrounding farms for their economic survival. The farm depression of the 1920s further frayed the economic fabric of rural America and increased resentment of urban and suburban America.

This resentment fueled the overwhelming rural support for two of the most controversial causes in 1920s America: Prohibition and the Ku Klux Klan (KKK). Historian Richard Hofstadter argued that Prohibition and the KKK both reflected a backlash from older, Protestant, rural America against the newer, urban, immigrant, Catholic and Jewish America. Prohibition was intended to tame the corruption and decadence of the cities by removing alcohol. But this extraordinary attempt at social scolding divided the nation bitterly, mostly by pitting rural supporters of Prohibition against urban opponents of Prohibition.

The Ku Klux Klan, which was estimated to have as many as four million members and sympathizers in 1924, often acted as a kind of shadow local government in many small towns in the South and Midwest, where the same people who served as mayors and sheriffs in the daytime put on the white hood of the KKK at night. The social and political influence of the KKK peaked in the 1920s, and its favored policies of segregation and intimidation of black Americans were backed by the rule of law in much of rural America. In its most savage form the specter of the Klan's bigotry encouraged the notorious riot at Tulsa, Oklahoma, in 1921 (75 blacks were killed and thousands lost their homes—44 blocks were razed) and the complete annihilation of the small black town of Rosewood, Florida, in 1924.

SEE ALSO:

Capone, Al • Democratic Party • Ku Klux Klan • Politics & Government • Progressivism • Prohibition • Republican Party • Smith, Al • Urbanization

BOOKS

Allen, Frederick Lewis *Only Yesterday*.
New York: HarperCollins, 2000

Belasco, Warren James *Americans on the Road: From Auto-Camp to Motel, 1910–45*.
Baltimore: Johns Hopkins University Press, 1997

Brophy, Alfred L. *Reconstructing the Dreamland: The Tulsa Riot of 1921: Race, Reparations, and Reconciliation*.
New York: Oxford University Press, 2002

Burnham, John C. *Bad Habits: Drinking, Smoking, Taking Drugs, Gambling, Sexual Misbehavior, and Swearing in American History*.
New York: New York University Press, 1994

Butsch, Richard (ed.) *For Fun and Profit: The Transformation of Leisure into Consumption*.
Philadelphia: Temple University Press, 1990

Carter, Paul A. *The Decline and Revival of the Social Gospel: Social and Political Liberalism in American Protestant Churches, 1920–1940*.
Hamden, Ct.: Archon, 1971

Clark, Norman H. *Deliver Us from Evil: An Interpretation of American Prohibition*.
New York: Norton, 1985

Cott, Nancy F. *The Grounding of Modern Feminism*.
New Haven, Ct.: Yale University Press, 1987.

Draper, Theodore *Roots of American Communism*.
New York: Octagon Books, 1977

Eagles, Charles W. *Democracy Delayed: Congressional Reapportionment and Urban–Rural Conflict in the 1920s*.
Athens, Ga.: University of Georgia Press, 1990

Ellsworth, Scott *Death in a Promised Land: The Tulsa Race Riot of 1921*.
Baton Rouge, La.: Louisiana State University Press, 1982

Ewen, Stuart *Captains of Consciousness: Advertising and the Social Roots of the Consumer Culture*.
New York: McGraw-Hill, 1976

Fass, Paula, S. *The Damned and the Beautiful: American Youth in the 1920s*.
New York: Oxford University Press, 1979

Fox, Stephen *The Mirror Makers: A History of American Advertising and Its Creators*.
New York: William Morrow, 1997

Galbraith, John Kenneth *The Great Crash, 1929*.
Boston: Houghton Mifflin, 1988

Ginger, Ray *Six Days or Forever? Tennessee v. John Thomas Scopes*.
New York: Oxford University Press, 1974

Jackson, Kenneth T. *The Ku Klux Klan in the City, 1915–1930*.
New York: Oxford University Press, 1967

Klein, Maury *Rainbow's End: The Crash of 1929*.
New York: Oxford University Press, 2001

Lemons, J. Stanley *The Woman Citizen: Social Feminism in the 1920s*.
Charlottesville, Va.: University Press of Virginia, 1990

MacDonald, J. Fred *Don't Touch That Dial! Radio Programming in American Life, 1920–1960*.
Chicago: Nelson-Hall, 1979

Nash, Roderick *The Nervous Generation: American Thought, 1917–30*.
New York: Rand McNally, 1990

Schlesinger, Arthur M., Jr. *The Crisis of the Old Order*.
New York: Houghton Mifflin, 2003

Schneider, Mark Robert *"We Return Fighting": The Civil Rights Movement in the Jazz Age*.
Boston: Northeastern University Press, 2002

Schudson, Michael *Advertising, The Uneasy Persuasion: Its Dubious Impact on American Society*.
New York: Basic Books, 1984

Sklar, Robert *Movie-Made America: A Cultural History of American Movies*.
New York: Vintage Books, 1994

Stearns, Marshall W. *The Story of Jazz*.
New York: Oxford University Press, 1977

USEFUL WEBSITES

Brief Timeline of American Literature, Music, and Movies, 1920–1929
www.gonzaga.edu/faculty/campbell/enl311/1920m.html

Cultural History of the 1920s
dir.yahoo.com/Arts/Humanities/History/U_S__History/By_Time_Period/20th_Century/1920s

Encyclopedia: 1920s
www.nationmaster.com/encyclopedia/1920s

Facts and Dates
www.fact-index.com/1/19/1920s.html

General USA History
www.teacheroz.com/generalUS.htm

Kingwood College Library
http://kclibrary.nhmccd.edu/decade20.html

1920s Details
http://din-timelines.com/1920de.shtml

The Lawless Decade by Paul Sann
www.paulsann.org/thelawlessdecade

Online Encyclopedia
www.yourencyclopedia.net/1920.html

The 1920s
http://www.state.sd.us/deca/DDN4Learning/ThemeUnits/1920s/general.htm

The Politics of Prosperity
http://us.history.wisc.edu/hist102/lectures/lecture15.html

The Rise and Fall of Jim Crow
http://www.pbs.org/wnet/jimcrow

The Roaring '20s and the Great Depression
www.snowcrest.net/jmike/20sdep.html

Mrs. Ruland's United States History Internet Resources
home.comcast.net/~mruland/USResources/boombust/boom.htm

Wikipedia
encyclopedia.calendarhome.com/1920s.htm

PICTURE CREDITS

Front Cover Images: **Daimler Chrysler/Library of Congress/Robert Hunt Library**

Bridgeman Art Library: Detroit Institute of Arts, USA 124; **Corbis**: Bettmann 11, 34, 66, 67, 81, 83, 85, 98, 115, 117, 120, 122, 156, Geoffrey Clements 118, Francis G Mayer 33, Museum of the City of New York 38; **Getty Images**: 7, 10, 125, 130, 152; **Library of Congress**: 6, 8, 12, 13, 14, 15, 17, 18, 23, 24, 26, 27, 29, 31, 36, 39, 41, 42, 43, 44, 47, 48, 49, 50 ,51, 53, 55, 59, 60 ,61, 62, 63, 64, 65, 70, 71, 73, 74, 77, 78, 79, 80, 84, 86, 88, 89, 90, 91, 93, 95, 96, 99, 101, 102, 103, 106, 107, 108, 109, 110, 111, 112, 113, 114, 116, 121, 126, 128, 129, 133, 135, 137, 138, 139, 140, 141, 143, 151, 153, 154, 155, 160, 161, 162, 163, 164, 165, 166, 167, 168, 170, 171, 173, 175, 176, 178, 180; **Los Angeles Public Library**: Shades of LA Archive 21, 22; **LP Pictures**: 5; **NASA**: 149; **National Archives**: 68; **Nobel Institute**: 30, 40, 146; **PhotoDisc**: Hisham F Ibrahim 172; **Robert Hunt Library**: 57, 145, 158; **Science & Society Picture Library**: Science Museum 147.

PRE-1920

1914
August 4 Outbreak of World War I between the Allies—Britain, France, Russia, Serbia, and Belgium (later joined by Montenegro, Japan, Italy, Romania, Portugal, and Greece—and the Central Powers—Austria-Hungary and Germany (later joined by Turkey and Bulgaria). The U.S. maintains an increasingly uneasy neutrality.

1915
May 7 German U-boat (submarine) torpedoes British liner *Lusitania* off the coast of Ireland. Among the 1,198 lives lost are those of 128 Americans. The United States calls for restraint, and Germany undertakes to avoid further attacks on noncombatant shipping.

1916
November 7 President Woodrow Wilson is elected for a second term.

1917
January 31 Germany announces that it will wage submarine warfare on all shipping.

February 3 The United States breaks off diplomatic relations with Germany.

February 5 The new constitution of Mexico asserts the nation's right to its own minerals and oil, thus setting the scene for a showdown with the United States.

March 1 The Zimmermann telegram from the German foreign minister to his legate in Mexico is intercepted and released to the U.S. press. It offers to help Mexico reconquer "the lost territory in Texas, New Mexico, and Arizona."

March 15 In Russia the overthrow of the czar marks the beginning of a revolution. The United States is sympathetic until November, when the communist Bolsheviks seize power.

April 2 The United States declares war on Germany; millions of U.S. troops are mobilized.

December 27 U.S. railroads brought under federal control for the duration of the war.

1918
January 8 Wilson outlines his vision of the postwar world in his "Fourteen Points" speech.

May 28 First World War I engagement involving U.S. troops at Cantigny, France.

November 11 Armistice ends World War I; the Allies are victorious.

1919
January 18 Paris Peace Conference is convened; Wilson attends in person.

June 28 The Versailles Treaty is signed.

October 2 Wilson suffers severe stroke.

November 19 U.S. Senate rejects Versailles Treaty and League of Nations.

1920

January 2 5,000 suspected communists in 33 cities are arrested in raids authorized by Attorney General A. Mitchell Palmer.

January 3 Red Sox baseball player Babe Ruth signs with the New York Yankees for $125,000.

January 16 Prohibition begins as the states ratify the Eighteenth Amendment.

March 1 U.S. railroads returned to private ownership.

March 19 U.S. Senate rejects Versailles Treaty for second time.

May 5 Anarchist Italian immigrants Nicola Sacco and Bartolomeo Vanzetti are charged with murder in Brockton, Massachusetts.

June 5 Census shows U.S. population 105 million. For the first time more than half the population (54 million) is urban.

June 12 Republican Party nominates Warren G. Harding as presidential candidate; joining him on the ticket is Calvin Coolidge.

June 15 Mob of 5,000 lynches three African Americans in Duluth, Minnesota.

June 29 Disorder at the Democratic Convention as the party debates Prohibition.

July 3 Bill Tilden becomes first U.S. tennis player to win Wimbledon.

July 5 Democratic Party names James M. Cox as its presidential candidate; his running mate is Franklin D. Roosevelt.

August 1–31 2,000 attend first convention of the Universal Negro Improvement Association.

August 6 Three killed in Denver, Colorado, as police fire on striking trolley drivers.

August 18 The states ratify the Nineteenth Amendment, which gives women the vote.

September 16 A bomb explodes on Wall Street, killing 30 people and injuring 300.

September 17 The American Professional Football Association is formed.

September 28 Eight baseball players for the Chicago White Sox are charged with fraud after their team's loss to Cincinnati in the 1919 World Series. They are dubbed "Black Sox."

November 2 Harding wins landslide victory in the presidential election.

November 2 KDKA in Pittsburgh, Pennsylvania, broadcasts the election results, the first commercial radio broadcast.

November 10 Woodrow Wilson wins Nobel Peace Prize.

1921

March 4 Harding is inaugurated as 29th president of the United States. He names Andrew W. Mellon as secretary of the Treasury and Herbert Hoover as secretary of commerce; his cabinet also includes Harding's friends and acquaintances—later dubbed the "Ohio Gang."

May 19 Congress passes Emergency Quota Act to limit the number of immigrants allowed to enter the United States according to nationality. No more than 3 percent of the total number of each nationality already resident in the United States in 1910 are allowed to enter each year. A maximum limit of 357,000 is also set. The act is a response to large increases in immigration after World War I.

May 23 *Shuffle Along*, the first all-black musical, opens on Broadway.

May 27 Emergency Tariff Act increases tax on wheat, sugar, meat, wool, and other agricultural products imported into the United States, with the aim of protecting the domestic market for American farmers.

May 31 Race riots break out in Tulsa, Oklahoma. Forty-four blocks of the city center, largely inhabited by African Americans, are burned overnight; about 75 people are killed.

June 30 Harding nominates former President William H. Taft as U.S. Chief Justice.

July 14 Sacco and Vanzetti are found guilty.

July 18 "Black Sox" trial begins in Chicago.

August 3 The "Black Sox" are acquitted but banned from professional baseball.

September 28 Margaret Gorman wins a contest in Atlantic City, New Jersey, to become the first Miss America.

October 5 Radio coverage of Major League Baseball's World Series begins.

November 9 The Federal Highway Act launches a program to regulate highways and create 169,000 miles (271,971km) of new roads. The work is to be carried out under the direction of the Bureau of Public Roads, in cooperation with the Association of State Highway Officials.

November 10 Margaret Sanger founds the American Birth Control League.

November 11 Washington Naval Conference convenes to limit the naval arms race and to work out international security agreements in the Pacific area.

December 13 The Four-Power Pact is signed by the United States, Britain, Japan, and France at the Washington Naval Conference. It states that all the signatories will be consulted should controversy arise over "any Pacific question."

1922

January 20 The House of Representatives passes an antilynching bill introduced by Congressman L.C. Dyer. The bill proposes fines for counties that fail to stop violence and lynchings within their jurisdiction.

January 26 Dyer antilynching bill is shelved after Southern Democratic senators threaten to filibuster.

February 5 First edition of *Reader's Digest* magazine is published.

February 6 Five-Power Naval Armaments Treaty is signed by Britain, the United States, Japan, France, and Italy at the Washington Naval Conference. It limits the number of battleships and aircraft carriers held by each power to an agreed ratio.

February 18 Capper–Volstead Act (also known as the Cooperative Marketing Act) gives farmers' cooperatives partial exemption from prosecution under antitrust laws—it also gives them highly favorable tax deductions. Its aim is to strengthen the position of farmers by enabling them to join together to market, price, and sell their produce.

April 29 Senate authorizes investigation into allegations of corrupt leases of naval oil reserves to private companies. Members of the government implicated in what becomes known as the Teapot Dome Scandal include Secretary of the Interior Albert B. Fall.

May 30 The Lincoln Memorial, Washington D.C., is ceremonially dedicated. The monument, designed by architect Henry Bacon, contains a statue of Abraham Lincoln by sculptor Daniel Chester French.

June 14 President Harding makes the first presidential speech to be broadcast on radio.

July 1 In an action organized by the American Federation of Labor (AFL), some 400,000 railroad workers strike to protest pay cuts.

July 1 The world's first shopping mall, the Country Club Plaza, opens outside Kansas City, Missouri.

July 9 Johnny Weissmuller becomes the first man to swim 100m in less than a minute.

August 2 Alexander Graham Bell, inventor of the telephone, dies.

August 28 First radio commercial is broadcast over WEAF in New York City.

September 19 Fordney–McCumber Act is passed to protect American farmers and businesses from foreign competition. It gives the president power to adjust tariffs by up to 50 percent.

October 7 Mrs. W.H. Felton of Georgia is sworn in as first female U.S. Senator.

1923

January 14 First wireless telephone call, sent via radio waves, made from New York to London, England.

March 1 The battleship USS *Connecticut* is decommissioned under the terms of the Washington Naval Treaty.

March 2 First issue of the weekly news magazine *Time* is published.

April 4 Brothers Albert, Sam, Harry, and Jack L. Warner found Warner Brothers movie studios in Burbank, California.

April 14 McMillan's Dancing Academy, Houston, holds a dance marathon; the winner dances nonstop for 65.5 hours. The dance marathon craze takes off.

April 18 Yankee Stadium opens in the Bronx, New York.

May 2–3 Lieutenant Oakley Kelly and Lieutenant John A. Macready make the first nonstop transcontinental flight from New York to San Diego in 26 hours, 50 minutes.

August 2 President Harding dies from a stroke or a heart attack in a San Francisco hotel. Thousands of mourners pay their respects to the president they praise as the "ideal American." Vice President Calvin Coolidge accedes to the presidency.

August 13 U.S. Steel reduces work day from 12 hours to 8 hours.

September 4 The first American airship, the USS *Shenandoah*, makes its maiden flight from Lakehurst, New Jersey.

September 18–26 Printers' strike stops publication of newspapers in New York.

October 15 Hearings on the Teapot Dome oil lease begin before the Senate Committee on Public Lands and Surveys. They contain the first of many disclosures that uncover the corrupt dealings of the Ohio Gang and discredit the Harding presidency.

November 9 Henry Cabot Lodge, the senator who led congressional opposition to U.S. involvement in the League of Nations, dies.

November 25 The British Broadcasting Company (BBC) makes its first transatlantic broadcast to the United States.

December 10 Robert A. Millikan awarded Nobel Prize for Physics for his work on the elementary electric charge and the photoelectric effect.

1924

February 3 Woodrow Wilson dies.

February 8 First U.S. execution by gas chamber. The sentence is carried out in Nevada on Chinese-born Gee Long for the murder of a rival gang member.

February 12 George Gershwin's *Rhapsody in Blue* is premiered at the Aeolian Hall, New York.

March 24 Harry M. Daugherty resigns as attorney general following his implication in the Teapot Dome Scandal.

April 6 Two U.S. Army planes leave Seattle, Washington, to make the first round-the-world flight. They take nearly six months to complete the 26,345-mile (42,397km) journey.

April 14 Construction of the Wilson Dam at Muscle Shoals on the Tennessee River is completed. It becomes a focal point for controversy over public and private ownership.

April 16 Metro Pictures Corporation, Goldwyn Pictures, and Louis B. Mayer Productions merge to form MGM film studios.

May 10 J. Edgar Hoover is appointed director of the Federal Bureau of Investigation (FBI).

May 26 Johnson–Reed National Origins Act limits the number of immigrants to 2 percent of each nationality resident in the United States as recorded in the 1890 census. The aim is to reduce immigration from southern and eastern Europe. Asians are almost completely excluded.

June 2 Indian Citizenship Act extends U.S. citizenship to U.S.-born Native Americans.

June 15 Ford manufactures its 10 millionth Model T automobile; more than half the world's cars are Model Ts.

June 24–July 9 Members at the Democratic Party Convention are split over their choice of presidential candidate. In the end they select compromise candidate John W. Davis.

June 26 *Ziegfeld Follies* opens on Broadway.

August 16 The Allies and Germany accept the Dawes Plan, which provides loans to Germany so that it can make reparation payments.

September 6 Nathan Leopold and Richard Loeb are sentenced to life imprisonment for the murder of 14-year-old school boy Robert Franks.

November 4 Republican Calvin Coolidge wins presidential election.

November 4 In Texas, Miriam "Ma" Ferguson becomes the first American woman to be elected a state governor.

December 13 Labor leader and president of the AFL Samuel Gompers dies.

1925

January 5 Nellie Tayloe Ross is inaugurated as the governor of Wyoming to complete her deceased husband's term in office; she becomes the second female state governor.

February 21 *The New Yorker* magazine publishes its first issue.

March 4 Calvin Coolidge is inaugurated as president with Charles G. Dawes as his vice president. Coolidge's inauguration speech is the first to be broadcast on radio.

March 18 The Tri-State Tornado hits Missouri, Illinois, and Indiana, killing about 700 people.

April 10 F. Scott Fitzgerald's novel *The Great Gatsby* is published.

June 13 Charles Francis Jenkins broadcasts the first synchronized pictures and sound over 5 miles (8km) from Washington, D.C.

June 18 Progressive politician Robert La Follette dies.

July 10–21 In the so-called Scopes Monkey Trial, in Dayton, Tennessee, teacher John Scopes is prosecuted for teaching Darwin's theory of evolution. Tennessee had passed a law in March that banned the teaching in its schools of material contradicting the biblical account of the divine creation of humans. The case hits the headlines. Scopes is defended by leading attorney Clarence Darrow. Although Scopes is convicted and fined, the prosecution's case is pilloried in the media. Scopes appeals and is acquitted on a technicality on January 27, 1927.

August 5 Interstate Highways Board designates 50,000 miles (80,000km) of roads "U.S. Highways."

August 8 20,000 Ku Klux Klan members march in Washington, D.C.

September 3 U.S. airship *Shenandoah* breaks up en route to Scottfield, St. Louis; 14 crewmen are killed.

November 22 Grand Ole Opry, Nashville, Tennessee, begins regular Saturday night broadcasts over new local radio station WSM.

December 8 *The Cocoanuts*, starring the Marx Brothers, opens at the Lyric Theater, Broadway; it runs for 375 performances and lands the stars a film contract with Paramount.

December 10 Nobel Peace Prize is awarded to Charles G. Dawes for the Dawes Plan.

December 12 First U.S. motel opened in San Luis Obispo, California.

1926

January 13 Mine explosion at Wilburton, Oklahoma, leaves 65 dead.

March 16 Robert H. Goddard launches the world's first flight of a liquid-fuel rocket on his aunt's farm in Auburn, Massachusetts.

March 17 Richard Rodgers's musical *The Girl Friend* opens in New York.

March 10
Hugo Gernsback launches *Amazing Stories* (cover April), the first science fiction magazine.

March 24 As consumerism increases, Marion B. Skaggs opens the first branch of the Safeways store chain in Maryland.

May 9 Richard E. Byrd and Floyd Bennet leave Spitsbergen, Norway, on what they claim is the first flight over the North Pole. Historians now believe that they did not actually reach the Pole.

May 20 Railway Labor Act creates a governmental board to intervene in railroad labor disputes.

May 20 Air Commerce Act makes the Commerce Department responsible for fostering air commerce, establishing airways and aids to navigation, and ensuring civil air safety.

July 2 Air Corps Act creates the Army Air Corps as part of the U.S. Army.

August 6 Warner Brothers debuts Vitaphone, a sound system providing movies with a synchronized musical accompaniment, in *Don Juan*, a lavish costume drama starring John Barrymore and featuring a score performed by the New York Philharmonic Orchestra.

August 23 Death of silent-screen star Rudolf Valentino; a nation mourns.

September 9 The National Broadcasting Company (NBC) is established as the broadcasting service of the Radio Corporation of America (RCA).

September 18–19 A hurricane hits southeastern Florida, devastating Miami and other newly built coastal resorts; 400 people are reported killed and 40,000 made homeless. The real estate boom in the state comes to a dramatic end.

October 20 Eugene V. Debs, labor organizer and former Socialist Party candidate for U.S. presidency, dies.

October 31 Death of Harry Houdini.

November 15 The NBC radio network opens with 24 stations; it is formed as a joint venture by RCA, Westinghouse, and General Electric.

1927

January 7 The first commercial transatlantic telephone service opens between New York and London, England.

January 11 Academy of Motion Picture Arts and Sciences is founded in Hollywood.

February 27 U.S. Marines arrive in Shanghai, China, to protect U.S. citizens and property from the Japanese.

April–June At least 300 people are killed in flooding on the Mississippi River.

April 5 Johnny Weissmuller becomes the swimming world record holder at every distance from 100m to 800m.

April 9 The death sentence is confirmed on Sacco and Vanzetti.

May 14 United States signs aid pact with Nicaragua, allowing U.S. intervention in the Cental American nation.

May 20–21 Charles A. Lindbergh makes the first nonstop solo crossing of the Atlantic Ocean, from New York City to Paris, France.

May 20–August 4 At the Geneva Arms Conference the United States, Britain, and Japan try unsuccessfully to limit the production of naval vessels.

May 26 The 15 millionth, and last, Model T Ford rolls off the assembly line at Highland Park, Michigan.

July 1 The Food, Drug, and Insecticide Administration is established. It is renamed the Food and Drug Administration (FDA) in 1930.

August 2 Coolidge announces that he will not run for president in the 1928 election.

August 23 Sacco and Vanzetti are executed in the electric chair in Massachusetts.

September 30 At the end of the baseball season Babe Ruth has hit a record total of 60 home runs; his record stands for 34 years.

October 6 Warner Brothers release the movie *The Jazz Singer*, the first "talkie."

November 22 George Gershwin's musical *Funny Face* opens on Broadway.

December 2 The Ford Model A, the successor to the Model T, is unveiled.

December 10 Arthur Compton and Briton Charles Wilson win the Nobel Prize for Physics for their confirmation of quantum theory.

December 12 Coolidge approves a $1 billion 5-year spending plan for the U.S. Navy.

December 27 *Show Boat* premieres in New York City. It runs for 575 performances.

1928

January 1 Five U.S. troops die in clashes with Sandinist rebel forces in Nicaragua.

February 29 U.S. Marine unit is ambushed by rebels in Nicaragua; five Americans are killed.

March 19 *Amos 'n' Andy* radio show premieres on Chicago station WMAQ.

April 23 Sandinist rebels capture U.S.-owned mines in Nicaragua, taking five hostages.

May 15 The Flood Control Act provides relief funds and a flood control program for the Mississippi River.

May 29 Chrysler and Dodge merge to become the third largest U.S. automobile manufacturer, after General Motors and Ford.

June 8–12 Republicans nominate Herbert Hoover as their presidential candidate. His running mate is Charles Curtis, whose mother was a quarter-blood Kansa Indian.

June 18 Amelia Earhart becomes the first woman to fly the Atlantic Ocean.

June 28–29 Al Smith is chosen as the Democratic presidential candidate.

August 27 The United States signs the Kellogg—Briand Pact, a multilateral agreement intended to eliminate war as an instrument of national policy.

September 11 The first television drama, *The Queen's Messenger*, is broadcast by station W2XAD from Schenectady, New York.

October 7 Albert B. Fall is brought to trial for his involvement in the Teapot Dome scandal.

October 15 The world's largest airship, the *Graf Zeppelin*, lands in New Jersey after a 111-hour flight from Germany.

October 25 Albert B. Fall is found guilty and sentenced to one year in prison and a $100,000 fine. He is the first cabinet member to be imprisoned for a crime committed in office.

November 2 Hoover wins a resounding victory in the presidential election.

November 7 Franklin D. Roosevelt is elected governor of New York.

November 18 Walt Disney releases *Steamboat Willie*, a cartoon movie with synchronized sound featuring Mickey Mouse.

November 26—December 23 President-elect Hoover makes a goodwill trip to Central America. He cultivates a less interventionist approach, which becomes known as the Good Neighbor Policy.

December 13 George Gershwin's *An American in Paris* is premiered in New York.

1929

January 17 Cartoon character Popeye the Sailor Man first appears in cartoon strip by Elzie Crisler Segar.

February 13 In one of his last acts as president, Calvin Coolidge signs a bill to build 15 cruisers and an aircraft carrier.

February 14 Members of Al Capone's gang murder seven unarmed members of the rival Chicago gang of Bugs Moran in what becomes known as the Saint Valentine's Day Massacre.

February 17 The first inflight movie is shown on a Universal Air Line flight from St. Paul, Minnesota, to Chicago, Illinois.

March 4 Herbert Hoover is inaugurated as 31st president of the United States.

May 16 Academy of Motion Picture Arts and Sciences awards the first Oscars.

May 24 *The Cocoanuts*, the first movie featuring the Marx Brothers, opens in New York. It is based on their vaudeville act.

June 15 The Agricultural Marketing Act aims to stabilize prices and promote farm cooperation in a bid to halt the recession that has affected farming throughout the decade.

June 27 H.E. Ives and technicians at Bell Telephone Laboratories in New York give the first public demonstration of color television. The first images are of a bouquet of roses and an American flag.

September 3 The Dow Jones Industrial Average closes at 381.17 points; it is the peak of the bull market.

October 24 "Black Thursday": Stock market prices tumble as investors rush to sell. Some 12.9 million shares change hands, an all-time record. Leading bankers try to restore confidence in the market.

October 29 "Black Tuesday": The stock market collapses. Some 16.4 million shares are sold in the day's trading at a loss of $10 billion.

November 7 The Museum of Modern Art, New York, opens.

November 13 The Dow Jones Industrial Average sinks to 199 points.

November 29 U.S. Admiral Richard E. Byrd becomes the first person to fly over the South Pole.

December 3 President Hoover tells Congress that the worst effects of the stock market crash are over, and that the American people have regained faith in the U.S. economy.

POST-1929

1930
June 17 The Smoot–Hawley Tariff is passed into law. It raises import duties to protect American businesses and farmers from foreign competition.

December 2 Hoover proposes a $150 million public works program to generate jobs and stimulate the economy.

December 10 Frank B. Kellogg is awarded the 1929 Nobel Peace Prize for the Kellogg–Briand Pact.

1931
May 1 Construction of the Empire State Building is completed in New York City.

October 18 Al Capone is convicted on five counts of tax fraud and given an 11-year prison sentence.

1932
January 2 U.S. troops leave Nicaragua.

November 8 The presidential election results in a landslide victory for Democratic candidate Franklin D. Roosevelt over Hoover.

1933
March 4 President Roosevelt makes his inauguration speech, which includes the famous line: "We have nothing to fear, but fear itself."

March 9 Congress begins its first 100 days of enacting New Deal legislation.

March 12 Roosevelt addresses the nation in the first of his radio "Fireside Chats."

May 18 Roosevelt signs an act creating the Tennessee Valley Authority, an ambitiously radical experiment in regional economic and social planning.

May 27 The Federal Securities Act is signed into law requiring the registration of securities with the Federal Trade Commission.

November 8 Roosevelt unveils the Civil Works Administration, designed to create jobs for more than 4 million of the unemployed.

November 16 The United States establishes formal diplomatic relations with the Soviet Union.

December 5 Utah becomes the 36th state to ratify the 21st Amendment, thus ending Prohibition; liquor is once more legal in the United States.

SET INDEX

Volume numbers are in **bold**. Page numbers in **bold** refer to main articles; those in *italics* refer to picture captions.

C

G

H

I

J

K

L

M

N

O

P

Q

R

S

W

X

Y

Z